THE WORKING POOR

Winner of the Myers Outstanding Book Award

Chosen as a Best Book of the Year by the *San Francisco Chronicle*, *The Washington Post Book World*, and *San Jose Mercury News*

"Sprawling, compassionate. . . . Describes with clear-eyed sympathy the individuals and families who sustain the seemingly limitless appetite for low-wage work and should provide ammunition to policy makers—if there are any—who wish to seriously engage the project of eliminating poverty in America."
                                                    —*San Francisco Chronicle*

"In the tradition of Michael Harrington, Edward R. Murrow and more recently Barbara Ehrenreich as it seeks to alert a complacent nation about the misery and deprivation in its midst. . . . By exposing the wretched condition of these invisible Americans, he has performed a noble and badly needed service."
                                                    —*The New York Times*

"Powerful. . . . Some may find in this eye-opening book reason to demand change. Others, with regret perhaps, will see it as an accurate description of the inevitable costs of free market capitalism."   —*Los Angeles Times*

"Moving and meticulous. . . . Unlike other sympathetic chroniclers of the working poor, he doesn't demonize their employers."
                                                    —*The Baltimore Sun*

"Masterly . . . a series of memorable portraits."
                                                    —*The Hartford Courant*

"This urgent new book obliterates the notion that impoverished people are simply lazy. . . . Shipler is a skilled interviewer whose knack for erasing himself from the picture lends this book an intimate quality."   —*Time Out New York*

"Shipler's report is gripping, his characters more alive than those found in many novels." —*Austin American-Statesman*

"Splendidly animated by Shipler's empathy—his ability to see people and more important to depict them, not as statistics or symbols of injustice, but as human beings."
—*The Miami Herald*

"*The Working Poor* will make any relatively well-off reader look at the struggles of the poor differently. . . . [It] deserves a place on the American bookshelf next to Barbara Ehrenreich's *Nickel and Dimed*." —*The Boston Globe*

"Shipler steers clear of diatribes, looking at human frailty and a spectrum of bosses and social services. With moving under-statement, he develops a compassionate picture of the working poor." —*The Star-Ledger* (Newark)

"A work of stunning scope and clarity. . . . He brings the reader close enough to the challenges faced every day by his workers to make them feel it when the floor inevitably drops out beneath them." —*The Buffalo News*

"The scope and importance of David Shipler's *The Working Poor* brings to mind Upton Sinclair's *The Jungle*."
—*Deseret News* (Salt Lake City)

"A powerful exposé that builds from page to page, from one grim revelation to another, until you have no choice but to leap out of your armchair and strike a blow for economic justice."
—Barbara Ehrenreich, author of *Nickel and Dimed*

"There is no better book on poverty in America than *The Working Poor* because it describes in vivid detail the sort of day to day problems and the cycles that these folks are involved in . . . really thought-provoking in a very important way."
—Senator John Edwards

David K. Shipler

THE WORKING POOR

David K. Shipler worked for *The New York Times* from 1966 to 1988, reporting from New York, Saigon, Moscow, and Jerusalem before serving as chief diplomatic correspondent in Washington, D.C. He has also written for *The New Yorker, The Washington Post,* and the *Los Angeles Times.* He is the author of three other books—*Russia: Broken Idols, Solemn Dreams*; the Pulitzer Prize–winning *Arab and Jew: Wounded Spirits in a Promised Land*; and *A Country of Strangers: Blacks and Whites in America.* Mr. Shipler, who has been a guest scholar at the Brookings Institution and a senior associate at the Carnegie Endowment for International Peace, has taught at Princeton University, at American University in Washington, D.C., and at Dartmouth College. He lives in Chevy Chase, Maryland.

THE WORKING POOR

David K. Shipler

THE
WORKING
POOR

Invisible in America

VINTAGE BOOKS

A Division of Random House, Inc.

New York

FIRST VINTAGE BOOKS EDITION, JANUARY 2005

A portion from chapter two previously appeared in *The New York Times Magazine*.

The Library of Congress has cataloged the Knopf edition as follows:
Shipler, David K. [date]
The working poor: Invisible in America / David K. Shipler.—1st ed.
p. cm.
Includes bibliographical references and index.
1. Poor—United States. 2. Working class—United States—Economic conditions.
3. Working class—United States—Finance, Personal. 4. Cost and standard of living—United States. 5. Wages—United States. 6. Income—United States.
7. Debt—United States. I. Title.
HC110.P6S48 2004
305.5'69'0973—dc21
2003056191

Vintage ISBN: 0-375-70821-9

Author photograph © Claudio Vazquez
Book design by Johanna S. Roebas

www.vintagebooks.com

Printed in the United States of America
20 19 18 17 16 15 14

FOR DEBBY

Contents

Contents

Author's Note

Most significant statistics have been updated in this edition. They show the basic landscape of poverty essentially unchanged, except that the contours of hardship have grown slightly more pronounced. Greater disparities of net worth separate the wealthiest and the poorest families, larger gaps in resources divide affluent school districts from others, more children miss school because of asthma, more Americans go without health insurance, more experience hunger, more are imprisoned, fewer workers are unionized, more illegal immigrants do essential jobs, and more of them die in the desert after crossing the border from Mexico.

Congress and many state legislatures have raised minimum wages, but they still leave most single-earner families below the poverty line. Astonishing percentages of adults who have been surveyed remain unable to perform everyday tasks in reading, math, and document comprehension, rendering them uncompetitive in a global marketplace. The subprime lending phenomenon, which began by exploiting low-income households, has reached into the middle class and jeopardized the entire web of financial markets, demonstrating that the ailments of the poor and the nearly poor cannot be quarantined. There is no refuge. There are only remedies.

D.K.S.
May 2008

Preface

Most of the people I write about in this book do not have the luxury of rage. They are caught in exhausting struggles. Their wages do not lift them far enough from poverty to improve their lives, and their lives, in turn, hold them back. The term by which they are usually described, "working poor," should be an oxymoron. Nobody who works hard should be poor in America.

In 1997, as the country's prosperity soared, I set out to find working people who had been left behind. I found them in black neighborhoods in Washington, D.C., and white towns in New Hampshire, in factories and job-training centers in Cleveland and Chicago, in housing projects in Akron and Los Angeles, in malnutrition clinics in Boston and Baltimore, in California sweatshops, and in North Carolina fields.

My purpose was to look into their lives as thoroughly as they would allow, to unravel the tangled strands of cause and effect that led to their individual predicaments. Some I encountered only once or twice, but others I have followed for five or six years into the present, checking with them again and again as the economic boom has collapsed and recession has set in, as they have gone through promotions and bankruptcies, marriage and divorce, childbirth and death in the family.

The rising and falling fortunes of the nation's economy have not had much impact on these folks. They suffer in good times and bad. Some, caught in paralyzing depression, feel resigned, helpless, and defeated. They are "tired of wishes, empty of dreams," in Carl Sandburg's phrase. Others, however, are proudly driven by their dreams and determination, by belief in the power of work. Rarely are they infuriated by their conditions, and when their anger surfaces, it is often misdirected against their spouses, their children, or their co-workers. They do not usually blame their bosses, their government, their country, or the hierarchy of wealth, as they reasonably could. They often blame themselves, and they are sometimes right to do so.

To spend years doing a dozen, fifteen, twenty, or more interviews with people, you've got to like them. So I am rooting for them, no doubt. But I have tried to see with clear eyes, not through an ideological lens. Indeed, devout conservatives and impassioned liberals will be bothered by this portrait of poverty, at least I hope so, for the reality I discovered does not fit neatly into anyone's political agenda. I want to challenge and undermine longstanding assumptions at both ends of the spectrum.

The subject is deeply emotional, reaching to the heart of what Americans believe about themselves, so I urge the reader who comes across a difficult fact to read on, to absorb all the contradictions of these lives into a larger insight. We need to get beyond partisan politics if we are to make headway against the problem.

It may seem odd to examine poverty by looking at those who live barely beneath or a little above the federal government's official poverty line, as most of these families do. They dwell in a border zone that defies ready definition. But that makes them significant, for as they attempt to escape, we see vividly the obstacles they have to cross. From the edge of poverty, we have an illuminating view of poverty's depths.

"Poverty" is an unsatisfying term, for poverty is not a category that can be delineated merely by the government's dollar limits on annual income. In real life, it is an unmarked area along a continuum, a broader region of hardship than the society usually recognizes. More people than those officially designated as "poor" are, in fact, weighed down with the troubles associated with poverty. Therefore, I use "poor" not as a statistician would. I use it as imprecisely as it should be used, to suggest the lowest stratum of economic attainment, with all of its accompanying problems.

No discussion of the working poor is adequate without a discussion of their employers, so they also appear in these pages—entrepreneurs and managers who profit from cheap labor or who struggle to keep their businesses alive. In addition, this journey encounters teachers, physicians, and other professionals who try to make a difference.

Although I have not sought to be demographically representative, most of the working poor in this book are women, as are most of them in the country at large. Unmarried with children, they are frequently burdened with low incomes and high needs among the youngsters they raise. A majority of those I write about are American citizens, but some are immigrants, both legal and illegal, whose labor is essential to the country's growth and comfort.

The people here are white and black, Asian and Hispanic. Poverty in America knows no ethnic or racial boundaries. African-Americans run up against special handicaps in the inferior public schools most of them attend, the decayed neighborhoods where many live, the stereotyping and racial discrimination they still suffer, especially as they try to move out of the ranks of manual labor into supervisory positions. The legacy of slavery has not yet dissipated, and America's long history of racial bigotry has still left blacks seriously overrepresented among Americans of low income. Yet poverty also contains universal hardships that afflict people of all races. Whites at the bottom of the working world are impeded by many, though not all, of the handicaps that blacks endure. Therefore, having written about black-white divides in my last book, *A Country of Strangers,* I now shift perspectives to the dynamics of poverty that are broadly shared across racial lines.

There are no composite characters in this book; I reject that device absolutely. Every person is real. Where someone has asked not to be named, I have used a first name alone, placed a pseudonym in quotation marks upon first reference, or used a randomly chosen first initial.

Among those who can be named, I have many people to thank. My wife, Debby, applied her skills as a teacher and social worker to open my eyes to intricate issues of schooling and parenting, and she applied her pencil deftly to the manuscript. She enriched my reporting by helping me understand the stories I was bringing home, and she pushed me to think and rethink what I was seeing. Two of my children, Laura and Michael, both graceful writers and keen observers, significantly improved the manuscript with their suggestions. It is a much better book because of them. My oldest, Jonathan, read it in its polished form and made helpful observations.

Many people assisted me with many hours of their time. Among those unmentioned or given insufficient gratitude in the text are David Allison, a friend and former New Hampshire legislator who introduced me to antipoverty workers there and made suggestions on the manuscript; Rebecca Gentes, Nancy Szeto, and Bob Olcott, who reach out to help the poor in New England; Roy Hong and Victor Narro, who head effective organizations to assist Korean and Latino workers in Los Angeles; my cousin Maria Wojciechowski, a fashion designer and manufacturer, who opened doors and enlightened me on the economics of the business; Monique Davis, Lourdes Castro, and Richard Caines of Jobs Plus in Los Angeles; the Reverend Richard Corbin of First Rock Baptist Church in Washington; James Beckwith, director of SOME's Center for Employment Training; Rufus Felder and Brenda Hicks, who provided keen insights into poverty in the nation's capital; Joshua Sharfstein, a brilliant, committed young pediatrician who commented on the manuscript and opened the way to the Boston Medical Center's clinics and research staff; Drs. Deborah Frank and Barry Zuckerman at the Boston Medical Center; Maureen M. Black, director of the Growth and Nutrition Clinic in Baltimore; Gwen B. Brown of the University of Delaware; Nancy Rice, director of day care at Akron's YWCA; Mary LaPorte, head of Cleveland's Center for Employment Training; Brent Schondelmeyer of Kansas City's Local Investment Commission; Anthony Marano and Theodore Hinton, perceptive school principals in Akron and Washington, D.C., respectively; and Julia Song, who interpreted for Koreans whom I interviewed in Los Angeles.

My agent, Esther Newberg, eagerly encouraged me in this project from the outset, and my editor, Jonathan Segal, welcomed the result with enthusiasm and sound advice. I am most grateful to both of them.

If this were a collection of short stories, they could be said to have character and sometimes plot, even family tragedy and lonely heroism. But there is no climax, and no tale ends. Lives continue unresolved.

D.K.S.

JULY 2003

THE WORKING POOR

Introduction

AT THE EDGE
OF POVERTY

Tired of wishes,
Empty of dreams
—Carl Sandburg

The man who washes cars does not own one. The clerk who files cancelled checks at the bank has $2.02 in her own account. The woman who copy-edits medical textbooks has not been to a dentist in a decade.

This is the forgotten America. At the bottom of its working world, millions live in the shadow of prosperity, in the twilight between poverty and well-being. Whether you're rich, poor, or middle-class, you encounter them every day. They serve you Big Macs and help you find merchandise at Wal-Mart. They harvest your food, clean your offices, and sew your clothes. In a California factory, they package lights for your kids' bikes. In a New Hampshire plant, they assemble books of wallpaper samples to help you redecorate.

They are shaped by their invisible hardships. Some are climbing out of welfare, drug addiction, or homelessness. Others have been trapped for life in a perilous zone of low-wage work. Some of their children are malnourished. Some have been sexually abused. Some live in crumbling housing that contributes to their children's asthma, which means days absent from school. Some of their youngsters do not even have the eyeglasses they need to see the chalkboard clearly.

This book is about a few of these people, their families, their dreams, their personal failings, and the larger failings of their country. While the United States has enjoyed unprecedented affluence, low-wage employees have been testing the American doctrine that hard work cures poverty. Some have found that work works. Others have learned that it doesn't. Moving in and out of jobs that demand much and pay little, many people tread just above the official poverty line, dangerously close to the edge of destitution. An inconvenience to an affluent family—minor car trouble, a brief illness, disrupted child care—is a crisis to them, for it can threaten their ability to stay employed. They spend everything and save nothing. They are always behind on their bills. They have minuscule bank accounts or none at all, and so pay more fees and higher interest rates than more secure Americans. Even when the economy is robust, many wander through a borderland of struggle, never getting very far from where they started. When the economy weakens, they slip back toward the precipice.

Millions have been pushed into a region of adversity by federal welfare reform's time limits and work mandates. Enacted in 1996 during an economic boom, the reform is credited by many welfare recipients for inducing them to travel beyond the stifling world of dependence into the active, challenging, hopeful culture of the workplace. They have gained self-confidence, some say, and have acquired new respect from their children. Those with luck or talent step onto career ladders toward better and better positions at higher and higher pay. Many more, however, are stuck at such low wages that their living standards are unchanged. They still cannot save, cannot get decent health care, cannot move to better neighborhoods, and cannot send their children to schools that offer a promise for a successful future. These are the forgotten Americans, who are noticed and counted as they leave welfare, but who disappear from the nation's radar as they struggle in their working lives.

Breaking away and moving a comfortable distance from poverty seems to require a perfect lineup of favorable conditions. A set of skills, a good starting wage, and a job with the likelihood of promotion are prerequisites. But so are clarity of purpose, courageous self-esteem, a lack of substantial debt, the freedom from illness or addiction, a functional family, a network of upstanding friends, and the right help from private or governmental agencies. Any gap in that array is an entry point for trouble, because being poor means being unprotected. You might as well try playing quarterback with no helmet, no padding, no training, and no experience, behind a line of hundred-pound weaklings. With no cushion of money, no training in the ways of the wider world, and too little defense against the threats and temptations of decaying communities, a poor man or woman gets sacked again and again—buffeted and bruised and defeated. When an exception breaks this cycle of failure, it is called the fulfillment of the American Dream.

As a culture, the United States is not quite sure about the causes of poverty, and is therefore uncertain about the solutions. The American Myth still supposes that any individual from the humblest origins can climb to well-being. We wish that to be true, and we delight in examples that make it seem so, whether fictional or real. The name of Horatio Alger, the nineteenth-century writer we no longer read, is embedded in our language as a synonym for the rise from rags to riches that his characters achieve through virtuous hard work. The classic immigrant story still stirs the American heart, despite the country's longstanding aversion to the arrival of "the wretched refuse" at "the golden door," in the words etched on the Statue of Liberty.[1] Even while resenting the influx of immigrants, we revel in the nobility of tireless labor and scrupulous thrift that can transform a destitute refugee into a successful entrepreneur. George W. Bush gave voice to the myth when he was asked whether he meant to send a message with the inclusion of two blacks, a Hispanic, and two women in the first senior appointments to his incoming administration. "You bet," the president-elect replied: "that people who work hard and make the right decisions in life can achieve anything they want in America."[2]

The myth has its value. It sets a demanding standard, both for the nation and for every resident. The nation has to strive to make itself the fabled land of opportunity; the resident must strive to use that opportunity. The ideal has inspired a Civil Rights Movement, a War on Poverty, and a continuing search for ways to ease the distress that persists in the midst of plenty.

But the American Myth also provides a means of laying blame. In the Puritan legacy, hard work is not merely practical but also moral; its absence suggests an ethical lapse. A harsh logic dictates a hard judgment: If a person's diligent work leads to prosperity, if work is a moral virtue, and if anyone in the society can attain prosperity through work, then the failure to do so is a fall from righteousness. The marketplace is the fair and final judge; a low wage is somehow the worker's fault, for it simply reflects the low value of his labor. In the American atmosphere, poverty has always carried a whiff of sinfulness. Thus, when Judy Woodruff of CNN moderated a debate among Republican presidential candidates in March 2000, she asked Alan Keyes why he thought morality was worsening when certain indicators of morality were improving: Crime was down, out-of-wedlock births were down, and welfare was down, she noted. Evidently, welfare was an index of immorality.

There is an opposite extreme, the American Anti-Myth, which holds the society largely responsible for the individual's poverty. The hierarchy of racial discrimination and economic power creates a syndrome of impoverished communities with bad schools and closed options. The children of the poor are funneled into delinquency, drugs, or jobs with meager pay and little future. The individual is a victim of great forces beyond his control, including profit-hungry corporations that exploit his labor.

In 1962, Michael Harrington's eloquent articulation of the Anti-Myth in his book *The Other America* heightened awareness; to a nation blinded by affluence at the time, the portrait of a vast "invisible land" of the poor came as a staggering revelation. It helped generate Lyndon B. Johnson's War on Poverty. But Johnson's war never truly mobilized the country, nor was it ever fought to victory.

More than forty years later, after all our economic achievements, the gap between rich and poor has only widened, with a median net worth of $1,430,100 among the top 10 percent and just $1,700 for the bottom 25 percent.[3] Life expectancy in the United States is lower, and infant mortality higher, than in Japan, Hong Kong, Israel, Canada, and all the major nations of Western Europe.[4] Yet after all that has been written, discussed, and left unresolved, it is harder to surprise and shock and outrage. So it is harder to generate action.

In reality, people do not fit easily into myths or anti-myths, of course. The working individuals in this book are neither helpless nor omnipotent, but stand on various points along the spectrum between the polar opposites of personal and societal responsibility. Each person's life is the mixed product of bad choices and bad fortune, of roads not taken and roads cut off by the accident of birth or circumstance. It is difficult to find someone whose poverty is not somehow related to his or her unwise behavior—to drop out of school, to have a baby out of wedlock, to do drugs, to be chronically late to work. And it is difficult to find behavior that is not somehow related to the inherited conditions of being poorly parented, poorly educated, poorly housed in neighborhoods from which no distant horizon of possibility can be seen.

How to define the individual's role in her own poverty is a question that has shaped the debate about welfare and other social policies, but it can rarely be answered with certainty, even in a specific case. The poor have less control than the affluent over their private decisions, less insulation from the cold machinery of government, less agility to navigate around the pitfalls of a frenetic world driven by technology and competition. Their personal mistakes have larger consequences, and their personal achievements yield smaller returns. The interaction between the personal and the public is so intricate that for assistance such as job training to make a difference, for example, it has to be tailored to each individual's needs, which include not only such "hard skills" as using a computer or running a lathe, but also "soft skills" such as interacting with peers, following orders willingly, and managing the deep anger that may have developed during years of adversity. Job trainers are discovering that people who have repeatedly failed—in school, in love, in work—cannot succeed until they learn that they are capable of success. To get out of poverty, they have to acquire dexterity with their emotions as well as their hands.

An exit from poverty is not like showing your passport and crossing a frontier. There is a broad strip of contested territory between destitution and comfort, and the passage is not the same distance for everyone. "Comfortable is when I can pay my rent with one paycheck—I don't have to save for two weeks to pay one month's rent," said Tyrone Pixley, a slender man of fifty in Washington, D.C. He was especially undemanding, having emerged from a tough life as a day laborer and a heroin user. "I don't want to have to scuffle," he said simply. "I want to be able to live comfortable, even if it's in a ten-by-ten room. And in the course of a month I can pay all my bills out of my pay. I don't have to have anything saved. For me to be comfortable, I don't have to have a savings account."

In such a rich country, most people have more appetite than Tyrone Pixley. Surrounded by constant advertising from television sets that are almost always turned on, many Americans acquire wants that turn into needs. "You're living in the projects, your mom's on welfare, so if you got six kids or five or seven, eight kids growing up, you be wantin' things all your life, and you can't have," explained Frank Dickerson, a janitor who dealt drugs in Washington to get things he didn't have. "You got kids want to have the nice tennis shoes, the jackets; they can't get that with a mom with six, seven kids on welfare. How they gonna get it? They may be getting older, growing up, they want to have nice stuff, so the only way to get that is turn to drugs. That's right. You go out there, you deal, and you get the things that you need. Car, apartments, clothes." Frank Dickerson spent three years in prison, but he and his wife also bought a house in the Maryland suburbs with the money he made from drugs.

Poverty, then, does not lend itself to easy definition. It may be absolute—an inability to buy basic necessities. It may be relative—an inability to buy the lifestyle that prevails at a certain time and place. It can be measured by a universal yardstick or by an index of disparity. Even dictionaries cannot agree. "Want or scarcity of means of subsistence," one says categorically.[5] "Lack of the means of providing material needs *or comforts*," says another.[6] "The state of one who lacks *a usual or socially acceptable* amount of money or material possessions," says a third (emphases added).[7]

By global or historical standards, much of what Americans consider poverty is luxury. A rural Russian is not considered poor if he cannot afford a car and his home has no central heating; a rural American is. A Vietnamese farmer is not seen as poor because he plows with water buffalo, irrigates by hand, and lives in a thatched house; a North Carolina farmworker is, because he picks cucumbers by hand, gets paid a dollar a box, and lives in a run-down trailer. Most impoverished people in the world would be dazzled by the apartments, telephones, television sets, running water, clothing, and other amenities that surround the poor in America. But that does not mean that the poor are not poor, or that those on the edge of poverty are not truly on the edge of a cliff.

"The American poor are not poor in Hong Kong or in the sixteenth century; they are poor here and now, in the United States," Michael Harrington wrote before Hong Kong's prosperity soared. "They are dispossessed in terms of what the rest of the nation enjoys, in terms of what the society could provide if it had the will. They live on the fringe, the margin. They watch the movies and read the magazines of affluent America, and these tell them that they are internal exiles. . . . To have one bowl of rice in a society where all other people have half a bowl may well be a sign of achievement and intelligence; it may spur a person to act and to fulfill his human potential. To have five bowls of rice in a society where the majority have a decent, balanced diet is a tragedy."[8]

Indeed, being poor in a rich country may be more difficult to endure than being poor in a poor country, for the skills of surviving in poverty have largely been lost in America. Visit a slum in Hanoi and you will find children inventing games with bottles and sticks and the rusty rims of bicycle wheels. Go to a slum in Los Angeles and you will find children dependent on plastic toys and video games. Living in Cambodia, my son Michael marveled at the ingenuity bred by necessity, the capacity to repair what would be thrown away at home; when his television remote stopped working in Phnom Penh, he got it fixed at the corner for a dollar.

In the United States, the federal government defines poverty very simply: an annual income, for a family with one adult and three children, of less than $21,100 in the year 2007. That works out to $10.14 an hour, or $4.29 above the federal minimum wage, assuming that someone can get a full forty hours of work a week for all fifty-two weeks of the year, or 2,080 working hours annually.[9] With incomes rising through the economic expansion of the 1990s, the incidence of official poverty declined, beginning the new decade at 11.3 percent of the population, down from 15.1 percent in 1993. Then it rose slightly in the ensuing recession, to 12.5 percent by 2003 and 12.3 percent in 2006.

But the figures are misleading. The federal poverty line cuts far below the amount needed for a decent living, because the Census Bureau still uses the basic formula designed in 1964 by the Social Security Administration, with four modest revisions in subsequent years. That sets the poverty level at approximately three times the cost of a "thrifty food basket." The calculation was derived from spending patterns in 1955, when the average family used about one-third of its income for food. It is no longer valid today, when the average family spends only about one-tenth of its budget for food, but the government continues to multiply the cost of a "thrifty food basket" by three, adjusting for inflation only and overlooking nearly half a century of dramatically changing lifestyles.[10]

The result burnishes reality by underestimating the numbers whose lives can reasonably be considered impoverished. More accurate formulas, being tested by the Census Bureau and the National Academy of Sciences, would rely on actual costs of food, clothing, shelter, utilities, and the like. Under those calculations, income would include benefits not currently counted, such as food stamps, subsidized housing, fuel assistance, and school lunches; living costs would include expenditures now ignored, such as child care, doctor's bills, health insurance premiums, and Social Security payroll taxes. When the various formulas were run in 1998, they increased by about three percentage points the proportion of the population in poverty, from the official 34.5 million to a high of 42.4 million people.[11] A later variation raised the poverty rate in 2006 by 1.9 percent.[12] Such a change would presumably make more families eligible for benefits that are linked to the poverty level; some programs, including children's health insurance, already cover households with incomes up to 150 or 200 percent of the poverty threshold, depending on the state.

Even if revised methods of figuring poverty were adopted, however, they would provide only a still photograph of a family's momentary situation. In that snapshot, the ebb and flow of the moving picture is lost. By measuring only income and expenses during a current year and not assets and debts, the formulas ignore the past, and the past is frequently an overwhelming burden on the present. Plenty of people have moved into jobs that put them above the threshold of poverty, only to discover that their student loans, their car payments, and the exorbitant interest charged on old credit card balances consume so much of their cash that they live no better than before.

When the poor or the nearly poor are asked to define poverty, however, they talk not only about what's in the wallet but what's in the mind or the heart. "Hopelessness," said a fifteen-year-old girl in New Hampshire.

"Not hopelessness—helplessness," said a man in Los Angeles. "Why should I get up? Nobody's gonna ever hire me because look at the way I'm dressed, and look at the fact that I never finished high school, look at the fact that I'm black, I'm brown, I'm yellow, or I grew up in the trailer."

"The state of mind," said a man in Washington, D.C. "I believe that spirituality is way more important than physical."

"I am so rich," said a woman whose new job running Xerox machines was lifting her out of poverty, "because—not only material things—because I know who I am, I know where I'm going now."

Another woman, who fell into poverty after growing up middle class, celebrated her "cultural capital," which meant her love of books, music, ideas, and her close relationships with her children. "In some senses, we are not at all poor; we have a great richness," she said. "We don't feel very poor. We feel poor when we can't go to the doctor or fix the car."

For practically every family, then, the ingredients of poverty are part financial and part psychological, part personal and part societal, part past and part present. Every problem magnifies the impact of the others, and all are so tightly interlocked that one reversal can produce a chain reaction with results far distant from the original cause. A run-down apartment can exacerbate a child's asthma, which leads to a call for an ambulance, which generates a medical bill that cannot be paid, which ruins a credit record, which hikes the interest rate on an auto loan, which forces the purchase of an unreliable used car, which jeopardizes a mother's punctuality at work, which limits her promotions and earning capacity, which confines her to poor housing. You will meet such a woman in Chapter One. If she or any other impoverished working parent added up all of her individual problems, the whole would be equal to more than the sum of its parts.

Consequently, most issues confronting the working poor are laced into most chapters of this book, even while each chapter throws a spotlight on one or another element of deprivation. In the chapter on work you will find stories of parenting; in the discussion of health you will see the matter of housing. Isolating the individual problems, as a laboratory would extract specific toxins, would be artificial and pointless. They exist largely because of one another, and the chemical reaction among them worsens the overall effect.

If problems are interlocking, then so must solutions be. A job alone is not enough. Medical insurance alone is not enough. Good housing alone is not enough. Reliable transportation, careful family budgeting, effective parenting, effective schooling are not enough when each is achieved in isolation from the rest. There is no single variable that can be altered to help working people move away from the edge of poverty. Only where the full array of factors is attacked can America fulfill its promise.

The first step is to see the problems, and the first problem is the failure to see the people. Those who work but live impoverished lives blend into familiar landscapes and are therefore overlooked. They make up the invisible, silent America that analysts casually ignore. "We all live in the suburbs now, not in the inner cities," proclaimed Professor Michael Goldstein of the University of Colorado, explaining on PBS why Woolworth's had been replaced by Wal-Mart in the Dow Jones Industrial Average.[13]

Tim Brookes, a commentator on National Public Radio, once did a witty screed against overpriced popcorn in movie theaters. Indignant at having been charged $5 for a small bag, he conducted research on the actual expenses. He calculated that the 5 $^1/_4$ ounces of popcorn he received cost 23.71875 cents in a supermarket but only 16.5 cents at prices theater managers paid for fifty-pound sacks. He generously figured 5 cents in electricity to cook the popcorn and 1 cent for the bag. Total cost: 22.5 cents. Subtracting sales tax, that left a profit of $4.075, or 1,811 percent.[14]

Evidently, the theater had the remarkable sense not to hire any workers, for Brookes gave no hint of having noticed any people behind the counter. Their paltry wages, which wouldn't have undermined the excessive profits, were absent from his calculation. The folks who popped the corn, filled the bag, handed the bag to him, and took his money must have been shrouded in an invisibility cloak. No NPR editor seemed to notice.

I hope that this book will help them to be seen.

Chapter One

MONEY AND ITS OPPOSITE

You know, Mom, being poor is very expensive.
—Sandy Brash, at age twelve

Tax time in poor neighborhoods is not April. It is January. And "income tax" isn't what you pay; it's what you receive. As soon as the W-2s arrive, working folks eager for their checks from the Internal Revenue Service hurry to the tax preparers, who have flourished and gouged impoverished laborers since the welfare time limits enacted by Congress in 1996. The checks that come from Washington include not only a refund of taxes withheld, but an additional payment known as the Earned Income Tax Credit, which is designed to subsidize low-wage working families. The refunds and subsidies are sometimes banked for savings toward a car, a house, an education; but they are often needed immediately for overdue bills and large purchases that can't be funded from the trickle of wages throughout the year.

Christie, a child-care worker in Akron, earned too little to owe taxes but got $1,700 as an Earned Income Credit one year, which enabled her to avoid the Salvation Army's used-furniture store and instead buy a new matching set of comfortable black couches and loveseats for her living room in public housing.

Caroline Payne's check went for a down payment on her house in New Hampshire. "I used my income tax and paid a thousand down," she said proudly. When she sold it five and a half years later and her daughter lent her money to rent a truck for her move, she planned to pay her back "when I get my taxes."

"I'm waitin' for my income tax to come in so I can pay my real estate taxes," said Tom King, a single father and lumberjack who lived in a trailer on his own land.

Debra Hall, who had started at a Cleveland bakery, was keen with anticipation after filing her first tax return. "I'll get $3,079 back! What am I gonna do with it? Pay all my bills off," she declared, "and I haven't had anything new in the house. Do some good with it, that's for sure. Minor repairs on my car. The bills are first, for my credit [rating], to get all my back debts paid. It will be well spent."

The Earned Income Tax Credit is one of those rare anti-poverty programs that appeal both to liberals and conservatives, invoking the virtue of both government help and self-help. You don't get it unless you have some earned income, and since its payments are linked to your tax return, you don't get it unless you file one. That leaves out low-wage workers—especially undocumented immigrants—who get paid under the table in cash and think they're better off avoiding the IRS. By filing, however, they would end up ahead, because they'd get to keep everything they earned and would receive payment on top of that. The benefits kick in at fairly high levels—at earnings of less than $38,646, for example, for a worker who supported more than one child in 2008. At the lower income levels, the Earned Income Tax Credit can add the equivalent of a dollar or two an hour to a worker's wage.

Enacted in 1975, the program was expanded under Presidents Reagan, Bush, and Clinton, and in 2005 paid more than $37 billion to 20 million households. Treasury officials worry about erroneous claims, honest or fraudulent, which may rise to 27 to 32 percent of the total.[1] On the other hand, an estimated 10 to 15 percent of those eligible don't file for it,[2] partly because employers and unions often don't tell workers that it exists. The presidents of two local unions in Washington, D.C., for example, one representing janitors and the other parking garage attendants, had never heard of the Earned Income Tax Credit until I mentioned it to them. And I have not yet come across a single worker or boss who knew that with a simple form called a W-5, filed with the employer, a low-wage employee could get some of the payments in advance during the year. When I mentioned the W-5 to Debra Hall and she then asked at her bakery, the woman who handled the payroll waved her away impatiently and said she knew nothing about it. Later, the tax preparer told Debra it was better just to wait and get the payment in one lump sum after she filed her return.

It sure is better—if you're the preparer. With cunning creativity, the preparers have devised schemes to separate low-wage workers from as much of their refunds and Earned Income Credits as feasible. The marvel of electronic filing, the speedy direct deposit into a bank account, the high-interest loan masquerading as a "rapid refund" all promise a sudden flush of dollars to cash-starved families. The trouble is, getting money costs money.

The preparers operate from sleazy check-cashing joints and from street-level outposts of respectable corporations. They do for a hefty fee what their clients could do for themselves for free with the math skills and the courage to tackle a 1040, or with a computer and a bank account to speed filing and receipt. But most low-wage workers don't have the math, the courage, or the computer, and many don't even have the bank account. They are so desperate for the check that they give up a precious $100 or so to get everything done quickly and correctly. "You get so scared," said Debra Hall, who paid $95 to have her simple return done after ending twenty-one years of welfare. "I don't know why it's so scary, but I'd rather have it done right the first time."

She was probably wise, because another disadvantage of being poor is that you've been more likely since 1999 to face an audit by the IRS. In that year, 1.36 percent of the returns filed by taxpayers making under $25,000 were audited, compared with 1.15 percent of those making $100,000 or more. The scrutiny was instigated by Republican congressional leaders who feared abuses of the Earned Income Tax Credit. In the face of bad publicity, the IRS shifted the balance in 2000 by auditing 0.6 percent of those under $25,000 versus 1.0 percent of those over $100,000. Thereafter, the audit rate tilted back and forth, to .86 and .69 percent, respectively, in 2001, then to .64 and .75 in 2002.[3] In other words, as the IRS lost enforcement personnel, it dramatically reduced its scrutiny of well-to-do taxpayers, whose returns were once audited at the rate of 10 percent. This despite the fact that audits at the upper levels of income naturally tend to recover more dollars in lost revenue.

Evon Johnson never dared do another return herself after the IRS charged her $2,072 in taxes, penalties, and interest. Newly arrived from Honduras, she was working from 5 a.m. for a cleaning service in Boston that never withheld taxes and never sent her a W-2. She didn't know they were supposed to do either. "I did my taxes, I fill it out, fine," she said. But not so fine, evidently. "Three years after or four years after, IRS contact me saying that I owe them . . . like, $2,072. 'Why do I owe you?' And they say: because I didn't declare my taxes. I say I did. . . . They say no. . . . I sent them a letter saying I was sending them $1,072 I think it was, 'cause I didn't have no money at the time, and I was going to make small installments for the rest of the money. . . . You know what they did? I had a bank account, and they took the money from my bank account—every penny I had." Ever since, she has happily paid $100 a year to a tax preparer, $100 a year for peace of mind. "I don't want the IRS back on me," she explained. "He do it and he sign it and put everything, so if any mistake, he gonna be the one who will have to deal with them."

By the end of February, H&R Block's storefront office on a dismal stretch of Washington's 14th Street looked like a well-used campaign head-quarters a week after Election Day. Most computer screens were dark, and the place was quiet and cavernous. All the desks were empty but one, occupied by Claudia Rivera, who used to prepare returns without charge at a library in Virginia. She and the manager, Carl Caton, didn't have much to do now that the rush had passed, so they were happy to sit at a keyboard and explain.

Each form the taxpayer needed carried a fee: $41 for a 1040, $10 for an EIC (the Earned Income Credit), $1 for each W-2, and so on. Electronic filing cost another $25. So a simple return with two W-2s filed electronically would run $78. But it didn't stop there. Block had a smorgasbord of services for people who lived on the edge. If you had no bank account, your refund could be loaded onto an ATM card that charged $2 per withdrawal. Or a temporary account could be opened into which the IRS payment could be deposited for a fee of $24.95. If you were enticed by Block's offer of a "rapid refund" and wanted a check in a day or two, you paid H&R Block an additional $50 to $90, depending on the amount you were getting. The fee on 14th Street could be as much as $50 on a $200 refund, up to $90 for $2,000 or more.[4]

This was actually a loan, and for a very short time. Filing electronically usually gets you a check in two and a half weeks, according to the IRS, and five days sooner if it's deposited directly into a bank account. At the most, then, the "rapid refund" loan, issued a day or two after filing, would run about fifteen days, which made the $90 fee on a $2,000 payment equivalent to an annual interest rate of 108 percent. At the least, the loan could run as little as four days, propelling the annualized rate to 410 percent on $2,000, and 2,281 percent on $200. (The highest percentage is incurred if the timing occurs perfectly: the return is filed by the IRS's weekly deadline of noon Thursday, the loan check is not issued until after banks close Friday, the taxpayer can't put it into his account until Monday, and the IRS is fast enough to deposit the refund directly with the lending bank the following Friday.)[5]

After a spate of lawsuits, a federal judge in Norfolk ordered Block to stop using the misleading term "rapid refund" in advertising loans, but Block continued with the ads by redefining "rapid refund" as a reference to electronic filing only. The company called its loan program a "refund anticipation loan," a distinction lost on many of the low-wage workers who ventured into Block offices in search of a rapid refund. In 2000 such loans went to 4.8 million taxpayers.

Among all the working people I interviewed who used the loan service, not one understood the terms or the options. Hector and Maribel Delgado, who earned about $28,000 a year picking and packing vegetables in North Carolina, were stunned when I sat with them in their trailer, looked over their tax return, and explained how it all worked. They had paid Block $109 to prepare their return, file it electronically, and give them an advance on their payment from the IRS of $1,307.05. The form they had signed disclosed a finance charge of 69.888 percent annually, but they had not understood it. Even as Block employees presented a contract in fine print, they were trained to avoid the word "loan," and say "two-day refunds" instead, a Maryland judge found in hearing a lawsuit on the lending practices. And the refund loans were lucrative enough to provide 8 percent of Block's entire profits in 1999, mainly because a Block subsidiary owned a 49.99 percent interest in the loans, made by Household Bank.

Something else illicit happened to the Delgados in the Block offices. Although they filed electronically in January, a time when the IRS promises checks within a couple of weeks, "We were told we'd have to wait six to eight weeks," Maribel said. This was patently false. "We needed the money to pay bills," she explained. "We send one part to Mexico, another part to here. We usually send $100 every two weeks to Mexico. We have a big family."

In 2000, after facing a decade of class-action lawsuits alleging misleading lending practices, H&R Block agreed to a $25 million settlement without admitting any wrongdoing. The only practice the company changed was to present the federally required truth-in-lending disclosures earlier in the process, according to a spokeswoman. Do employees at least explain the terms verbally? "A lot of it depends on questions customers ask," she said. "If they ask questions, preparers are supposed to answer." Many customers simply do not know what questions to ask.

Poverty is like a bleeding wound. It weakens the defenses. It lowers resistance. It attracts predators. The loan sharks operate not only from bars and street corners, but also legally from behind bulletproof glass. Their beckoning signs are posted at some 10,000 locations across the country: "Payday Loans," "Quick Cash," "Easy Money." You see them in check-cashing joints and storefront offices in poor and working-class neighborhoods. They have organized themselves into at least a dozen national chains, and they charge fees equivalent to more than 500 percent annualized interest.

They also provide a much needed service. Say you're short of cash, and the bills are piling up, along with some disconnection notices. Payday is two weeks away, and your phone and electricity will be shut off before then. The guy at the local convenience store, who has a booth for cashing checks, throws you a lifeline. If you need $100 now, you write him a check for $120, postdated by two weeks. He'll give you the $100 in cash today, hold your check until your wages are in your bank account, and then put the check through. Or you can give him the $120 in cash when you get it, and he'll return your check. Either way, 20 percent interest for two weeks equals 1.428 percent a day, or 521 percent annually.

If you're still stuck after payday, if your paycheck doesn't quite cover your needs, or if your check for $120 bounces, no problem. The guy behind the bulletproof glass will gladly roll over your loan—for another $20. This pattern prevails in Illinois, for example, where state examiners found that rollovers made up 77 percent of all payday loan transactions. The average customer had ten such renewals, which meant paying fees totaling up to twice the amount borrowed.[6] Eventually, you may have to borrow from another payday loan merchant to pay the fees at the first. And so on and on and on.

Furthermore, the loans are not technically loans in some states, because there's a check. And if a check bounces, more severe penalties apply than those for unrepaid loans. Borrowing $300, for instance, an Indiana woman paid a $30 fee and wrote a check for $330. When the check bounced, her bank and the payday loan establishment charged $80 in fees. Then the lender took her to court, won triple damages of $990, lawyer's fees of $150, and $60 in court costs. The total charge on the $300 loan: $1,310.[7]

Con artists have also enticed the working poor with false promises of outright grants from foundations; all people have to do, the mailings promise, is pay $19.95 to $49.95 for a list of foundation names and addresses, then write heart-rending letters. "There are literally hundreds of private foundations that are anxious to donate money by mail to people who have genuine reasons for needing the money," says one solicitation. "Many foundations are not concerned with what you wish to use the money for as long as it is something legal . . . to pay off bills, go on vacation, meet emergency need or to buy anything that you might need." This absurd assertion has swamped foundations large and small with desperate pleas for cash to repair houses, pay medical bills, and pay off debt. In 2001 an Ohio judge sentenced one operator to five years in prison for bilking people out of at least $500,000 this way. A New Jersey man was raking in $30,000 a week, a prosecutor charged.[8]

Another marvelous setting for scams is the workplace. Korean restaurants in Los Angeles have come under scrutiny for their inventive ways of swindling waiters and cooks, almost all of whom are Korean or Latino, said Roy Hong, head of Korean Immigrant Workers Advocate. Many are paid a flat monthly wage, which is customary in South Korea, and have to work up to twelve hours a day, six days a week, violating state wage laws. Unlike the 2008 federal minimum wage of $6.55 an hour, California's minimum of $8.00 applies to waiters, so many restaurateurs cook the books by faking time cards to show employees working shorter shifts.

Some restaurants also file W-2s that exaggerate the amount of tips paid to workers, a way of transferring part of the tax burden from the business to the employee. When a customer puts a $20 meal on a credit card and adds a $2 tip, for example, the owner pays the worker the $2 tip but tells the IRS that $3 went for the tip and $19 for the meal. (Businesses, as well as individuals, get audited more frequently when their incomes are under $25,000.)

In campaigning for Korean workers, the association has uncovered a pernicious scheme in the custodial business. Korean mom-and-pop janitorial contractors in Los Angeles offer their newly arrived compatriots a tempting deal. Eager for jobs, devoid of English, and frightened that their illegal status may be discovered, the recent immigrants are enticed by the proposition that they can become subcontractors making $1,000 or more a month cleaning commercial buildings where dentists and doctors, lawyers and executives keep their offices. All they have to do, the contractor explains, is put up two and a half months' wages as a contracting fee.

Many Koreans come to the United States with extensive family ties for pooling money and cushioning financial hardship. So the up-front funds can usually be scraped together. "They give away the last bit of their savings in the hope that they too can start a janitorial company," Roy Hong noted. The immigrants usually work at night, cleaning the offices, and everything goes along nicely for a few months. But then the contractor may delay a wage, saying he hasn't yet been paid by the building management. "The next thing you know, you're owed several thousand dollars, and you wonder what happened," Roy explained. Finally, "three or four months later," he said, "the contractor shows up. 'You're out of here. Give me the key.'

" 'What did I do?'

" 'There's been too many complaints.' "

And the next "subcontractor" is offered a tempting deal, if he'll just put up two and a half months' wages.

Behind respectable facades, some major institutions also have their way with the poor. Few banks want depositors who keep low balances, so in states where no laws require otherwise, banks set high minimums and charge prohibitive fees. Many impoverished neighborhoods have no branches at all. This forces low-income families into the expensive check-cashing services, whose outlets have multiplied across the country.

Even where state law requires "lifeline" accounts for the poor, they are rarely advertised because banks tend to lose money on them. Branch officers often don't know about them, and most potential depositors don't either. The best-kept financial secret in New York is the state requirement that banks offer accounts with a $25 minimum opening deposit, a one-cent minimum balance, and eight free withdrawals a month for a $3 monthly fee. Most depositors are kept ignorant of such terms, and major banks report few people opening those accounts.[9]

One reason may be that many workers prefer to earn under the table and keep their finances unrecorded. Others may believe folklore they've heard about unscrupulous banks. "We have our little methods of stashing stuff," said Wendy Waxler, a single mother who had just moved off welfare to a job. "What I plan on doing is getting a safe. It won't draw interest. But at the same time, if the bank go bankrupt, I still have money! You know, I know how they do that money exchange with the bank. It's your money but it's being bought by somebody. It's some kind of system they go through, so when you get there and you say I want all my money, you can't get it right away, you have to wait a certain amount of days so they can get it back. That's what I was told. It's some kind of money something exchange of hands."

Wendy was wrong about the waiting period, but her suspicions were understandable. At the confluence of private industry and government, American society devises numerous techniques of separating the working poor from their meager cash. State lotteries do a booming business at the corner stores in poor parts of town as people pray for the right number to come up and deliver them from hardship. Businesses large and small practice American consumer culture's universal deception: the sweet-sounding come-on that doesn't quite resemble the fine print. Everything is strictly legal; it's just that you have to listen and read carefully before signing, and you have to be a little savvy about the ways of the commercial world. In Debra Hall's case, the enticement was a cellular phone that she got for her daughter, who was in her early twenties. It seemed ridiculously cheap. "It was easy to get," she recalled. "I didn't have the credit, and they still gave it to me. The contract, she just filled it out and I signed it. I didn't take time to read it. . . . The lady made it sound so good. It was gonna be $9 a month. That turned out to be a tale." Debra had somehow missed a digit. "It was $89 a month. I got tricked into a three-year contract. They give you like two thousand minutes. My calls over the weekend were supposed to be free. They weren't. It ended up costing me. I done made two payments toward them. They called me, threatened to take me to court, but they accepted I made two payments. I told the man I feel like I got ripped off."

By contrast, Ann Brash did read her contract when she took over a lease on a Jeep Cherokee. She knew the terms were unfavorable, but she felt forced into an unwanted choice. Ten years earlier, a divorce had plunged her and her two children into poverty and temporary homelessness. Child support payments plus a pittance as a freelance copy editor brought her about $10,000 a year until she landed a full-time editing job at $23,000. She simply needed a reliable vehicle to get to work through the snows of New Hampshire.

"I have a Toyota," she said. "Something's wrong with the starter, and one front panel in the door is pretty lacy with rust. I don't think it's going to pass inspection. . . . Something's wrong with the front end at the moment. I know the brakes need to be redone." She had no savings, no credit, no money to make the repairs. Her teenage children, Sandy and Sally, offered to give up their driver's licenses for a year to cut the insurance premium, hoping that she could replace the car with the money saved.

Then, "a car fell into my lap," she said. "A nice young man in Plainfield wouldn't continue leasing his Jeep. He got married and had too many expenses. He had put quite a bit down on it, and I think there were fifteen months left on the lease, and the [car dealership's] chief person called me and said, 'Would you like to take over his lease for him? It won't require any down payment or anything like that.' So that's what I've done. Did it last week. Seems a little silly to be driving this gas-guzzling huge yuppie car."

The lease ran $293 a month, which was barely manageable for her, and at the end of the lease loomed a crisis. If she wanted to keep the car, she would have to come up with $17,000; if not, she'd have to pay 15 cents a mile over the 36,000 she was allotted, or $2,500 for the nearly 53,000 miles on the odometer. "So, because I hadn't $2,500 to pull out of my pocket, I needed to buy the thing," she said. "My credit is awful." Having defaulted on $18,000 in student loans and $12,000 in credit card debt, she could get a car loan only by enlisting a couple from her church as co-signers. Even at that, the interest rate would have been 24 percent; it dropped to 19 when the man agreed to put his name first as the owner. Payments were $394.45 a month, and they would last until the Cherokee was likely to collapse into a heap of junk.

High interest may be the most ubiquitous trap for low-wage workers. Married, Ann was in the middle class, with all the perks of easy credit. Divorced, she sank rapidly, and for a while, the only barriers between her and utter destitution were four thin pieces of plastic: one from Discover, another from Citibank, and two from Sears. As the balances ran up, she restricted the use of her cards to essentials such as car repairs or purchases that she could justify as contributions to her children's physical health and intellectual well-being: a set of cross-country skis, a computer for Sandy, who later won full financial aid at Dartmouth. "Credit cards went for things like a bicycle," she insisted, "not for potato chips or little Barbie dolls, but things like books, for things that would make them larger and their lives larger, that would contribute to their growing."

The current moment always chafed against the uncertain future. "Christmas was always huge in gift giving," she confessed, "because I thought there may not be a next year."

"Each year you said we can't do it again," added Sandy as he stared at his laptop in the living room.

Ann's relatives were critical of her. "If we decided to splurge and get a box of raspberries in the middle of the winter, that would be just unforgivable, because we didn't have the means to do that," she said. "We shouldn't have those kinds of choices. And I often hear people say, 'Well, look at them, I think they're on welfare. They have food stamps. What are they doing with a television?' I know from the everyday grind of not knowing what's going to happen next that people need some way to relieve that pressure and that pain—and it is pain. Some of us can do it in healthy ways, like putting cross-country skis on a credit card—and that's not very responsible, but it's pretty healthy." She laughed, but not merrily.

The real price was reflected in those bills with the snowballing balances. Since her credit rating was not exactly AAA, she was being charged up to 23.999 percent interest. What's more, while she was faithfully paying the finance charge and minimum almost every month, she did not always get her salary in time to meet the deadline; as a result, she gradually realized, the card companies were adding late fees to her principal, then charging the exorbitant interest on that ever-growing principal. Long after she stopped using the cards, the balance continued to rise.

This has become a chronic problem across the country as lenders search credit records for minor delinquencies to label them "subprime." If you're in that category you get charged higher fees and interest, but you may not know it, because few states require lenders to reveal the score that determines a consumer's credit rating, even when the borrower sees his credit report. The score, running from a low of 375 to a high of 900, is based on five factors: punctuality of payment, the amount of debt, how long credit has been used (the longer the better), how much new credit has been requested (the less the better), and whether the borrower uses a mixture of credit (mortgages and auto loans are preferred over credit cards). Often, the lenders get the facts wrong, of course, and it's to their advantage. Subprime lending grew from about $37 billion to $370 billion from 1994 to 1999, with major banks among the culprits, according to *Consumer Reports.* Setting the stage for the 2007–08 wave of foreclosures, lenders "relaxed the old standards of sound lending by luring consumers into debt waters well over their head, but they didn't relax the old strict standards of loan repayment. The result: Easy-money lenders point fingers at the subprime class they helped create, then punish those borrowers with significantly higher interest rates and fees. College students—and now even 16-year-olds—are a new target for subprime lenders."[10]

Sandy Brash, an Ivy League student with no money at all, "gets an offer a day, at least," said his mother. Because of the aggressive soliciting and the easy credit, even teenagers were declaring bankruptcy, a financial counselor told Ann. She found the notion of bankruptcy abhorrent. She sat one day at the dining room table in her shabby, $400-a-month apartment, her head in her hands, compiling the modest figures for her tax return and tracking her expenses. On a pad of white lined paper, she had written lists of numbers, none of them very large. "I don't know," she said. "I don't even feel like trying; I feel that hopeless. There's no way out of this." Many people get out by declaring bankruptcy, I said. "It sounds like taking welfare, and I don't want to do it," she retorted. "I just want to pay what I owe." Her voice rose onto a high note of anxious melancholy. "But I can't do it with these kinds of rates. I knew that it was gonna take me about an extra thousand dollars a year to get the kids by over those growing years, but I just couldn't find a way around it. And so I did it. And I knew I'd have to pay the piper. So. There it is."

In one respect, Ann was typical of the low-wage working people I spoke with across the country—in New Hampshire towns, North Carolina fields, and Los Angeles housing projects. They were white and black, Latino and Asian, native-born and newly arrived in America, and they were not gripped by rage. Ann did not point a finger of blame. She did not make sweeping criticisms of society at large. "I got myself into this, I made the choices," she said plainly. "In spite of the fact that the credit card companies are taking advantage of people, that they're really awful in charging such awful interest rates, I made the choice of using them. I haven't used them in a couple of years. And plus I can't answer the phone." She did not answer the phone because she hated to hear the bill collectors. "They have all kinds of tones of voices," she said. They left alarming messages on the answering machine, like, "Call this number immediately."

Always when she talked this way she then apologized for "complaining." But I was an instigator in her complaints, I suppose, for I kept asking questions. What does this feel like? What do you think about? How foreign does the zone along the edge of poverty seem to someone who grew up in middle-class comfort? "Nobody really wants to know that sometimes $2 is a significant amount, and $25 always is tremendous," she said, as if this condition still amazed her as well. "Tell me it's not true for ordinary, everyday people. Is it the same? I mean, normal life"—she gave a despairing laugh—"before life was like this. I can't remember. I can't remember what it was like. I mean, every day and every night when I'm trying to fall asleep, there's this worry hanging. Is the car gonna make it through because I haven't maintained it properly? How am I gonna get this? I know I have to do this. How am I gonna get it done? How am I gonna stretch to get these bills paid? If one extra thing happens—."

In May, three months before her car lease expired, her ex-husband's $100-a-week child support payments were scheduled to end because Sally would turn eighteen. It was a deadline of sorts, and Ann finally conceded that bankruptcy had to be considered. It went against her grain, but she couldn't make the numbers add up another way. She then discovered that she was too poor to declare bankruptcy; she would need $700 for the lawyer and $200 as a filing fee. She went to a financial counselor instead.

The counselor was accustomed to working with credit card companies to lower the interest rate to zero if the principal could be paid off in regular installments. But Ann turned out to be too poor for that option as well; looking at her low income, her expenses, and her complete lack of assets, the counselor told her that she would not be able to make the payments. So he advised her to stop paying her credit card bills, pay the rent and electricity first, save the money for bankruptcy, and file when she had enough. Gritting her teeth to "put the moral question aside," as she described it, she stopped paying the credit card bills in March, took sums out of her food money, saved for seven months, and finally in October had pulled together the $900 required to file. It was no cause for celebration. "I take home about $860 every two weeks," she explained. "One half of the biweekly check goes to rent, the other half to the car. Then there are utilities and transportation costs to get back and forth to work. I can't replace underwear. We're not having Christmas this year, though we will try to have a meal. I'm sorry, I don't mean to complain."

On the surface, it seems odd that an interest rate can be determined by the condition of an apartment, which in turn can generate illness and medical bills, which may then translate into a poor credit rating, which limits the quality of an automobile that can be purchased, which jeopardizes a worker's reliability in getting to work, which limits promotions and restricts the wage, which confines a family to the dilapidated apartment. Such are the interlocking deficits of poverty, one reinforcing the other until an entire structure of want has been built. Such was the prison of Lisa Brooks.

She was only twenty-four, but a blemish of weariness tainted her youthful face, and her blond hair was stringy with the carelessness of stress. She worked hard and well as a caretaker at a halfway house for mentally ill adults. She was good with them, kind and firm, but she was paid only $8.21 an hour, which put her and her four children a couple of thousand dollars a year below the federal poverty line.

She lived in a rough section of Newport, New Hampshire, in the kind of housing shown by recent studies to cause and exacerbate asthma in children. Lisa had never noticed any mold, mites, mouse droppings, or roaches, which have been linked to asthma. But she did notice that her nine-year-old son, Nicholas, got worse after they moved into a damp, drafty apartment in an old wooden house on Beech Street.

Nicholas, home with his blind grandmother, had sudden trouble breathing on two occasions. She called 911, and each time an ambulance whisked him to a hospital, once to Claremont and once to New London. In each emergency room, he was treated with oxygen and steroids. But the family's health insurance, for which Lisa paid $97 every two weeks, refused to cover the ambulance charges of $240 and $250, arguing that the doctor had never obtained the proper authorization. Lisa did not understand the insurance rules and procedures and did not know how to appeal. "I fought with the doctor's office and the insurance company," she complained, "and they still said no matter what, I had to pay for it."

She could not pay immediately or all at once, for she operated close to the edge of insolvency. So the charges went onto her credit report. When she tried to move to decent housing by applying for a loan to buy a mobile home, she was denied because her credit record showed the overdue ambulance bills. When she tried to buy a more reliable car, which she needed to get to work, she was also denied. So when her 1989 Dodge Caravan developed fatal electrical problems, she had no choice but to go to a used-car lot that didn't do credit checks but charged her 15.747 percent interest. She paid $5,800 for a 1995 Plymouth Neon that had 82,000 miles, a bad alternator, and other troubles that cost $100 to $200 a month to repair.

On the day Lisa told me about her high-interest loan, I happened to receive an unsolicited offer from my insurance company of an auto loan at 7.5 percent, less than half of her rate. I didn't need the loan, and that's why my rate was so low. In a free market economy, people are like corporations issuing bonds: the less secure they are financially, the more interest they have to pay when they borrow.

Poor people and investment bankers have one thing in common: They both expend considerable energy thinking about money. They have to juggle, predict, and plan, and every decision has magnitude. "If you are starving, you become interested in food. If you are struggling to pay the bills, money becomes tragically important," observed Sebastian Junger, who had the experience before his best-seller, *The Perfect Storm*, suddenly made him a millionaire.[11] Many of those for whom money is tragically important make their choices with enormous care, scouring the papers for sales, clipping coupons, perusing secondhand stores with a canny eye for bargains. Others, however, allow their cash to hemorrhage, never knowing the benefits of saving because they have never had enough to save.

They are caught between America's hedonism and its dictum that the poor are supposed to sacrifice, suffer, and certainly not purchase any fun for themselves. So Ann Brash gets raised eyebrows when she buys raspberries, and many others come under criticism for such indulgences as cable TV. The monthly cable bills cause acid indigestion in some people who do anti-poverty work, and the harshest critics seem to be those who were once poor themselves.

If you sit with a group of dedicated men and women who are trying to help impoverished families, you often notice that one or two among them have apparently been licensed to pronounce stern judgment on their clients' profligate spending. Invariably, the faultfinders display their credentials: a childhood on welfare, an unwed pregnancy, an unhappy intimacy with the culture of hopelessness. Their previous poverty confers an authenticity that commands respect. Having found their way out of the quagmire, they cannot stand to see those left behind, who remind them of themselves, wasting their chance.

So it was that Nancy Szeto spoke up in a discussion at Valley Regional Hospital in Claremont, New Hampshire. Nancy was the streetwise case manager at Partners in Health, a clinic and medical program that served a poor white population abandoned by closing textile mills and shoe factories. She had grown up in the projects in South Holyoke, Massachusetts, and knew all the tricks of staying alive by selling food stamps, stealing off clotheslines, "shopping" by eating quickly off the shelves of supermarkets. She listened for a few minutes to her colleagues' polite analysis of medical problems and services, then cut through the niceties.

"If they're gonna get any money from the state, they should be forced to go through budget counseling," she declared. "I see so many people spending $150 on a phone bill, and all of them have $90 on a cable bill."

"And they all have call waiting," added a caseworker, her tongue loosened by Nancy's outburst.

The others chimed in with stories and complaints. The principal of an elementary school told of trying to call the home of a little girl who was sick only to discover that the phone had been disconnected. "The girl said, 'Yeah, we couldn't afford both the cable bill and the phone bill,'" the principal told the group. The others nodded knowingly.

"They don't have milk, but they do have cable," said Brenda St. Laurence, a home visitor in a program for young mothers at risk. Her clients seemed to love her sweet toughness, which they took as affection unlike anything they had ever received. Brenda applied her lessons from a working-class childhood of frugal self-help and self-denial, of her parents' pride in the hand-me-downs and the hand-sewn clothes and the refusal to take welfare or food stamps. Her formula for survival consisted of good choices and hard work. "We're imposing our values on their priority," she declared without apology. Her clients wouldn't buy health insurance because the expense seemed overwhelming, she complained, but they would buy $200 VCRs and television sets.

"It's instant gratification and an escape," one of her colleagues remarked.

Yes, and why not? some might ask. There are worse ways than television to escape, and why should the poor not share in that vast common ground created by American TV? It is worth remembering that not many decades ago, a welfare recipient wasn't allowed to have the unwarranted luxury of a telephone. The prohibition succumbed to the argument that a phone facilitated job searches, not to mention summoning help for a sick or injured child.

Many middle-class anti-poverty workers feel no right to dictate that the poor shall not purchase middle-class pleasures. It strikes some aid-givers as condescending across class and sometimes cultural and racial lines. The inhibition seems less common among the formerly poor who are now providing assistance, and who often cite good reasons to second-guess the spending habits of their clients—people who are fleeced by corporate and freelance rip-off artists and also fleece themselves by ill-conceived buying. Having seen recovering addicts and alcoholics squander money, for example, some drug and alcohol treatment programs require working residents of halfway houses to turn over their wages for deposit in escrow accounts.

Brenda couldn't make her young mothers do that, but she tried to guide them. "I make them write a list before going to the grocery store," she explained. It was a frustrating effort. "Money saved for bills goes for sodas, cigarettes. They all have pets."

By contrast, the families she admired were those often seen by the principal: working poor parents too proud to use the free lunches for which their children qualified. "They will pack a good, nutritious lunch for their kids," the principal said. "They won't send the Twinkies. They'll send a nice sandwich, a piece of fruit."

That kind of quiet good sense is always less memorable than excess, so the anecdotes around the table may or may not have been representative. The profligate were the ones who stood out to Nancy, who remembered a man requesting help to pay for prescription drugs. Pharmaceutical companies are willing to donate medicine that is nearly outdated, and she routinely worked overtime on the intricate paperwork needed to make the case in situations of particular need. But when she learned that this man had contracted to bring every available television channel into the comfort of his living room, she blew. "I said I'm not gonna waste any time working on his $40 medicine bill if he's gonna spend $90 a month on cable."

Nancy would have liked Leetha Butler, a grandmother who sat smoking in a cool breeze on the concrete patio behind her apartment. This was Benning Terrace, a poor, largely black section of Washington, D.C. Outside the recreation center, just after a July midnight not long before, her daughter Diane had been killed in a drive-by shooting, leaving Leetha with the three grandchildren, four, eight, and sixteen. The circumstance forced her to hone her expertise in saving money, and she was a font of unsolicited advice to her neighbors. If people were hired to run seminars on the subject, which they should be, Leetha would have been the most venerable professor.

Because she drew Social Security, she got less in welfare than her daughter had—$379 compared with $500 a month. Her daughter had received $400 in food stamps; Leetha got $180. She and her husband, now deceased, had worked as custodians, and then she cooked at the Paradise Restaurant. She had no pension.

"It's not tight with me, because I'm an old country woman who knows how to be economy," she declared out of syntax and puffed on her cigarette. Her résumé may have read country woman because she came from Mississippi forty years ago, but she had the cunning of a field commander who knew when to feint and advance and pull back as she played the needs and wishes of her grandchildren. "They don't want for nothin'," she said proudly. They were not allowed to go to the ice cream truck when it cruised temptingly through the neighborhood; it was cheaper to keep ice cream, cookies, candy, and soda at home. She watched for the sales, of course, and could recite the prices of ketchup and Coke in the Safeway, Giant, and Shoppers Warehouse. "I get the papers on a Wednesday and get me a pad and write them down. Coke is $1.89 a box. When they have it on sale for 69 cents, I buy two or three cases. Kmart has ketchup and mustard, 69 cents a bottle. The cheapest you can buy it at Safeway is $1.23." When roast beef was on sale, she bought a lot of it. "I dice it up and use it for stew beef. I dice it up and make pepper steak. When sales be, I buy in quantity. I don't have a car, but I gets around. I get on that iron horse—the bus." If she bought more than she could carry, she paid some fellow $5 to bring her home.

"I went to the thrift store Sunday, and I bought four sets of sheets with pillowcases, four mattress covers, eight coffee cups, and a single bed, and all of that come to $43 and something. My neighbor, she used to go to the store every day, and I said, 'You're just wasting money.'" Leetha Butler would tell anyone who would listen how to do it.

Anti-poverty workers often wish that schools would give required courses in responsible budgeting, but sometimes the opposite occurs. A school in Washington, D.C., preparing fourth-graders from poor families for the Stanford 9 Achievement Test, used a workbook containing this exercise:

> Victor loved money above all things. He had few friends. He never spent any of his money having fun. He never gave any money away to people who were in need. *He just worked very hard and saved. Needless to say, Victor was often unhappy.* [emphasis added]
>
> Dorian was completely different. He liked to have fun. He liked to go to movies and plays. He worked hard, but money wasn't very important to him. Whenever anyone asked to borrow some money, he was happy to help out.

Having confused thrift with stinginess, hard work with misery, and extravagance with generosity and happiness, the exercise asked students to choose the best description of the difference between Victor and Dorian. The correct answer: "D. Dorian helped others and Victor didn't."[12] Teaching children charity shouldn't require denigrating hard work and saving. You don't have to idolize money to need some of it, as the families of these children knew, and if you don't have any, it does take on a certain importance.

Barter is a frequent answer to the lack of cash. Sometimes it looks like a simple favor, as when Marquita Barnes, one of Leetha Butler's neighbors, got her car fixed for a minimal price from a mechanic friend, or lent her car to another friend who did some shopping for her. She and another woman traded day care for the other's kids, and no money changed hands. In other cases, the swaps become explicit. Nancy Szeto worked in a doctor's office in exchange for her hysterectomy. "Lynn," a middle-aged librarian, retained bartering habits from her dirt-poor childhood in Tennessee, and so did her schoolteacher husband, who came out of poverty in Eastern Europe.

"I have a friend who is a better seamstress than I," said Lynn, "and if she will sew sometimes for me, I will clean her house." Her husband used his amateur carpentry skills to make cupboards, bookcases, and the like out of wood scraps he picked up from behind a cabinetmaker's shop. He bartered a kitchen cupboard for a blueberry pie from "a lady that makes the world's best blueberry pies," Lynn said. "We barter for repair of the car sometimes." And her nephew built them a computer in exchange for bookcases in his office.

Lynn lamented the decline of such homespun, marketable know-how. "I have actually made all my clothing in some years," she noted. "I have grown and canned all the vegetables that we have had, he has rebuilt or built every house that we have had, and I have never had anyone in my house to repair any kind of appliance or anything." They had adjusted very tentatively to their rise into the middle-class. "It's just now in our late fifties that we have given ourselves certain luxuries," she said. Such as? "Such as, we paid $8 for a bottle of wine at Christmas, and we shared that. We still have a little bit left, here it is in January. I had a little glass last night." Her thrift made her proud, though it grew out of fear of destitution. "It doesn't matter how much money you make, it's how you spend it," she declared. "And it goes for millionaires to the most poverty stricken people in this country. And I think this is an American problem . . . this advertising, you got to have this, you got to have the newest, the latest, the best, and so on—and that is, I think, an American problem."

Overspending is certainly not the exclusive province of the poor. Tom Wolfe, capturing the opposite side of Horatio Alger's America, deftly caricatures the foibles of the affluent. *"I'm already going broke on a million dollars a year!"* the bond trader screams to himself in *The Bonfire of the Vanities*:

The appalling figures came popping up into his brain. Last year his income had been $980,000. But he had to pay out $21,000 a month for the $1.8 million loan he had taken out to buy the apartment. What was $21,000 a month to someone making a million a year? That was the way he had thought of it at the time—and in fact, it was merely a *crushing, grinding burden*—that was all! It came to $252,000 a year. . . . So, considering the taxes, it required $420,000 in income to pay the $252,000. Of the $560,000 remaining of his income last year, $44,000 was required for the apartment's monthly maintenance fees; $116,000 for the house on Old Drover's Mooring Lane in Southampton ($84,000 for mortgage payment and interest, $18,000 for heat, utilities, insurance, and repairs, $6,000 for lawn and hedge cutting, $8,000 for taxes). Entertaining at home and in restaurants had come to $37,000. This was a modest sum compared to what other people spent; for example, Campbell's birthday party in Southampton had had only one carnival ride (plus, of course, the obligatory ponies and the magician) and had cost less than $4,000. The Taliaferro School, including the bus service, cost $9,400 for the year. The tab for furniture and clothes had come to about $65,000. . . . The servants (Bonita, Miss Lyons, Lucille the cleaning woman, and Hobie the handyman in Southampton) came to $62,000 a year. That left only $226,200, or $18,850 a month, for additional taxes and this and that . . . garage rent for two cars ($840 a month), household food ($1,500 a month), club dues (about $250 a month)—the abysmal truth was that he had spent *more* than $980,000 last year. Well, obviously he could cut down here and there—but not nearly enough—*if the worst happened!*[13]

In real life, the numbers were lower for Willie and Sarah Goodell, but the pattern was similar. They were barely out of their teens, with three small children and their own missed childhoods to make up for. Both of them had inherited destructive behaviors from their upbringing—he drinking, she violence—and were busily reenacting them in their young adulthood.

They lived upstairs in Sarah's grandmother's beaten-up house. As if the weathered building had no purpose but to fade and sag, it stood sadly among the tightly crisscrossed streets of old homes in the center of Claremont, New Hampshire. The grandmother had no money to repair the place, so nothing much worked: the shower, the washer and dryer, the kitchen sink. Windows were broken, and the living room had no carpet—only bare linoleum—but plenty of toys were stacked along the wall, and a tall rack of music CDs adorned a cabinet containing a stereo and a large television set. The two oldest children, ages three years and eighteen months, wore no clothes, only diapers.

Like many New England mill towns, all that is left of Claremont's quaintness are the pretty sounding names: Sugar River, and streets called Summer and Pleasant and Pearl. Most of the decent jobs in mills and factories have disappeared, leaving a gritty struggle to find work that barely pays a living wage. Willie and Sarah, who lived on Pearl Street, were luckier than most because Willie got a job through Sarah's stepfather installing sheet metal roofs on candy factories and pharmaceutical plants being built in Massachusetts. Although it took him two and a half hours to drive each way every day, he could make $13 to $20 an hour, which added up to $31,000 in his best year. The trouble was, they spent it all, scratching little pleasures out of a constant, grinding, and unsatisfying chore of buying:

$50 a week on cigarettes alone; clothes, shoes, CDs here and there; almost every dinner out at McDonald's, Pizza Hut, or Taco Bell. They had no bank account.

Willie was lanky, mild, easy, with glasses and a mop of light brown hair. He often wore a slight smile that made him look a bit lost, as if he had suddenly awakened to find himself in a mysterious mess. His kids were hellions, and Cody, the three-year-old, already had wild anger in his eyes, already shouted with a rage that sounded as deep as a man's. He hit his younger sister, who in turn hit the baby. Cody actually looked like a good buddy of Willie's, and sure enough, turned out to be the buddy's son. But Willie was an honorable man, and he adopted his wife's firstborn.

Sarah had short, spiky, reddish hair; a ring through her right ear; and another through her right eyebrow. Her face was very pale and often sullen, her pasty complexion betraying her preference to stay inside, usually in bed, rather than take her restless kids into the country daylight to run off their energy. She spoke in a morose and despairing tone, almost a whine.

"I got molested twice as a child," she told me the first time we talked. "When my mom and dad broke up and my dad moved out, my mom decided that she wanted to be a kid again 'cause she had me when she was eighteen. She went to bars quite a bit. I was nine years old, and I stayed home by myself. So that was real hard. I was in foster homes, group homes. I was molested by an uncle and a family friend. I have a lot of mental health problems because of my upbringing. That's why I can't work. I suffer from severe anxiety, panic, post-traumatic stress syndrome, all kinds of different stuff. I have a severe drug phobia, too, so I go to see counselors, but I can't take any medication." She lit a Marlboro with a lighter. Nicotine was a drug she didn't fear.

Sarah also went to bars quite a bit, because she also needed to be a kid, she explained. By twenty-one her marriage to Willie would collapse and she would have four children by three fathers. She fed the kids junk food and a constant stream of inconsistency, one moment allowing them to run wild, the next scolding them angrily for the same behavior. Threats of punishment—being deprived of a trip to rent a movie, being sentenced to bed—came and went like blowing leaves, creating no consequence.

Brenda, the home visitor, worried about the dangerous conditions. I saw them too while the couple was still together. Cody turned on an electric fan one day, stuck his fingers close to the blades, and received a mild rebuke. He climbed onto the sill of a window without a screen. Willie said firmly, "Get out of the window," and Cody ignored him with impunity. Brenda once arrived at the house to find Sarah asleep and Kayla, at eighteen months, chewing on a cigarette and putting a Bic lighter in her mouth. She played in the dirty toilet while Cody pulled his chair up to the stove with the burners lit. I saw Kayla hit the baby in the face with a sneaker and pick up a plastic bench, ready to slam it onto the baby's head. Cody screamed, and Willie stopped her. But less serious behavior seemed to get more serious scolding: Kayla was permitted to eat cheese while walking around the living room, and then got a harsh reprimand for the natural result of dropping cheese all over the living room floor. Neither Willie nor Sarah nor the kids seemed to know how to play; their few expensive toys were mostly just dragged noisily around the house. Willie's idea of a fun Saturday outing, after his license was suspended for drunken driving, was to walk with the children to Wal-Mart. Brenda's agency and the state's protective services tried unsuccessfully to get a judge to remove the children from the home.

Sarah's marriage was stormy while it lasted. Having grown up watching her mother hit her stepfather, she explained, she did the same to Willie. "I beat the hell out of him. He goes through about four pairs of glasses a year." Since she could stand a few paces back from herself and see clearly what she was doing, I asked, couldn't she change? She answered in a small voice, "I feel absolutely helpless."

To avoid her violence, Willie bought her off. "I know I could put money in the bank," he said, "but what's easier, puttin' money in the bank or havin' a mellow home life? Really." With a wan smile, he looked over at Sarah. They had just kept a month's accounting for me, and Willie and Sarah both thought they could have cut a lot of their spending if they'd tried. "Six hundred of it," Willie estimated. What would that have done to their lives? "It would have been terrible," he said. "You tell him," he suggested to Sarah, who kept silent. "She can't—you know, with her problems and stuff, it seems like, being depressed all the time, if she's not spending money she's not happy."

But buying a couple of CDs didn't make her happy for long. "For the day," she said.

"Till she's out of the store," he countered.

Their routine living expenses were not exorbitant. They included $300 a month rent to Sarah's grandmother, about $100 for the use of her phone, and nothing for electricity and cable TV. But Willie's long commute usually cost several hundred dollars a month in gas, except when he hitched a ride with fellow workers, as he had to do after his license was suspended. The couple paid $220 a month for a car they couldn't afford to insure, about $200 a month on laundry because their appliances didn't work, and $200 a month to eat out because the gas company wouldn't turn on their gas until they paid $400 in overdue bills. Also, Sarah rarely felt emotionally well enough to cook, and Willie was too exhausted when he got home from a fourteen-hour day.

Furthermore, they liked to spoil themselves sometimes. "We're both young," Willie explained, "and because neither one of us really had everything when we were kids, I suppose we do sometimes go overboard with birthdays and Christmas and stuff."

Their accounting, from mid-April to mid-May, showed that they had added enough outflow to their rent, car payments, and other recurring bills to use up almost all of the $2,500 Willie had earned.

Groceries (includes diapers and cigarettes)	$467.19
Movie rentals	$53.93
Eating out	$214.45
Miscellaneous	$785.09

The groceries included expensive items, such as $3.99 a day for Lunchables, the only kind of lunch that Cody would not hurl around the room of his preschool. The Miscellaneous category comprised fifty-two entries, most of whose details neither Sarah nor Willie could remember a month after listing them. They ranged from $2 and $5 for instantly forgotten things to $161 for concert tickets (to hear Ozzy Osbourne), a $52 outfit for a wedding, and numerous presents at $45 and $50 for birthdays, weddings, and one of those occasions cleverly invented by the manufacturers of nonessential items: Mother's Day.

Their main effort at economizing came at Willie's expense. Instead of smoking Camels, his favorite, he agreed to smoke Marlboros at $4 a carton less. Cutting out smoking altogether did not make it onto the agenda. Forgoing restaurants, prepared foods, and junky snacks seemed an impossible sacrifice, and Sarah angrily spurned advice on this point from Brenda the home visitor. "Her plans on a budget are: You eat hamburger and mashed potatoes for the week and stuff like that, and that's just not the way I want to live," Sarah scoffed. "I like to be able to eat what *I* like."

Even if Sarah and Willie had been models of frugality, their lives would still have been shackled to a heavy history of debt. From leaner days before he'd landed his roofing job, Willie owed $700 on a phone bill, $5,000 on a repossessed car, and $10,000 in medical bills. He could not get a phone; she could, only because her phone debts were run up before she became legally responsible at age eighteen. Eventually, she would probably have to try a ruse employed by some parents in this situation: open telephone accounts under a child's name and Social Security number.

Willie's medical bills were incurred in a fashion typical of working people without health insurance. He could not afford to go to the dentist, his teeth were decaying, and he was on the road working construction jobs. Whenever an abscess developed, he went to the nearest emergency room for painkillers and antibiotics. The law requires hospital emergency rooms to treat everyone, covered or not, but they can then send bills, which are usually whoppers. The charges were all beyond Willie's reach, and they ruined his credit rating.

"Poor," Sarah said in describing their socio-economic level, and then laughed a high-pitched, nervous giggle.

"We'd put ourselves poor," Willie echoed, "but I know if we were smart people, we could be very well off. Sometimes I bring home $700 a week. I know I could be very well off. But, you know, neither one of us can just sit home and say, OK, this is what we've got for dinner, and that's it." He smiled sadly. "If we had $10 in our pocket and we were sick and tired of sitting in the house, we'd go out and spend $10 on ice cream and supper. I guess it's easier to make life easier by doing something that costs money."

Sarah offered her definition of being poor: "We don't have any money saved. We don't really have a home we can call our own."

"It's our own fault," said Willie. "I'm not blaming it on anybody else."

Willie's earnings from working with sheet metal were high enough to put his family above the federal poverty line but low enough to get them some benefits. The children were eligible for SCHIP, the federally funded State Children's Health Insurance Program, and Sarah got milk, cereal, peanut butter, baby formula, and other foods from WIC, the Special Supplemental Nutrition Program for Women, Infants, and Children. Some years, when they filed their income tax return, they received not only a refund of taxes withheld, but the additional Earned Income Tax Credit.

One year, they used part of their check from the IRS to get tattoos. "It's like we're still kids ourselves," she said, "so we've got to act like kids once in a while." Willie got a wizard etched on his arm. Sarah pulled her shirt up in back to show hers: a heart made of thorns.

Chapter Two

WORK DOESN'T
WORK

It is not easy for men to rise whose qualities are thwarted by poverty.
—Juvenal, *Satires*

Christie did a job that this labor-hungry economy could not do without. Every morning she drove her battered '86 Volkswagen from her apartment in public housing to the YWCA's child-care center in Akron, Ohio, where she spent the day watching over little children so their parents could go to work. Without her and thousands like her across the country, there would have been fewer people able to fill the jobs that fueled America's prosperity. Without her patience and warmth, children could have been harmed as well, for she was more than a baby-sitter. She gave the youngsters an emotionally safe place, taught and mothered them, and sometimes even rescued them from abuse at home.

For those valuable services, she received a check for about $330 every two weeks. She could not afford to put her own two children in the day-care center where she worked.

Christie was a hefty woman who laughed more readily than her predicament should have allowed. She suffered from stress and high blood pressure. She had no bank account because she could not keep enough money long enough. Try as she might to shop carefully, she always fell behind on her bills and was peppered with late fees. Her low income entitled her to food stamps and a rental subsidy, but whenever she got a little pay raise, government agencies reduced the benefits, and she felt punished for working. She was trapped on the treadmill of welfare reform, running her life according to the rules of the Personal Responsibility and Work Opportunity Reconciliation Act of 1996. The title left no doubt about what Congress and the White House saw as poverty's cause and solution.

Initially the new law combined with the good economy to send welfare caseloads plummeting. As states were granted flexibility in administering time limits and work requirements, some created innovative consortiums of government, industry, and charity to guide people into effective job training and employment. But most available jobs had three unhappy traits: They paid low wages, offered no benefits, and led nowhere. "Many who do find jobs," the Urban Institute concluded in a 2002 report, "lose other supports designed to help them, such as food stamps and health insurance, leaving them no better off—and sometimes worse off—than when they were not working."[1]

Christie considered herself such a case. The only thing in her wallet resembling a credit card was a blue-green piece of plastic labeled "Ohio" and decorated with a drawing of a lighthouse projecting a beam into the night. Inside the "O" was a gold square—a computer chip. On the second working day of every month, she slipped the card into a special machine at Walgreen's, Save-A-Lot, or Apple's, and punched in her identification number. A credit of $136 was loaded into her chip. This was the form in which her "food stamps" were now issued—less easy to steal or to sell, and less obvious and degrading in the checkout line.

The card contained her first bit of income in every month and permitted her first expenditure. It could be used for food only, and not for cooked food or pet food. It occupied the top line in the balance sheet she kept for me during a typical October.

"2nd Spent 136.00 food stamps," she wrote. So the benefit was all gone the day she got it. Three days later she had to come up with an additional $25 in cash for groceries, another $54 on October 10, and $15 more on the twelfth. Poor families typically find that food stamps cover only one-half to three-quarters of their grocery costs.

Even the opening balance on the card was chipped away as Christie inched up in salary. It makes sense that the benefit is based on income: the less you need, the less you get. That's the economic side. On the psychological side, however, it produces hellish experiences for the beneficiaries. Every three months Christie had to take half a day off from work (losing half a day's wages) and carry an envelope full of pay stubs, utility bills, and rent receipts to be pawed over by her ill-tempered caseworker, who applied a state-mandated formula to figure her food stamp allotment and her children's eligibility for health insurance. When Christie completed a training course and earned a raise of 10 cents an hour, her food stamps dropped by $10 a month.

That left her $6 a month ahead, which was not nothing but felt like it. Many former welfare recipients who go to work just say good riddance to the bureaucracies that would provide food stamps, medical coverage, and housing. Some think wrongly that they're no longer eligible once they're off welfare; others would rather forfeit their rights than contend with the hassle and humiliation. Quiet surrender ran against Christie's grain, however. She was smart and insistent, as anyone must be to negotiate her way through the system. She never flinched from appealing to higher authority. When she once forgot to put a utilities bill in her sheaf of papers, her caseworker withheld her food stamps. "I mailed it to her the next day," Christie said. Two weeks passed, and the card remained empty. Christie called the caseworker. "She got really snotty," Christie remembered. " 'Well, didn't I tell you you were supposed to send some documentation?'

"I was like, 'Have you checked your mail?' " No, as it turned out, the caseworker's mail had piled up unread. "She was like, 'Well, I got people waiting up to two, three months on food stamps.' And she didn't get back with me. I had to go to her supervisor." The benefits were then restored.

It is easy to lose your balance having one foot planted tentatively in the working world and the other still entwined in this thicket of red tape. Managing relations with a boss, finding reliable child care, and coping with a tangle of unpaid bills can be daunting enough for a single mother with little such experience; add surveillance by a bureaucracy that seems more prosecutor than provider, and you have Christie's high blood pressure.

While she invoked the system's rules to get her due, she also cheated—or thought she did. Living with her surreptitiously was her boyfriend, Kevin, the father of her son. She was certain that if the Housing Authority knew, she would be evicted, either because he was a convicted felon (two years for assault) or because his earning power, meager though it was, would have lifted her beyond eligibility. So slight are the margins between government assistance and outright destitution that small lies take on large significance in the search for survival.

Kevin looked like a friendly genie—a solid 280 pounds, a shaved head, and a small earring in his right ear. His income was erratic. In decent weather he made $7.40 an hour working for a landscaper, who rewarded him with a free turkey to end the season at Thanksgiving—and then dumped him onto unemployment for the winter. He wanted to drive a truck or cut meat. He had received a butcher's certificate in a training course during imprisonment, but when he showed the document from the penitentiary, employers didn't rush to put a knife in his hand.

The arithmetic of Christie's life added up to tension, and you had to look hard through her list of expenditures to find fun or luxury. On the fifth she received her weekly child support check of $37.68 from Kevin (she got nothing from her daughter's father, who was serving a long prison sentence for assault). The same day, she put $5 worth of gas in her car, and the next day spent $6 of her own money to take the day-care kids to the zoo. The eighth was payday, and her entire $330 check disappeared in a flash. First, there was what she called a $3 "tax" to cash her check, just one of several such fees for money orders and the like—a penalty for having no checking account. Immediately, $172 went for rent, including a $10 late fee, which she was always charged because she never had enough to pay by the first of the month. Then, because it was October and she had started to plan for Christmas, she paid $31.47 at a store for presents she had put on layaway, another $10 for gasoline, $40 to buy shoes for her two kids, $5 for a pair of corduroy pants at a secondhand shop, another $5 for a shirt, $10 for bell-bottom pants, and $47 biweekly for car insurance. The $330 was gone. She had no insurance on her TVs, clothes, furniture, or other household goods.

Utilities and other bills got paid out of her second check toward the end of the month. Her phone usually cost about $43 a month, gas for the apartment $34, electricity $46, and prescriptions between $8 and $15. Her monthly car payment ran $150, medical insurance $72, and cable TV $43. Cable is no longer considered a luxury by low-income families that pinch and sacrifice to have it. So much of modern American culture now comes through television that the poor would be further marginalized without the broad access that cable provides. Besides, it's relatively cheap entertainment. "I just have basic," Christie explained. "I have an antenna, but you can't see anything, you get no reception." And she needed good reception because she and Kevin loved to watch wrestling.

One reason for Christie's tight budget was the abundance of high-priced, well-advertised snacks, junk food, and prepared meals that provide an easy fallback diet for a busy working mother—or for anyone who has never learned to cook from scratch. Besides the staples of hamburger and chicken, "I buy sausages," Christie said, "I buy the TV dinners 'cause I might be tired some days and throw it in the oven—like Salisbury steaks and turkey and stuff like that. My kids love pizza. I get the frozen pizzas. . . . I buy my kids a lot of breakfast things 'cause we're up early and we're out the door. You know, those cereal bars and stuff like that, they're expensive! You know? Pop Tarts, cereal bars, Granola." The cheaper breakfasts, like hot cereal, came only on weekends, when she had time. "They eat the hot cereal, but during the week we're on the go. So I give them cereal in the bag. My son likes to eat dry cereal, so I put him some cereal in the lunch bag. Cocoa Puffs. They got Cocoa Dots." She laughed. "Lucky Charms. He's not picky. My daughter's picky." Those candylike cereals soak up dollars. At my local supermarket, Lucky Charms cost dearly: $4.39 for a box of just 14 ounces, while three times as much oatmeal goes for nearly the same price, $4.29.

Recreation for Christie and Kevin centered on food and drink. When her eleven-year-old daughter brought home a good report card, they rewarded her by scraping together a little cash for an evening at a modest restaurant, either Mexican or, if it was Wednesday, at Ryan's down the street. Wednesday was steak night at Ryan's, a big, boisterous, all-you-can-eat family place at the edge of the black neighborhood where they lived. The buffet counters, heaped with steaming potatoes and green beans and slabs of beef, were encircled by a jovial, multiracial crowd of grandparents, parents, and kids jostling one another with friendly apologies as they carried away piles of stick-to-your-ribs food for just nine bucks apiece.

As an occasional present to themselves, Christie and Kevin invited friends over, lit a charcoal fire in the metal barrel that had been made into a grill behind her ground-floor apartment, and feasted on barbecued chicken and ribs and lots of cans of Miller's. Did they drink to get drunk?

"Mmmmmmmm," Kevin replied in a long, low hum.

"Mmmmm," said Christie. "Not around my children. I go to the club for that. Then I come home and go to sleep." She gave a delighted laugh. She liked Boone's Farm wine, Manischewitz Cream, and Paul Masson brandy, which explained the entry in the records she kept for me: "15.00 on bottle" on October 12. But she was no alcoholic, and she and Kevin swore that they had stayed away from drugs despite the constant temptation in a neighborhood crawling with pushers.

"Christie likes to have fun," her mother said tartly. Her mother, "Gladys," had dropped out of high school, spent years on welfare, and nurtured the fervent dream of seeing her three children in college. The ambition propelled two of them. Christie's brother became an accountant, and her sister, a loan officer. But Christie never took to higher education. She began reluctantly at the University of Akron, lived at home, and finally got fed up with having no money. The second semester of her sophomore year, she went to work instead of to school, a choice that struck her then as less momentous than it turned out to be.

"She didn't take things as serious as they really were," Gladys complained. "Now she sees for herself how serious this is." Just how serious depended on what she wanted to do. She loved working with children but now discovered that without a college degree she would have trouble getting hired at a responsible level in the Head Start preschool program, much less as a teacher in a regular school; she was limited to a YWCA daycare center whose finances were precarious. Since 95 percent of the Y's children came from low-income families, the fees were essentially set by the center's main source of income, Ohio's Department of Human Services, which paid $99 to $114 a week for full-time care. Given the center's heavy expenses, the rates were not enough to pay teachers more than $5.30 to $5.90 an hour.

Christie's previous jobs had also imprisoned her close to the minimum wage as a hostess-cashier at a Holiday Inn, a cashier at Kmart, a waitress in a bar, a cook and waitress and cashier in various restaurants. She had become a veteran of inadequate training programs designed to turn her into a retail salesperson, a bus driver, and a correctional officer, but the courses never enabled her and her classmates to pass the tests and get hired. She had two words to explain why she had never returned to college. "Lazy. Lazy."

It was strange that she thought of herself as lazy, because her work was exhausting, and her low wage required enormous effort to stay afloat.

When the bills would inundate her, she explained, "I pay that one one month and don't pay that one and play catch-up on this one, one month. I play catch-up pretty much. I rotate 'em around. You got a phone bill. You got to pay that every month. If you miss a payment, pssshhh. It's double the next month and triple the next month. The next thing, you got a disconnect. I live on disconnect notices. And I pay my bill every month, but get a disconnect every month, because everybody wants you to pay on the first of the month. I don't get paid on the first of the month. I can't pay ten people on the first of the month. I get the disconnect notice, and I get very, very close. I call, I make payment arrangements. I'm like, 'Hey, please give me a break. Don't turn me off yet. I'm gonna send ya something,' you know. The car dealer man, I might not take him all of my 150, but I take him something. They're funny guys. They work with me, they're real nice. And he said, 'Well, Miss V, what do you have for us today?' One thing the guy said, he said, 'I notice you come every month with something.' And I do. I come with the majority. Every month. I'm like, 'Hey, I gotta buy food, fellas.' "

Her strained schedule made her vulnerable to fees and fines, including one that ended her children's summer day care. Because she couldn't afford the $104 a month it would have cost to put her kids part-time in the Y's day-care center, her mother watched them after school. In the summer they went to a Boys and Girls Club for a token $7 each. But the club had a strict rule about pickup times—3 p.m. except Friday, when it was 1. One Friday, her mother forgot the earlier deadline. Instead of calling Christie at work, the club started the clock running, imposing a fine that began at $10 apiece for the first five minutes and continued at a lower rate until her mother finally appeared, more than an hour late. It reached $80 per child, an impossible amount for Christie to afford, so her children could not continue. In her life, every small error had large consequences.

Christie seemed doomed to a career of low pay without the chance of significant promotion, no matter how important her jobs might be to the country's well-being. At her level in the economy, everything would have to be perfectly aligned to open the door to comfort. After the missteps at the outset of her adulthood, she would now need the boost of higher education or the right niche of vocational training. By itself, hard work alone would not pay off. That lesson, tainting such a revered virtue, is not one that we want to learn. But unless employers can and will pay a good deal more for the society's essential labor, those working hard at the edge of poverty will stay there. And America's rapturous hymn to work will sound a sour note.

Work didn't work for Debra Hall either. Like many welfare mothers forced off the rolls into the labor force, she found almost everything in her life changed except her material standard of living. She had to buy a car to get to work, wake up before dawn, struggle to learn new skills, and weave her way among racial tensions on the job. Her budget had more complexity but no surplus. Her major gain was emotional—she felt better about herself—and so, on balance, she was tentatively glad to be working.

Debra was fortunate enough to live downstairs in a two-family house owned by her mother, in a Cleveland neighborhood of faded comfort. With her meager wage on the open market, she would have been confined to a dreadful flat. Here, the houses needed paint and their roofs needed shingles, but the rooms were spacious and the streets were not so hard. Across her stoop wafted the sweet smell of marijuana being smoked by two young women sitting on the steps next door. A curtain was drawn across Debra's large front window.

Inside, the living room was dark at the height of the afternoon. She had been sleeping on the couch since returning from her 3:30–11:30 a.m. shift in a bakery, and she still wore her white uniform shirt with "Debra" on a label stitched above the right-hand pocket. Her black hair was straightened, and a perpetual smile illuminated her broad face, touched by a flicker of sadness now and then as she managed to laugh pungently through the tales she told of hardship.

The television set was on, and an upright vacuum cleaner stood in the middle of the living room floor. Decorating an end table were pictures of her two children: a younger son who was handicapped by Down syndrome, and an older daughter who was progressing modestly at the lower levels of a banking career. "Thank God she didn't get on welfare," Debra declared in her deep voice.

It was the birth of her daughter, when Debra was eighteen, that launched a twenty-one-year career of welfare checks and "under-the-table-type jobs," as she put it, including positions as a housekeeper and bar hostess that paid her in unrecorded cash. The widespread practice of holding undeclared jobs while getting welfare meant that "welfare-to-work" should have been called "work only," for it slashed people's actual incomes. "I got used to that, having the extra money," Debra explained. "I could make like, per week, probably like $120 'cause they would pay you like $30 a night, plus tips. . . . So I got used to that and got stuck on it and forgot about the outside world."

The letter reminding her of the real world came from her caseworker. At age thirty-nine, Debra had no skills to speak of. She had dropped out of community college—"I wasn't puttin' anything into it," she confessed. She judged herself "lazy" and had never tried to learn a trade. She had lived off her welfare check, her illicit earnings, and her Supplementary Security Income (SSI) payments from Social Security for her son, a teenager who was in special schooling. Welfare reform was now catching up with her. The 1996 act allowing states to impose time limits and work requirements gave Ohio the right to demand that Debra get a job or do job training.

She found her way to the Cleveland Center for Employment Training, whose board members were executives of local industries that needed machinists, welders, and other laborers, and because she liked wearing jeans and sneakers instead of dress-up clothes, she chose warehouse work—"shipping and receiving," in the trade vernacular. As part of its real-life training, the center dispatched UPS packages for companies in a small industrial park, so Debra learned how to type, how to operate the computerized UPS system, how to keep an inventory, how to run a forklift. The course "settled me down and made me want to learn and want to do something as far as getting into the workforce," she said. It was the first time in her life that she felt motivated, and it made her think that welfare-to-work wasn't a bad idea. "People will want more," she predicted, "and be able to teach their kids that's growing up to want more. . . . And if they put us into these training centers and show us that we can do it, we can show our kids."

That's how it looked when Debra was still a trainee. It didn't look as bright once she got into a job. First, the car she had to buy to avoid a long bus ride to work was not cheap and not reliable. Then, UPS had no openings, so she took her forklift certification, her carefully prepared résumé, and her newly acquired interviewing skills to Orlando Bakery. Poised to answer all questions brilliantly, she never got to speak. A man guided her quickly around the plant, and then asked, "Can you start at seven?"

She was stunned. "All this rehearsing I did to talk and everything like that, and he just asks me can I start at seven." She gave a sour laugh. "I thought I was being hired as a forklift operator," she continued. "I was wanting to run a forklift 'cause they have forklifts. They have them in shipping and receiving, the dock area where the trucks pick up. You have to load the trucks up and everything. But it's all men!" she yelped. When she arrived at work the first day, she was put on an assembly line. "Excuse me, heh," she told a supervisor. "You just hired a woman that can drive a forklift."

" 'Oh, we don't have any openings for a forklift operator.' "

On-the-job training could be summed up in a single command: copy the worker next to you. Debra watched closely and began by flipping bread on the dreaded garlic line, a conveyor that required employees to start at 7 a.m. and stay until the entire day's production was packaged, usually about 5 p.m. and sometimes as late as 6. "Everybody there can't stand it," she said. "The garlic loaves, the sticks, garlic sticks, garlic rolls—and every chance they got they was coming over with a different type of bread to see if they could make it garlic." After the bread passed through a slicer, "you have to separate it, lay it flat, then it's two people next to the one that's separates it, make sure it lays flat and don't go down double. Then it goes through the butter. You know, they have butter like a fountain. It goes through, then it goes through the freezer, then you got four people there that stacks it. Then you got a person that stands there makes sure it goes through, then they pack it."

The workers were unionized, but the conditions were unworthy of a union contract. The pay was $7 an hour, including a paid lunch hour and a fifteen-minute break after nine hours of work. Benefits didn't kick in until an employee had been on the job for six months. It wasn't hard labor, but it challenged Debra's mental and physical agility. "The first day I worked there, I'm like, I'm not gonna get this. It was terrible." She was laughing again. "I'm like, oh, God, my whole body was sore. And just lookin' at the conveyors 'cause the stuff is steady movin', you know, and it's movin' fast 'cause it's comin' past you. . . . I was crying almost. I was like, I can't do this."

After a while she was offered a welcome chance to move off the garlic line, and even though it meant getting out of bed at 2 a.m for her shift, she would be doing less stressful work: packing bread into bags and cartons. The respite from tension was short-lived, however. No sooner had Debra learned the packing task than she was yanked again into panic when a supervisor abruptly assigned her to a machine that she was untrained to operate. "I didn't even know the name of the machine," she said. "I just happened to hear them say, 'You be Number Two.' I was like, 'What you all be talking about?' " Number Two was, indeed, the name of the machine, a huge piece of equipment that needed somebody to "flip switches," Debra explained. "You have to feed the bags in, make sure the zip locks that close the breads is on. You have to set the machine a certain way—different kinds of bread, hamburger buns, hot dog buns. You know, different parts of the line you have to set the slicer to slice the bread. You have to know how deep."

She was having nightmares. "I'm still disoriented because I can't think. All I keep doing is feel like I'm floating, because of this machine. . . . I done had dreams where my supervisor was fussin' because this didn't go right. You know what I'm saying? The job came home with me. . . . This doesn't make sense for this little seven dollars." A few months later her wage went to $7.90.

Being black, Debra also felt herself on the wrong end of subtle racial strains. "Seems like they're too lenient on the Hispanics," she asserted. "I was next to one, and she wouldn't keep up. You know, bread was piling all up, and she puttin' 'em in boxes, and flattening them out, and he come over and raise hell." She pretended to speak no English, so Debra became the target of the complaint. "Hold on!" she objected. "She can understand as much English as I can understand. Don't come over here pressing me because she won't keep up! I done made three boxes to her one. But she runs off that Spanish, gets a Spanish partner, and they get to going on and on and on and on, you know what I'm saying? Oh, my God, yeah. It's a lot of that, a lot of that."

Debra had no confidence that she could move up in position and pay. Whenever she asked supervisors about the salary at their level, they'd answer vaguely, "It varies." She couldn't get specific figures, so she had no sense of what her goal might be. She seemed doomed to repeat her family's inability to emerge from low wages. She barely knew her father and couldn't remember what work he did. Her mother had cleaned houses and had drawn a welfare check. Two of her brothers had been shot dead, one in a bar fight, the other in his car. A third was in prison for burglaries, a fourth worked as a truck driver, and a fifth did maintenance at a retirement center. One sister worked in a factory, another in a bar, and a third took care of her grandchildren. Debra's daughter had taken the modest step from bank teller to a promotional sales job, but Debra was mostly delighted that she had avoided pregnancy. "I was lucky. I just did a lot of preaching to her," Debra said. "I did escape being a grandma early."

Debra's cash flow was so anemic, compared with her expenses, that she barely had a bank balance. Her wages from the bakery were deposited directly, but they were gone as soon as they hit the ledger. "I have maybe $8 in the account every week," she said. "You can't get less than ten from the money machine, so if I have five, I can't get five." If she went to a teller, the bank levied a $3 charge. She was so low one January that she had to pay a $15 fee for a two-week $100 advance from a storefront payday loan operation.

Her fellow workers in the bakery were trapped in gloom. Nothing there encouraged her. As she began the job, one employee after another cautioned her: "You don't want to work here." She heard the warning even from an assistant supervisor who had been her high school classmate.

"Debra, I know you don't want to work here," she remembered her classmate saying.

"How long you been here?" Debra asked.

"I've been here twelve years," her friend replied.

"And I didn't have anything to say," Debra remarked to me, "but my mind was saying, 'What the hell you doing here so long?' "

The new millennium arrived in a crescendo of American riches. The nation wallowed in luxury, burst with microchips, consumed with abandon, swaggered globally. Everything grew larger: homes, vehicles, stock portfolios, life expectancy. Never before in the sweep of human history had so many people been so utterly comfortable.

Caroline Payne was not one of them. A few weeks after New Year's Day, she sat at her kitchen table and reflected on her own history. Two of her three goals had been achieved: She had earned a college diploma, albeit just a two-year associate's degree. And she had gone from a homeless shelter into her own house, although it was mostly owned by a bank. The third objective, "a good-paying job," as she put it, still eluded her. Back in the mid-1970s, she earned $6 an hour in a Vermont factory that made plastic cigarette lighters and cases for Gillette razors. In 2000, she earned $6.80 an hour stocking shelves and working cash registers at a vast Wal-Mart superstore in New Hampshire.

"And that's sad," she declared. "I got thinking about that the other day.

I'm only making eighty cents more than I did more than twenty years ago." Or less—the equivalent of $3.70—taking into account the rise in the cost of living. And she did not know then how much sadder it would become.

Caroline's was the forgotten story of prosperity in America. With indifference, the economic boom at the turn of the century passed her by. The reasons were not obvious, but they were insidious. She was not the victim of racial discrimination—she was white. She was not lazy—she was caustic about colleagues and relatives who were. She was punctual, rarely out sick, willing to do night shifts, and assiduous in her work habits. The Wal-Mart manager, Mark Brown, called her "a nice lady" with lots of enthusiasm. "She's self-driven," he observed. "She's always willing to learn and better herself. She's got potential. She can definitely move up."

But she did not move up. She had never moved up. And that ceased to amaze her, it had been going on for so long, in job after job after job. She was astonished only by Mark Brown's praise. "I'm surprised," she remarked when I told her what he had said. She was stacking blank videotapes on a shelf. "I didn't think they liked me here. People don't usually say nice things about me."

Somewhere along this track that leads nowhere, a good many Americans give up on the dream. They sink back onto welfare, or they stop imagining themselves as foremen or department heads or office managers. Caroline was fifty, with so many years of disappointment that her moments of despair seemed quite reasonable. She had been treated occasionally for depression, and she once tried to commit suicide with an overdose of aspirin. Still, she kept striving. She called herself "luckylady" in her e-mail address. She said, "Have a wonderful day" on her answering machine. She did not have big thoughts about corporate profits or dark judgments about society's unfairness; she just tried for basic financial security. Her persistence seemed so incongruous that it played like a dissonant melody against the monotone of job stagnation. Again and again, she applied to manage one sales department or another at the store, and again and again she was passed over in favor of men—or, she observed wryly, women who were younger and slimmer.

"I work my butt off, excuse my language. I'm there most of the time," she said sharply, "but that don't matter to them." She was paid a dollar an hour more during nighttime shifts, nothing close to what her flexibility was worth to a store that stayed open around the clock. Trying to get ahead, she was always available to change hours and fill in, even during evenings when she had to leave her fourteen-year-old daughter, Amber, home alone. Without a car, Caroline had a twenty-minute walk each way, trekking back and forth at odd times of night in all kinds of weather. One cold February day, walking gingerly along icy streets to save her temperamental back, she trudged from her house to her job at her normal time of 10 a.m., only to be told to come for a shift beginning at 1 p.m. instead. So she made her way home and then returned to the store: three trips consuming one hour before earning her first dime of the day. This she did willingly—even after the store had hired a man, whom she knew, at a wage higher than hers. "He's working in electronics at night, but you go in and he's standing around looking at them TVs or doing something else," she said in a soft whine. "He doesn't keep busy or do anything, and they don't say nothing. And I've complained about it, and I've been practically told to mind my own business."

Nor could she compete with the slender women, who received flirtatious attention from the assistant manager. "You notice a lot of these young girls get these jobs," Caroline declared. "My age shows on me terribly. I've had people think that I'm Amber's grandmother, I've had such a hard life."

The people who got promotions tended to have something that Caroline did not. They had teeth. Caroline did not have teeth. If she had, she would not have looked ten years older than she was. But her teeth had succumbed to poverty, to the years when she could not afford a dentist. Most of them decayed and abscessed, and when she lived on welfare in Florida, she had them all pulled in a grueling two-hour session that left her looking bruised and beaten. Under the state's Medicaid rules as she understood them, a set of dentures would have been covered only if she had been without any teeth at all; while some of them could have been saved, she couldn't afford to do less than everything. In the end, unfortunately, the dentures paid for by Medicaid didn't fit and made her gag, so she couldn't wear them. An adjustment would have cost about $250, money she didn't have.

No employer would ever admit to passing her over because she was missing that radiant, tooth-filled smile that Americans have been taught to prize as highly as their right to vote. Caroline had learned to smile with her whole face, a sweet look that didn't show her gums, yet it came across as wistful, something less than the thousand-watt beam of friendly delight that the culture requires. Where showing teeth was an unwritten part of the job description, she did not excel. She was turned down for a teller's position with the Claremont Savings Bank, which then hired her for backroom filing and eventually fired her from that. Wal-Mart considered her for customer service manager and then promoted someone else, someone with teeth.

Caroline's was the face of the working poor, marked by a poverty-generated handicap more obvious than most deficiencies but no different, really, from the less visible deficits that reflect and reinforce destitution. If she had not been poor, she would not have lost her teeth, and if she had not lost her teeth, perhaps she would not have remained poor. Poverty is a peculiar, insidious thing: a cause whose effects then cause the original cause, or an effect whose causes are caused by the effect. It depends on where in the cycle the analysis begins. Like most of the forgotten America, Caroline was a bundle of causes and effects.

Depression, a frequent companion of poverty, afflicted Caroline in paralyzing bouts of self-neglect, according to Brenda St. Laurence, the caseworker and home visitor who helped Caroline for years. "A lot of times she doesn't wear her deodorant and really needs to, doesn't take a shower, her hair will be really messy," Brenda said. "She's a heavy smoker; her clothes will smell smoky at times." I never saw Caroline in that condition during five years of interviewing, but Brenda came from the same world as her clients and easily moved into their lives. Brenda was not a graduate-degree professional from an affluent upbringing; she had a high school diploma and a working-class background. She did not condescend, but she did judge, and with enough affection to be regarded warmly by those she tried to assist. At Caroline, she directed more understanding than blame. "When you are a depressed person," Brenda observed, "you can't get motivated."

Like many laborers stuck at low levels, Caroline was the victim of many factors: appearance, yes, but also a heavy burden of childhood, marital, and educational handicaps that included difficulty reading and writing. All her deficiencies intertwined with the injustices and the ruthlessness of the free market. At times, personal trials distracted her so intensely that she could not concentrate on her work. And so, as the country's economic power rushed forward, she was caught in a back eddy of stagnant wages and limited horizons. The recession that followed the boom made little difference at her lowly position; she continued to move laterally among her modest jobs, from store to factory to store. Her pattern mirrored the broader experience of low-income single parents nationwide, whose employment rate and hourly wages barely changed during the recession.[2]

Caroline's father had been a school janitor and her mother, an occasional factory worker. "We didn't have a lot of love and security that kids need," she remembered. Nor was there material plenty. "When I was a kid, I never had much." Long after that early void, neediness remained. "I always wanted things," she admitted. "I can get spending and overdo things sometimes."

Even in her late forties, she was like a teenager craving instant gratification, said Brenda, who worked with Caroline on budgeting and tried to rein in her spending. "She likes her credit cards," Brenda remarked. "She said that she deserves these things. She said she works hard, she wants nice things before she dies. Of course," Brenda added, "I come from a family of eight where you just bought the necessities. Food was the most important thing, paying the rent was the second thing, keeping light and heat."

After Caroline bought her house, Brenda saw her mature. But it was hard to break the patterns of childhood, and the debts of the past did not disappear easily. Caroline's family had moved repeatedly and disrupted her education. She spent first and second grades in a four-room schoolhouse in Meriden, New Hampshire, then repeated second grade there because of reading problems. "I'm a slow reader," she confessed, "and I have to have it quiet, and I read word for word. I'm self-conscious about it." She didn't remember her mother or father ever reading to her. "With us kids, she was not really a mother." In third grade, she and her family lived over a shoe store in downtown Leominster, Massachusetts, with sirens and traffic and no place to play. The following year they moved to a trailer park in Keene, New Hampshire, where she spent fourth, fifth, and sixth grades.

One day as a sixth-grader, walking home from a playground, she was slapped with terrible news. A sympathetic friend of her sister's said how sorry she was to hear that Caroline's dad was leaving. What? Caroline had been given no hint of this. "And I ran the rest of the way home," she recalled, "and I remember opening that trailer door, and I just looked at him—we had a double-decker—and I ran up the stairs, and I cried and I cried." And the seed of distrust was planted.

"There was really no communication in that family, and it was very hard. And my dad come up and tried to talk to me and things then, and he said he was really surprised that it bothered me the most, because I used to be the tomboy one, you know. But I think underneath I was never really happy, but I would always smile, and I think I was puttin' on a front making people think I was, when I really wasn't."

From then on, she wrote in a college essay, she felt like "nothing but a piece of furniture being shoved around in all directions." The rootlessness made her friendships transitory. She spent seventh and eighth grades with an aunt back in Meriden, while her brother and sister were farmed out to other homes. Her mother remarried. "My stepdad drank a lot," she said. "He tried to get fresh with me and things like this, and I was scared and never told my mom, you know? And I got to the point where I hit him."

Then, since Caroline did not want to live with her stepfather, every year of high school was spent in a different place. As a freshman, she stayed in Lebanon, New Hampshire, with a woman for whom she had been a baby-sitter. She did most of her sophomore year back in Keene, then went to live with her father, first in Woodstock, Vermont, in her junior year, then as a senior in Northfield, Massachusetts, where she proudly graduated. "I'm the only one out of three kids that actually ended up graduating from high school," she boasted. "My brother ended up going in the service, and my sister got married at fifteen. And I'm not trying to brag, but I felt good 'cause my mom and dad never graduated from high school neither. It took me an extra year 'cause I stayed back in second grade."

Two months after her commencement in 1969, Caroline got married. "And now there's times I wished I hadn't," she declared. "I was young, and I think it was because I wanted that security, and I thought I loved the guy, maybe at the time. I had a strong belief that when you get married it's supposed to work; I had real old-fashioned, strong beliefs. And I think it was so easy for me to latch onto people because I haven't had lots of love and security and communication and things. It was almost like if a guy gave me affection, I'd latch onto almost like the first one that come along. And that's not good. I've learnt over the years, it's not good."

The marriage produced three children, lasted fourteen years, and finally sank into a swamp of suspicion created by her husband's infidelity. She worked night shifts in factories to put him through engineering school, took care of the kids and the animals they raised, and in the end caught him out all night with another woman. The relationship was then corroded by distrust until it disintegrated.

Because she could not afford a lawyer and just wanted out of her marriage, she ended up with only $400 a month in child support and no share in their house. "It was a nice place," she said sadly. "It was a log home that we had built when I was pregnant. We had to put in our own bridge, and I had always wanted a covered bridge made out of logs. Never did get one. But at the time I couldn't afford the taxes and everything." Immersed in the memories, she was quietly weeping.

Proudly and foolishly, Caroline rejected an offer from her ex-husband's parents to put a trailer on their land for her and the kids. Taking care of her was not their responsibility, she felt. So she took a small apartment and bounced between welfare and dead-end jobs, supplementing her income by scavenging for cans. "We'd go and watch a ball game at school, and I'd take bags and stuff them in my pocketbook," she recalled. "After the ball game I'd be going around poring through the garbage cans pickin' out five-cent cans." Her older daughter would ride her bike as far ahead of her mother as possible to avoid any hint of association. "I figured, that few cents buys some milk, buys some bread, things that you need, you know what I'm saying? It all helps. But it embarrassed her. She hated it as she got older."

Alone and scared, Caroline married again, and this time it was worse. Vernon Payne insulted her, hit her, flew into jealous rages—once when he thought he saw her talking to a young man outside the nursing home where she worked. The "man" was actually a woman with her hair cut short. The marriage lasted two years. "At times I hated men," she said. "Men were no good, they just lied, and you're not gonna tell me no different." On the rare occasions when she voted, she made a point to vote only for women.

Yet she remained hungry for a man in her life and duplicated the pattern so often seen among single mothers who carry the wounds inflicted by men. Women of limited means who crave and cannot create loving partnerships dominate the ranks of the poor, for they are not just single mothers. They are also single wage-earners.

Amber, Caroline's fourth child, was born into the troubled second marriage. Except for a clubfoot, the petite, dark-haired girl seemed healthy. Only gradually did telltale signs of trouble emerge. She was late walking compared with Caroline's other children, and a little later to be potty trained. That struck her mother as nothing more than a normal variation among children. "She could watch TV and remember a lot of things she saw," Caroline recalled. Then, a test in a preschool program found some learning "delays."

After the divorce Amber spent every other weekend and a week or two in the summer with her father, Vernon. She once came home with a burn on her finger, and someone filed a complaint with Vermont's child protective services. "They came right there and took me in a room right at work and threatened they were gonna take Amber away from me even before I got home from work," said Caroline. The authorities had both the wrong crime and the wrong culprit, as it turned out later, but their suspicions were kept alive by persistent anonymous reports. Caroline suspected her own mother, "a back stabber," in Caroline's words. "Even if I just grabbed ahold of Amber, like her arm like this, she would say, 'Oh, don't hurt that kid!' " The state pursued the matter, and Caroline found herself in a fight for her daughter. "I had to go to court, I had to go to parenting classes, to keep Amber."

Family turbulence can rarely be walled out of the workplace. An employee with desirable skills or a powerful position may have enough value to be tolerated through a difficult time. But Caroline had so little capital of that sort that she could not purchase an employer's patience for her personal trials. When her life at home got stressful, her life at work got perilous. That meant marginal performance, no advancement, and a rolling career of short stays in jobs with no accumulation of seniority.

"You're all nerved up, you're stressed, you don't know what somebody's gonna pull on you next," she said. Even at the factory in the middle of the night, she would cry and cry, "and people would know things were wrong."

Amid the struggle, Caroline somehow did a training program in office skills, got off welfare, and landed a decent job as the front-desk receptionist in an insurance company. (She still had her teeth.) She answered phones, sorted mail, typed up initial files for insurance policies. "It was quite an experience," she said, and she would have continued if the pressures over Amber hadn't damaged her work. "They were giving me some warnings," she said, "that I wasn't doing so good, and I think it was being upset at all these problems." She was obviously going to be fired, so she quit—"got done with the job," as she put it.

She searched intensively for good office jobs, applied for one after another, and heard nothing. She would call to find out why. Again and again, she would be told that another candidate had a college degree. So she decided to get one, and enrolled at Vermont's Johnson State College. She obtained a student loan and began classes in business and accounting.

And then she noticed that Amber, who was nearly five, was masturbating. "Kids experiment anyway, but she was doing it excessively," Caroline said. "It was more and more obvious. I'd give her a bath and she'd be touching herself. There was these little signs, but it was hard to prove anything because she was not old enough to come out and tell me, and it would be my word against theirs. But I had this funny feeling." Often, at the end of a weekend with her father and his wife, "she'd come right to me real quick, you know? And I'd say, 'Give your father a kiss,' and she'd kind of back away."

So, one day when her father brought her home, Caroline took her into the bathroom. "I noticed she was red, front to back. And this was not right." Alarmed, Caroline asked a college friend, Tina, to talk with Amber alone and see what she could learn. "And Tina said, 'You won't believe the things she told me.' " They took the little girl to the hospital, where a doctor confirmed that she had been penetrated. The police were called, Caroline's welfare caseworker was summoned. As Tina and the caseworker questioned Amber, Caroline and a police officer watched and listened from behind a one-way mirror. The girl repeated what she had told Tina, and a restraining order was issued against Vernon Payne. To escape, Caroline moved with Amber to Florida for several footloose years that disrupted Caroline's education, and Amber's as well.

Nearly a decade later, when Caroline told Amber that her father had died, the girl, then fourteen, said in a sudden burst of relief, "Good, good."

Amber's "delays" became more pronounced in Florida. Further testing when she entered first grade measured her IQ at 59, in the low range of mild mental retardation, a handicap more prevalent in lower-income households. But she did not get the consistent special schooling that might have helped her, because Caroline repeated her parents' syndrome of uprootedness by moving from place to place: a tiny apartment, a trailer with a woman friend, a filthy trailer of her own, a place with a male friend, and another trailer—all in New Port Richey, Florida—then to a cousin's in Winter Haven and back to New Port Richey. In three years, Amber attended three or four different schools. Caroline then headed north to New Hampshire, where she moved a few times from one school district to another. Altogether, she estimated, Amber had been in seven or eight schools. "She was probably like this little rag doll that just got brought anywhere," said her caseworker, Brenda, who pressed Caroline to settle down and resist her urge to keep moving; otherwise, Brenda told her, teachers and counselors could not get to know Amber well enough to provide fruitful help. The argument took hold after Caroline became a homeowner, until that achievement was reversed by misfortune and miscalculation. "She's very good with Amber," Brenda said then. "I work with so many families. Sometimes I wish I had another Caroline."

There was no clear evidence on the extent to which educational stability might have aided the girl. Her middle-school principal called her condition "a language-based learning disability." She could barely read and write, could not easily tell time from clocks with hands, and was unable to understand that she had enough money if she gave a storekeeper $10 to buy something for $4. Yet she could play the flute if her mother wrote the letter for each note on the musical score. She took gymnastics lessons at a dance school, for which her mother paid by cleaning the school's studio once a week. And Amber could give a lucid verbal account of a class trip to Montreal, for example; if you heard her talk, you wouldn't suspect retardation. With sweet courtesy, she eagerly helped her mother around the house, and she could cook for herself in a microwave. But she also had epilepsy, and the risk of a seizure prompted doctors to advise that she not be left alone. The logistical maze of arranging care for Amber around constantly shifting hours of work had Caroline tangled in anxiety.

Social Security provided Amber with SSI, a monthly disability payment, but that didn't give Caroline the means that an affluent parent would have to muster an arsenal of expensive private tutors and therapies. Nor did Caroline have the skills and sophistication to help her child extensively at home, as school officials urged. "They came right out and told me in one of the meetings that it was my job to teach my daughter to read," Caroline complained. "I said, 'Wait a minute. I'm a single mom. I bring up my daughter . . . I do my job . . . I pay my taxes in full. You do your job.' They gave me a dirty look. They didn't say nothing."

Brenda, her caseworker, hit the same wall. "I would say to Caroline, 'At night, please sit and read to your daughter, even if it's ten or fifteen minutes.' She'd say, 'That's not my job. That's the teacher's job.'"

So Amber had only the meagerly funded special education classes in the public schools of Claremont, a town so strapped for financing that it led a group of communities in a celebrated victory before the New Hampshire Supreme Court to win state grants for impoverished school districts. The court's ruling was not implemented effectively, however, and Claremont—ranking 236 out of New Hampshire's 259 municipalities in per capita income—still badly underpaid its teachers. Amber felt herself standing still, and she was furiously frustrated, especially after she entered high school and was consigned to a vocational-technical department that taught cooking, check-writing, and other basic skills of independent living—but little or no reading.

Whether her capacities could have been expanded by the kind of training that money could buy was an open question. Would affluence have made any difference to Amber? Her pediatrician, Steven Blair, who had treated her since she was nine, paused for a long time, considering his answer. "Minute differences," he said finally. "Not substantial differences." On the other hand, specialists in mental retardation generally argue for "individualized therapeutic and educational services for the child in conjunction with flexible support services for the family," as Jack P. Shonkoff puts it in a basic pediatrics textbook. "Such services are delivered best when they focus on the family as a dynamic system and view child and family adaptation as interdependent and mutually influenced by the environment in which they live."[3] That was as realistic in Caroline's case as suggesting a long vacation in Paris.

To flee with Amber from Vermont, Caroline had to suspend her studies, which she later resumed in Florida, at Webster College, completing a two-year associate's degree in office technology and information processing. She also ran up a debt of $17,000 in student loans, a sum that rose to $20,000 as she deferred payments. Contrary to conventional wisdom about education as a good investment, Caroline's degree turned out to be a colossal waste of money. She never landed a job in her field of training, never got one that required anything more than a high school diploma. She would have benefited with a bachelor's degree, of course, but the associate's degree proved useless as a credential.

When she moved back north from Florida to New Hampshire, Caroline lived for two weeks with her aunt, applied for welfare, and had a typical brush with governmental absurdity. She was told by officials that the best way to get welfare benefits and subsidized housing was to move into a homeless shelter, so she did. That made her an emergency case. In just three weeks—a hundred times faster than if she had lived in a major American city—she had a Section Eight voucher that paid most of her rent in a privately owned apartment. Then she set about working toward her dream: a house of her own.

For seven days a week she worked two part-time jobs—one in a store for $5.25 an hour, the other for "four something" an hour answering phones and doing other chores at the local lodge of the Loyal Order of Moose, where she was also a member. In two years, Caroline paid off most of her back bills and put herself in a position to start thinking seriously about finding a house to buy.

She did not quite realize it at the time, but she had assembled an essential structure of attributes to open the door to a mortgage. They included a record of diligence on the job and connections with people of influence—both intangible benefits of being in the workforce. Furthermore, she had a reliable monthly check in the form of Amber's Social Security payment. Very few low-wage workers can claim a steady income from the government or helpful personal contacts.

The key individual for Caroline turned out to be her boss at the store, also a real estate agent, whose good friend happened to be president of the Sugar River Savings Bank. The banker met Caroline and was impressed. "She seems like the type of woman who would go hungry to pay the bill," he told her boss. Not quite, though. She had two or three bills to take care of to burnish her credit check, so she spent a year on those while the house she wanted stayed unsold. The price dropped, and she finally got the bank's approval for a mortgage.

It didn't hurt that Amber's Social Security payment of $514 a month would be deposited directly into an account at Sugar River Savings, from which the mortgage installment would be automatically withdrawn. (The SSI check rose to $736 after Amber's father died, but the money flowed in and out, which usually left an account balance of under $100.) Using those funds for mortgage payments was legitimate, Caroline reasoned, because Amber would eventually inherit the house—an assumption that, in the end, couldn't survive the family's poverty. It was a terrible fact that a mortgage would not have been forthcoming without Amber's disability.

The snug, gray clapboard house, built in 1891, was nestled among others on an icy street. It was about to be improved, courtesy of a federal program that would replace the siding, repaint the trim, and remove lead paint inside—testimony to Caroline's skill at securing government aid. The windows were now insulated with plastic sheeting stapled to the frames, and over the side door hung a "Merry Christmas" banner. In a different place at a different time, the house would have been considered quaint and charming enough to be worth plenty. But sitting in a sad, old neighborhood near the center of a New England town that had been left behind, it was worth just $37,000 when Caroline discovered it in 1997. With $1,000 from her income tax refund to cover closing costs, she became the owner—along with the Sugar River Savings Bank.

There was no price tag on her satisfied sense of possession and autonomy. She proudly conducted a tour: the two beige couches in the living room, the flowery wallpaper, the yellow curtains, the old TV set and VCR, Fluffy the cat with a red collar and a bell, the pantry and storeroom behind the kitchen, her adult son's crossbow for deer hunting, the cellar with a washer and dryer and oil furnace, the upstairs where colorful afghans she had crocheted lay folded waiting to be given to Amber's teacher and school bus driver and principal for Christmas.

Caroline worked in a clothing factory, sewing for $6 an hour. She was laid off. She worked a few hours a week at the shelter where she had lived, helping applicants to the fuel assistance program. When winter ended, she was out of a job, so she worked at Tambrands, a factory that made Tampax, for $6.50. Sitting for hours at a time, she began to get acute pain in her legs and finally had to go to the emergency room. Her back was the cause. "And so the doctor says, 'I want you to take one night off and rest as much as you can. Stay off your feet. Stay off your legs.' " She called Tambrands, owned by Procter & Gamble, to tell them she wouldn't be in on Sunday because of her back. Monday morning the phone rang: Her services were no longer needed. So she went back to the sewing factory and got laid off two or three times. Working at the edge of poverty means working on the coldest side of corporate America.

The Claremont Savings Bank, which had rejected her as a teller, called to invite her to apply for a filing job. She was hired for twenty-five hours a week at $7 an hour, with the prospect of going to $10 or $11. Mercifully, it was less painful because she could alternately stand and sit as she went about her main task of taking cancelled checks in a tray to a large open drawer where customers' accounts were separated by dividers. Each account had a signature card, so Caroline—and others working the same job—were to verify the signature on each check, then file it in the proper account.

She liked the position. The bank was a short walk from her house. She had bought the right clothes. She would learn other tasks. She had $2.02

in her own bank account. Her mother was dying. Her tortured relationship with her mother was coming to an end—except, of course, it would never quite end but would rather be frozen in whatever emotions had been created over the years. And when her mother died, Caroline was thrown unknowingly into depression. She heard the diagnosis when she went for counseling. "I didn't realize that I'd been in depression. I didn't realize, OK?"

People at the bank were beginning to notice mistakes. "We know that on average, three or four times a year we will get a call that a customer has gotten wrong checks," said a bank officer, preferring not to have her name published. "In a period of eight weeks, we got three or four calls. We started monitoring and had people double-checking, and we isolated it and found where the error was coming from."

Caroline was called in for a talk. "They said I wasn't catching on fast enough," and she admitted that she may have made errors. But others were filing too, she noted. "I was gettin' the blame for it, and I felt it wasn't all me, you know what I'm saying? And in the meantime I was dealing with my mother being in and out of the hospital, dying, and they had told her she was gonna die but we just didn't know when."

It was hard to get the checks mixed up, the bank officer insisted, because they were different colors. Maybe Caroline's attention wandered, the officer speculated. "She had difficulty learning what we needed her to do. There were other functions we needed her to learn how to do, but we could never get to that. We would ask people to start assembling statements to be mailed to customers, researching any errors. . . . We couldn't even get to that. Microfilming. There's a systematic way to microfilm work and file it away. She really had difficulty learning to do that, so we stopped having her do it. So she was only doing filing, and that was not working out well. . . . She wasn't receptive at all to the fact that she was making mistakes. It was definitely her. To be honest with you, I was surprised she had trouble because I thought she could do it. In fairness to her, we had just come out of a situation where we had to do a lot of handholding. She came in after that other person was gone, and I think everyone was exhausted and didn't have the energy to spend the time with her." After eight weeks Caroline was fired.

Her back was killing her, and she applied for SSI disability payments through Social Security. She was afraid to get another job while she waited for the decision, lest she undermine her case, so she went back on welfare and waited and waited. She thereby became typical among low-income laborers who develop back problems, apply for SSI, and don't work for months while hoping for approval. When Caroline was finally turned down six months later, she got a job at Wal-Mart.

Now the problem took a different form. Thanks to a chiropractor paid by Medicaid, Caroline's back had improved. But then she got a rude lesson in welfare law: "I just found out I have no medical insurance anymore," she said desperately one day. She had fallen ill, had seen a doctor, had been given a prescription, and had gone to the pharmacy to have it filled. There she learned that her Medicaid had expired because she had gone to work (Amber's continued because of her disability). "I didn't know that," Caroline declared. She had to pay $11 for the medicine and cancel an appointment for an eye exam the next day. More urgently, "I got to stop going to the chiropractor and everything now," she said, "and that's what kept me going to work, because I can't afford to pay it. I owe him 150 already."

Wal-Mart offered health insurance, but she found the premiums too expensive. Besides, she couldn't handle the $250 annual deductible, so she joined the growing ranks of the 45 million uninsured Americans, who included the many low-wage workers passing up insurance that their employers made available. They did short-term calculations that made the weekly cost seem high, without figuring the long-term cost of large medical bills. It was a gamble, and Caroline was lucky. Through the following year her back pain eased enough to permit her to continue working. She drifted along with no insurance and never went for regular checkups and did not get seriously ill.

Anyone who walked all the way around the outside of the Wal-Mart superstore on Route 103 would walk a mile, Caroline said. The place was immense. It sold everything from lawn mowers to ground beef, underpricing smaller stores that were struggling to survive in the center of town. Its 300 to 330 employees, who came and went seasonally, wore Wal-Mart's uniform of blue smocks and friendly smiles, trained as they were to be surprisingly helpful to customers.

Mark Brown, the manager, could pay his people more without raising prices, he conceded. He sat at a table in the store's snack bar, watching the part of the grocery section he could see, listening to the public address system's calls for help at the registers, his eyes darting around this corner of his fiefdom like a school principal waiting for the next catastrophe. He was thirty-one, but he looked as young as a college kid and spoke with the twang of his native southeast Missouri. He had come from another store in Georgia and was learning to ski here in New Hampshire.

His employees started at $6.25 an hour, earned an extra dollar at night and another 25 cents "for going to the front end," which meant working one of the twenty-four cash registers. And if he started them at $8 an hour, say, instead of $6.25, how would that change the economics of the store? "Hmmm. I don't think it would change at all." He wouldn't have to raise prices? "No. We've got a corporate pricing structure. And the way we do things, we go out and we check our competition every single week. Every department manager in this store goes out once a week and checks competition, and that's what determines our prices. We have a core price structure that we set regionally, by areas. Definitely the base price here would be probably higher than what it is in Arkansas, where there's a cheap cost of living. So it would be higher here, but it would still be standard to this area. And then after they give us that base, then we go out and check our competition, and if we're gettin' beat, we lower our prices."

So there's enough profit to absorb an increase from $6.25 to $8? "There would be, because if we were having to raise our wages, then evidently everybody else would be too, and if we make sure we're low enough, our competitors' customers are gonna shop with us." Would wage increases have any effect at all? "We'd have to cut corners on other things like, you know, we may not be able to put all the pretty balloons up all over the store. The non-necessities we'd have to cut back on."

Three days later Wal-Mart Stores, Inc., announced a net income of $5.58 billion for 1999, up 26 percent from the previous year.

Caroline was bouncing from one department to another, from one shift to another, but her pay stayed within a narrow range, beginning at $6.25, going to $6.80, sometimes up to $7.50 if she worked at night. So unpredictable were her hours that she couldn't work a second job, which would have helped her cash flow. She kept applying for higher positions and kept hearing that she needed a bit more experience.

"I did make Cashier of the Month for November," she reported happily. "I've collected over fifteen hundred dollars for the World War II veterans memorial in Washington. That's what got me Cashier of the Month." She also persuaded customers who checked out at her register to buy a total of seventy-two tickets to a Bruins game in Boston to raise money for the Claremont fire department, and that won her a weekend getaway from Pepsi. She could take herself and three other people to a paid stay in any Marriott she chose, anywhere. "But I have to get there," she said. That was the catch. So it was going to have to be nearby, someplace that somebody would drive her. Hawaii never entered her mind, not even New York; she considered only places in New Hampshire. "I think there's one up here in Lebanon," she said. "If I could get somebody to take me to Manchester, Amber likes to look at the malls. I've never been down there. Just to look at things." In the end, Caroline, Amber, a friend of Caroline's, and her child drove north to a hotel in Bethlehem, New Hampshire, where they visited a small shopping center in North Conway.

"I bought this," said Amber. "It's a lamp. It's one of those bunny lamps that goes round and round. And I bought a sweatshirt that I took with me on the trip."

"That jacket I was wearing that was ripped on the side for two years," said Caroline, "I bought me this winter coat at one of the stores in the mall. Originally it was a hundred-dollar coat, OK? It was marked down to $79.99, but they were having a big discount so I got it for $31.99. So that wasn't bad."

Wal-Mart had such a big turnover of personnel that Mark Brown didn't feel comfortable saying how high it ran. But he was clear about the reasons in the years of prosperity. "A lot of it, I think, has to do with the fact that our economy's so strong today. You could go anywhere in this town, anywhere outside of town, and you see the signs, 'Now Hiring, Now Hiring.' I mean, if they're not treated right, all they got to do is just walk out the door. It's very competitive, very competitive." So Wal-Mart tried to hold people by providing them with a share of the company's profits. Eighty percent came in stock, the rest in cash, maintained in an account in which an employee began to be vested after a year, and was fully vested after seven.

But this enticement was not working for Caroline. She had taken out a second mortgage, for $19,000, to replace her roof, doors, and windows, and she needed money now. "The way they schedule your hours," she said, "sometimes it's ten to seven, sometimes it's nine to four, sometimes it's seven to four, sometimes you work later in the evenings, and you never know what day. You don't always have the same two days off. Like I was supposed to have last Sunday off because of Amber's recital. I asked for it off. Well, I got home and later that night there was a message on my phone: 'Can you please come to work for a while?' I did. I did. It was overtime. I never said no to them. But why couldn't they have the decency to pay me a little bit more?"

That was the way the store treated "associates" when the economy was booming. In more depressed parts of the country and during recessions, however, some Wal-Mart managers were accused of forcing employees to work before punching in or after punching out to avoid paying overtime as required by law. "Wal-Mart management doesn't hold itself to the same standard of rectitude it expects from its low-paid employees," wrote Barbara Ehrenreich, who worked at a Wal-Mart in Minnesota while researching her book *Nickel and Dimed*. "When I applied for a job at Wal-Mart in the spring of 2000, I was reprimanded for getting something 'wrong' on this test: I had agreed only 'strongly' to the proposition, 'All rules have to be followed to the letter at all times.' The correct answer was 'totally agree.' Apparently the one rule that need not be slavishly adhered to at Wal-Mart is the federal Fair Labor Standards Act, which requires that employees be paid time and a half if they work more than forty hours in a week." Workers were warned against "time theft," which meant "doing anything other than working during company time, anything at all," she reported. "Theft of *our* time is not, however, an issue."[4]

Caroline never had the overtime problem in her New Hampshire store, but in six Southern states employees filed a class-action suit against the company for ordering them off the clock as their weekly time approached forty hours. Their attorney calculated the benefits to the firm: If each of 250 hourly wage "associates" in a single store worked just one hour of unpaid overtime a week, that would total 250 unpaid hours a week, 1,000 a month, 12,000 a year—and there were over 300 Wal-Mart stores in Texas, producing savings in that state alone of more than $30 million that should have been paid to employees.[5]

Caroline did not suffer from any violations of law, as far as she could tell, but her career went nowhere. Mark Brown, the manager who liked her, got transferred to Pennsylvania, dimming her prospects for advancement. So after a year and a half at Wal-Mart, she signed up with a temp agency, which found her a $7.50-an-hour daytime job Monday through Friday assembling wallpaper sample books. And she had the pleasure of telling Wal-Mart's assistant manager that she was leaving for higher pay.

"I'm just hoping they'll be sorry someday," Caroline said.

"Because they don't know who they're missing," Amber added. "She's such a nice mom, and she's pretty cool."

After a month the agency tempted Caroline with a job back at the Tampax factory for $10 an hour, the most she had ever earned. She took it, but there was a problem: Procter & Gamble had organized the factory on rotating shifts. One week she left the house at 5:30 a.m. and got home at 2:30 p.m., the next week she left at 1:30 p.m. and was home by 10:30 p.m., and the third she left home at 9:30 p.m. and returned at 6:30 a.m. Putting aside the question of sleep, stamina, and the basic requirements of an orderly life, the "swing shifts," as they were called, raised havoc with Caroline's arrangements for Amber. She had rented rooms to boarders occasionally or taken in homeless families so Amber wouldn't be alone. But these situations never lasted long; Caroline found the people intrusive or bossy or dishonest.

One family staying with her as she worked the swing shifts became difficult, and she kicked them out. "The people were sort of homeless," she said. "I was kindhearted, you know me, took 'em in. They had three little kids. He was on probation, a car accident, something. . . . They were paying $100 a week. They didn't pay the last two weeks. They said they would stay for the winter. I only intended it to be a short-term thing. The little kids destroyed wallpaper in my house and other things. . . . On top of that, come to find out, he had got another girl pregnant and had another baby." Furthermore, they were getting checks from welfare and food from WIC, while he had his own business laying flooring and carpeting. "They make good money," Caroline said resentfully, "and I'm wondering if they reported it all. They're not married. People scheme the system like this, and they get away with it."

Without the boarders, though, Caroline had nobody to look after Amber, so she very reluctantly left the girl home alone during her evening and nighttime shifts. While Caroline was running the machines that put tampons into boxes, she was worrying about Amber, and with good cause. "I don't think she should be left alone now," said her pediatrician, Steven Blair, who feared that given her epilepsy and cognitive problems, "she could be in trouble pretty easily." She could stay home by herself for "a short evening," he believed, "but I wouldn't leave her for many hours at a stretch."

Amber happened to tell her teacher how scary it was being home alone after dark. The teacher was alarmed. "She can't take care of herself," said the principal of Claremont Middle School, Donald R. Hart. "She's fourteen, that's our concern. No young lady, middle school student, should be left alone at night. She gets scared, she's had people knock on her door at night. We would still have the same reaction with a normal fourteen-year-old. When you look at statistics when kids get themselves into trouble with drugs, alcohol, sex, it's after school hours in the home." So, what did the school do to help? It summoned up a dreaded specter from Caroline's past: The teacher threatened to report Caroline for neglect. "We have a legal obligation to report if neglect is going on," said Hart. "We would be breaking the law if we suspect neglect, abuse, or anything like that."

It was late in October of 2000, the height of the presidential election campaign, and the country seemed consumed by politics. Not Caroline. Her voice trembled with rage and fear as she searched frantically for a way to keep both her job and her daughter. The celebrated New Hampshire primary had long since passed without so much as denting Caroline's consciousness. She didn't bother to see any of the candidates as they crisscrossed the state, and, looking back, she was not even sure whether or not she had voted. "I can't remember," she said frankly. "I might have been working. I don't think I did." And now, even with Al Gore and George W. Bush arguing and preaching and promising intensely on the TV in her living room, Caroline had no spare room in her thoughts for either of those men. "I haven't really listened to them," she said. "Right now it's the least of my concerns. They're all liars in a way. They tell people they'll do this or that. I have no use for Clinton, because he did not set a good example by running around with that girl. I think his wife's a fool to stay with him."

Clinton wasn't running, of course. No, but she felt that Gore shared responsibility. "He's the vice president. He must have a good idea of what's going on in there. He's next in line. Why couldn't he have stepped in and done a little more and straightened things out?" For that reason, Bush struck her as preferable, but she obviously didn't know about his affluence. "I want a motivated person like me that has been through these situations and knows what it's like out here. It will never happen. If I vote it will be straight women. I'd like to see a woman president. I would not like to see some rich person in there. I'd like to see somebody who has sense enough to help these people who need the help, you see what I'm trying to say?

The system needs to be straightened out. They need more resources to help these people who are trying to help themselves." November 7 came and went without her vote.

Faced with the threat of being reported to the state's child protection agency, Caroline stopped going to work and started working the phones and surfing the internet trying to find care for Amber. Unlike most of America's low-wage laborers, Caroline had a computer, bought on time with a Sears credit card. Mostly she liked to play games and send e-mails, and even search for men on-line, but now the machine became a tool in a desperate task. She found the website of one agency after another, made calls, and came up empty-handed: the Governor's Office of Disability, Parent to Parent, Social Security, Health and Human Services, Family Assistance, the Parent Information Center. "They're all trying to find help, and there doesn't seem to be help out there," she said. She was told that Amber was too old for welfare's child-care support and too young for Social Security's.

All she really needed was a month, because a young couple she knew in Massachusetts planned to move up and live in her house while they worked—and they could be there evenings and nights with Amber. But when Caroline called her boss at the factory, he told her that he could not leave the position vacant for a month and had asked the temp agency to find someone else; he needed workers.

At school, the principal, Donald Hart, raised the issue with his "wrap-around team," comprising a school psychologist, a local counseling agency representative, a juvenile protection worker, and a guidance counselor. "I've asked them what is out there for services for Amber while Mom is working," he reported, "and there is just nothing out there."

"And I don't have any extra money to pay anybody either," Caroline added. "And I'm trying to do the best I can and get caught up on little bills. And now I don't have a job, and I'm gonna have to go apply for welfare. You pull yourself up and then somebody has to knock you down. If I don't work, it's [also] neglect: not feeding or clothing my child."

Perhaps the most curious and troubling facet of this confounding puzzle was everybody's failure to pursue the most obvious solution: If the factory had just let Caroline work day shifts, her problem would have disappeared. She asked and got brushed off, but nobody else—not the school principal, not the doctor, not the myriad agencies she contacted—nobody in the profession of helping thought to pick up the phone and appeal to the factory manager or the foreman or anybody else in authority at her workplace.

Indeed, this solemn regard for the employer as untouchable, off limits, beyond the realm of persuasion unless in violation of the law, seems to permeate the culture of American anti-poverty efforts, with only a few exceptions. Even the most socially minded physicians and psychologists who treat malnourished children, for example, will advocate vigorously with government agencies to provide food stamps, health insurance, housing, and the like. But when they are asked if they ever urge the parents' employers to raise wages enough to pay for nutritious food, the doctors express surprise at the notion. First, it has never occurred to them, and second, it seems hopeless. The suggestion makes them shrug. Wages are set by the marketplace, and you cannot expect magnanimity from the marketplace. It is the final arbiter from which there is no appeal.

Perhaps they're right. With Caroline's permission, I called her supervisor at the factory, just to ask why they had swing shifts. I assumed that it was hard to find people willing to work only evenings or nights, so a rotation expanded the labor supply. The supervisor never called back. After leaving many messages, I finally got a call from the human resources manager, a curt woman named Deborah Garrity. Since Caroline was a temporary worker hired through an agency, Garrity said, the factory had no responsibility for her and could not comment on her working hours, or even on the reason for the swing shifts. The following week was Caroline's turn for the day shift anyway, and the temp agency had not yet found a replacement, so she went back to work. The school had not yet made a report of neglect, but the prospect hung over her.

The company did have a rationale for the rotating shifts, I later learned from Kevin Paradise, the Human Resources Leader of Tambrands factories in New Hampshire and Maine. "Rotation allows greater exposure of employees to the overall business," he explained. People on perpetual night shifts tended to lose the big picture, to be less aware of a factory's mission, and to leave problems for the succeeding shifts. He called this "a separation from the cultural standpoint." Nighttime workers were also less likely to be promoted, because at night they didn't have contact with management. These reasonable arguments did Caroline no good.

And then a little miracle happened. A woman with whom Caroline had worked at the homeless shelter happened to know someone from her church who offered to take Amber whenever necessary to her farm outside of town. So the job was saved. And in the end, the young couple moved early from Massachusetts, and Amber didn't need the farm option. And when the couple was eventually evicted by Caroline, who felt they were snooping into everything, she found a woman nearby who would take Amber for $50 a week. That effectively reduced Caroline's hourly wage by $1.25, but she was still ahead financially.

"God works in mysterious ways," she declared. "I have a guardian angel." Even with the angel's help, though, she didn't hope to be rolling in money. "I don't want to," she replied. "I want to be average. I think rich people have a lot of problems too. I wish for a normal life."

But hers was a normal life in the forgotten America, and in such lives, small blessings had a way of shimmering elusively, then evaporating. For months, Caroline had looked forward to requesting a permanent job at the Tampax factory. At first, she was told that she could apply after working five hundred hours as a temp, then she was told one thousand hours, and then she learned that a young man had been hired permanently after only a month as a temp worker. When she questioned the procedure, a supervisor barked, "We hire who we want." Furthermore, the application required her to take a written test without being paid for the time she would spend. And her pleas to work a day shift were rejected, even though a few people were being put on steady hours.

So she left Procter & Gamble and returned to the factory that made books of wallpaper samples, working 7:30 a.m. to 4 p.m. Monday through Friday and dropping from $10 to $7.50 an hour. She tried to look on the bright side. She was saving $50 a week in child-care expenses, her daughter was more content, and her income had the chance of declining enough that she would qualify for fuel assistance, a government program that subsidized the cost of heating oil. It was February, after all.

As the recession set in, Procter & Gamble closed the Tambrands factory, which made Caroline feel smart about having resigned. Otherwise, she didn't notice the economic downturn. "I can't see much difference," she remarked. "I've always struggled, and I'm still struggling." She continued to move horizontally from job to job. She felt free to walk out of the wallpaper factory after a squabble, got hired by a manufacturer of photo albums for $7 an hour, and then worked as a cashier at a Cumberland Farms convenience store and gas station for $7.50. "The only thing I don't like is a drive-off," she said—the driver who fills the tank and speeds away without paying. "You can lose your job if it's more than five bucks, if you get too many of them." How many would be too many she did not know, however: The boss kept the employees off balance by never telling them.

She was still living on the edge, perhaps one drive-off away from unemployment, unable to keep up payments on her debts. Life seemed oppressive and dangerous. Every dollar that was coming in was going out, and she still owed about $12,000 on her credit cards, $20,000 on her student loans, and $54,000 for two mortgages on her house. Nothing in her job prospects suggested that she would ever be able to make any headway against the weight of all those debts. She was trapped in the inescapable netherworld of work, and as the grinding fact of that stagnation gradually infiltrated her understanding, as she finally accepted the improbability of advancement, she began to think about the unthinkable: bankruptcy. Under the law, her student loans would not be forgiven, and her mortgages could not be avoided without losing her house. But the credit card balances would go away, and that would ease her burden.

The trouble was, Caroline did not feel morally right about taking the step. She had recently purchased new appliances on time from a local store, and Brenda told her that declaring bankruptcy was a form of stealing. "It hurt my feelings when she came out and said that," Caroline admitted, but it also struck a chord. Her spending had been undisciplined, she knew, though she thought she had improved. She needed a fresh start. Painstakingly, she saved until she had $800 for filing and lawyer's fees, and made the move. "It was hard, and I got real depressed," she said. "It was my pride, and I didn't want people to know about it."

Amber was chafing against the limits of her schooling. She hungered to read, but the high school provided only one hour of tutoring a week. She craved more math than she could get. She yearned to be in the main part of the school, not in the vocational and technical wing, where students were stigmatized as stupid and many seemed considerably less able than she. "Beth," a counselor at a community center, concluded after intervening with the school: "They did not have here in this district what Amber needed and wanted very desperately. What she needed and wanted was to be more in the mainstream, and this was really not allowed, and that was a shame, because she had so much to offer." Amber also needed "continuous, intense reading instruction," Beth observed. Instead, she was taught what she already knew: cooking, shopping, doing laundry. When school officials received pleas from the counselor, who had previously worked as a para-professional with emotionally handicapped kids in a nearby town, "they laughed at me," Beth said in surprise. Perhaps they wouldn't have laughed if Caroline had been wealthy enough to hire a psychologist or a lawyer to make her case and bring pressure, as the affluent must often do.

Whether or not Amber could have been mainstreamed was an open question. The school psychologist, who had done a battery of tests the year before, had confirmed Amber's mild to moderate retardation, with IQ scores ranging from 43 to 57 in a variety of areas from numerical operations to written expression. "Amber did not know her birthday," the report stated. "She had difficulty with word finding. Amber's math skills are dependent on using her fingers to add and subtract."

Whatever the best course, Caroline gradually lost confidence in the Claremont system's ability to provide it. She had no money for a private school, but she did have a daughter-in-law in Muncie, Indiana, who agreed to take Amber temporarily while her husband served in the army. The public school there sounded promising. "I spoke with the superintendent's office," Beth said. "They told me what school it would be. I spoke to the special ed teacher there. She was very helpful, and I explained exactly what Amber needed. [She said,] 'We have programs here. She'll be at the high school with everybody, will be expected to do as much as she is able.' "

By September, Amber was in Indiana, ecstatic with school, enrolled in an adult literacy class, and slated to begin three tutoring sessions a week in reading and math. She soon moved into higher-level special ed classes, was scheduled for tests in the spring, and felt herself progressing. Her brightened mood on the phone buoyed her mother's spirits. But the advances would come at a high price.

Caroline had heard that jobs were plentiful in Muncie, so she prepared to follow her daughter there. To leave, however, she had to sell her precious house, for she could not comfortably rent it out from a distance. Tenants might do damage, and she had no money to travel back and forth to oversee repairs. It took a few months until a buyer could be found to invest in this struggling town, and Caroline had to settle for a break-even sale at $79,000, an amount that should have brought her a nice profit over the $37,000 she had paid. She made nothing, though, not a penny. In effect, she said sadly, "I gave it away."

The responsibility that she had demonstrated as a homeowner had lifted the value and, ironically, had stolen her equity. She had maintained and improved the house sensibly for the long term. She still owed about $34,000 on the first mortgage, and the second mortgage of $19,000 carried a pre-payment penalty, which forced her to pay just over $20,000 to get out of it. The federal grants of $17,000 for lead paint removal and new siding required pro-rated reimbursement if the house was sold within ten years and five years respectively, so she had to pay back nearly $16,000. In total, she owed about $70,000. After adding the real estate agent's fee, taxes, and other closing costs, she ended up short $300, which the agent kindly absorbed by reducing the commission. Five and a half years of mortgage and interest payments had yielded nothing, and one of her dreams was gone.

As the New Hampshire winter arrived in early December, Caroline left with pockets nearly empty. She could not even afford to rent a U-Haul truck. Her older daughter, who had a good job with Verizon, lent her $700, and a couple of friends donated their vacation time to drive the truck and Caroline to Indiana, by way of a slashing blizzard in upstate New York. On the move again, as she had been since childhood, she was happy to see a little of the country.

Muncie was not gentle, though. "I miss my house, and I miss my friends," Caroline lamented, "but I had so much overhead, I'm glad to be out of that." After six weeks with her daughter-in-law, she found a small apartment in a public housing project in a hard section of town. "It's not the best neighborhood," she observed mildly. It was riddled with drug dealers and prostitutes, and a shooting had just occurred two blocks from the convenience store where she was working. "Jobs don't pay nothing around here," she had discovered. Her hourly wage, $5.45 without benefits, meant a downward slide even from the $6 at the Vermont plastics factory more than a quarter century before. "I just can't get ahead," she said.

Six months later, Caroline's skill in hunting for government aid brought her a couple of important finds. First, she was accepted into public housing in a safer neighborhood. "It's really nice," she said. Second, she managed to get Medicaid to contribute over $400 for a new set of false teeth, provided that she could come up with $322 to cover the balance. She did not have that kind of money in her anemic bank account, so her older daughter gave her a loan. The teeth gave her confidence. "They fit nice, and I still got to get used to them," Caroline reported hopefully. Once they felt comfortable, she planned to try them out in a few job interviews. She found work at a convenience store, went to $7 an hour, and was training to be an assistant manager. That was the optimistic side of her balance sheet.

The debit side was severe, however. The benefits of moving to Muncie were beginning to look dubious. "I think it's harder to make friends here," she observed. "I don't get out much." The finances were harder. She was stunned by Indiana's income tax (New Hampshire had none), plus the city and county taxes. Her low wage didn't keep up with the outflow. "I'm broke," she said flatly. Furthermore, the reason for the move—Amber's life prospects—now seemed less certain. She was learning more, but Caroline could no longer afford the $140 a month for Amber's reading tutoring. Besides, Caroline said, "the school told me I was wasting my money." Amber would never learn to read.

Money may not always cure, but it can often insulate one problem from another. Parents of means could have addressed Amber's difficulties without uprooting themselves and discarding their assets. They could have purchased services; brought their own skills to bear; and walled off their house, their jobs, and their lifestyle from the intrusion of hardship. In the house of the poor, however, the walls are thin and fragile, and troubles seep into one another.

Chapter Three

IMPORTING THE THIRD WORLD

Give me your tired, your poor,
Your huddled masses yearning to breathe free,
The wretched refuse of your teeming shore.
                                        —Emma Lazarus

Luxury is produced by humble hands. Not only in the squalid factories of
"developing" countries but on American soil too, wealth and poverty inter-
sect. Where immigrants have come seeking lives of plenty, they bring their
deprivation with them, creating islands of hardship amid the surging tides
of prosperity. For a paltry wage, albeit one far greater than at home, they
feed and clothe and comfort the Americans they wish to emulate.

So it is in potato fields and sewing lofts, in cleaners and restaurants,
and in the manicured gardens of suburban affluence. In Los Angeles,
among shabby blocks around Spring and 8th, garments to be sold lucra-
tively on Fifth Avenue and Wilshire Boulevard are sewn together by
struggling Mexicans and Thais, Hondurans and Koreans. By the time the
graceful dresses and tasteful blouses are pressed and hung on mannequins
in glistening windows, all the stains of suffering have been erased.

A New Yorker can wander the sprawling expanse of Los Angeles searching in vain for a city. Vast stretches of low houses and warehouses, broad highways and scattered factories spread carelessly eastward from the Pacific as if land were an infinite resource. The garment district, however, is an exception; it has a taut urban feel. Structures are tall enough to cast shadows across streets, and streets are filled with a rainbow of complexions, a babel of tongues. Even without approaching the cluttered vibrancy of Manhattan's garment district, this neighborhood would make a New Yorker feel almost at home. Hand-pushed trolleys hung with clothing weave in and out of truck traffic among buildings exhausted from hard use. At lunchtime, creaky elevators traveling down from ten, twelve, thirteen stories disgorge the industrious, the slick, the honorable, the corrupt—in sum, a global population, the faces mostly Asian and Latino with smatterings of black and white. A couple of taco vans take up strategic positions in an alley and along a parking lot; workers and their bosses eat lunch quickly, then return to lofts crammed with sewing machines and bolts of fabric.

In her nine years since coming from Mexico, Candalaria worked here, moving from one to another sewing job as small companies appeared and evaporated like beads of sweat in the wind. She was quick, and she had better have been, because she was paid by the piece: three-quarters of a cent for each fly she sewed with a machine onto a pair of jeans. The arithmetic was coldly simple. "I have to do a hundred flies to get seventy-five cents," she noted. To make California's minimum wage, which was $5.75 at the time, that added up to 767 flies an hour, allowing her just under 5 seconds for each fly. "I'm pretty fast at this," she bragged, much faster than workers new to the industry. "I can do four cuts a day; each cut is twelve hundred to sixteen hundred pieces." At the highest end, that came out to about $6 an hour for an eight-hour day.

There was a catch, though. Her supervisor, a Vietnamese woman named Anh, kept track of the difference between Candalaria's piecework earnings and the minimum wage. If she didn't make the minimum wage on a certain day, Anh paid her anyway, and Candalaria owed her the difference. If she made more than the minimum wage, she owed Anh the excess. Even though this put a ceiling on her wage, it was a better deal than the below-minimum piecework pay that many garment workers received. Those who could not maintain the pace were fired.

Candalaria started work at 7 a.m., but Anh didn't let her punch in until 9 to make sure the records showed fewer hours. So quick and nimble were

Candalaria's fingers that Anh accused her of fabricating tickets to exaggerate her production. The allegation led to arguments, and Candalaria once pulled out the notebook in which she had listed her hours. "The boss tried to take it from me," she remembered, "and tried to get me to sign something saying I'd faked the tickets." Constant chicanery gave the sewing loft the uncertainty of a dusty marketplace where no price was fixed and no bargaining power was had by the seller. Without immigration documents, Candalaria had no legal right to be in the United States or to sell what the American economy needed: cheap labor at the bottom rungs of production. So she had stayed in this sweatshop for a year and eight months. Was there a chance of finding a better job? She laughed at the silly question, and so did several men who were sitting with her. They worked at various sewing companies.

"When I put a label on a pair of pants, I get four cents," said Juan. This, after his nine years of experience in the garment district. "They pay a total of $2 to all the people who work on a pair of pants."

"I produce loops," said Jesus. "I get nine cents per pair of pants. Most of the factories don't pay minimum wage, but for people like Juan, he'll be able to reach that level. Someone who's new can't do that much." The inexperienced, those with less dexterity on the sewing machine, made as little as $3 an hour, he said.

Paying so little may seem like a boon for a boss, but he isn't always delighted. Low piecework wages reflect low productivity, and the sewing factories have deadlines to meet. Juan's employers, therefore, "expect workers to produce enough to reach the minimum wage," he explained, and they fire anyone who consistently falls short. When the state raises the minimum wage, the employer usually raises the required speed of production and leaves the rate per piece unchanged, workers' advocates report. That circumvents the law, of course—the law enacted by government, that is. More potent is the law of economics. Global manufacturing has put the five thousand sewing factories in Los Angeles in cruel competition with those in Honduras, Cambodia, and other Third World countries where living standards and labor costs are exceedingly low. Mexicans get about $4 a day for factory work; in Cambodia, where teachers earn $15 to $25 a month, Cambodians who sew garments get $30 to $45 a month, or 16 to 23 cents an hour. One response has been to import some features of the Third World into the United States.

Few American demonstrators against globalization and the World

Trade Organization seem aware that if they want to protest sweatshops, they don't have to look for exploitation in poor nations; they can find more immediate targets by walking along 8th Street in L.A., where the bad publicity would surely provoke speedier results. Protesting globalization is like protesting the monsoon season. What's the point? The rain is going to come anyway, and it yields both hardship and benefit—destructive flooding that also produces enough water to grow rice. The best approach is to channel it, control it, prevent it from inundating the defenseless.

That is what several organizations in California have done since they formed a coalition called Sweatshop Watch[1] to lobby and litigate on behalf of garment workers. The organization has persuaded some laborers to overcome their fears of deportation and to expose both their direct employers—small sewing shops—and the larger, brand-name designers and manufacturers. Those big names often hire the abusive sewing contractors to do their dirty work by underpaying workers to assemble garments. In 2000 a Latino couple and their daughter, who were paid as little as $3 an hour, won a settlement of $134,000 from three manufacturers, John Paul Richard, Francine Browner, and BCBG Max Azria. The manufacturing firms had hired a private company to monitor conditions at the sewing contractors but did nothing when the monitor reported problems.

The most infamous case to date began in rural Thailand in the late 1980s, when Thai con artists recruited impoverished young people, most of them women, with promises of well-paid sewing jobs in the United States. Upon arrival, the workers were practically enslaved in a two-story apartment complex in El Monte, just east of Los Angeles. They ate, slept, and worked behind razor wire and windows covered with plywood. For seventeen or eighteen hours a day, they were forced to sew and assemble clothing for major American manufacturers, including Tomato, Clio, B.U.M., High Sierra, Axle, Cheetah, Anchor Blue, and Airtime. The apparel was sold at Sears, Target, May's, Nordstrom, Mervyn's, Miller's, and Montgomery Ward.[2] The workers' wages amounted to less than a dollar an hour, from which the Thai organizers subtracted the cost of groceries, inflated by a factor of four or five. Without medical care, the laborers suffered from various ailments; because of untreated gum disease, one had to pull out eight of his own teeth.

"They were told that if they tried to resist or escape, their homes in Thailand would be burned, their families murdered, and they would be beaten," writes Julie Su, one of their lawyers.[3] They were shown pictures of a man who had been badly battered after an escape attempt, and they were threatened with the dreaded Immigration and Naturalization Service if they complained—threats that came true, in a way. In 1995, seven years after the involuntary servitude began, and three years after the INS had received its first report on the problem, federal and state agents finally raided the place, "freeing" seventy-one hapless workers only to imprison them in a federal penitentiary pending deportation. The INS, bound by law to detain and deport illegal immigrants, thereby reinforced the intimidation commonly used by employers to enforce their workers' silence. The official toughness "could only serve to discourage workers from reporting labor law, civil rights, and human rights abuses, and push operations like El Monte further underground," Su argues. "The INS, we asserted, ought not conspire with exploitative employers." It took an entire week of vehement demonstrations by Sweatshop Watch members before the tormented Thai workers were released by the immigration agency.

In the end, their captors were jailed for two to seven years, and the workers won $4 million settling a civil suit. Most significantly, the manufacturers, who were two steps removed from the El Monte factory, did not escape responsibility. That was a breakthrough against high-rolling brand names that try not to sully their labels.

In the usual routine of the garment business, the manufacturer, or designer, draws the pattern and uses huge jigsaws, run either by hand or by computer, to cut thick stacks of fabric along the lines of the pattern. The cut pieces of clothing are then shipped to a contractor whose employees sew the pieces of each garment together, often on an assembly-line basis. It is at that level of assembly that most abuses occur. The contractor charges the manufacturer a per-garment price, and so is motivated to keep labor costs close to the bone. The manufacturer throws up his hands in a mock pretense of ignorance and helplessness over his contractor's relations with his employees. In the El Monte case, however, lawyers for the Thai workers argued successfully in court that the manufacturers could not plead such ignorance, having delivered cut pieces to a couple of small contractors in the garment district with demands for such a quick turnaround of finished apparel that they had to know the work would be farmed out to some larger operation—in El Monte, as it happened. The Thai laborers were joined in their lawsuit by the contractors' Latino employees, who were badly underpaid. It was a rare instance of inter-ethnic cooperation in

Southern California, where workers' rights campaigns are usually organized into separate movements by Koreans, Latinos, Cambodians, and others.

Publicity over abuses led to state legislation in 1999 holding clothing manufacturers and retailers responsible for their sewing contractors' compliance with minimum wage and overtime laws. Enforcement has been less than thorough, however: A year after the law was enacted, state and federal investigations found that only one-third of the sewing contractors inspected in Los Angeles were observing labor laws, down from 39 percent the year before.[4]

The economics of the garment industry, like the market forces that govern much American enterprise, work against decent wages at the bottom because competition is fierce, margins are razor thin, and many employers feel vulnerable. They don't think they could stay in business without hiring undocumented immigrants, but they risk prosecution and the confiscation of their stocks of clothing for doing so. Many small sewing contractors are recent immigrants themselves; a good number arrived from Hong Kong as the British colony was turned over to China. Some undoubtedly get rich on the backs of their Korean, Chinese, and Mexican workers, but others make considerably less than a fortune. "Many contractors are just able to cover their own paychecks," said an industry spokesman, Joe Rodriguez, who headed the Garment Contractors Association of Southern California. "One guy told me he was paying himself $36,000 a year. That's why things like health insurance are a pipe dream."

In average times, Joe Zabounian paid himself up to twice that much, but it was not a lot for a man who had owned a business for twenty-five years. He and his wife together took $5,000 or $6,000 a month out of their small, eighth-floor sewing loft called Adrienne, where about fifteen employees (down from twenty-two in better days) used old machines to stitch the hems and seams of evening gowns and other apparel more elegant than any of them could ever afford. Joe was a sad-eyed, melancholy man wrapped in grayness—a gray crew cut, a gray-blue short-sleeved shirt, and jeans. Several decades ago he arrived from Beirut, where his family had been in the retail business. "Actually, men's wear, not ladies'," he explained, "so it's something new for me. I still don't know how to sew to this day. But I know if something is wrong, something has a problem, what needs to be done on it."

The people who did know how to sew, all of them women, were skilled and longtime employees who earned at least the minimum wage,

Joe said, but usually didn't go above $7 to $7.50 an hour. "I've had girls here for twenty years," he remarked. "They average about ten years, probably." In other words, upward mobility didn't exist. They got no fringe benefits, and when there was not enough work, he had to call and tell them not to come in for a couple of weeks.

Paying by the piece rather than the hour would have made his calculations easier, for he would have known precisely how much each garment would cost to assemble. But he couldn't follow his preference because the high quality of the work he got from designers was "too intricate," he noted. "It's too complicated, more time consuming. You can't really put a time on how long it should take. You estimate, more or less." That forced him to keep as many as 60 to 70 percent of his employees on hourly wages. The others, on piecework, sometimes asked for more when the job was taking longer than expected, and occasionally Joe could raise their rate. "It depends on what I'm being paid. If my margin is very low on it, I can't do very much, even though I try to balance it. Maybe I lose fifty cents and give them the fifty cents. That happens sometimes." Could he have gone back to the designer and asked for more per garment? "That's a rare happening. Basically you're stuck with the price. Sometimes you take work just to have work for the girls. You break even, but you keep your girls busy. I've done that many times."

This niche of high-quality designer work that had to be done quickly and well was what kept Joe in business while most of the large-scale, mass-produced sewing had gone south to Mexico or west to Asia. If the stitching could be relatively shoddy and the manufacturer could wait many months for the finished goods, it was worth shipping the pieces to low-skilled operations overseas. But when the shifting taste of the fashion world had to be satisfied in weeks, manufacturers used Joe and other contractors down the street or downstairs.

They paid a premium to do so, but not much of it filtered down to the women behind the sewing machines. That black strapless gown on the rack would ultimately sell for $200 or $300, Joe figured, and he charged just $20 to sew it together, which was about 15 to 20 percent more than it cost him to make. Labor accounted for some 70 percent of his expenses, so he couldn't raise wages without making himself uncompetitive or cutting severely into profits. Another contractor might do the dress for $10, he said, but the quality of work would be lower.

The sweatshops that cheated their workers were irksome to Joe because he paid his employees more and had to charge more for the finished garments. He simply could not compete in dollar terms, only in quality. "Six months, a year they open up a shop," he said of the sweatshop owners, "they work there, then they shut it down and go somewhere else. . . . This corner space back here was shut down maybe three, four times within three years. They'd open up for six months, shut it down, open up for six months and shut it down. New names, new owners. People come for their payroll, the place is closed, nobody's there, they don't get paid." If you're an owner who doesn't pay your workers for two weeks, Joe noted, "You're talking maybe $20-, $30,000 that goes into your pocket. All that stuff happens."

When Joe was hiring undocumented workers, he didn't think much of the law against hiring undocumented workers. Now that his were all documented, he thought the law protected him. But it was still absurd, he felt. "There's a demand, absolutely," he said, "I doubt that there's any American that would work for $7 or $8 an hour, $6 an hour. It's just not gonna happen. This industry would shut down." His supposition is only half right. Half of all new workers entering the American economy are immigrants, yet many Americans in many businesses do work at such wages. Garment manufacturing is a case study in the difficulty of bringing economic justice to the rank and file in an industry squeezed by global competition. The hard rules of the marketplace will yield only to stricter government regulation and a measure of conscience.

At the upper levels of fashion, some designers such as "Nicole" allowed a sense of guilt and concern about wages and working conditions to creep into their consciousness, and they took care to check on their contractors. They could afford to do so.

Slender and meticulously dressed, Nicole tried to look chic even in the disorder of her workshop. She had done her dark hair in careful curls, had painted her lips bright red. She had a steely mind for both business and morality. She could have had garments assembled for half the price, she estimated, by using unscrupulous sewing firms. "There are definitely a lot of shops out there that are disgusting," she said. "You wouldn't even want to meet the person who runs it, because they're like a slumlord, you know? That is just so unappealing to me that I would never even go there. It's not worth it. I think that it's really heinous and indecent, and I think that it exists in a multitude of industries." She observed acidly that nobody seemed to hear much about exploitation that produced radios or widgets, but when the luxury and glamour of elegant clothing were created in sweatshops, the paradox was too searing to ignore.

Nicole tried to do right by avoiding "handmade" fabrics, which to her meant textiles produced in China or India by exploited child labor. "I don't buy things that are touted as being handmade," she declared, "when I know that handmade means literally on the dirt floor with a bucket of fish heads as payment." She paid her own employees a minimum of $8, and her best sample makers got up to $13 and $14. "The stores say, 'If you were 20 percent cheaper, we'd buy more,' " she noted, but "we pay a higher salary 'cause they deserve it. They do really great work. My regard or my esteem for what these women do is that it's a craft. It's not about getting people in to crank out the best for as little as possible. It's really about paying them pretty much top dollar and expecting professionalism and integrity back, which is what I get every day."

Fine sentiments do not stand firm against the economic imperatives of running a business, however. And economic behavior is heavily psychological, as anyone who has played the stock market knows. When you have started a business from nothing, as Maria Wojciechowski had, you feel instinctively how tenuous prosperity can be, and that translates into anxiety about how much you can afford to pay your employees. Maria was tall, blond, and still willowy enough to be the model she once had been, and she was doing well now—extremely well, with profits of half a million dollars annually for a line of women's clothes called Maria Bianca Nero, which she designed, manufactured, and sold in Bloomingdale's, Saks, and a hundred other stores. Yet the hard beginnings still weighed on her judgments; they made her cautious about raising wages (she'd rather have given bonuses, which could be skipped in a bad year) and resistant to taking loans (she kept cash reserves to buy material and meet payrolls). Her office, which doubled as a large work area, was furnished like the apartment of a kid who just got out of college; her desk was an old door supported by two black filing cabinets. Her mindset had not caught up with her success.

She had begun by making basic mistakes. She opened a small store, drew patterns, bought fabric, took everything to a woman who had a little factory in her house, and gave her an order: ten smalls in black, three mediums. Then Maria picked up the finished dresses and sold them in her store. She had only a vague idea of what they were costing her. She paid the woman's rent, plus $20 to $25 an hour—a fortune in the garment business. After three years she realized that a dress she was selling for $200 was probably costing $250 to make. Furthermore, burglars broke into her store twice and took most of her stock. The second time, luckily, she had the new season's inventory in her apartment, and she decided to give up the retail operation and go wholesale instead. Working with her husband, Yannis, she contracted with a sales representative for a 10 percent commission. "We put a little line together and we gave it to her," Maria remembered, "and she sold it, and we filled the orders little by little and just started very, very small." They lived on a shoestring and didn't even have medical insurance. What they did have, however, was Maria's creative, somewhat conservative eye for dress designs that were mildly inventive but not flashy. Step-by-step, her ideas caught on.

In retrospect, the basic lesson she learned seemed to be straight out of Entrepreneurship 101: "The whole key to having your own business is your overhead," she said, and a big chunk of overhead is the cost of labor. "When we first started, we had no overhead. It was me and Yannis. We didn't pay ourselves. We took whatever we needed to, like, eat. We didn't have any employees, and we had very little overhead for the rent—$250 a month. So we knew that we didn't really have to hardly sell anything and we were still going to be in business 'cause we only had these expenses every month. So that's the key. And then as you grow, you still want to keep your overhead to a manageable level . . . to absorb the bad times 'cause you don't want to have to fire everybody and start all over again. You want to be able to, like, OK, we're not making any money, but I don't have to let anybody go yet."

The same game of cutting overhead was played by every company at every step in the production and sales process, of course. The industry thus resembled the food chain, with each lower creature more helpless than the one above, and the most helpless of all on the bottom, sewing together ritzy garments for minimum wage or less.

The carnivorous nature of the companies above and below Maria led her to price her goods defensively, with plenty of markup. Retail stores devised endless methods to avoid paying the agreed price. If they sold the garment at a discount, they cut their payment. If they didn't sell it within a certain period, "they want this thing called markdown money," Maria explained, "where they take a little bit more money off your check." If apparel was defective, they claimed damages. " 'Well, this zipper's been broken on twenty garments; I had to fix them and it cost me $300, so I'm gonna pay you $300 less for your line.' They'll nickel and dime you for everything. And then, 'We need special items for promotion.' 'The store manager had a special thing,' or 'The person who bought the most of Bianca Nero got free gifts, so we gave away ten free gifts, so we knock another five hundred off.' You can go and fight them, or you can just say that's the way it's done. . . . You're lucky if you get the money back. So you've got to cushion the price."

To figure the price she began with the cost of fabric, on which Yannis, using a computer, laid out parts of garments, fitting them together like pieces of a jigsaw puzzle to minimize waste. Then she estimated the price a sewing contractor would charge for assembling the apparel. "You go, well, I made something similar, and I paid $10, so let's cost it at $10. Then it takes one zipper or three buttons or whatever, and you add up your little trims or whatever."

This "costing" did not include her rent, utilities, insurance, employees' salaries, or other ongoing expenses, nor did it take into account the mistakes made by sewing contractors. "They cut the wrong color, they cut the wrong fabric. They sewed it wrong, you've got to redo it. It came in damaged. There's a lot of waste," she said, "so you've got to absorb some of that cost." Her goal was to sell to the store at a price that would get her double the money she spent on a specific garment. Therefore, in the bizarre arithmetic of manufacturing, she didn't multiply her cost by 2; she multiplied it by 2.5, hoping that the extra markup would cover her contractor's mistakes, her sales rep's commission, and the store's imaginative ideas for avoiding full payment.

"Let's say the garment costs $15 and you charged it at $37.50," she explained. "You're hoping you'll make maybe $15. You paid $15 for it, and you want to try to make another $15. So that $7.50 is your cushion. You've got to pay $3.75 to the rep, they get 10 percent, so that basically leaves you only $3 something for discounts and cushioning." Then, to get the final selling price, the store multiplied Maria's price by 2.1 or 2.2—or even 3.0 in fancy shops, so a typical dress that cost Maria $60 to make was sold to the retailer for $150 and to the customer for over $300.

There was also the tyranny of time, which all businesses suffered. "You have to start making it four to six weeks before you actually ship it," Maria explained, "and you don't get paid for at least another four to ten weeks after you ship it. So there's like a three-month period of when maybe you've actually paid for the stuff before you see your money. So if you have like double the amount of business next month as I had this month, I'm gonna need to fork out a double amount of money; I'm not gonna see any money back for three months. I've got to carry myself, pay my workers, pay my bills, have to have a surplus of money to last for those three months before I get paid back." Many manufacturers "get factored," she said, meaning a bank fronts the money and takes 4 to 5 percent of the profits. She had avoided that.

Sometimes the three or four contractors Maria routinely used complained that they hadn't made anything on a job because it had taken longer than expected, and sometimes she paid them more than the agreed rate. But since costs were critical, and since her own employees' salaries were part of that constant overhead that she had to watch, she deemed it imprudent to raise wages above the going rates in the industry, even if her sympathy often pulled at her to do so. "I always want to give them more," she said, "but then I think: I've got two kids. What if things don't go well? I've given away all my money. You see how they live. They're taking the bus, don't have a car. It's an awkward thing. We're doing well; we've only been doing really well for two years. You just got to go slowly. What if you start paying someone, say $20 an hour, and your business starts going bad? I mean, I have to like cut down their salary?" she asked. "Or I have to now fire you because you're getting this great big salary but people aren't buying my product?" High wages would have increased her risk.

"I think the first person we hired was a sample maker," Maria said. That was in 1993, for $12 an hour, a bit high at the time. "She's still making the same amount of money," but with bonuses on top. "Sometimes we give like $800, $1,000," twice a year, in June and December. That way, lean times would mean bonus cuts, not necessarily wage cuts or layoffs.

Winston Churchill once remarked that democracy was the worst system ever devised, except for all the others that had been tried from time to time. The same could be said about capitalist free enterprise: It's the worst—except for all the others. It has a ruthlessness about it, a cold competitive spirit that promotes the survival of the fittest and the suffering of the weak. But it also opens opportunity unparalleled by communism, socialism, or any other variant so far attempted. The sense of injustice that it fosters derives from its lack of egalitarianism—that exalted ideal that other systems also fail to practice. The American ideal embraces an equality of opportunity for every person but not an equality of result. In fact, free enterprise thrives on difference—the difference between the owner and the worker, the educated and the less educated, the skilled and the less skilled, the adventurous and the timid, and ultimately the rich and the poor. That differentiation, particularly the freedom to hire labor at relatively low cost, has fueled the entrepreneurial risk-taking so essential to a robust, decentralized economy. It is a highly regulated economy, woven with legal and contractual restrictions on abuse. But those regulations, aimed at protecting health, environment, and employees' well-being, are kept in check by constant debate across the American political spectrum; they have not been allowed to suffocate private business, which needs space to maneuver, invent, and grow.

Like most employers, Maria saw no alternative to the discrepancy among various grades of workers, and she was devoted to preserving the differences. "You certainly don't want to pay someone who is doing shipping or a tedious manual job a huge salary," she declared. "It's almost not fair. Someone who went to college, studied, tried to make something of their lives, those people should be rewarded and they should be making the better salaries. The person that dropped out of high school . . . I mean, that doesn't make sense 'cause then, in fact, no one's gonna go to college. That's like the way it works. If you go to school and get a good education you're gonna get a better paying job."

The head of a temp agency in Kansas City shivered at the notion of paying the people she placed more than $6 to $7 an hour. "You'd fall out of whack," she said, and falling out of whack was a disturbing idea. "You're offsetting the entire pay scale. They're making three, four, five dollars more an hour than they maybe should be. A clerical person that I would typically pay seven, if I paid them ten, now I have to pay my accountants thirteen, fifteen, seventeen dollars an hour. Now you're pulling up the whole pay scale."

The words "should be" were significant. Another Kansas City employer, Paul Lillig, used the same phrase to lament the rise in the hourly rate—from $6 to $9—being earned by the few workers who could operate an inserter machine for handling mail. "Pretty soon we've got these people who are being paid more than they really should be paid," he declared. Other employers echoed the conviction that there was a "right" wage for a job, and that if they raised their manual laborers' pay, they would have to do the same for their foremen, accountants, and executives to maintain a substantial distance between salaries. In other words, the national ethic is ambivalent, decrying the disparity on the one hand (as some CEOs get five hundred times their workers' lowest wage) and, on the other, embracing the differences as virtuous. It is somehow morally wrong not to pay an accountant more than a secretary.

The disparities in earning power were even enshrined in the formula used to calculate compensation after the terrorist attacks of September 11, 2001. The survivors of a thirty-year-old married father of two who was killed in the World Trade Center, for example, would receive $1,066,058 if he had been paid $25,000 a year, and $3,856,694 if he had been paid $150,000. Everyone's life had a price.

Some employers even use the earning gap to argue against narrowing it, noting that raising wages at the bottom would have a direct impact on prices for the same people. Randy Rolston, president of a mail-order stationery company, Victorian Paper, put it this way: "If you move the minimum wage up, where they are spending their money is back within the minimum wage realm. . . . They can't afford to go to a nice restaurant. If they go out to dinner at a Wendy's or a McDonald's, well, you raise the price there. . . . You go to the grocery store, they've got to buy their food, you raise the price there. When the wages are raised, prices would have to be raised. People are either gonna go out of business or they're gonna raise the prices. The inflation it would cause would be a low-end inflation. Those are the businesses that they usually patronize."

The economy resulting from the wage differentiation has been agile in responding to need, demand, and the impulse for innovation. Unfortunately, it has also increased the disparity between wealthy and poor—and, in an ominous harbinger of a troubled future, has not enhanced the opportunity for upward mobility during a worker's lifetime, especially among Third World immigrants impeded by low education and low skills. In a booming economy, practically anyone who wants to work can get a job, but usually at a low wage without much prospect of promotion. Except in certain growth industries such as health care, with high turnover and a demand twenty-four hours a day for a variety of talents, the entry-level job often turns out to be the dead-end job.

It is mobility that has created the global reputation of the United States as a land of opportunity, and it is that impression that has generated the popular view of a society more open and less stratified than others. At the beginning of the twentieth century, the son of Polish immigrants could drop out of school after the eighth grade, work on the Jersey City docks for eight cents an hour, and rise to become president of Bethlehem Steel's steamship lines. That's what my grandfather did. Not today. Most modern American mobility is generated by economic growth, not by any absence of boundaries between races or classes. That economic expansion, rapid enough after World War II to open broad avenues of advancement, has slowed since the 1970s, leaving many workers behind, especially men and women with nothing more than high school diplomas. More mobility occurs between generations than within generations. It is a sad truth now that a young person with limited skills and education arriving on these shores—or entering the workforce from a background of poverty—will start on the bottom rung only to discover that the higher rungs are beyond his grasp.

Nowhere is the stifling frustration more obvious than in the ethnic enclaves that serve America's economy. Formidable walls surround the subcultures of Koreans, Chinese, Vietnamese, Mexicans, Hondurans, Ethiopians, and others who populate the ranks of low-paid workers. Those who lack fluency in English, proper immigration papers, or advanced skills cannot easily scale those walls; they are imprisoned in an archipelago of scattered zones of cheap labor that promote the country's interests. They are not Americans, but they are an essential part of America. They sustain not only the garment industry, but also the restaurants, farms, parking garages, landscapers, painting contractors, builders, and other key contributors to American well-being.

"They treat 'em like shit," said Roxie Herbekian, a gangly, fast-talking union organizer and president of the Parking and Service Workers Union in Washington, D.C. She represented parking garage attendants in Washington, northern Virginia, and suburban Maryland, most of whom were Ethiopian immigrants, plus some West Africans, Latinos, and African-Americans. "People are routinely fired without good reason," she contended, "and there's a lot of racist division of work. It's very hard for people of color to get out of the garages into anything higher [such as] a supervisory position, a management position, accounting." Many workers "feel this wall of disrespect," she said. "A lot of the immigrants, particularly from Ethiopia, are professionals. There's a lot of lawyers, a lot of pharmacists, people that were highly trained . . . and then they're working these jobs, and some young white kid is the supervisor and treats 'em like they don't know anything."

Parking attendants get minimum wage—in the District of Columbia that is a dollar more than the federal minimum—but a lot of their time is off the clock, Herbekian complained. It may take a cashier twenty minutes after she punches out to complete forms and deposit receipts in the bank, but those minutes go unpaid. One big company had "forced breaks," she said. "They automatically deduct an hour and fifteen minutes for breaks—well, people don't get the break." They had to work right through most of it. Personal connections also count. If you have friends who can get you a late afternoon or evening shift parking cars downtown, you'll get up to $200 a week in tips from people retrieving their vehicles. But you need the contacts, and you need to be a man. Women are usually confined to the tipless position of cashier.

A fine-boned woman named Leti, fatigue and defeat etched in her ebony face, worked twelve hours a day as a cashier in a Washington garage. Although she spoke good English, she had never finished high school in Ethiopia, and her long hours and two children hadn't left her time to get her degree here. Seventeen years ago she arrived in the United States on a tourist visa, and two years later managed to get her green card, which signified her legal status as an immigrant. But neither the card nor her English nor her long time in the country opened doors. "I feel like I came last year," she said. "Nothing has changed."

In Los Angeles, "Nara" and her husband were also stuck. Her piercing eyes were bright with anger, her words bitter. For twelve hours a day six days a week, she worked as assistant cook in a Korean restaurant, where customers' tips were not shared with the staff in the hot kitchen. In the evenings, because her husband refused to cook for himself, she got home and had to prepare dinner for him and their son. "Cooking all day and then at home is like being in hell," she said angrily. During one of her many fights with her husband, she shouted at him, "Why did you make me come here?" He walked out and didn't return for ten days.

In 1991 he came from South Korea with $20,000; she arrived six months later with $15,000. Now their savings had dwindled to $5,000, and they had moved to a smaller, cheaper apartment where they slept in the living room, letting their boy of thirteen have the one bedroom. In Seoul, the husband ran an import-export business dealing mostly in sunglasses; in

Los Angeles, he picked up odd jobs as a welder. She was a dress designer but without English couldn't get such work here, so she felt confined to the subculture of Korean restaurants in the "Koreatown" section of Los Angeles. "I went to a language institute for three months," Nara said through an interpreter, "but I forget very easily. I'm too old." She was forty-five. "I live in Koreatown; I can get along without English." She could get along, but she couldn't get out.

When they both had work their income didn't look bad on paper. She made between $1,700 and $1,800 a month, though her long days meant that the hourly rate barely reached California's minimum wage of $6.75 and omitted overtime, which the law required. He could earn $1,000 to $2,000 a month welding gates and fences, so together they may have taken in nearly $40,000 a year. That was a graphic illustration of the virtue of having two wage-earners and the hazards of being a single parent: At those low wages, single parenthood would have been a prescription for poverty.

Still, they felt pinched. Los Angeles was an expensive place to live. Public transportation was so bad that they had to own two vehicles, a truck and a car. Their jobs provided no health insurance, so they spent large sums on Korean doctors and dentists. As illegal immigrants, they got virtually no government benefits (which Nara insisted she would have refused in any case). Moreover, a psychological confinement imposed a mood of defeat. Marginalized, cloistered, and stagnant, Nara simply wanted to go back to South Korea; her husband wanted to stay.

Jung Hee Lee also felt trapped. A sinewy, diminutive woman with a wan smile, she arrived from South Korea with her husband in 1995; he was on a student visa to study computer science at UCLA. "We sold our house in Korea," she explained. "We had planned in Korea that if we sold the house, that's a lot of money, so we could come here and study for about three years comfortably. Both of us would study. We never imagined that I was going to work. It wasn't in the plan. But when we got here, that money ran out quickly, in a year." They were stunned by the cost of living. From a three-bedroom, two-bathroom house in Korea they descended to a one-bedroom apartment in Los Angeles. Their two children had beds; the parents slept on the floor.

She went from bank teller in Korea to waitress in Los Angeles, earning less than the minimum wage and spending hours delicately navigating the slippery floor tiles of a restaurant kitchen. One day, carrying a tray, she lost her footing and fell. Crockery crashed to the floor, and dreams shattered. Her back was injured so seriously that she could not work for a year. Desperate for money, her husband had to drop out of school and get a job—and the college degree was relegated to a distant hope. Jung's employer did not carry worker's compensation; she had found a lawyer who had agreed to take only a contingency fee if a lawsuit were successful, a process that was likely to run for at least five years.

Here again, the family's income was respectable enough, but the ambitions they brought with them to America had been extinguished. The husband, now a manager for a garment contractor, made about $2,000 a month, much better than most garment workers, and Jung was back waiting tables six nights a week in a Korean restaurant, where tips were often good enough to practically double her $800-a-month salary. Nevertheless, the money all disappeared, and they couldn't save. Without health insurance, their medical bills were huge. The tension in their life ground at their emotions. They would have returned home, but they felt ashamed to do so in defeat.

"If you look at the wages earned, it's not bad," she said. "But the problem is you work long hours. Most of the time you're at work, and who's going to take care of the children? So you end up spending about $500 a month for child care, and I don't have much time to spend with my family or husband. So it ends up, going to work, going home and sleeping, and coming out again. There's no time to cook so they always have to go out and eat," she said of her husband and children. That was expensive, and their diet and health suffered as a result.

"My husband is a salaried man, but he doesn't have any social life. He has friends, but he can't hang out with them. He has to come home and take care of the kids. So my husband and I have lots of trouble—arguments. He has no days off. . . . In Korea, we never argued. I've heard from other immigrants that the first five years of immigrant life you and your husband will argue, but if you can get past that you will be together."

But "together" was a relative term. Her husband was out of the apartment by 7:30 or 8 a.m. and back about 8:30 p.m., when she was still at work. "I walk in the door around twelve or one o'clock, I open up the door and my husband's snoring and everyone's asleep, and I feel like, why am I living? I get very depressed. In Korea, at least we spent evenings together so we'd have things to talk about. But right now we have nothing to talk about with each other. There's no time to talk, and there's no content to discuss." In one respect Korean immigrants are becoming assimilated into America: Their divorce rate is about 50 percent.

The salvation of immigrants to the United States has almost always been deferred to the subsequent generations. If the parents cannot speak English, the children can. If the parents are confined by long hours and low wages, the children are freed to find a way up along the path of higher skills and education. It's hard to make comparisons with earlier eras, but in today's ethnic enclaves the assumptions are not completely intact, the confidence is not entirely unshaken that the next generation will succeed, advance, emerge into the shared sunlight of the country's prosperity.

Indeed, when I asked Jung what she foresaw in her children's lives, she answered curiously; she described how active she had become in campaigning through the Korean Immigrant Workers Advocate to improve working conditions in Korean restaurants. That battle, if won, would make her children's lives better, she believed. So, I asked, she expected them to be working in restaurants? "There's no guarantee that they will not be working in a restaurant," she said sadly. "Of course, I would love to have my children go to Yale, Harvard, Columbia, New York University, and become a doctor, a lawyer, but—right now my son's dream is to become a police officer. My daughter's is to become a teacher in elementary school. But in looking at their future employment, who knows? They could end up working in the restaurants."

Chapter Four

HARVEST OF SHAME

These are the forgotten people, the under-protected,
the under-educated, the under-clothed, the under-fed.
—Edward R. Murrow, "Harvest of Shame," 1960

If the cinder-block barrack had been filled with migrant workers, the impression would have been less severe. We would have talked with the men and women, joked with them, listened to their stories. We would have been busy with their laughter and leathery faces and weary eyes, not focused so intensely on the crude dark rooms, the rusty bunk frames, the stained and stinking mattresses, the grimy kitchen sink, the torn screens, the row of toilets without partitions. The presence of people would have softened the stark conditions in which they lived. But this was December, and North Carolina's growing season was over, cut short this year by a hurricane that flooded fields and ruined crops. A remnant of the last harvest—a small pile of dusty sweet potatoes—huddled against an outside wall. Late on a sunny Wednesday, the "camp" was vacant. In the emptiness, the echo of hardship reverberated.

Like most such camps, this one was way out of sight and hard to find.

Pastor Tony Rojas had brought us from Newton Grove in a van big enough to negotiate the merciless dirt road that twisted through deep ruts and puddles until it emerged at the edge of a vast field. There, in a weedy lot less than twenty feet from where Thanksgiving yams were grown, stood the building, as dismal as a neglected barn. Long and narrow with a peaked roof, its single story had many doors, each opening into an unpainted cinder-block room resembling a cell. Each cell smelled of mold, was lit by a bare bulb on the ceiling, and contained two or three bunks, not enough for the laborers who crowded in here. The pastor gave the workers clean sheets, he told me through my son Michael, who was interpreting from Spanish.

A sad scene from this building was hung like an icon of misery on the office wall of Father Tony, as he was known. It was a large color photograph of a young man sitting here on the floor among bunks with filthy mattresses. One day, visiting the office, the man was stunned to see himself depicted in such surroundings. He told the pastor that if his family saw the picture, they would never let him come here again. "The mattresses are nauseating," Father Tony told us before we saw for ourselves. "They are sticky. They smell disgusting. It is horrible to be there. They prefer to sleep on the floor. They are afraid of getting a disease by sleeping on the mattresses."

Father Tony was a native of Colombia in his fifties, a Catholic priest turned Episcopalian. He had a broad brown face that vividly registered all the pain, amusement, outrage, and inspiration that the migrants brought him as he tried to render help through the Episcopal Farmworkers Ministry. They were vulnerable and strong, adrift and steady. At the height of the picking season, he said, twelve to fourteen men were crammed into each twelve-by-fifteen-foot cell, fewer women in their respective cells. Summer was fiercely hot. There was no air conditioning, and not even a fan, unless a worker happened to bring one with him. But migrants travel light—a pair of shoes, two or three pairs of pants. Men and women are stuffed into a van or a pickup, moving with the seasons from the citrus groves of Florida to the North Carolina fields of cotton, tobacco, green vegetables, strawberries, and sweet potatoes, sometimes to the apple orchards of Pennsylvania and New York, and then back southward again. In late fall, some cut Christmas trees. You can hardly go through a day, much less observe a holiday, without the fruit of their labor in your life.

The farm owners usually provide housing for the migrants—either barracks like this one, run-down trailers, or dilapidated wooden farm-houses that look like shipwrecks on a horizon of tilled earth. We turned off the main road past a neat subdivision of brick homes decorated for Christmas, and a rutted dirt road led to a pair of decaying houses that seemed abandoned. Screens were torn, doors were half off their hinges, the paint looked decades old; the inside was bare, dirty, gray, and dark. So many workers lived here, Father Tony said, that they slept in the hallways. Years ago someone climbed to the peak of one roof and installed a handmade sign reading, "Motel Six."

"They smile every day," Father Tony observed, even though across a field, behind trim white fences, they could see mahogany-colored horses gamboling before an ample house painted gleaming white.

Sometimes, as in the case of the cinder-block camp, the owner rents housing to a *contratista*, a contractor who collects, transports, and organizes the teams of farmhands. Some farmers charge their migrants rent; some don't. Some pay them decently and co-sign loans for cars and trailers; some don't. Some are simultaneously cruel and caring, ruthless and paternalistic.

Unlike the decrepit wooden houses, this barrack clearly had one function from its conception. Whoever owned it—Father Tony didn't know his name—must have understood what he was doing when he designed this harsh building, for its configuration could have had no purpose other than to house workers—and to deprive them of their dignity. It was not an old structure, just chillingly efficient. The kitchen contained one gas stove and hookups for five others, which were supplied in season by the contractor. The common room, also used for dining, was furnished with two picnic tables and a bulletin board where the required notices were posted in Spanish and English on the minimum wage and the rights of migrant workers. Typed in English only was this warning:

MEN
Stay out of the women's bathroom.

WOMEN
Stay out of the men's bathroom.

If caught you *will* be fined $30.00.
Everybody has there [*sic*] restroom so stay in your own place.

The men's bathroom had one sink, four toilets in full view, and four showerheads in a stall too cramped for four people to shower at once. The women's bathroom had the same arrangement, with two toilets and two showerheads. It looked as if nothing had ever been cleaned or repaired. There was no privacy, no comfort, not even the quiet sense of sparse simplicity that could be found in a primitive village. There, at least, human beings live. Here, they were kept, warehoused, stored like seed and fertilizer.

Father Tony knew to let us wander through the rooms in silence, as if we were visiting a memorial at the scene of a crime. Independently, Michael and I were suffused with the same recollection, which we learned later by comparing notes: of another kind of camp where the greatest crime occurred. And then we apologized to ourselves for feeling the parallel, which of course was no parallel at all. No injustice that happened here approached what happened there. And yet the sensation of standing where something terrible had taken place was not dissimilar. Even in the emptiness, you were somehow a witness.

Claudio and his eighteen-year-old wife had lived here. He was an unsmiling man of twenty-four, dressed in a sweater and camouflage fatigues. A mustache and a thin beard defined his narrow face, which looked gray in the pale December light. The previous summer, the young couple set out on their journey to a new life in America by agreeing to pay a coyote, a smuggler of humans, to sneak them across the border from Mexico near Laredo, Texas. The price was $1,300 for Claudio and $1,400 for his wife, rates that had doubled in the last decade. "He charges more for women; it's more work," Claudio explained.

They didn't have the cash, so the fee was advanced as a loan to be repaid in three months by withholding installments from their paychecks. For collateral, Claudio's father had to sign over his house and seven and a half acres of land in Mexico, putting Claudio and his wife into a modern form of indentured servitude. They could not fail to work, because they had no money; they could not fail to pay, because his father would lose his property. It was typical of the arrangements through which Mexicans cross illegally into the United States.

The journey can be difficult and dangerous, and has become more so as the U. S. Border Patrol has beefed up surveillance of the frontier, especially in urban areas. Deflected into remote regions of desert, immigrants traveling with too little clothing or too little water have succumbed in rising numbers to the cold and the heat of the wilderness. In the five years following the introduction in 1993 of new technology and additional manpower to monitor the border, the number of deaths from exposure jumped from six to eighty-four. In the year from October 2004 to October 2005 alone, 473 people died.[1] As small comfort, the numbers murdered by thieves or killed in road accidents have declined.[2]

Claudio and his wife had the luck of a relatively easy trip. They hid from border agents in Texas during daylight and walked in darkness, but only for three nights and for short distances. At a predetermined location, a *contratista* met them with a van and drove them (for no extra charge, Claudio was pleased to say) to a farm in South Carolina to spend a month removing stakes and plastic sheeting from tomato fields. He was not quite sure how their wages were figured. "We never knew how they were paying us," he admitted. "They didn't tell us." It wasn't by the hour but by the row, he thought. All he knew was that it was a lot more than Mexican wages, and—as he was now learning—minuscule by American standards. He and his wife together, working the same rows, received about $250 for the two of them—but only every other week, really, because the contractor withheld half their earnings for the coyote: "One check for us and one for him," Claudio said.

Then they were moved to the cinder-block camp in North Carolina. Up at five every morning, they were driven by van to some distant farm a couple of hours away—he didn't know the farmer's name—where they spent eight or nine hours walking behind tractors that were unearthing sweet potatoes. They gathered the potatoes by hand and filled bushel-sized pails as fast as they could for 40 cents a bucket. He could fill about thirty buckets an hour, he said, "if the field is in good shape and there's a lot." So that would be $12 an hour, I said. "No," he replied and looked confused. "No, it was less because in order to make $50 in a day we had to work really hard all day." Either Claudio's arithmetic was weak or the contractor's was cunning. Neither Claudio nor his wife had gone past the sixth grade; the contractor, on the other hand, knew how to invent deductions to list on the pay stub, leaving about $40 for each day of labor. That was still as much in a day as Claudio earned in a week doing farm work in Mexico, so he displayed no hint of grievance. "In the checks there were a lot of discounts," he said dispassionately, "like cleaning. They did a discount of rent, of light, of all those things." He could not remember how much.

Cleaning. Rent. In the squalid cinder-block camp for which Claudio and his wife paid involuntarily, they were lucky enough to be placed with another married couple in a cell for just the four of them. Many later arrivals were jammed into the small rooms, he said, where they slept on floors, sometimes on flattened cardboard cartons laid over the raw concrete. "What we made wasn't enough to buy food," he remarked. Then the hurricane's torrent of rain flooded everything except the camp, which sat marooned like a derelict in a sea of muddy water. Work was halted. The migrants played cards and waited. Claudio and his wife still owed the coyote $2,300.

After a month the young couple learned in a phone call to Mexico that their fourteen-month-old daughter was ill; they had left her with his parents. They needed to send $50 for treatment. So they stopped waiting for work and left the cinder-block camp, setting out on foot. Few migrants here have their own cars; most are trapped in remote locations, dependent on contractors to take them periodically to a grocery store or a Laundromat in town. But their contractor didn't come, so the young couple hiked for miles into Newton Grove. At a gas station, they met a Mexican man who took them into his home until the network of hard-luck migrants stranded by the storm began to function. Two other Mexican men invited them to share rent in a tiny, weather-beaten house in the scruffy town of Wade. That is where the thin December light now filtered onto Claudio's gray face. He had no work. For a while he had been employed by a roofer for $250 a week, then for a woodcutter whose truck broke down and put him out of business. A week ago Claudio's wife was hired by a meat-cutting plant; he wasn't sure how much she would be paid. She wanted to return to Mexico. The coyote was waiting for his money, but he had given an extension because of the hurricane.

Having just visited the barrack the day before, I tried now to see it through Claudio's eyes. He was a taciturn man, not given to introspection or graphic description, so the questions had to be specific but not leading. I wanted to know how he felt living there, without suggesting how I thought he should have felt. He conveyed a sense that the squalor of the camp was overshadowed by the lack of work, for work was the entire purpose of his coming. Were the conditions in the camp what he expected when he came, or were they worse? "For me it wasn't good because there was no work there," he replied. Aside from the fact that there wasn't work, did he have any complaints about the camp and the way it was? "Like what?" Well, whatever occurred to him. Was there anything about it he didn't like? "The only thing was that there was no work."

The following April we again encountered a curious absence of anger. Pedro, twenty-five, was sitting on a bunk in an eight-by-ten room in another cinder-block building, this one on Burch Farms between Mt. Olive and Faison, North Carolina. The inside was painted a dirty robin's-egg blue; the outside, a faded pinkish cream. On the door to room 13, someone had pasted a bumper sticker: "Eat More Sweet Potatoes." The first spring lettuce, kale, and turnip greens were poking up through rows of plastic strips that made the sweeping fields look like washboards glinting in the sunlight.

Pedro wore a little gold cross in his left ear and a dirty Cleveland Indians baseball cap. He had just moved in as a refugee from another house called El Infierno because of the rough bunch there who drank and fought with knives. He had no bed and slept on the floor. After his fifteen-year-old cousin was stabbed and wounded, Pedro got his contractor to switch him to this place with a less exciting name: "the camp." It was grim but quiet so far. Both beds in this room had mattresses; one bunk was propped up on cinder blocks. A colored drawing of Jesus was stuck to the wall with gray duct tape. In the corner, strung between two nails, a black electrical cord no longer attached to an appliance was used to hang towels and jeans. He kept all his other possessions in two black plastic milk crates, a cooler, and a few plastic bags; on top of a crate was a fairly new baseball mitt and a ball signed in big letters, "PEDRO, TE AMO," by his girlfriend back in Mexico. He hadn't seen her in a year.

This was census season, but Pedro didn't exist. He hadn't received a form and hadn't seen a census-taker. Luckily for him, the Immigration and Naturalization Service didn't know he existed, either. But the Internal Revenue Service and the Social Security Administration did, because they got a portion of his wage, duly withheld each week by his employer, who paid him the minimum of $5.15 an hour. Pedro would never see any Social Security benefits, of course, and he didn't dare file a tax return, even though he might have been entitled to a refund. The IRS is not supposed to tell the INS, but who believes that?

After the hurricane, Pedro decided to stay on for the winter, packing sweet potatoes and radishes that survived the flood. He worked sixty hours a week, earned nine times what he had made in a Mexican slaughterhouse, and managed to send $300 to $500 a month to his parents, who were using the money to build him a house there. "God willing, two years from now," he hoped, he would go home to Mexico, live in his new house, and harvest corn and beans on his family's farm. That was the closest Pedro came to a complaint.

The owner complained about this building, though. Jimmy Burch griped loudly when he drove us past it in his pickup-truck tour of the large farm he owned with his two brothers. "See the beer cans and shit in the yard?" he said in his country twang. "I paid $60,000 to build that ten years ago. I been fined prob'ly $25,000 for that camp. Beer cans in the yard, torn screen. I say, 'They did that, not me.' Don't matter. They fine me." The fines were levied by the state Department of Labor, which licensed the housing but seemed ineffectual in enforcing decent standards. Jimmy would have liked to give the building to somebody. "It just gets trashed every weekend. I get tired of pissing my money away. Just keep it up to minimum standards and don't worry about it. The stove my grandma gave me lasted forty years. The stoves in these camps won't last twelve months."

Jimmy was a rather round man, not tall, but he carried himself with a tautness that said: in charge. His light brown hair was unruly, his face ruddy. His alert blue eyes, constantly sweeping the gleaming rows of red lettuce, had a piercing acuity that enabled him to see—and to know what he was not seeing. He talked constantly while he drove in his mud-spattered black Chevy pickup, suddenly whirling off the pavement onto a dirt road, then spinning into a field, first running straight so his wheels straddled the rows of greens, then knifing diagonally across the jouncing rows until he got to a couple of men with a tractor and trailer piled with irrigation pipe. He talked with the older worker in a trashy Spanish so corrupted by North Carolina drawl that Michael couldn't understand a word. The younger one, looking frightened, hung back and said nothing. Jimmy was down to earth and above the landscape, comfortable and wary in his natural habitat.

The one place he wanted us to get out was a dirt yard near a trailer, where he stopped his truck. "This is where we started," he said. He was fourteen when his brother David, a helicopter pilot, was shot down and killed during the 1968 Tet Offensive in Vietnam. His family used the life insurance payment to buy this piece of land—fourteen acres, later expanded to thirty-five, which produced enough vegetables to put all five sons through college. "We thought we were rich," Jimmy said, looking down at the dirt. "They spent all their money on us, my parents did. They didn't have any damn money left over."

With 2,000 acres now, he and two of his brothers grew cucumbers, peppers, squash, eggplants, various greens, and sweet potatoes, which found markets from Boston to Miami. They grossed $15 million a year and usually made a net profit of 3 to 4 cents on the dollar, before taxes. That margin is typical for many businesses, but in agriculture it's vulnerable to weather, of course. The floods produced a loss of $1 million last year, he figured, and he received just $17,583 in federal subsidies, including $8,095 in disaster relief.[3] "Horrible. Lost all the fall greens, all the fall cucumbers and squash. We saved most of the sweet potatoes. We were lucky," he added incongruously. "That's the way it goes with Mother Nature. He gives and he takes it away." So do the oil companies: Jimmy was spending $3,000 a week more on fuel this year than last. The cost of seed, fertilizer, and pesticide had doubled in the last decade.

Furthermore, modern farming is a tricky business of calibrated timing to hit the market with the right vegetable at the right moment in a season that rolls relentlessly from south to north. "You only got a window you can plant in," Jimmy explained. "You got to plant in your window. If you don't, you know you're not gonna make anything. Florida's got their time. Georgia's got their time. We've got our time. Then it goes into Jersey and Michigan. Everybody's got their slot for the vegetable deal. If you overlap, you always get murdered in the marketplace. Prices go to hell." The only way to survive is to average out the bad years with the good. "It's like going to Atlantic City. Very little difference. Very little difference. Don't get me wrong, we've done very well. . . . You work a lot of years, you hit the hot markets, make a lot of money one year, pay off all your debts and go again. Fortunately, I've had enough of them years, I can pay off them debts and go again." The loan officer was interested enough to drive out and look over the crops once in a while. "I'm on a first-name basis with my banker," Jimmy said laughingly. "We know each other well. But I've never failed to pay him, so he don't never fail to lend it to me."

Jimmy wheeled his truck through a mustard field and stopped at the end of an array of rows lush in kale and other greens. A team of men was cutting by hand and packing the crisp new growth into crates. He paid them a dollar a box, he said, and most workers did about ten boxes an hour, the quick ones, fifteen. He sold the greens for $5 a box but added hastily,

"I'm not gettin' rich here, you know. The box costs $1.10, the labor's a dollar, twenty-five cents for the ice, you figure a buck and a half to raise it. If I make fifty cents a box, that's about all I can get." Given those figures, the profit actually worked out to more than twice that much; math seemed to be a fuzzy science in these parts. "I'd like to charge ten bucks but the market won't allow it." Could he have paid the workers less than a dollar a box? "Hmmmm. I probably could. I know I could. Sometimes. But hell, I want to keep these people here year-round. I want a stable workforce." That's why he grew a sequence of crops: to have a steady demand for labor to keep a core of good workers busy. It's a reason other farmers raise tobacco, which can be planted before, and harvested after, cucumbers, for example.

Burch Farms employed 115 to 120 people year-round and added another 100 or so from May through November. Labor accounted for about 25 percent of the farm's expenses, so there was an obvious incentive to keep wages down. On the other hand, Jimmy professed a passionate desire for reliable workers who would stay on or return year after year. "They're not up here to make me rich," he said. "They're here to make a living for themselves. That's the way it is. They got their own dreams, you know." So he tried to pay them enough to compete with a factory wage; that meant field hands got a piece rate that he thought allowed them to average $10 an hour ("They have to hustle, but they do it"), and packers started at minimum wage but went to $6 or $7. He was planning to add health insurance for his full-time employees. "You want to keep 'em you got to pay 'em more. Not anybody gonna stay here for minimum wage. Hell, they can't live on minimum wage." In fact, the minimum wage has an impact on wages above it. If it were raised by a dollar, he figured, employees making more than the minimum would have to be raised by at least fifty cents. The reason was simple, he declared: "Nobody works for you 'cause they love you."

Another way to keep good people was to help them buy homes and settle here, a point he made by driving through a cluster of trailers the locals called Little Mexico. "I co-signed with all these people here with these trailers," he explained and then gestured toward a nice old single-family house. "I gave the house away." He kept title to the land but charged no rent for it. He had learned that many Mexicans who began as migrants would stay put if they found congenial work, and by giving them housing, offering financial advice, and co-signing their loans, he helped employees he valued to abandon the wandering life, put down roots on his farm, and remain obligated to him. He had done this for about twenty people, he bragged, and the benefit seemed mutual. He pointed to another house, where a shift foreman and his wife lived. "I went to the courthouse and give it to him. He has the title. That way I don't have to put up with government bullshit no more. . . . That way if there are beer cans in the yard, I say, 'He owns the house.' And you didn't see any beer cans in the yard, did you? Ownership makes a big difference."

The risk to him was minimal. A trailer cost "around $20,000 if you buy it new," he said, pointing to one after another on Mexico Lane. "This one was used, I think he paid about ten for that one. He bought his new, I think it was eighteen. These are people who are married, wife and children. They don't want to stay in a barracks anymore. They want some privacy. They don't want their young 'uns around them boys on the weekend drinkin' and raisin' hell." Jimmy had never been cheated on a house. "For cars, yes," he said. "I don't co-sign for cars anymore. They have some strange idea that when the transmission or motor blows up, the payments stop. I don't know why they think that way. I don't co-sign car loans no more. Got burned two or three times. Never been burned on a house, though, never." He was selective and not altruistic. "It's after they been here awhile, you get to know 'em. It ain't something I do for somebody who just walks up here and says, 'How about helpin' me out?' I ain't into that."

He helped out the Delgado family when their kerosene heater exploded and their trailer burned up. They had no insurance. "He lent us money to get a car, lent us room in the camp, co-signed for a loan for this trailer," said Maribel, a young mother whose face lit up when she talked. With her husband, Hector, she was sitting in the kitchen at the end of the long trailer opposite the two bedrooms. In the middle was an ample living room. The "mobile home" was hardly mobile. It sat on cinder blocks on land that Jimmy Burch and his brothers still owned, land the Delgados wished they could have bought. The land had to be cleared and a well dug, which cost $2,500 on top of $4,000 for the trailer.

Jimmy had a stake in this family, whose long-term loyalty was an asset. Maribel's father still worked on the farm, as he had for years, and she worked in the packing plant for $6.25 an hour. Hector got that dollar a box for picking greens, but he couldn't reach the $10 an hour Jimmy boasted of; it was more like $6 an hour, he figured. At the height of the harvest, the work ran to seventy hours a week. "When there are no vegetables, when there's snow," he said, "we aren't working at all." And they tried to send $100 every two weeks to their relatives in Mexico.

The Delgados had no medical insurance, but Medicaid provided coverage for their three children, who had been born in the United States and therefore had American citizenship. The family's income was probably low enough to entitle them to food stamps, which had been repeatedly denied by self-important clerks who kept telling Maribel that it was the wrong day or that she wasn't a "real" resident (though she, too, was a U.S. citizen). Such benefits are not available to undocumented immigrants, and are granted to legal immigrants only if they are children, elderly, or disabled and arrived before welfare reform was enacted: August 22, 1996. The denial is designed to discourage illegal immigration, but it doesn't work.

Maribel demonstrated that no obstacles were imposing enough to serve as deterrents. She came to the country as a teenager, crossing the Rio Grande several times with her father, a migrant worker. Attacked by armed robbers, hunted at night by Border Patrol officers with searchlights, her group was caught and deported. Later, she tried again, but the river was full and roaring and carried her downstream so violently she thought she was drowning. Finally reaching the bank back on the Mexican side, her group was attacked again, and one man was stabbed. On the third attempt, "we passed through a very strange place full of narco-traffickers," she said. "The person who brought me here, I think he knew them and they let us through." She lived with her mother in Brownsville, Texas, then applied for the 1986 amnesty granting legal status to certain undocumented immigrants. She received her green card, certifying her right to be in the country, and seven years later she gained citizenship; as a result, Hector obtained documentation as well.

These folks now seemed like the salt of the earth, the models of elemental striving through a hardscrabble life of incremental gain. The key word is incremental. If theirs was the beginning of the classic immigrant journey from penury to prosperity, it was hard to see. Maribel and her husband were doing the same work as her father, so there had been no intergenerational mobility there, unless the mere fact of moving to the United States could be considered advancement. She was satisfied with her children's rural school, but whether it put them on a path to college was questionable. From their trailer on a shabby lane in Little Mexico, the horizon of opportunity looked very close and confining. They could not gaze out to an expansive distance of possibility.

For most such workers, attainable progress occurs only within the enclave of farm labor: from field hand to tractor driver, from picker to supervisor, from migrant to *contratista*. Severino Santivanez had made that move from migrant to contractor. He oozed success, though he had only a fraction more than the men he supervised. He was somewhat portly, with a bit of a beer belly that he revealed by wearing his white shirt open to the button just above his navel. He flashed a gold tooth when he smiled, which he did frequently as he half sat, half leaned on the driver's seat of his truck, the door open in the late afternoon shade.

It was parked outside the group house where he had lived in 1989, and where he now housed his crew, currently nine men from the same town in the Mexican state of Vera Cruz. "I like this house," he said, "because the water is cold, perfect for drinking. It's a strong house." As proof, he noted that it was still standing, which was remarkable since it looked long abandoned. He claimed that a tornado swept by some years ago and left it intact.

The house was also a firetrap. It felt like a half day's journey from the nearest fire department, at the far reaches of narrow blacktop roads that crossed endless flat fields, passed tight clusters of houses, then turned to dirt and wandered among fields just being planted with tobacco. The house had a single story and used to be white. The remaining paint was peeling, exposing the weathered wood beneath. One of the windows was sealed with a piece of cardboard where glass should have been. In front, nailed to the stump of a telephone pole was a faded green piece of plywood with a rusty basketball hoop attached. The men had no basketball. Inside the torn screen door was a space—once the dining room, perhaps—with four beds, saggy mattresses, and a rusty refrigerator. The former living room had a boarded-up fireplace and four beds. There were no closets. Nails had been hammered into walls, and wire coat hangers hung on them bore layers and layers of shirts and pants.

Severino didn't pay anything for this house. The farmer magnanimously gave him the use of it, paid the rent for the house where Severino lived, and also paid Severino 50 cents an hour per man in his crew. So, at the peak of the season, when his crew grew to twenty-seven men, he was making $13.50 an hour, about the average wage in the United States. It wasn't bad for a man with a first-grade education who could hardly read or write. "I learned more here 'cause I had to write the names," he said, showing a list of his crew members, now working for Jimmy Burch. Only by chance did he achieve this rank. After more than a decade migrating among farms from Florida to North Carolina, he rose to supervisor, and one day the grower asked him to bring more field hands. So he did, and he had a new career.

His men here were gloomy. They all missed their families and yearned to go home to Mexico, each on a different, carefully planned timetable: next January, a year, two years from now. They sent home about 70 percent of the money they made, but the experience provoked reflections on where priorities lay. "I learned to value the family," one young man declared. "Here it's material and it's money, and that's not life. It's sustenance. It's like eating and clothing are the most important. The spiritual and the family, you can't buy it with money. That's the biggest thing there is."

Living miles from the nearest town, with no transportation except what Severino provided, the men felt they had relinquished independence. "I depend on everybody here for everything," one said. At home, "you have freedom," he added. "You can go there, you can go here. I don't have to be ten to fifteen kilometers outside a town. I feel pressured here for the money. It's like being in the house, all you see is the wall. Outside, the wall, it's like being in prison here. Truthfully, it's like prison. We can't go to centers of fun, entertainment. We can't go together into a store because the immigration will take you away."

Not a single one of the men would advise any other friends or relatives to make the journey to work in the United States. "My brother wanted to come, and I told him not to come," one said.

"For my family, I would say that nobody else should come here," said another. "If they have work there, it's better for them to keep it and not come here."

They were also jittery. A couple of Sundays before, Severino had taken them from the trailer where they were living to a Laundromat in Goldboro. By the time they returned, their trailer had been consumed by an unexplained fire; all their belongings, except for the clothes that were on their backs and in their laundry bags, had been reduced to smoldering ashes. The casualties included their only television set, which they'd bought in a Florida Wal-Mart for $288.86. A lanky guy pulled out the receipt, then said, "For me, material things aren't important. At least it didn't get us while we were sleeping."

And that's what made them nervous. Severino had moved them into this house, but they could see how quickly a fire would spread through the bare wooden walls and floors. They wondered about a fire at night. They had no phone, no vehicle. They were miles from the nearest neighbor and could see no other house from theirs. I asked a woman who had brought us here, who worked for a fledgling union called FLOC (the Farm Labor Organizing Committee), if she could get them two or three smoke detectors. She replied firmly that it was the owner's responsibility. The owner wouldn't do it, I said, and I suggested that she go buy a few for ten bucks apiece and give them to Severino. That would have violated some peculiar ethic of accountability, and she clearly had no intention of doing so. I asked Severino. He said maybe he had one somewhere.

When we drove away in the gathering dusk, the men stood outside and said farewell. Even in a crowd, they looked lonesome.

Ramiro Sarabia was short, stocky, and solidly built, and he wore a black mustache. Bill Bryan was lean and clean-cut, and he wore gray slacks and a white tennis shirt that made him look like a 1950s character out of *Ozzie and Harriet*. Ramiro's well-worn office, once the living room of a gray house that sat near the base of the town's water tower, had the feel of an old shoe with too many miles on it. Bill's office, at the heart of the Mt. Olive Pickle Company's processing plant, was crisp and fancy, carpeted wall to distant wall. Its centerpiece was a conference table, of dark wood, covered with jars of the various pickles and relishes that his company produced.

Since 1998 the men had been cordial opponents in an unusual labor-management dispute. Ramiro, FLOC's field organizer in North Carolina, had tried to unionize field hands, but not by the traditional bottom-up approach of forging disgruntled workers into a phalanx that demanded their employer's recognition. Migrants are difficult to organize; they don't stay long, they can't risk a strike or dismissal, and most are vulnerable to deportation. So while Ramiro had signed up about half of the six thousand workers he wanted to represent, he was really attempting a top-down approach, trying to start negotiations not only with the direct employers— the farmers—but with the man who bought their cucumbers: Bill Bryan, president of the major business in the little town of Mt. Olive, North Carolina. The farmers Bill bought from were not regarded as wealthy enough to sustain a union contract without Mt. Olive paying more for their cucumbers, FLOC believed. Furthermore, the growers were numerous, far-flung, and impervious to public embarrassment about working conditions. So Ramiro wanted Bill's company as one party in a three-way contract including FLOC and the farmers. That would have raised wages, improved benefits, and brought decency into the fields and barracks.

No way, Bill said with the kindly sincerity of a scoutmaster explaining why it was up to the older boys to decide who got the leaky tent. "We don't believe that we should interfere in the relationship between other employers and their employees," he explained. "If you go out on a farm and convince the farmers and the workers that a union's in their best interest, we're gonna respect that, just like we'll respect it with the other people we're doing business with. We've got some union suppliers; we've got some non-union suppliers. On the ag side, the only unionized supplier we have would be in Ohio, where FLOC is based. And in that case, the supplier . . . came to us several years ago and said for several reasons, he was looking at negotiating a contract with FLOC, he thought that was in his best interest, and what did we think of it? And we said, 'Well, we think you have to make a decision that's in the best interests of your operation and do what you think is best. As long as you continue to be the kind of supplier you've been, with the quality and the service level and being competitive, we think—that's not a problem with us, we'll continue to do business with you.' We still have a good business relationship with that supplier." But Bill said he was not about to force farmers to unionize their own workers.

FLOC figured that in agriculture, as in the garment industry, it was the brand-name producer, highly sensitive to bad publicity, that would get suppliers to shape up. Furthermore, Ramiro argued that Mt. Olive was not as far removed from the growers as it pretended; it often signed contracts for a certain quantity of cucumbers at a certain price before the farmers even planted, making the growers little more than subcontractors. Mt. Olive "dictates conditions for growers and workers alike," said a FLOC position paper. In rebuttal, Bill noted that his suppliers grew lots of crops besides cucumbers—everything from tobacco to sweet potatoes—and so were truly independent.

The unorthodox labor-organizing tactic that treated the processor as the effective employer had worked for FLOC in parts of Michigan and Ohio near its home office of Toledo. Campbell's signed on after a boycott, then escaped from the arrangement by halting purchases of tomatoes in the region. Heinz, Vlasic, and Dean Foods had three-party contracts with FLOC and farmers for cucumbers in that area. But FLOC hadn't made a dent in little Mt. Olive. Eastern North Carolina is to labor unions what the Wild West was to string quartets, and Ramiro received a rough education in the resilience of small-town politics and economic interests. After a year of fruitless meetings in which Bill didn't budge, FLOC launched a boycott of the Mt. Olive Pickle Company's products. Ramiro and his colleagues circulated dramatic leaflets, sent around open letters, and solicited support for the boycott from churches and area colleges. Bill countered with contributions to those worthy institutions, Ramiro contended. Indeed, Bill was a prominent citizen, generous and important and well liked. The town even put on an annual pickle festival. But the boycott finally succeeded. In 2004 Mt. Olive signed a three-party contract with FLOC and a growers' association to pay farmers more for cucumbers, contribute to workers compensation insurance, and establish grievance procedures.

FLOC and other farm unions have not limited themselves to wages and contracts. They have also focused on the pesticides and herbicides that have damaged men and women and children who have harvested bounty from the American earth. Even as government has removed from the market more and more of the "hot stuff," as Jimmy Burch called the most deadly chemicals, some farmers (not he, Jimmy insisted) have used the permitted compounds irresponsibly. Spraying in the wind, sending workers into fields too soon after application, failing to provide sinks and showers and laundries, many growers have exposed their employees—and their employees' children—to untold health risks. Of particular worry are children who live in camps among the fields, who play outside in the weeds and soil, who put their hands in their mouths, who crawl around floors where parents have tracked the toxic residues, and who are especially vulnerable during their growing years when their brains and bodies are developing.

The most obvious effects of poisoning are "vomiting, nausea, dizziness and headaches, fatigue, drowsiness and skin rashes," as well as bronchitis and asthma, according to a study of incidents in California. Less visible and more serious problems may include "childhood brain tumors, leukemia, non-Hodgkin's lymphoma, sarcoma," and damage to the immune, endocrine, and nervous systems, though these "are very difficult to link definitively to pesticide exposure," the report concedes, since they develop long afterwards, possibly resulting from years of cumulative contact. The toxins may be responsible for the higher incidence of birth defects among farmworkers, recorded at three to fourteen times the rates among the general U.S. population.[4] The statistics are incomplete, however, because many symptoms go unreported. Most field hands have no health insurance, and the nearest free clinic may be far away. Unless they're very sick, they usually don't want to miss a day's pay and risk dismissal.

The United Farm Workers of America, the union founded by Cesar Chavez, has complained that California does not vigorously enforce its own laws. Where farmers fail to post warnings that fields have been sprayed, for example, and ignore the mandatory waiting periods before resuming hand harvesting, minuscule fines of $200 or $300 are levied. Only when overt illness results can the fines reach $2,000, the union reports.[5] The victims are invisible, after all.

The children of migrants can also be invisible in schools, which they may attend only for a few months before moving on. The United States has a keen interest in educating these youngsters, for most of them will remain in the country and grow up to become working citizens. Severe disruptions in their schooling do not contribute to the society's well-being. Yet only a few small programs, funded mostly by the U.S. Department of Education, seek to address the problem by providing kids with laptops for learning on the web, for example, or by sending traveling mentors and instructors who keep the studies going as families follow the growing seasons from south to north to south again. Teenagers have been able to graduate from high school through these efforts, which exist in Florida, Illinois, Kentucky, North Carolina, Oregon, and elsewhere. But the number of students enrolled is too small to release the vast majority from the educational deficits that confine them to a predetermined path.

Blacks used to work these North Carolina fields, first as slaves, then as free citizens who were imprisoned by the unyielding laws of economics. "They were treated pretty tough," said Jimmy Burch, who saw some of his fellow farmers drive the workers ruthlessly. "They worked all week, and all they got was the wine and their meals, or marijuana and their meals, whatever the thrill of the week was," he recalled. "You say, 'Well, this guy's taking advantage of them.' And he is. And on the flip side of the deal is, where else is he gonna go? Where's he gonna go? What's he gonna do? I mean, he ain't got no marketable skills. He's got a roof over his head. Might not be a nice roof, but it's a roof. He's warm at night, he gets fed every day. To me, it would be a shitty existence, but for some of these people, I guess it's all

right. I guess. Kind of sad to say that. I guess it's better than being homeless in New York or Washington, waiting for somebody to hand you fifty
cents or a dollar."

Today, after massive black migration from farms to cities and from
South to North, most field hands are Mexican and Central American, the
bulk of them here illegally; less than 2 percent arrive through a limited
visa program known as H2A, whose red tape is formidable. If they complain about employers, they risk not being hired and issued the visa the following year. The remaining 98 percent come without visas, and if the laws
against employing them were enforced efficiently, agriculture in North
Carolina and certain other parts of the country would shut down, farmers
believe; machines cannot replace hands in harvesting crops that are easily
damaged. Jimmy argues that since the United States grants visas liberally
to foreigners who write videogame software, it should do the same for foreigners who harvest food.

Being undocumented is precarious. Fearing deportation, you will think
twice about contesting your wages or working conditions. You will be ineligible for government benefits except free school breakfast and lunch
programs, emergency Medicaid, immunizations, and treatment for com-
municable diseases. And you'll suffer from less obvious inconveniences,
such as the lack of a bank account, which will cost you in fees when you
transfer money. In other words, American government and business gain
financially from your inability to legalize your presence in the country.

Some 6.6 million Mexicans are thought to be living as undocumented
immigrants in the United States, immigration officials estimate, and about
52 percent of the country's 1.6 million farmworkers are here without permission, the General Accounting Office figures.[6] They send more than
$9 billion a year to Mexico to help their families with food, clothing,
medicine, and housing; the flood of cash exceeds the government budgets
of some Mexican localities. Most workers seem to focus on the immediacy
of however many dollars they can earn today, not on some elusive career
ladder. A young man named Abel was a case in point. He knew how to
repair farm machinery, but he didn't advertise his skills and preferred to
stay in the fields. If he became a mechanic, he imagined, "They'll be paying me the same as everyone else and I'll have to work harder, do more difficult work."

Abel and many others have a single purpose—not to gain a foothold in
the United States, not to enter the mainstream, but simply to make

enough money to sustain their impoverished families back home. The common ground of America looks too remote from the twilight margins where they reside.

Earning minimum wage in the cotton fields, Abel and his two cousins worked from seven to seven in the planting season, and from seven in the morning until midnight seven days a week during the harvest from October to December—a peak of labor intensity that saw nine brothers and cousins cram into a tiny grimy trailer sitting among the fields of cotton and tobacco. On this farm, the grower followed the law and paid them overtime of $7.50 for each hour over forty a week, and he didn't charge them for gas, electricity, or rent for their dingy quarters. That was a better deal than they could get during their winters picking oranges in Florida, where the grower charged them each $40 to $50 a week for housing. At the busiest times, they sent about half their earnings to Mexico as a lifeline to keep their parents out of destitution; in slower months, they sent practically everything home, holding out about $30 a week each for food and $200 a month for payments on the old cars that all three of them managed to buy. The jalopies were not a luxury; they got the men to painting and construction jobs in periods between farm chores. Nevertheless, all that labor yielded only modest results: In three years, the cousin who had been here the longest, Rolando, had saved only $2,000 of the $5,000 he needed to build a house in Mexico. "If you would give me the 3,000," he said to me with a laugh, "I would go back right now."

The price they paid was figured in loneliness, separation, and isolation from anything resembling community. No substitute could be found among the rough and transitory flows of migrants from south to north to south again. Abel put it succinctly: "We're single, and we're looking for girlfriends."

As the men send dollars home, 10 to 25 percent of the money is siphoned off by Western Union, banks, and pharmacies in both the United States and Mexico through unfavorable exchange rates and exorbitant fees for wire transfers. People without bank accounts get hit with the highest charges: Their average remittance of $300 dwindles by $80 to $90 as it travels electronically to Mexico, according to the Texas Credit Union League.[7]

To open an account, a bank usually requires a Social Security number. To get a valid number, an immigrant must be in the country legally, so an undocumented immigrant cannot get a valid Social Security number. No problem, said Abel, and he pulled out a Social Security card. He and his two cousins were sitting at a scarred round table in their trailer. All three were here without permission from the U.S. government, doing jobs essential to the U.S. economy. And all three had bank accounts. Social Security cards are not very elaborate, and to my untrained eye this one looked real. So did Abel's more complex, laminated green card bearing the seal of the Immigration and Naturalization Service. Together they cost $100—a package deal—and Abel said he could have paid more if he had wanted higher quality. "We present it for work, that's all," he explained. "After that we don't really carry it."

Producing such documents is part of a charade: The workers know that the farmers generally know that the cards are phony, and the farmers know that the workers know they know, but the little card shuffle seems to exempt the employers from the fines under federal law. Those doing the hiring have dutifully checked the documents, after all. The immigration agency is usually content to deport the workers without going after the employers as well. A noted exception came in the form of a federal grand jury indictment of Tyson's Foods and six employees on charges of arranging to have illegal immigrants smuggled into the country and provided with false documents. The case was thin, however, and despite testimony by several employees who pleaded guilty, a federal jury acquitted the company and the three managers who were brought to trial.[8]

The only authentic piece of identification illegal immigrants can obtain is a driver's license, and that has become more difficult since the terrorist attacks of September 11, 2001. A license is not a necessity for the newest arrivals who don't have cars and don't drive farm equipment, but it's essential for those who want to step off the migrant train and stay in one place for a while, or move up a rung on the job ladder from field hand to tractor driver. Certain states require a Social Security number, and one that's false can get the applicant arrested on the spot for fraud. Among the tighter rules since September 11 is Pennsylvania's practice of stamping "non-citizen" on immigrants' licenses, which are now timed to expire when their visas do.[9] This provokes some to drive without licenses and encourages ethnic profiling by the police, who park outside trailer camps and stop drivers who look Hispanic. The Justice Department has asked police to enforce immigration laws, which have targeted people from Muslim countries especially.

The crackdown also generates some migration within the migration—

a trip from Ohio, Tennessee, or South Carolina, where the rules are strict, to North Carolina, for example, where lawsuits against the state used to guarantee that anyone without a number was allowed to fill in the blanks with zeros. Even here, though, you needed two forms of I.D., and that could be a hassle. A voter's identification card from Mexico counted as one, and a Mexican birth certificate was acceptable. Otherwise, a title to a car would suffice, along with the voter's I.D., but that required a certificate of insurance, which in turn required identification, and on into a labyrinth. After September 11 and the rising fear of immigrants, North Carolina imposed new requirements: proof of state residency and either a valid Social Security number or Individual Taxpayer Identification Number, available with some difficulty from the IRS. Then Congress stepped in, barring states from issuing licenses to illegal immigrants after 2008.

Father Paul Brant put fifteen hundred miles a week on his aging van crisscrossing the countryside of eastern North Carolina on behalf of these folks: saying masses; doing counseling; arranging medical care; and helping people get driver's licenses by pleading, urging, demanding that the motor vehicle administration adhere to its own regulations. He was a Jesuit priest who got his start helping the poor in the Bronx—a tall bear of a man with a flushed, puffy face and a constant smile in his blue eyes. He wore a pleasant squint of jolly compassion behind narrow-rimmed glasses, the thinnest wisp of a gray beard, and a T-shirt that said, "Festival Latino Wilmington '98." His fluent Spanish tumbled along in a very American accent.

He had just had a go-round with the bureaucrats on behalf of Patty and Gloria, whose lack of English required them to take the tests in Spanish, as North Carolina law allowed. Two years before, an examiner in the Kenansville office flatly refused to use Spanish for the test on road signs, even though he had cards with translations sitting on his desk. Now, a more amenable woman, whom Father Paul had helped get the job, was on duty. But he decided to phone ahead anyway, just to be sure. He never identified himself when he called, because he wanted to know how the agency responded to everyone, not just to an activist priest. He found out. Not recognizing his voice, the examiner told him that while applicants could take the written test in Spanish, the signs test had to wait for an interpreter, available only on Fridays. Puzzled, Father Paul called the state capital in Raleigh to see if the rules had changed. They had not. A supervisor contacted the hapless examiner to ask why she had refused to give a test. Her nose was out of joint when the priest walked into her office with

Patty and Gloria. Would he please call her supervisor and get her off the hook? she asked. "I will," he said to me, "but what she told me when I was there was different from her knee-jerk response before she knew who it was."

The other bureaucracy that bothered Father Paul was the Roman Catholic Church: the officious parish priest, the inflexible diocese, the hierarchy that seemed indifferent to the special needs of the transient Hispanic faithful. The church, for its part, seemed barely to tolerate Father Paul, an itinerant priest without a parish, as he journeyed along the edges of society, rocking the boat.

"What I like most is people empowerment," he declared. "I like to get organizations up and running to help address an unmet need, and a lot of that's needed in the Catholic Church 'cause there are lots of unmet needs. But I'm always in trouble with my superiors as a result—not my Jesuit superiors, but the other ones. They don't like waves. They don't like change. It's really amazing, the bureaucracy—no matter where it is, it's the same. It resists any kind of innovation, any kind of change."

Migrants who want to marry, for example, run into a six-month waiting period imposed by the diocese to make them stop and think. It sounds sensible, but six months is a whole growing season, and the bride, the groom, or their family members will probably be long gone by the end of it. Most of the marriages that don't last have been arranged at age fifteen or sixteen, Father Paul argued, and he believed that devout Hispanic adults usually go solemnly enough into matrimony not to need the forced period of reflection. "When a Hispanic couple comes to you and says they want to get married in the church, you're pretty sure they're ready to make a lifetime commitment," he insisted. "But these pastors who don't work with Hispanics much are saying, 'Well, number one, I don't speak Spanish; number two, there's a regulation. No.'" He gave an exasperated laugh. "Most of the priests around here who don't work with Hispanics are very much by the book, and they won't make any exceptions for anything. And they don't ask questions; they just say no. So that's driven a lot of people away."

Those failed child marriages can present a problem, given the church's opposition to divorce. A second marriage cannot be performed in a Catholic church unless the first is annulled, and that must be done by the diocese in which each individual resides—not so easy when the wife, for example, is back in Mexico or Honduras. "Our diocese did not have any provision for handling annulments for couples unless both of the partners were living in this diocese," Father Paul said, "and it requires a special appeal to Rome in order to change jurisdictions, and have this diocese take charge of annulments that properly belong to another diocese. So for two years I presented it to the people in charge of our tribunal: that it was an unjust situation because even if they could do the communication with the diocese in Latin America, most of the dioceses do not have a tribunal. They can't afford to put three priests or two priests in an office to handle marriage cases. So they don't have anything. Basically, then, it becomes impossible for the couple to be freed from a previous marriage bond and be able to marry again. So now they've given me permission to do that. They say, 'Be sure to tell them it's gonna take an extra year because we have to go to Rome and ask for a change of jurisdiction and then we have to start the process after we've gotten that.' "

Most of his time was occupied by secular issues, though, and they ran the gamut of farmworkers' difficulties. One was the lack of community, intimacy, and trust, especially among young men traveling without families. "The kinds of problems that are exacerbated would be the ones that could be settled if the patriarchs were around—the *abuelos,* the grandparents," he noted. "I'll ask them after they've shared something profound with me, 'Do you have any other . . . accountability partner, somebody they'd feel comfortable saying the same things to? Do you have anybody of confidence that you can talk to?' And they'll say no."

So Father Paul tried to fill the void, both by offering good advice and by handing out narrow cards the size of a bookmark, produced on the computer in his cluttered yellow house. Migrants could carry the card, which bore an iconic image of the Virgin Mary and a prayer in Spanish appealing for help in abstaining from alcohol and drugs. Alcoholism was rampant, Father Paul observed. Cocaine and marijuana arrived with young workers, many of whom were addicts before they came, he said; some kicked the habit once they were here, though it was harder to make that happen in the absence of family and community. Health problems became severe, not only because of drugs, alcohol, and the denial of medical insurance, but also because farm work had a high incidence of accidents.

Father Paul was a fixer, an arranger, a middleman, a negotiator, a finder of dentists who would permit payments on an installment plan, doctors who would reduce their charges for uninsured workers, sometimes to zero. And he was a financial counselor, transcending cultures to explain patiently to these folks that here in the United States it was better to pay a little on a bill periodically than to wait and pay nothing until you had it all. He taught them something about the country they served.

The migrants, so essential to America, journey along its edge, touching its wealth as tangents barely touch a circle, never penetrating, never looking out from inside. And so they do not see themselves the way they are seen, and they do not apply to themselves the measurements that America applies to their suffering.

When a migrant stops moving, however, he starts to enter America. He looks around. He settles in. Perhaps he opens a little store to sit incongruously on a North Carolina crossroads to stock jalapeños and other foods familiar to his countrymen. Perhaps, like Agustin Baltazar, he just keeps working year-round on the same farm, and he begins to wonder how to see himself.

Agustin was straddling the line, inside and outside. He and his wife and three children lived in a small white frame house, decorated with flashing lights and a lovely Christmas tree, owned by his boss, a chicken farmer who charged no rent. A handsome guy of thirty-three, Agustin had to spend every penny he earned. Nothing was ever left over. Yet he was not sure where to place himself in the hierarchy of classes.

"I cannot say that I'm poor, poor, because I have a car," he explained. "The most important is that I have my children and my wife. I have a life that continues, so I can't say that I'm so poor. I also recognize that I don't have money. I have something to eat, and my children have their clothes and their shoes, and I feel good. If I say I'm poor, I don't know, maybe. If I say I'm really poor, it would be bad before God, and if I say I'm rich it would be too proud. So I cannot classify myself."

Chapter Five

THE DAUNTING WORKPLACE

People who don't call when they can't come to work probably don't think they're important enough to matter.

—Ann Brash, *after plunging into poverty*

They were a tough bunch. They had survived crack wars, homelessness, and prison, but now they were venturing into truly frightening territory—the unfamiliar world of work. They were terrified.

The sixteen men were callused addicts, alcoholics, and ex-convicts who had done some hard living on the streets of Washington, D.C. All were black. On a Wednesday evening, they gathered for the weekly meeting of their support group in a halfway house within sight of the glowing dome of the United States Capitol. They filled the chairs around the edge of the room, sat on the floor, leaned against the walls, and began to confide in one another about their feelings.

Fear had been a taboo subject in their former lives, where "bad" was good, and the best defense was a threatening posture of aggression. To be safe, they had to look mean, act dangerous, and never admit to being scared. Mothers taught that lesson to their sons, brothers to their brothers.

Tonight, however, the men sat in a circle of security where they had discovered that candor could be therapeutic. They could talk comfortably here. Their treatment program required them to look for jobs, find work within a month, get apartments, and move out on their own. Each task seemed formidable, and they were nervous.

The job hunt is never pleasant, even for a white, middle-class college graduate with high credentials and a sense of ease in the workplace. But for these men, the workplace was like a foreign culture. They entered it burdened by their personal histories of repeated failure: failure to finish school, failure to resist drugs, failure to maintain loving relationships, failure to hold jobs. Nothing in their track records predicted success, and no brave promises could paper over their doubts about themselves. Their brash, streetwise armor seemed a thin veneer. Underneath, they were as tender as babies, deeply vulnerable. They admitted gently that they were afraid of making the phone call, of getting no reply, of filling out the application, of going to the interview. They waited tensely for the inevitable question about a police record—afraid of telling the truth, and afraid of lying. "You got to put down, have you been arrested? I always have a feeling I'm not gonna get hired here—sitting there looking at people's faces and knowing I'm not gonna get hired," said Wayne, his eyes lowered to the floor. "So I pick up little [jobs] here and there—McDonald's. It's a fear of rejection, and it's holding me back."

"Each step is an obstacle to me," a tall, sinewy man confessed. "The interview is an obstacle. I'm kind of shaky with dealing with rejection. I know there're gonna be some problems. I'm gonna run from it or deal with it. I still get feelings when I know I got a job and then I don't get it. I still feel disappointed. There's this worry with me in the way I feel and the way I perceive things. I still have to work on this. Thanks for letting me share."

"Thanks for sharing," the group replied in unison.

The room contained a smattering of successes. One man wore a dark blue uniform with a triangular red shoulder patch reading "Prince Security Incorporated." Another had found work moving office furniture at $6.50 an hour. A third, however, had been turned down as an airport baggage handler because of his criminal record.

Even getting hired wouldn't have ended the anxiety for some of the men in the halfway house. A couple of them were scared of success in being accepted, for they doubted that they were up to the job, whatever job. For at least one of them, though, work itself became therapy. "When I got there I was afraid—oh, no, I can't do this," he admitted. "But every day it comes back a little more. Damn, I forgot I had this in me. It makes me feel good."

Talking about fear took a lot of courage.

Across the continent, Camellia Woodruff carefully missed her orientation for a sales job in the jewelry department of Macy's. She was a lithe black woman of twenty-six who moved like a self-conscious dancer through the yards of Imperial Courts, the Los Angeles housing project where she lived. Attempting a stylish look, she straightened her hair, twisted it into a bun, slicked it down, and pasted a lock at an angle across her forehead. She wore dangling gold earrings. Then she tried to ward off male attentions. Anxiety and anger were transmitted through all four limbs, constantly in motion, gracefully threatening, as if to say, "Get out of my face!" She gave her voice an edge as cold as a blade.

In her living room, she sat down briefly on a blond wooden TV stand—the only other piece of furniture was a white plastic lawn chair—but she could not stay still. As she talked, she fidgeted by mopping and sweeping, pacing and gesticulating. She turned sharply on a burly man who came to her door, cutting him with contempt: "I'm in the middle of an important conversation!" He scampered away.

Camellia had dropped out of school in the eleventh grade, then "started getting into street life," fell into an abusive relationship, and saw her mother die of a drug overdose. She had not married, had no children yet, loved taking care of friends' little kids, and had worked sporadically at low-wage jobs. She'd lasted at each one for quite a while, by her definition. "I've worked for a long time," she boasted. "Four, five, six, seven, eight months." Her horizon was not very far away; she had never considered where she wanted to be ten years out. "Getting up for work every morning seems hard," she said. Her dream job? "I would love to work with kids, like a teacher's assistant or child care."

Isolated in the projects, many like Camellia lack the encouragement and connections to find decent work until a helping hand gives a push or opens a door. The help for Camellia came from Glenda Taylor, a caseworker at the project's federally funded Jobs Plus program, which was designed to overcome the array of barriers to employment. Those obstacles, not always visible to an outsider, were clear to Glenda from her childhood just a few blocks away in this neighborhood of Watts. When she enrolled at San Diego State, she had become the only girl in her large family to go directly from high school to college. Then, having escaped from Watts, she returned to help. Like a tracker with a keen eye, she could read the telltale signs of dysfunction among young people here, the inner anxieties that smothered initiative. "Fear." That was the first barrier on her list. "A tendency not to want to go out there, because you're scared, you're afraid," she said, then added frankly: "Another issue is, people are just plumb lazy."

Or, she observed, they've never been in a family where they've seen anyone going to work. "It becomes a cycle. . . . I think kids role model after what they see, and the first thing they see is in the home. . . . My dad got up at four, five o'clock in the morning every morning, and he was a construction worker."

Many felt inadequacy and rage, she added. "They just build up anger inside of them, build up this sense of low self-esteem, which will not give them a desire to want to go further, because they think that they can't. There's no one saying that you can; there's always someone saying 'Oh, you can't, you won't.' And so when you constantly hear that and even go to school and you hear it, because you're reacting and so the instructor thinks that they're doing something by saying, 'Oh, you're not gonna be anything, you're just gonna be trouble,' well, eventually that's what's gonna happen."

She tried to break the cycle for Camellia by using a contact. From part-time work at Macy's, Glenda knew a manager, vouched for Camellia, and got her a job selling jewelry—a position with some prospect for advancement.

Camellia had misgivings. Two days before her orientation, she told Glenda that she wasn't going because of an embarrassing shoplifting charge on her record, which she was sure would mean rejection. "But I think it would be very helpful if you went anyway and just let them deal with that," Glenda advised her. "Sometimes when you're honest or you're up front about it, they'll be honest and up front themselves." But would they have hired a shoplifter? "I don't think so," Glenda told me later. "I personally don't think that they would have, but I also don't think that you can keep hiding behind your past. You've got to break open and let yourself experience some things." Furthermore, the door was not completely closed. The manager was willing to go ahead if her superiors approved, and Macy's protected itself by impressing new employees with an intimidating display of the store's high-tech security. "It's the fine jewelry department, so they have a camera four ways. Every bay you're at,

every side, the camera's beaming down at you," Glenda said. "The registers, if they so much as suspect you, in the computer room they can pull
up your register from their office and see that you're not making a good
transaction."

Pushed relentlessly to attend her orientation, Camellia started out by
bus, she claimed, but never arrived. "Once I got down there I couldn't find
anything," she said. Did she call? "No. I don't know. I don't think that's the
job I like to do. I'm an outside type of person. I heard it was on commission, and I don't think I could sell stuff well." The job would have paid a
base salary plus commissions.

So, she had thought up four reasons not to appear at her orientation:
shame over shoplifting, distaste for being cooped up indoors, self-doubt
about her sales skills, and losing her way. She could not find her way
through the thicket of tangled anxieties and excuses. And she never called
Glenda to tell her, to thank her, to apologize. Only several days later
did Glenda learn of the missed appointment from the manager, leaving
the obvious question of how to help Camellia now. Glenda's answer: "Keep
hugging her."

A few months later, Glenda was transferred to another housing project
and moved out of Camellia's life.

At Imperial Courts, shabby little apartment buildings were separated by
weedy lawns where children scampered and clusters of young men stood,
postured, and glared. Aesthetically, the compound was less dismal than the
brick jungles of high-rises that were designed in Middle Penitentiary Style
for Chicago and New York. Socially and economically, however, this was a
wounded community. Domestic violence ran rampant, and of the 1,462
residents (two-thirds black, one-third Latino), only 54 were employed full-
time and 12 part-time—and that was in the booming years of a prosperous
economy, just before the recession began in 2001.

Nevertheless, adults who were looking for jobs fell into a peculiar pattern, here and in other low-income housing developments: They did not
want to leave their compounds. The outside culture, with alien rules and
fearsome challenges, seemed so daunting that residents preferred work
inside the projects, preferably for the Housing Authority, according to
Glenda and caseworkers elsewhere. Despite the run-down buildings, the
broken people, the gangs, the pushers, and the gunfire after dark, the proj-

ect was the comfort zone. "It's like a shield where they can feel very protected," said Truong Cam, a Vietnamese immigrant in Los Angeles working where he grew up: at William Mead Houses, a project surrounded by factories that wouldn't hire its residents. "Everything that's in the development, it's like a little town, a little city, everybody knows each other," he observed. "When you refer them outside, even four or five miles from here, they don't want to do it. The fear of meeting new people, experiencing different stuff ... the fear of even asking for an application, because they have low self-esteem. They think, 'Oh, they're not going to give me this job because I live in the projects or something.' That's how a lot of them think."

Employers rarely see those corrosive suspicions of worthlessness that course beneath the surface. They see the surface behavior: the employee who shows up late or not at all, who lacks a "work ethic" and the "soft skills" of punctuality, diligence, and a can-do attitude. Sometimes they see a worker who takes no initiative, relates badly to his colleagues, has bursts of temper, cannot take an order from a boss without a spasm of anger. If employers had to choose, many would prefer low-wage workers with those "soft skills" rather than the "hard skills" of reading, writing, and math.[1] A lot of menial jobs don't need writing or math, but they all require people to show up on time. "Basically the only skill that you require is a work ethic—and sometimes you have to teach that," said Bryan Hagin, a Burger King manager in Maryland.

The soft skills should have been taught in the family, but in many cases, the family has forfeited that role to the school. In turn, the school has forfeited the role to the employer. The employer simply does not know what to do. When Bryan opens a new Burger King, for example, he spends six months or more going through hundreds of workers until he boils down his labor force to a core of dependable employees. Some of his new people don't even brush their teeth. They look "like they just rolled out of bed, put the uniform on, and came to work," he lamented. "And you have to teach these people these skills: 'Listen, man, you come to work for me, you've got to wash your hair and make sure it's combed over. If you're a guy, you've got to shave.'" He starts his workers at $6.50 an hour and has to hire three for every one that he needs during the course of a year, making his turnover rate about 300 percent.

The notion that grown adults would have to be taught such basic elements of workplace behavior stunned C. Mitchell Ball when he took over

Jackson County Rehabilitation Industries, an on-the-job training center in eastern Kentucky that had contracts with nearby companies. "I thought that was the craziest thing that I had ever heard," he said. For a long time he refused to believe that his trainees, all poor Appalachian whites, needed to learn what he felt he had always known instinctively. "*I* knew what time I was supposed to be at work," Ball declared. "*I* knew that I couldn't miss for just any reason. *I* knew if I had car problems I'd call someone or at least call in or fix the car. If I was sick I knew to call in. If child care became a problem with the first option, then I went to plan B. And I was a little slow being convinced, having worked all my life and even before I was old enough to work—did a lot of hard work, farming and so forth—I was really hard to convince. Surely not. People know to get up. They know to comb their hair. They know to wash their bodies. I'm not being nitpicky here, but I'm telling you the truth. It took me a while to realize that there was a need for soft skills and job readiness skills, job preparation skills."

Among those lacking such skills, the dropout rate is high. Paul Lillig needed about 200 people to operate Docusort, a firm he founded in Kansas City, Missouri, to bar-code and sort outgoing bulk mail for corporate clients. So he hired 250, most of them poor blacks and immigrant Vietnamese, paid them minimum wage, and usually ended up with the requisite minimum of 200 on any given day. "We would go through somewhere between 3,000 and 4,000 W-2s at the end of the year," he grumbled. "Today they worked, tomorrow they wouldn't." He observed his employees as prone to friction along racial lines, inclined to blame others for their own mistakes, and "very fragile, very fragile." He ultimately replaced almost all of them with machines, which were easier on the balance sheet and the nerves.

Employers in three focus groups that were arranged for me in Kansas City griped about their workers' tardiness, absenteeism, lack of initiative, fistfights, drug use, and high attrition. Several employers did not get to complain, though, because they never showed up at the meetings they had agreed to attend. Two wandered in late. By contrast, all the former welfare recipients who committed themselves to a group discussion came punctually. To complete the irony, one of the latecoming employers, Brad Casey, who owned a document-imaging company, denounced workers who had been on welfare. "Just coming to work every day is a new paradigm," he said of them. "And on time!" he added straightfaced, without the slightest hint of a sheepish smile.

Some employee "problems" may be little more than the fantasies and exaggerations of managers who harbor prejudices about minorities, women, and welfare recipients. Established American stereotypes hold that blacks are lazy and incompetent, women are too obsessed with their families to be productive employees, and welfare recipients are unwilling to work. Therefore, when such a case is actually encountered, it resonates with the longstanding expectation and becomes memorable. When employers are questioned closely, they sometimes turn out to be generalizing from a couple of extreme examples.

On the other hand, real problems do exist. "I've got a woman with seven children, and she's on the phone constantly with her children," complained K. B. Winterowd, who owns CISCO, a construction supply firm in Kansas City. "Her supervisor has difficulty communicating to her that, you know, 'Let's take some breaks in the day and then take calls from your children.' Instead, she spends half of her time on the phone dealing with personal crises and problems. That's true with a lot of the employees that come out of this." By "out of this" he meant out of the welfare ranks, from which he hired, both for the larger good and for a $3-an-hour subsidy that Missouri paid companies as an inducement. But he found the performance so poor and the supervision so costly that he could not help ranting against government handouts to folks on welfare and raving in favor of handouts to him. "If you'll pay a full-time supervisor for every six people I hire," he declared as if speaking to the state, "and you pay me for a full year for the full salaries of those six people, I will provide society a basic function."

The horror stories are legion, especially from employers who hire from homeless shelters. Nobody from a shelter had ever succeeded at John Knox Village, a retirement community in Kansas City, according to Sharon Eby, the human resources director. One, a nurse's aide, "just did really bizarre things," she said. "She sat at the nurses' station one day and took her shoes and socks off and was picking her toes at the nurses' station. And you know it was one thing after another like that. They tried a lot of correction and so forth, from the standpoint of, you know, 'This isn't appropriate,' and it just didn't seem to help. And one day she called from a car somewhere and said that she didn't have anyplace to go, she couldn't even go to the shelter, and she tried to talk a vice president into putting her up someplace. . . . They ended up putting her up someplace out there at the village. Then it turned out there was a party in her room. It was one crazy thing after another."

Whether because of mental illness or a web of other problems, some people "are just not employable," asserted Randy Rolston, president of Victorian Paper, "no matter what kind of incentives you give employers, no matter what you threaten them with." His conclusion flew in the face of the experience of his own company, which sold stationery and greeting cards by catalogue, and had hired successfully with the $3-an-hour subsidy. "We were pretty lucky," he conceded. "We've had one person that's been with us for about two years now, and she's great. She's one of our best employees." She was promoted to the creative job of making up gift baskets. Nonetheless, his imagination had no trouble conjuring up the specter of hopelessly incompetent workers. "Their grandmothers were on welfare, their mothers were on welfare, they're on welfare," he declared. "It would be sort of like us taking them to a foreign country. This is what they've grown up to be and this is the life that they've led, and to pull them out of that and to give them some type of responsibility is just completely foreign to them and will never work. . . . There's no role models that they've ever had, and they're expecting the employer to be the role model, the provider."

Expecting the employer to be anything other than irritated may be expecting too much. Laborers at the bottom are often seen as expendable, and employees coming out of poverty are rarely armed with support networks, coping skills, and backup mechanisms to insulate their workplace from their personal difficulties. Only in a tight labor market, where an enterprise seeks people avidly, is the entrepreneur likely to invest in training and retaining somebody in the lower ranks. Globalization magnifies these tendencies, for Americans with deficiencies cannot compete in a world where Cambodians and Filipinos will do the same low-skilled work for much less than a decent living standard in the United States requires.

Few supervisors display much insight into why employees use the slightest excuse not to show up—and don't even bother to call. It may be complete indifference to the obligations of a job, as many bosses believe, or ignorance of workplace customs. But something deeper may also be going on, as Ann Brash observed. Having descended into poverty after growing up in middle-class comfort, she felt a smothering sense of worthlessness that gathered around her like a heavy cloak. "People who don't call when they can't come to work probably don't think they're important enough to matter," she explained simply. "It's more than low self-esteem. It's invisibility."

When I quoted Ann's observation to employers, some of them said, "Oh!" as if a light bulb of revelation had just been turned on. They suddenly understood something. The feeling that you don't matter, that you aren't seen, that you have no value in the running of a store or a factory, means that you can miss work casually because the boss can't possibly care whether or not you're there. Only with dramatic steps can such lack of self-regard be countered, as Michael Summers, president of the Summers Rubber Company in Cleveland, had learned from his father. An employee who didn't come to work would get a call. If his car had broken down, Michael sent someone to pick him up. If he had a doctor's appointment at 9 a.m., "You say, 'Fine, we'll see you at 10 when your appointment's over.' One, it calls their bluff, tells them, 'We expect you here. If we didn't expect you here every day, you wouldn't be [working] here. . . . But we rely on you, we depend on you, and when you're not here it creates hardship and cost. And you got to be here. And if you can't be here you got to tell us what's going on.' You got to pound that into this group 'cause they're not used to being accountable. That is a problem with that group."

His was a small business of sixty employees, founded by his father and grandfather to produce hoses and fittings for hydraulic, chemical, and fuel lines used in heavy industrial machinery. Every single man or woman who stood at a workbench or sat at a desk or drove a forklift was vital to getting shipments assembled, packed, and out on time. That meant that every absence left a gaping hole in the process. Either it had to be filled by somebody else who was pulled off another job or it delayed production. "My father, who ran this business for years, he reminded me when I first showed up, he said, 'You're gonna be like a parish priest,' " Michael recalled. "You turn your collar backwards, and you gotta deal with the issues 'cause they're blocking performance. He needed the guy's skills, the guy was in jail, he'd post his bail so he could come in and weld the metal hose for us."

As a CEO, Michael was thoroughly unpretentious. His Spartan office had a spectacular view of the parking lot. The reception room was spare: four black vinyl and wood chairs, magenta wall-to-wall carpet, cheesy white walls with little blue and black specks, a reception window that had sliding glass and a little silver bell on the counter with a plunger on top—like an old-fashioned hotel bell. Behind the window sat a redheaded receptionist who seemed bored. On the wall hung a framed photocopy of the front page of the *Cleveland Plain Dealer* of October 1, 1949, the day the company was founded. A banner headline read: "500,000 Quit Jobs in Steel Strike."

Back then, boys could learn by working on their cars without expensive tools, computers, and complex training, and many who discovered their mechanical talents followed their fathers happily into the factories, where they found financial security, a sense of professionalism, and a pathway up. Michael Summers was young, but he had a sense of that history, and he missed it. "Kids today do not have the ability to work on mechanical things," he said. "We're in a throwaway society where the lawn mower breaks, you don't tear apart this little two-cycle engine. You throw it out and you get another one. So a kid sees his father—if he has one—throwing away everything and buying new, and his expectation is, what do you mean we make things? What do you mean we take things apart and fix them? [We have a] shortage of tool and dye makers and fluid power mechanics, the guys who are basically screwing things together and building systems. People who are good at that are good because they like it, they have an aptitude for it, and they've had exposure to it. There are a lot of kids who [would] be good at it, but they have no clue that they have mechanical interest."

Add family dysfunction, survival instincts from the street, and the culture shock of entering the workplace, and you have a dearth of qualified labor. "The family issues become overwhelming to them, and the job is secondary," Michael observed. "So a person will be at work for a month, and then all of a sudden they won't show up, and then they show up two days later and you say, 'Where were you?' and they say, 'Well, my car broke and I had to fix it.' Or, 'Somebody got sick and I had to stay home with them.' And you discuss the issue and you try to explain: 'You don't understand. That might have been an important family problem, but you've got to work around that. You cannot *not* show up here, especially if you don't call.' "

Typically, members of what he labeled "the non-job-ready group" started work with an enthusiasm that usually lasted a month or two, Michael noticed. "And then there's friction: with other co-workers, with the supervisor who's giving them a hard time or doesn't understand them, and they don't know how to deal with that. And the reaction is, 'I'm out of here.' And I think our challenge as employers to deal with this very delicate work group is to learn how to shepherd them through that emotional crisis. It's almost guaranteed it's gonna happen. 'Somewhere in the first six months, you're gonna emotionally be very upset with what's going on here. Let's understand that up front. Now, here's how we're gonna handle that. You're gonna come in and tell me what's going on, but you're not gonna *not* come into work. That can't be an option here.' "

None of the supervisors at Summers was black, and that, Michael conceded, subtracted from the counseling tools that good management required. "Our supervisors, the first-level supervisor, does not have the training or the sensitization to deal with it in that way. They're being beaten on for raw performance issues, and they lose tolerance real fast with that, and they'll say, 'You're out.' And if you have cultural differences—you've got a white middle-class male and a young black male—big communication problem, big culture problem. Low tolerance of poor performance on the part of the supervisor. Inability to comprehend and understand. The employee, a young black male, will say, 'This is a hostile environment to me.' "

So, did it help to make employees feel essential? "People who are abusers of the employer relationship leave," Michael said. For others, who had ambition, "It gives an alternate view of the world."

It has been argued that workers feel devalued when they are paid low wages, and that higher pay would be the most tangible way for management to express its need for the people who actually do the production or provide the service. In the Summers case, though, as in many other small enterprises, the profit margins provided little cushion. A raw recruit, a new warehouseman, started at $8 or $8.50 an hour and could be making $12 in about two years, Michael said. He pulled out a spreadsheet showing the income and expenses of his $10-million-a-year company. "If you think in terms of a sales dollar," he explained, "60 cents goes for the material we make, 25 cents goes for people, and that puts us basically at 85 percent right there." Most of the rest of the incoming dollar was consumed by "utilities, phone costs, communications, maintenance, repair, training," he added. Then he pointed to a number all the way down at the bottom right-hand corner of the spreadsheet: the company's profit of 3 percent. "In this business, this is a middle position," he said. "It's not a high performer or a low performer. So 3 cents in distribution after tax is considered pretty good. And it's that 3 cents that fuels our growth."

In a bountiful year, Michael Summers, the son and grandson of the founders, the chief executive officer of this successful enterprise, takes home for himself between $80,000 and $100,000, "which frankly I think is great pay," he declared. It was about six times the salary of his beginning employees. "Of course we read about the big spreads, where it's five hundred times," he said with a grimace. "I happen to think that's a little criminal. I personally, I can't justify that that guy is worth that much money to any company, you know, $10 million or whatever it is—that's absurd. But that's also not the norm. The norm is us."

If employers don't think they can spare the money to make their workers feel wanted, they may look for other ways. The Landmark Plastic Company in Akron, facing a turnover rate of more than 100 percent a year, decided to ask people in exit interviews why they were leaving, and the answers surprised the managers. In its sprawling factory with its two hundred employees, Landmark made throwaway plastic pots and trays for plants at nurseries. Little plastic chips, arriving in cardboard barrels, were heated and formed into small pellets, which were heated again; driven by hydraulic force into molds; and pressed into black, white, or green plastic pots of various sizes. Huge machines, their innards a maze of hoses and thick pistons, generated thunderous roars and hisses, and those on the floor almost had to shout to be heard. The air was misty with a plastic dust that a factory safety officer, Ken Slone, called a "gray hue," and which the federal Occupational Safety and Health Administration considerately labeled "nuisance dust" so that it was not ruled as dangerous. Masks were available for workers, but none was wearing one; everyone had the required safety glasses, and a few had put little green or orange rubber plugs in their ears. Every six seconds a $200,000 machine called the Husky was spitting four plastic pots onto a short conveyor belt, which lifted them to the eye level of a woman and dumped them onto a broad tray in front of her. As they toppled down, she gave them a cursory inspection, stacked them inside one another, and then packed them into a cardboard box behind her. Every two hours she got a fifteen-minute break.

It was not the mind-numbing routine, the noise, or the plastic dust that departing workers complained about, however. It wasn't even the low starting wage of $7 an hour. It was something less tangible—"that they didn't feel needed, necessary, or wanted," reported David Bokmiller, the unsmiling, tough-minded manager of manufacturing services. "And that's what most people want in life," he continued. "They were ignored, just another body. The supervisors weren't doing the job because they were busy doing what supervisors had to do. So we looked back and looked through the whole matrix and said, all right, what's distracting the supervisor? Why is the supervisor not able to do the humanistic things that he needs to do? 'Cause he's too tied up in technical things." The company's answer was to assign each new employee a "sponsor," a peer who would "be their friend, so to speak, and their guide for ninety days during their probationary period," David said, "make sure they're comfortable, make sure they got friends, get them connected with other people, make sure they're not left standing around or wondering, have lunch with them, take breaks with them, hopefully engage them socially, or try. Just to make them feel connected, wanted, needed, help them understand rules, policies. We've had people on exit interviews tell us they were here ten days and never met the supervisor. I mean, that's kind of a horror story, but we hear that, and it's true." If the employee stayed at least ninety days, "that sponsor gets a $100 reward."

Trying to lock employees in "golden handcuffs" by improving benefits and raising pay would not do the trick, David insisted. "I can go out to people earning $7 an hour. 'Here's $2 an hour [more].' Trust me, I would get nothing more for it except a higher labor cost," he said. "If we increase the unit cost per hour, my customers won't pay that. I have to find a way to absorb those increases." Then he added reflectively: "It's not what you pay people. It's what they cost you. You pay people what they're worth, they don't cost you anything. You pay people too little, it can cost you everything."

As the unemployment rate falls, quality does also. It's one of those cruelties of free market economics: the better the times, the more difficult the employers' search for high-caliber workers, especially at low wages. So, if the bosses aren't going to pay more, they at least have to do some handholding. Few seem interested, according to Carla Tillmon of the Kansas City Full Employment Council, which saw few managers attend its training sessions on how to supervise former welfare recipients. "It makes me mad that there are some employers out there who want the earth, moon, and the stars for $6 an hour," she declared. "They want a high school degree, job experience, et cetera, really good work experience, no gaps in employment. You have to forgive some things and go forward."

In Kansas City, where federal welfare reform stimulated intense cooperation between corporations and job-training programs, executives who railed against welfare were often challenged to make good on their opinions. "I say, OK, put your money where your mouth is," declared Terrence R.

Ward, assistant to H&R Block's chairman. "The typical welfare recipient is a single mother, high school dropout, competing at a second- or third-grade level. You say she ought to get a job. How are you going to make it happen?" He got evasive answers. "If they say, 'We can't hire them,' I say, 'So you want to perpetuate welfare.' 'Well, no.' 'Well, take your choice. It's one or the other. The only thing missing is a job, and you can provide that.'"

Employers also have to provide what Ward called "tough love and a nurturing attitude," that combination of discipline and compassion that makes for good managing as well as good parenting. The approach was forced on Sprint as the economy prospered. Paying $7.45 an hour, the company could no longer attract enough operators to its call centers in the suburbs, where the unemployment rate dropped to 1 percent and the annual turnover rate reached 80 percent. So, to draw workers from mostly black inner-city neighborhoods with double-digit unemployment, Sprint opened a call center with great fanfare in the heart of Kansas City's historic jazz district, installing cubicles crammed with computer equipment on the third floor of an old brick building at 18th and Vine. The company reduced its educational requirement from high school diploma or G.E.D. to "seeking a G.E.D." It raised the starting wage to $8.25 and assigned a couple of no-nonsense black women to supervise the forty-five employees, virtually all of whom were also black women.

"They don't trust anybody," said Hazel Barkley, the operations manager. She came to the office as if dressed for church, carrying with her that caring firmness of the teacher who is now feared and then remembered fondly after years have passed. She saw two pervasive problems among the mothers coming from welfare. One was an absence of any belief in others, a profound distrust. The second was a conviction that backing down meant weakness. Those two disabilities stole from her employees the ability to manage their anger and to form collegial connections in the workplace. She lectured them. She demanded that instead of screaming and yelling, "You be the bigger person and walk away," as she put it. "If we can help them up front with that, we probably wouldn't have a turnover rate." It was running at 48 percent a year, better than in the suburbs, but still too high.

To avoid hiring angry people, hurried employers look for clues that often amount to stereotypes. Violence has a longstanding place in many whites' images of blacks. So, if you are black, if you are a man, if you are large and strong, or if you have a prison record, you are likely to be perceived as a person with a temper, a vein of rage.

Kevin Fields fit neatly into all those stereotypes. He loved to watch wrestling on television, and he was built like a wrestler himself—tall, a beefy 280 pounds, shaved head, small gold ring in his right ear. And when prospective employers asked whether he had ever been convicted of a felony, he told them honestly that he had spent two years in the penitentiary. When they asked him what for, he told them the truth.

"It was assault," he said. "It was five guys against me, and I had a baseball bat. They threw a bottle up against my car, and it broke, and the girl I was with at that time, the glass splashed on her, and like, hey, that's very disrespectful, you know? They tell me, 'Get back in the car before we kick your so-and-so.' OK, fine. So I reach in my backseat and grab the bat out, and I guess it happened then. When I left, everybody was layin' there, and then I had the police lookin' for me. My mother taught me: turn myself in."

Typically, the employers had a follow-up question. "It always comes up, you know: 'What if something happened here, what would you do?'" Again, Kevin answered truthfully. "I always tell them I'm gonna stand up for myself because I'm a man," he said. "You know, I ain't gonna let nobody run over me." Didn't he ever think of lying, just a little, and say he'd walk away or stay cool? "No, I ain't gonna let nobody just do anything to me without me saying anything about it," he declared. He almost never got the job. The best he could do was to mow lawns.

Some firms automatically reject applicants with prison records, some do not. "In our industry they have to be bondable," said the head of a Kansas City temp agency. "Bondable means able to handle checks, handle cash, confidential information for the companies. . . . As far as a conviction for an offense, of course, we ask them why. That usually is an immediate heads-up for us, especially if it's dealing with anything regarding stealing, anything you were convicted for, anything that would impose a liability issue." The John Knox Village retirement home and other health care facilities were governed by Missouri law's prohibitions. "You cannot have a felon working for you who has been convicted of an A or B felony—crimes against persons, property, or any sexual offenses," said Sharon Eby. No statute prevented Randy Rolston of Victorian Paper from hiring ex-convicts, but "it's better just to avoid it," he said. "We have a company that for $50, they give us their full police records."

As the economy faltered and the threat of terrorism grew, employers were tightening background checks. In Washington, D.C., nobody with a history of drug use or violence could get hired as a certified nursing assistant, for example, although that course was popular with job-training programs. Because of concerns over liability, building owners grew less willing to overlook the rap sheets of applicants for maintenance jobs—another favorite of training centers. People with prison records could work as day porters or floor waxers, but not at jobs with unfettered access to offices or apartments.[2] Some firms even rejected people who had sued former employers for racial discrimination or sexual harassment.

But Bryan Hagin had a different approach in looking for workers at his Burger King. "I have hired people from halfway houses and guys who have just gotten out of jail," he said. "Guys have come to work with bracelets on their ankles. 'Who's doing your monitoring?' There are a couple of companies around the city that do it. 'When are you supposed to leave? When are you supposed to be home?' If you can find that out you can help them along. Some people appreciate it. Most don't."

He pointed to a success that began as a simple request from one of his workers who had a friend, a young woman crack addict in a rehab facility. "Look, she just got out of jail," the worker told Bryan. "She needs a job. Can you help her out?"

"I interviewed her and she seemed like a generally OK person," Bryan recalled. "She wasn't like wonderful or anything," but he hired her as a favor to his employee. At work, he fell into long personal conversations and came to respect the battle she was waging. "She understood that I needed her as much as she needed to work and that I depended on her. When she realized that, she just took off in terms of her abilities. It was really—it made your heart feel good that you were able to pull somebody off the streets. She invited me to her graduation from rehab. She was really proud of herself, and she should have been. It was a really difficult situation for her. She really turned herself around. I won't say that working at Burger King did that for her, but I think it gave her a great sense of self-worth, and she was able to pick herself up off the ground and get her life together.

"She moved on to a different position in a different company. I still speak to her from time to time. She's a receptionist with a real estate firm, and she also does something else, she works for a hotel. She does well. I mean, it's not fantastic. She's not working in Silicon Valley, but she's doing well for where she was."

In the rough-and-tumble marketplace, then, low-skilled workers can often be rescued by a low-cost gamble, a few minutes of attention and teaching. "One young lady we were about to terminate 'cause she couldn't get to work on time," said Hazel Barkley of Sprint. "She'd never ridden a bus" and simply did not know how. So her supervisors showed her. "Now she can read a schedule, she takes the bus, she's fine."

In other words, when chance happens to match a needy worker with a hungry and compassionate employer, both can benefit. In mediocre economic times, John Knox Village, the Kansas City retirement home, never suffered from the fact that it stood beyond the reach of public transportation; in a tight job market, the home could keep its 1,000 jobs filled with people who had their own cars. But when the economy flourished, Knox had to dip into the reservoir of inner-city labor, and a critical shortage of personnel erupted. "When the bottom fell out of the labor pool and our unemployment rate dropped below 5 percent," said Sharon Eby, the human resources manager, "we were just not able to get people, and so openings would just stay open, and from week to week we would run with a hundred openings." She finally realized that transportation was a major obstacle, and she found the solution in the home's own fleet of vans and buses that were used to take retirees on outings. She mobilized the vehicles to make runs to and from the inner city.

That kind of stopgap measure by a single company is a Band-Aid, not a cure. It doesn't heal the economic ailment caused by America's preference for the automobile; it doesn't address the long-term disadvantage of the laborer who is too poor to own a reliable car. It doesn't shift tax revenues away from highways into mass transit. It is a perfect example of the limitations of the private sector's ability to address a social problem. The solution doesn't last past the economic boom.

When Bryan Hagin of Burger King said that the only thing he required was a work ethic, he was inadvertently defining the limits of his employees' possibilities. From flipping burgers, you don't rise into management, not unless you have a college diploma and a lot of attributes besides punctuality. The hardscrabble route upward has become a rough pathway that can rarely be negotiated without the proper credentials.

The diploma, in Bryan's view, does not indicate what you know but how hard you try. "When I see someone with a college degree," he said, "the first thing I think of is: This person's persistent. To get through college is amazing. And if you're able to graduate, even if you just have a poli sci degree, at least you got out. And you're successful. That means you can be successful somewhere else."

The "soft skill" of persistence, though, is produced by the "hard skills" supposedly learned in school and in training on the job. Nobody who sees herself as incompetent is going to be persistent, punctual, or positive, or have any realistic hope of advancement. Employers complain about applicants who can't fill out applications, high school graduates who can't spell "high school," but they still hire such people—without much likelihood of promotion. Sharon Eby didn't care that housekeepers and food service workers couldn't spell. "They're not having to write on the charts," she noted. "As long as they can read order changes and those kinds of things, then that's really what makes the difference." That kind of job runs no farther than the end of a blind alley.

"I have an issue with a cashier right now," Bryan said. "Wonderful personality. Guy's amazing, customers love him. But if he doesn't have that keyboard to make the change for him, he's stuck. He just can't get it in his head." And sometimes the cash register isn't available. "Say, for instance, you work at a register and, 'Hey, Bryan, I need some fives.' I pop the drawer open. I take some money out and give you some five-dollar bills, and the way I pop the drawer open is I hit the cash key. So the amount is up there but there's no amount tendered, so they don't know how much change to give. There's that hesitation, and you tell them how much it is. . . . So what have I done? Taught him second-grade math. Bring him problems. 'Solve these for me.' " Customers may love him, but he won't be a manager.

Nor is he so unusual. Some 55 percent of American adults cannot total the cost of office supplies ordered from a catalogue, nor can they tell when to take medicine in relation to meals as instructed on a label. According to the Department of Education's 2003 National Assessment of Adult Literacy, 43 percent cannot summarize the experience required in a job ad, 34 percent cannot follow directions with a map, and 22 percent cannot figure weekly earnings from hourly wages. Therefore, they cannot compete on the global playing field. Because American living expenses are high, American workers doing unskilled labor need higher pay than their counterparts doing the same job in, say, Sri Lanka. Unless there is a geographic necessity that the job be done here in the United States, it will rush out of the country down to the lower wage level as inexorably as a river flows to the sea. That's why recipients of food stamps who have a question and dial an 800 number in New Jersey get answers from somebody in India. That's why Paul Lillig's Docusort transmits images of envelopes from Missouri to Mexico, where workers at computer screens type in zip codes to produce bar codes. As the American economy craves more and more workers with skills, those without will have less and less opportunity to move upward.

Studies show that the workers who take advantage of employers' programs of tuition subsidies and other educational incentives tend to be the workers who already have the most education. It's as if education were like capital; the more you have, the more you get. Employees who are just coming out of poverty, or who hover on its precipitous edge, rarely have the luxury of planning ahead or calculating the advantages of such benefits with deferred impact as health insurance, life insurance, and retirement plans. "Entry-level people who are working out of desperation or need, they don't have career goals," David Bokmiller observed. "They don't know what a career path is. They're making minimum wage to eke out a living or support a bad habit—or if they don't work they go back to jail. . . . They don't have their heads in their jobs. They just decide not to come to work. . . . Their lives are a wreck." Observing the personal and family problems that often come crashing in on his low-wage employees, Paul Lillig put it another way: "Work is not their number one job."

Bryan Hagin could usually tell quickly in the interview. "You try to ask the right questions," he said, "intuition, kind of feel it out. . . . A good question to ask is, 'Today's Tuesday. What's a typical Tuesday for you? What do you do?' If they can rattle off six, seven, eight things they do in a row, if one of them's going to the probation officer, then you know where you need to be. But if one of them's like, 'I get off at my grandmother's house and I go down to the local kitchen and get breakfast or something— or I go down to Manpower and do some paperwork and try to look for some jobs,' you kind of get a read for where they are, what their ambitions are."

Then, too, Bryan used his own eyes and tried to make sense of what he saw. "You look for the visual cues, his body language and things, try to figure out what's really going on. A lot of times, you can interview someone with their head pointed to the floor the entire time. What does that mean? Does that mean they're deceitful, or does it mean they're painfully shy?" Or could it mean that they are full of fear about their inability?

Chapter Six

SINS OF THE FATHERS

I'm not gonna let you get too close, because if people get too close to me, I'm in danger. I'm in danger of being robbed. I'm in danger of being mugged. I'm in danger of being taken for granted.

—"Peaches," a homeless working woman

The ten-year-old girl sat on an idle swing, chatting with the caseworker on the swing beside her. "How many times," the little girl asked, "have you been raped?"

The question came casually, as if it could merely glide into the conversation. The caseworker, "Barbara," tried to stay composed.

"I said that I hadn't, and she was surprised," Barbara recalled.

" 'I thought everybody had been,' " she remembered the girl saying.

"Her friends talked about it in school," Barbara observed. "It's an everyday thing."

That was Barbara's introduction to the epidemic of sexual abuse that infests uncounted homes in America. The girl was the first of Barbara's cases in a mentoring program for children at risk, referred by teachers who saw telltale signs of trouble in their students' lives. Of the thirteen boys and girls whom Barbara tried to help in a New England town, twelve had been sexually molested, she said. They usually told of the experience when they were sitting next to her, on swings or in a car, so that they did not have to see the reaction on her face. The ten-year-old was being raped by her father. He was sixty-seven.

Barbara wondered what kind of adult she would grow up to be. She was in and out of foster homes while her mother succumbed to alcoholism. "For a sweet little girl," Barbara said, "she's really screwed up. In her twenties she'll be a survivor."

A survivor. That was Barbara's most hopeful prognosis, and she was almost right. At eighteen, the young woman was pregnant and unsure which of three men was the father.

A surprising number of women at the edge of poverty turn out to be survivors of sexual abuse. Like huge financial debt, their trauma weighs them down long after it occurs. Unlike debt, it cannot be erased by declaring bankruptcy. Their future is crippled by their past, which forces its way into their explanations of who they are, sometimes candidly in the first discussion, sometimes obliquely in the fourth or fifth encounter. Even though I never posed the question, sooner or later most of the impoverished women I interviewed mentioned that they had been sexually abused as children.

Only half an hour after I had met a young mother named Kara King, she told me her story. I had merely asked her about her family. "My father molested me as a child," she said plainly. "My husband doesn't know that. I was twelve. He fondled me over a year's time. My father was drunk. I locked myself in my room. I woke up with him on top of me, I pushed him off. He said, 'That's the way a father and daughter are.'

"You know it's not right," Kara continued, "but you don't know who to tell. I stayed at a friend's house. I told my mother, and she said, 'That's OK, my father did that to me when he was drunk, but it won't happen again.' "

When a woman discloses such intimate humiliation to a stranger, she reveals its magnitude. She cannot help tracing many of her handicaps to the legacy of disgrace and self-loathing imposed by her childhood assailants, and the disabilities can be life-altering: her unwise choices of male partners, her deep distrust, her emotional distance, her failure to form attachments. The abuse seems too central to conceal.

Sexual abuse afflicts all classes, all races. The more open societies in this more open era tend to discuss the problem more frankly, and so Americans have grown increasingly aware and alarmed. Victims have overcome their misplaced shame to indict priests, uncles, family friends, and fathers. Yet much remains hidden, so the questions outnumber the answers. Are poor children any more vulnerable than rich? Do families lacking material means also lack the means to protect their children from such indelible harm? Is molestation more prevalent in disrupted households with single mothers, transitory boyfriends, alcohol, drugs, and absent adults working long hours in late-night shifts?

What is well known is that the trauma debilitates in ways consistent with handicaps frequently seen among the poor. A child who is sexually abused is invaded by a sense of helplessness. If that feeling continues into adulthood, as many victims testify it does, it may break the belief that life can be controlled. Lost is the very notion that real choice exists, that decisions taken now can make a difference later. A paralyzing powerlessness sets in, and that mixes corrosively with other adversities that deprive those in or near poverty of the ability to effect change.

Molestation in childhood damages the capacity for intimacy in adulthood, and thereby damages a household's economic potential. About 53 percent of all poor families are headed by single women, and another 9 percent by single men, which means that 62 percent have only one wage-earner, a huge handicap at low rates of pay. The women, who usually end up caring for the children, may or may not receive adequate child support from the fathers.

Sexual abuse is one reason, among others, for the failure to create healthy partnerships. An abused child's sense of powerlessness may lead to surrender and to a method of escape that psychiatrists term "dissociative," in which the victim mentally stands aside watching the assault occur. The same phenomenon has been observed in victims of other trauma, including war. This out-of-body experience generates protective feelings of indifference and emotional detachment that can remain for years after the event, even for a lifetime. Children are especially vulnerable. "Repeated trauma in adult life erodes the structure of the personality already formed," notes Dr. Judith Lewis Herman, a psychiatrist at Harvard Medical School, "but repeated trauma in childhood forms and deforms the personality."

> The survivor's intimate relationships are driven by the hunger
> for protection and care and are haunted by the fear of aban-
> donment or exploitation. In a quest for rescue, she may seek out
> powerful authority figures who seem to offer the promise of a spe-

cial caretaking relationship. By idealizing the person to whom she becomes attached, she attempts to keep at bay the constant fear of being either dominated or betrayed.

Inevitably, however, the chosen person fails to live up to her fantastic expectations. When disappointed, she may furiously denigrate the same person whom she so recently adored. Ordinary interpersonal conflicts may provoke intense anxiety, depression, or rage. In the mind of the survivor, even minor slights evoke past experiences of callous neglect, and minor hurts evoke past experiences of deliberate cruelty. . . . Thus the survivor develops a pattern of intense, unstable relationships, repeatedly enacting dramas of rescue, injustice, and betrayal.[1]

Abuse in various forms may lead to early sexual involvement. One study found that "emotional deprivation, particularly at an early age, may predispose adolescents to seek emotional closeness through sexual activity and early parenthood."[2] Another, based on a sample of 1,026 young African-American women in Memphis, found that while nonsexual physical abuse had no correlation with early pregnancy, sexual abuse did. Girls who had been molested as small children tended to have consensual intercourse at a slightly younger age (a mean of 14.9 versus 15.6 years old), and they became pregnant earlier (at 16.7 versus 17.4). "Clinicians should consider a report of child sexual abuse from an adolescent to be a red flag for early sexual activity," the report concluded. "Such adolescents should receive appropriate family planning counseling and be referred for mental health counseling to reduce the risk of premature pregnancy."[3] They should be, but they rarely are, especially if they're poor.

Among low-income families, then, sexual abuse emerges as one mechanism transmitting poverty to the next generation. Abuse occurs among the affluent too, but the well-to-do have other mechanisms to propel their children forward despite what happens inside their own suffering. Parental ambition and high expectations, the pressure to succeed, the access to education, the drive for professional achievement all add up to a sense of entitlement and opportunity. Survivors often engage in anxiety-ridden efforts to please, which in certain families means excellent academic performance.

The dynamics can be quite different in low-income families, where the abuse is added to a pileup of multiple stresses. Overall, one in four or five girls is sexually abused, researchers estimate from polling, but the percentage may run higher among low-income single mothers. Journalists covering welfare reform have encountered many poor women who mention being sexually abused, seeking protection from their mothers and being disbelieved, having their sense of safety shredded and the refuge of their home undone. One white reporter who had written on the subject looked confused when I told him about the girl on the swing in New England. But was she white? he asked. Yes, I said, it was practically an all-white town. Kara King and many of the other women who had talked with me about having been abused were white. Well, he confessed, he'd thought the problem had something to do with black culture. He seemed taken aback by his own prejudice.

Wendy Waxler, just off welfare in Washington, D.C., had finished outlining her tight budget during our second conversation when she began to talk about the assaults that were woven into her childhood memories. Nearly thirty years had passed, and she was now determined to mask the scars by forcing herself to recover from failure, to work hard, laugh hard, and be a model to her handicapped daughter.

She knew nothing of her biological mother, only of the two foster homes where she had spent her first four years. "They believed in beating us for every little thing," she said of that initial family. "They had this two-year-old. She was a foster child, too. . . . I remember one day; it comes like it's a reoccurring dream. It's like it won't let me forget. [The foster mother] took the little girl down in the basement and beat her. I think the little girl peed on herself or something, and she got mad 'cause she got to clean it up. All of a sudden, I couldn't hear no more screaming. The lady came upstairs, but the baby didn't. I got scared, and I guess she saw the expression on my face. She said, 'What, you don't want to be here anymore?' And I think I told her no. She told them people to come get me, and they did, and I went to the next foster home." Wendy never learned whether the little girl had lived or died.

The second family provided no sanctuary. They had another foster child, Paula, and two teenage sons who ran loose and free. "These boys used to take me and Paula in the basement, pull down our panties, and do—." Wendy couldn't finish her sentence. "Stuff like that you never forget, I don't care how old you get. You never forget. Until the day you die, you never forget."

Again she was rescued, this time when she was adopted by a divorcée without children. "By the time she got me she said I looked anorexic," Wendy recalled. "She said my hair was all over the place, my clothes were dirty, and she said my teeth were green. She said it was a wonder they were still in my mouth. She said, 'I saved you.'"

But not from everything, it turned out. When her adoptive mother regularly dropped her off with a baby-sitter, Wendy was often left alone with the baby-sitter's sons. "They used to do the same thing," Wendy remembered, "take me in the bathroom or whatever, make me do weird things. . . . That was the first and only time I experienced anal sex. I think I was in second grade. . . . And my mother never believed me. She didn't believe me. Thought I was lying 'cause when she asked the lady, the lady didn't know anything about it."

Like many abused women, Wendy had trouble with men, with intimacy, with trust and love. Her mother struggled mightily to keep her off the fast track to poverty so frequently taken by teenagers who get pregnant, have babies out of wedlock, drop out of school, hook up with abusive men, go on and off welfare, drift in and out of low-wage jobs. Her mother expected her to go to college, and Wendy had been accepted by Howard University when, on her high school graduation day, she learned that she was pregnant. She was terrified of telling her mother, and once she did, her mother insisted on an abortion.

Wendy resisted, then reluctantly went ahead. She had been carrying twins, she was told later. "After the surgery I turned around, and there's a jar with these body parts all in it," she remembered vividly. "I felt that was really cruel, because if you're gonna have me go through something like that, don't leave the result right there." A chasm of disrespect opened between Wendy and her mother.

Each pregnancy ended badly, like each relationship. Neither could be brought to fruition; for many years there was no birth or marriage, no successful pregnancy or loving partnership. A baby was stillborn. An engagement was ended by Wendy when the man hit her. Because she feared that another baby would die, that she would suffer and fail without support, she had two more abortions. Alone, estranged from her adoptive mother, and financially fragile, she could not afford Howard's tuition, transferred to the University of the District of Columbia, and dropped out before getting her degree. Then she met another man she wanted to marry—and cancelled the ceremony when she found his flaw. "It was like a week before the wedding," Wendy said. "It turned out he was on drugs, and I had to let him go. But I still had the baby in my stomach. I ended up losing the baby, the baby died. That baby lived for eight hours and died."

She had worked odd jobs at US Airways, Kentucky Fried Chicken, and elsewhere, but she couldn't make enough to keep her own housing. Moving in and out with men, she was occasionally homeless, living in shelters. She got pregnant again and decided this time that even without the father's committed caring, she would have the baby. "I said if I get rid of her, I'll never forgive myself. If I let this happen again. And I made that promise to never to do this again. And I had to tell myself: Stop running. The fear should be over now. Handle this. The whole time I was pregnant, regardless of what happens, I was gonna love this child and take care of this child."

The child, a girl she named Kiara, came three months early and weighed two pounds one ounce, born at D.C. General Hospital when Wendy was staying in a shelter. "Because I was homeless, they treated me like I was dirt," she said. "The nurses acted like I didn't know anything, I was a dumb so-and-so from the street." She spoke up for herself and insisted on respect. She didn't get it.

Her daughter's birth was not a happy event. "Because she was coming so early, they tried to tell me I wasn't having contractions. I had contractions for three days. They tried to tell me I didn't know what I was talking about, that I had an infection. And I told them if I had an infection and I been taking this medication for this infection for three days, why is it still up there? . . . They all hooked me up to the monitor and left. I couldn't page the nurses. For one thing the equipment wasn't working. They didn't come check to make sure I was OK. And I had to actually take both monitors, wrap a blanket around me, go in the hall, go all the way down the hall to the nurses' station and say, 'Excuse me, I've been calling you for three hours. I need more lubrication for the baby's heart monitor—the beeping from this monitor is driving me crazy. I'm having contractions. I need somebody to check and make sure everything is OK.' You know.

"And they said, 'Why are you in the hallway?'

"I said, 'Because I've been trying to get your attention. I've been yelling. I shouldn't have been yelling.' . . . I said, 'You treat me like I'm a paying patient, OK?' And this went on until she was born. . . . See, that's the way they treat people who don't have money."

Then came the alarming news. A homeless shelter was no place for a newborn, she was told, and the premature baby, once released from the hospital, would have to go to a foster home until Wendy had a place to live. "I told them, 'No way,' "Wendy declared. " 'Nobody's gonna raise my child but me. I've been in foster homes. I know what they're like.' " Only a single alternative presented itself. "I bit my tongue. I bit my lip: I called my mother. I said, 'Look, I had the baby, I know we've had our differences, but I am not having anybody raise my child except me.' I said, 'I need to stay there until I find an apartment. As soon as I've healed enough, I'll go look for an apartment,' which I did. My mother agreed with me. And I think that's when I first got respect from my mother."

There was a second blow: At eight months, Kiara was diagnosed with cerebral palsy, caused by a brain injury before or during birth. The little girl grew into a cute, smiling, drooling toddler—except that she couldn't toddle. She would never walk; she was destined for a wheelchair. At nearly four, she could barely talk and would never do so fluently.

Were it not for these handicaps, the typical pattern might have been broken, for Kiara was experiencing nothing close to Wendy's early trauma. "I spank Kiara," Wendy admitted, "but she got to really, really do something wrong. I don't spank her for every little thing. I may just pat her leg a little bit. I don't use belts. I don't use paddles." Whatever devotion Wendy's mother had shown by being tough and concerned had compensated for some of those early years of deprivation and abuse, Wendy believed.

Even as she struggled into loving motherhood, however, Wendy could not pull herself out of the abused past that foiled her search for a loving partnership with a man. When she finally married, she chose badly. Her husband, suffering from depression and rage, became more adversary than ally. Two months after the wedding, he quit his job at a delicatessen because he "wanted to live off me," she said. They had a healthy baby, but he sat at home, refused to help with child care, complained about the food she cooked, and called her office colleagues to make jealous threats about fictitious advances that he imagined they were making. "He was very insecure," Wendy said. "He would get mad at me 'cause I kept telling him, 'Get your black ass out there and get a job!' " He drank. He tried to hit her, "but I beat the snot out of him," she said, laughing angrily. "I picked up the phone and beamed him between the eyes." She laughed again. "I punched him in the face, I tried to hang him with a hanger." She let out a joyous roar of delight. "I hit him upside the head with a frying pan . . . a big old cast-iron frying pan." She laughed and laughed. He fled, and she filed for divorce.

Survivors of sexual abuse have often been observed as extremely protective of their children, sometimes excessively so, peppering them with "no, no, no," in a manner that destroys the youngsters' creative inclination to explore and learn. Wendy displayed some of that anxiety, but it was hard to tell how much derived from her own history and how much from her older daughter's disease. Doting and dutiful, Wendy was determined to maximize whatever possibilities Kiara had in life, just as she was trying belatedly to maximize her own. She now had a reason to be a role model.

"I feel that everybody has their mishaps, everybody has their setbacks or whatever. It will take a real strong person to overcome those," Wendy said bravely. "By her seeing me overcoming mine, I'm hoping that'll influence her to overcome hers."

"Call me Peaches," said the woman with the hard pain in her eyes, the small scar over her left cheekbone. She must have chosen the pseudonym in irony or in yearning. She was too bruised, too bold, too callused, too frightened, too worldly-wise. She was living in a homeless shelter and running Xerox machines for a fancy law firm in Washington, D.C., a job that delighted her and put her on track toward satisfaction. The office where she worked was located in a temple of prosperity. Its vast marble lobby was framed by massive columns, a wall of palms, and a crystalline glass tower opening to views of sky and buildings. The place where she lived, in a dangerous neighborhood, was populated by broken women who stole one another's food.

"I have no idea who my parents are," Peaches said. "The people that adopted me died before I was five." The foster family that then took her in, on Maryland's Eastern Shore, inflicted debilitating cruelties. They were black, as she was, but evidently not as dark, for they ridiculed her color. "I've been locked out of the house, told that I was nothing," she said, "just like my mother: black, ugly, bony—just worthless. So what the heck, I just existed within that household."

And she existed to support the household. In the summers, she said, "I worked from the time I was eight years old in a factory filling buckets with scalding hot tomatoes. That's how you have to get the skin off, put it in a bucket. Now this is a bucket the size that you use to mop a floor. You got ten cents for a bucket, push and pull. You can imagine . . . just pushing and pulling buckets on and off, pans on and off, doing that hard work, six o'clock in the morning until the evening. . . . Illegal labor, but I had to work. That was my summer."

She still wore the brands of punishment imposed by her foster mother. "I got scars all up my arm," Peaches said, showing the twisted shapes like burnished metal. "Didn't press the collars right, I got burned, because I didn't do it right. . . . If I ever breathed sideways I'd get a whippin'." Adolescence overtook her with confusing stealth. "They didn't really give any input to me," Peaches recalled. "I'm a woman, and as young women do, you come into a change where you have your menstrual cycle. I didn't know what was happening to me. It wasn't told to me. It was like, 'Oh, what did you do now? Oh, come on.' There wasn't any, 'Now, this is what you do, this is what I expect, you're a young lady.'"

Her childhood suffering did not end with the end of childhood. She mentioned no sexual abuse, but the anguish of the physical and emotional battering continued to reverberate. "People look at me strange," she remarked. "It's like, 'You act as if you haven't interacted with people, you have a disability.' Well, I haven't. I never went to a movie. I never went to a circus. My girlfriend treated me to a circus, I was in my twenties, about twenty-seven . . . I cried because I'd never been to a circus. That was something new to me. I really didn't hang around with a whole lot of people. I stayed at home because I didn't have really any choice.

"I noticed something else about myself. When people talk about their friends, their buddies, the relationships that you have from high school, I don't have much to say because I didn't get to interact, so I didn't develop those kinds of friendships. . . . The last couple of years I went to an integrated school. Well, heck, I didn't feel worthy among black people, so you know I didn't feel worthy among white people. So I was even more isolated. . . . I didn't know what I was worth, because I was always told I wasn't worth anything."

After Peaches graduated from high school, the foster family kicked her out. "The first time I had sex I got pregnant" and got a scolding, she said. " 'You're just like your mother, no good, blah blah blah.' I'm like, well, excuse me, nobody really sat and told me anything about myself to make me feel like I was worth the while for anything, so an older man had sex with me. I didn't like it. It hurt." She did not have the baby, on this or any other occasion when she got pregnant. Instead she joined the Job Corps, where she was raped by a pimp who wanted her as a prostitute, and she rapidly descended into hell. Along the way, she tried to hold onto fragments of independence. "I've prostituted myself," she confessed, but not for a pimp, she asserted, only as her own boss. "I couldn't see me doing it for nobody else."

In a desperate search for a touch of caring, Peaches picked one wrong man after another and was whiplashed between a dream and a fear—the dream of having an idyllic family and the fear of creating a home like her foster home. "I've been pregnant several times, but the only thing I think that kept me from having children was the fact that all of this replayed in my mind. And if I was not going to have a man and have a home like I envisioned that a home could be from watching TV—'Hello, honey, I'm home,' instead of, 'M-F, you so and so,' . . . I was not going to bring a child into this world," she declared. "Now, I wanted that textbook family with the husband and wife and home and maybe a dog and a cat, two kids, and a car and a house. But I could never really get ahold of it. I could never get ahold of it. That thing eluded me. I fought, I cried, I agonized over it, but it just eluded me, because I had too many things going on with me. I didn't know what it was. I just exist through life, go from day to day, just work, go have your drink, party every Sunday through Saturday. . . . If someone would just come in and at least pretend that they love me, I can make it work. I would give and give and give and give until it hurts. And it did. It hurt me."

Without much sense of self, she gravitated to men who enjoyed controlling her—men who evidently had no control over anything else in their lives. One of them, with whom she spent many years, off and on, shared her view of herself as a person of little value. "The gentleman that I stayed with, he got me to the point where I wished I could just fade into the wall," she said. "Please just don't let him say anything else to me."

If she put a sweater on, he would say, "You don't need that. Take it off." If she left the house, he would shout, "Where you goin'?"

"I had to sneak and make a phone call on the street," she said. "If I tried to get away from him, he'd follow behind. And looking back, how in the world did I get to this point? What can I do? 'Don't sit here, don't sit there.' . . . Going from man to man that didn't see me as really being anything. I couldn't understand why. I'm a nice person. Well, maybe I'm not a nice person. You know, maybe something's wrong with me. Well, there is something wrong with me. That's what I've always been told. I was going crazy."

Peaches was robbed and beaten by the men whose affection she craved. "Looking at the pictures, the few that I have left, I see that I wasn't a bad-looking child," she said in surprise. "I wasn't a bad-looking woman. At some points in my life I was a very good-looking woman—nice figure, hair down my back. But I never felt that way, because if somebody took my looks into account, the only thing they wanted from me was my body. If I couldn't give that, fine, there was no use for me."

When they had used her up, employers also disposed of her. "I really don't work that well with people, and that held me back," she explained, " 'cause I didn't really know the ins and outs of working with people." For a dollar or two above the minimum wage, she felt she did well selling women's clothes at Lord & Taylor and other stores. But long waits for buses in the winter dawns and nights aggravated her asthma, which made her miss work and got her fired. It was another case of the far-flung effects of disparate problems: poor public transportation causing poor health causing job loss.

"I've drunk. I've smoked some pot—thank God nothing else," she said. "I've partied from Sunday to Saturday, ain't leaving much room in between." She ended up on the streets of the nation's capital, where her neighbors looked through her. "They wouldn't say a word. They saw me walking the street, dirty, matted, wouldn't say, 'Whatcha do? You need a sandwich?' People that I knew. Even not knowing you, 'Ma'am, excuse me.' Something. Just an invisible person."

She sneaked into an unfinished basement to stay. Then she went into a dreadful shelter where "the sheets that I got to put on the little wafer-thin mattress was bloody. When you shook out the sheets there was mice turds in it. . . . When they served you food, you had a plate, you didn't even have utensils. But I was hungry as heck 'cause I hadn't eaten all day, so I'm sitting there eating with my hands, and I looked, I said, 'I can't do this.' So I went back and stayed in the little half-done basement with the dust, spent my little money, got me a blanket 'cause I was cold." She then returned briefly to an abusive man "because I needed to go somewhere where I could actually take a bath, and I just creep up against a wall and hope and pray that he didn't touch me. . . . He put me back out on the street, and I walk the street, eat as I could, bought my food as I could. I mean, money goes fast when you're on the street."

She stole to survive, but she felt devalued and thus ineligible for anything luxurious, so she stole modestly to match her low opinion of herself. "I've stolen food. I've stolen clothes," she admitted. "Nothing exciting, 'cause, see, I didn't, I never really went into nice stores." She gave a little laugh. "If I'm a black and ugly little person with stick legs, that's not for me. There's no way possible that I can go there. But see, I could go to McBride's, I could go into Kmart and steal some clothes. . . . I wouldn't steal a steak. I'd steal some bologna." She laughed at herself heartily, bitterly. "I wasn't good enough to even steal something good enough." Her laughter grew until it mangled her words and consumed her: "If I was gonna steal something, I could steal a steak at least, and not bologna. Heck, I could spare ninety-nine cents to get some bologna!"

The sins of the fathers and of the mothers take many forms, not just sexual, and abuse visited upon the sons and daughters can lead to self-abuse. Where a sense of worth should be, a void is created, into which alcohol and drugs often flow as swiftly as air rushes into a vacuum, rapidly destroying the chemistry of a functioning family. And since childhood feeds into adulthood, resonating and repeating themes, a youngster's experience of neglect and cruelty can eventually shape the way she raises her own child; the injury may be passed down through the generations.

How it happened to Marquita Barnes she was not quite sure, but she had seen her family life disintegrate since her grandparents' day, and she worried that the failures would extend to her children.

Both sets of grandparents had owned single-family houses in a solid blue-collar section of Washington, many of whose African-American residents were secure in civil service jobs. Twenty years later, however, Marquita was living in a public housing project where another young mother had recently been gunned down in a drive-by shooting. As if she were afraid to let the outside world in, Marquita kept her blinds drawn, her windows tightly shut. No fresh light or clean air relieved the stale darkness. She sat uncomfortably on a folding metal chair. A bike in her kitchenette was draped with clothes, and clean laundry lay folded on the brown couch in her living room. She had a gray cat, a fish tank, pictures of her kids in cardboard frames, and a phone that never stopped ringing. It was usually for her teenage daughter, who had followed Marquita's example by dropping out of high school. The glowering girl answered her mother, and others, in curt monosyllables.

This family had turned the American Dream on its head. Over three generations, and now into a fourth, it had experienced declining achievement and well-being, defying the country's ethos of optimism about upward mobility. "I always thought my grandparents were rich," Marquita said. "Every time we went over there, we could have whatever it was that we wanted, you know, and there was plenty of food. My grandmother had about eight kids, and there was still plenty." Her other grandparents "always had, too," she remembered, and one of her favorite places had been her grandfather's workshop in a garage "that he had made hisself," loaded with "stuff you could mess with in there." The recollections made her laugh with a nostalgic warmth that she could not summon up about her later life.

One grandmother had been a nursing assistant, Marquita recalled, and a grandfather had worked at the water department. His son—Marquita's father—had followed in those footsteps, but that was where the security of job and home had come to an end. Her father never lived with her mother, and her mother's sporadic work—at the Government Printing Office and doing laundry—had placed her and the children on welfare from time to time. "My mother was an alcoholic," Marquita said bluntly.

As the older daughter in the middle of three children, Marquita was taxed with undue responsibility for her age, and unwanted embarrassment as well. When her mother descended into drunkenness and stopped performing basic chores, Marquita took her older brother and younger sister grocery shopping. She went on search missions for her mother at neighbors' apartments, banged on doors, and threatened to call the police in the hope of getting her home before she was too far gone. "I didn't want any of my friends to see her acting like that," Marquita said. Children saddled with grown-up burdens cannot succeed, and that is often their first failure, the root of inadequacy.

"I ran away a lot," she recalled. "I ran away a lot to go and stay with my father. And once I got to stay with my father, I didn't want to stay with him either. . . . I went and stayed with my grandmother. I wound up back with my mother. [Then I] went to stay with some friends and come to find out that a good friend I was staying with, her nephew was trying to creep into bed with me at night, and I explained it to her, and she was like, 'Why would this young boy want to be in the bed with you?' So, OK, I got to leave here, you know. It was a struggle. Me and my mama, we never really got along too well. I guess it was basically because I just wanted a normal family."

A normal family was not to be, only hard memories and wistful plans. "I was basically ashamed sometimes for being without a hat and stuff," she remembered, "always swearin' [that] when I got to the point where I could do something on my own, I was gonna take my brother and my sister, they would live with me, and everything would be much better." Slowly the senior relatives died off, those who remained grew apart, and Marquita was left in that limbo of "just basically havin' to fend for yourself," as she put it.

Fending for yourself is a frightening demand that makes a child feel powerless. Marquita did not do it very well. Instead, she took another step into the decline: The first time she had sex, she got pregnant. In October of her sophomore year, she dropped out of high school to have the baby, the first of four children by three fathers. She never considered abortion, and her reasons echoed those often given by teenagers who see their babies as badges of maturity and autonomy: "I could say to my mother, 'Now I'm grown, I can do what I want to do, I can do this and that, I have some kind of little income, I have a little leverage right here.' I guess that's what that was."

Marquita went on welfare, and her poverty forced her to live in Brentwood, a mean section of Washington infested with drugs. She called it "a trap," for it confined her and swallowed her dreams. A neighborhood can have a deep impact, determining neighbors, friends, diversions, temptations, and this one took its toll. With no job to go to, Marquita was surrounded all day by a culture of dealers and users who populated a seedy strip of stores and crowded the hallway of her building. "I guess I was like twenty-seven at the time," she said. "I wound up using. I got caught up in it. . . . I got into that real heavy, smoking coke, smoking reefer, stuff like that." The first high from smoking crack was amazing and indescribable, and it was followed by a constant search for the beginning. "You're just chasing it, 'cause you never get that first high. . . . You're trying to find that high, which you never do. . . . I would do anything to get what I wanted, such as, I'd sell my kids' stuff, Christmas stuff, whatever I had, get money from somebody."

Addicts say that crack erases even the powerful mothering instinct, and it happened to Marquita. She grew oblivious to her children, was evicted from her flat, and was taken in by a man down the street. Although her youngsters were with her, their condition so worried Marquita's sister and a girlfriend that they called D.C.'s Child and Family Services Agency. "I was still using," Marquita said. When the investigators arrived, she was out for two or three days buying and smoking crack. She returned to find the children gone, the oldest to stay with an aunt, a son to his father, and the youngest two into a foster home. It was a body blow, but not enough to knock her out of her addiction. That had to come later, and only then could she wonder how anyone could endure "what you have went through and what you put your kids through," as she told herself. "How could I have done that?"

A recovering drug user or alcoholic will often tell his story as a morality tale with elements of a religious parable: the temptation, the fall, the confession, the penance, the salvation. So it was, for example, with a tall man named Joshua, who followed his father into alcoholism, then wandered in and out of homelessness and unconsciousness. One Christmas Eve, drinking heavily with buddies in Lafayette Park across from the White House, he passed out, was stripped of his shoes and most of his clothes, and awoke Christmas Day in a hospital with doctors fighting to save his frost-bitten feet. Half of each one had to be amputated, and that was enough to provoke his resurrection. Time in a hospital can also be a time of forced detoxification. He dried out and got a maintenance job.

So, too, Marquita had to hit a low before she could rise again. There, on the bottom, came flashes of lucidity and common sense. She was awakened by two realizations: One, her addiction had cost her the affection of her father. "When I started using drugs, our relationship died," she said sadly, "and that hurt me a lot, because I was always Daddy's little girl. He would do anything in the world for me." Two, she ended up in the hospital, and that cleared both her body and her mind.

"I had went with this guy one night," she said. "He had bought me some stuff, and when we got to his house I did what I had to do with him, and he went to sleep. . . . I took his keys and took his car and went and got myself some. My intentions were good—to bring his car back." But when she arrived in the drug-selling neighborhood and asked someone there to park the car, he drove it off, popped the trunk, and stole her friend's tools. She exploded into a fury, driving her fist through one car window and her leg through another. She was so high she felt no pain. "With my hand bleeding, my leg bleeding, I still wanted to smoke, I didn't want to go to the hospital, none of that crap."

The car's owner then appeared. She expected a bruising from him, but instead he took her to the hospital with a surprising kindness so potent that it cut through her calluses and softened her into reflection. "And that like touched my heart, you know, 'cause most people would want to beat the crap out of you." She told herself: "I don't need no more signs or nothing—I do not want to die. And that was it."

The number of addicts seeking treatment far exceeds the number of beds, so the centers can be choosy. They look for clients who are serious, and Marquita set out to portray herself as such. She found a good program that would not charge, then called day after day until she impressed the intake people with her determination, and when a bed finally opened up, she went into a five-day detoxification session, followed by twenty-eight days of rehabilitation and a year in a transitional house. By contrast, the affluent can usually buy their way into treatment.

Marquita's treatment center was located far from the old neighborhood where her addicted pals hung out, and that imposed a crucial separation from the network of ill-considered friends. Divorce from the drug crowd is an essential step for those who wish to kick the habit, but it carries the hardship of isolation. It left Marquita essentially alone. Without a family intact, she depended for years on an artificial "family," a support group of recovering addicts who met weekly.

As she advanced, she kept her eyes fixed intently on the goal of getting her children back. In foster care, luckily, they had escaped the kind of damage done to Wendy and Peaches and others. Marquita's two youngest were placed with a foster mother who provided a core of caring and became Marquita's benefactor, friend, and confidante. "She's a blessing to me," Marquita declared. "She said, 'I'll tell you what you can do. You can come on up to my house and you can work for me watching the kids.' Watch my own kids plus her foster kids she was gonna adopt!" With powerful generosity, she amazed Marquita by paying her about $200 every two weeks. "She was like a second mother to me. She's a very sweet soul," Marquita said four years later. "We go places together, do everything together. I love her to death." From the foster mother, Marquita learned something about mothering.

But she also needed money, and without a high school diploma, or even its G.E.D. equivalent, her job prospects were humble. Emerging from treatment, she found work doing laundry and cleaning bathrooms at a nursing home in Bethesda, Maryland. She got an apartment in public housing. She recovered all four of her children. And with her children under her care again, her long commute to Bethesda without a car became burdensome. After six or seven months, she moved to a job in the warehouse of Hecht's department store, where she was paid $7 to $8 an hour to mark merchandise and unload trailer trucks. Still, she spent an hour each way on a series of buses, and the working times were inconsistent—a day or two here, then nothing until the weekend, then full days the following week. The low wage and the scattered hours produced too little cash to be worth the erratic absences from home. She calculated that she would do better on welfare, so she went back to "P.A.," as she called public assistance.

And there she would probably have remained for many years had it not been for the 1996 welfare reform law, which required her to get a job. Had it also required her to study and get her G.E.D., or to train in a salable skill, the reform might have made a more significant impact. She took the G.E.D. exam once, failed the math, and was afraid to spend the $20 fee to take it again. The very subject made her look pained and scared. "There's just a thing about me and math that don't click together," she said. "When it comes down to math, I never got out of being illiterate in that area. I can do certain things, but when it came down to fractions and multiplication, I got stuck." She had plans, though. "I can get $20 to go and take a G.E.D. test," she said. "So there's really nothing stopping me from doing it except me being afraid to just go in and do it." When? "I don't know. Probably this month, probably next month. Most likely probably next month." More than four years later, she had still not dared to try the test again.

When welfare forced her into the workplace, the best she could find was four hours a day at $6.15 faxing, filing, mailing, photocopying, and sitting at the receptionist's desk of the Metropolitan Boys and Girls Club, a job with no light of promotion at the end of the tunnel. In fact, there wasn't even a tunnel, just a windowless reception area boxed in by dead ends.

Life at home was no better. Her sister—the sister who had rescued Marquita's children—was now strung out on drugs, living on the street and in crack houses. So Marquita now rescued her sister's teenage son and brought him to live in her small apartment, where they waited for the day when her sister hit bottom and found that moment of lucidity.

To make matters worse, Marquita's daughter Kiyonna began to duplicate some of Marquita's patterns. The girl hated school, dropped out in her junior year, and went to work cleaning houses. Marquita, seeing her own mistakes being replayed, grieved and raged and pleaded with Kiyonna to go back into the classroom. The girl stubbornly refused. At least she wasn't pregnant, Marquita noted, but that consolation did not last long. Within a couple of years, Kiyonna gave birth to one child out of wedlock, then to another two years later. She went on welfare, thereby extending the syndrome to three generations in a row. "Not good," Marquita observed sadly, "not really good."

And yet, that newest generation was dividing itself at a fork in the road. Along the fast track of bad decisions and corrosive failures that led to poverty, there appeared an occasional exit opened by wise choices and small successes. While Kiyonna seemed to be speeding toward lifetime destitution, her teenage brother Garry took a different course, thanks to a smart move by Marquita and Garry's father. Of the three fathers of her four children, only one was able to help. Kiyonna's father was "deceased," Marquita pronounced formally, and another was "incarcerated." But the third, Garry's, was concerned enough to offer his suburban Maryland address so that his son could enroll in a good high school and escape from D.C.'s inner-city system. Marquita happily embraced the opportunity— not only for his better education but also to pull him from the whirlpool of the drug-laced neighborhood. It worked. Garry graduated, went on to college in Nebraska, and began to think about becoming a teacher.

Then Marquita took an exit herself. She studied hard for her commercial driver's license and, on the third attempt, passed the test. She went to work for the post office, though the unrelenting overtime hours were tough on her kids, and she disliked the laborious task of sorting and carrying mail. So she started driving a bus for Washington's public school system at the comfortable wage of $15 an hour plus benefits. Everything went well until she slipped up one morning after delivering kids to school. She forgot to check that all the children had gotten off. A little boy in the back had fallen asleep, and only after she returned the bus to the yard did she discover him there, snoozing peacefully on a seat. She took him directly to school, but no matter: An important rule had been broken, and she was fired. Perhaps at another time, she would have quietly sunk back onto the welfare rolls, but that wasn't an option under current law, so she got a job at a private school driving what she called "a limousine bus, a luxury bus with thirty-five passengers," to transport children to and from school every day. She earned $13 an hour but no benefits. The privileged children never saw her scars.

Her mother, who had created that crucial vacuum in Marquita's child-hood, died at age fifty-nine, a victim of kidney disease. Her passing did not erase the past, however. "Look in the Bible," Marquita remarked. "You're my father, and you have did this awful crime or something like that, or you have sinned, that sin would go passed on, if the family's not livin' the right way or something like that. So it continues on. And it some-times goes down to that. It might skip a couple of generations and go to another generation, you know." She gave a sour laugh. So it continues on.

The psychological techniques that help a child cope with sexual or physical abuse do not work when the child herself becomes a parent. The dissocia-tive reaction, the emotional closedown, interferes with the grown survivor's responses to her own children. She may be defensive and overprotective, emotionally unavailable, and ill-equipped to sustain empathy. Everyday stress can reactivate the post-traumatic symptoms.

Here again, the dynamics may vary with socio-economic level. While a child of privilege can be damaged by a parent's inability to nurture, his access to good education, special services, therapy, and other opportunities may help him survive more successfully than his counterpart in or near poverty. Without the buffers of family affluence, achievement, and ambi-tion, a child is dangerously exposed.

This does not mean that poor people are automatically worse parents than rich. It means that neglectful parenting can have more damaging results in poverty. A family, like a house, can withstand only as much wind and weather as its construction and maintenance allow; the storms that rage around the poor would test the resilience of any structure. As Ameri-cans of all classes know from their own high divorce rates, family can be a fragile thing indeed.

There is no more highly charged subject in the discussion of poverty, for impoverished families have long been stigmatized as dysfunctional. The father is a drunken or addicted ne'er-do-well, if he's around at all, and the mother an angry shrew or submissive incompetent. The parents don't read to their children, don't value education, don't teach or exhibit morality. That is the image. Absent from the picture are the devoted grandmothers and parents who love zealously, the sensible adults who make smart choices within limited means, the supportive web of relatives, all of whom could overcome with more help from the society at large.

At the extremes of the debate, liberals don't want to see the dysfunctional family, and conservatives want to see nothing else. Depending on the ideology, destructive parenting is either *not* a cause or the *only* cause of poverty. Neither stereotype is correct. In my research along the edges of poverty, I didn't find many adults without troubled childhoods, and I came to see those histories as both cause and effect, intertwined with the myriad other difficulties of money, housing, schooling, health, job, and neighborhood that reinforce one another.

The interactions were described by Dr. Robert Needlman, a behavioral pediatrician who sees children from all socio-economic levels in Cleveland. "Horrendous parenting can cause severe behavior problems that have, as part of them, difficulty in paying attention," he said. "It takes a lot of psychological health to be able to go to school and pay attention to a teacher, and care and do the work. The kids who do that are healthy. Really bad parenting can prevent that." And what prevents bad parenting? "It's really a lot easier to be a good parent if you're well rested, you can afford baby-sitters, and you have someone to clean your house. People who have those psychological resources that allow them to be good parents quite often have the resources that allow them to be relatively secure financially."

Some parents never play with their children, so when their children become parents themselves, they have no experience to bring to the important job of playing with children of their own. The disability can be dramatic enough to be recorded on videotape, even when the parent knows the camera is rolling. Such has been the discovery of a Baltimore malnutrition clinic that tapes low-income families with their kids to show parents their mistakes.

In one recording, a little boy sits in a highchair playing with his food but not eating. His mother watches for a moment, then pulls out a magazine and reads. Nothing ever goes into his mouth, and she pays no attention.

In the second session, the same boy sits on the floor, putting blocks in a plastic bucket. His mother watches, yawns, puts her head down, and closes her eyes. She has no interaction with her son.

The third session finds both mother and child sitting at a low table, each playing separately with plastic blocks. The staff has told her, "Play with your child," but she evidently thinks that means to play as if he weren't there, or to play as if she were a child herself. Having built a stack of blocks, the boy says proudly, "Look, Mommy."

She mocks him, repeating in a sarcastic tone, "Look what I did, Mommy." Then, without including her son, she tries to assemble the blocks into a formation pictured on the bucket's label. The boy reaches for a block on the table in front of her. She snatches it away and snaps, "No!" Then she even dismantles the stack of blocks he's made to use a couple of them in her construction, all the while saying to him mockingly, "Look, Mommy! Look, Mommy!"

Again in the fourth session, they sit at the low table, each doing a separate puzzle. The mother holds hers on her lap, tilted up so her son can't see it. The boy picks up his puzzle, which is all together, then turns it over and dumps the pieces on the table with a clatter.

"You're gonna pick them all up!" she says harshly. "You're making a mess!"

The boy plays nicely and quietly, putting all the pieces carefully together again while the mother continues with her own puzzle, ignoring her son except to scold him.

Can anything be done about this? Can parents so deeply deprived be taught how to nurture? Jackie Katz thought so. Just before 9:30 on a May morning, she strode up to Delaware's Webb Correctional Facility, a small building made of old brick, just around the corner from a bowling alley between Newark and Wilmington, and surrounded by a chain-link fence with concertina wire. She pushed a button and was buzzed into a tiny anteroom, where she faced a wall of wire mesh and a heavy door reinforced by three-quarter-inch bars. The face of a clean-cut guard appeared behind a small window. He recognized Jackie, turned a key, and swung the door open for her. Inside, she handed over her keys and driver's license, submitted to a scanning with a handheld metal detector, and signed the visitors' log. Under the column headed "Purpose of Visit," she wrote, "Parenting."

Tall, slim, with long brown hair straight down her back, Jackie had grown up poor; her father had died in prison when she was eleven. She had not been parented very well herself, and she had taken the deprivation as a series of lessons that she now passed on to others. In a large cell upstairs, where the sky came in through many big, barred windows, seven men in pristine white jumpsuits stood and chanted, "Good morning, Jackie! Good morning, Guest!" They then took seats on double-decker bunks made up in neat military style. They were about to finish sentences for selling crack, forging checks, possessing deadly weapons, and other nonviolent crimes, but all hardness dissolved when they talked about their children. They missed their kids acutely and waited eagerly for "play days," when Jackie and other facilitators taught them how to give their youngsters undiluted, constructive attention—something most of them had never done outside the prison walls. Now they were meeting with Jackie alone, without their kids, for the twelfth and final session of a weekly parenting course, a time for summing up what they had learned.

As children, many of these fathers had never played with an adult, Jackie said, only with other children. The same was true of many welfare mothers whom she also taught; Delaware required them to receive parenting instruction along with their checks. Their upbringing had given many of them no model to emulate, no intuitive knowledge of how to give their children the companionship, the deference, the empowerment that adult-child play promotes. A child's play is critical in fostering cognitive development and problem-solving skills—and also in building cooperative relationships with important grown-ups.

On play days, Jackie explained, the children were told that their fathers or mothers "are gonna pay real close attention to what you want to play." The fathers, in turn, were urged not to impose their own wishes but to "let the kids lead the activities." Through their play, children were trying to figure something out, she told them, so let them do so, and give them plenty of encouragement. "We tell them to recognize what they like about their child during that time," Jackie said, "to be their cheerleader. They might just get on a pogo stick, or might just play basketball. You play up to their level, but you let them win." She recommended that the parent comment positively on what his kids were doing: "You may say, 'Wow, I didn't know you could do that.' "

Parents were advised that an occasional period of undivided attention was a vital resource to a child, like food and shelter. Finding fifteen or thirty or even sixty minutes at home for such "special time" was essential, "and during that time you're not adjusting the drapes or answering the telephone or picking up toys in their room," said Gwen Brown, a professor of education at the University of Delaware and director of Parents As Counselors and Teachers, a family support network that ran Jackie's classes. "You're just paying attention to them," Gwen insisted. "It's an agreement to be completely for them and with them," a hard thing to do in a house full of many children, she acknowledged. When parents complain, " 'Oh, they're just trying to get attention,' that's because it's attention that they need. When they grow up, people will pay $100 an hour just to get attention that they need."

If the inmates sitting on the bunks were to follow all the advice that Jackie gave as she reviewed the course on its final day, they would probably have been model fathers. But they had already gotten into trouble with their wives by giving them tips over the phone, from inside the penitentiary, far removed from the whirl of daily family life. Andrew, a gambling addict in jail for forging checks, had scolded his wife by phone when he heard her snarl at one of the children: "Get away from me! You've been around me all day!" He said to the class: "That makes me so angry, because I'd just as soon she ignored me and paid attention to them."

Jackie told the prisoners that a parent was the youngster's first teacher, counselor, and disciplinarian. In "taking care of the emotional needs of our children," she advised, listening was central. "Sometimes it takes a long time listening," she said. "You're going to have to listen to a lot of messy feelings, but eventually you may hear what's really going on. If we don't listen to problems about a broken lollipop, 'Somebody doesn't like me,' the little things, we're surely not gonna hear about the larger problems later." As fathers, then, they had to be around to listen after their release; kids with dads did better, she told them. "You don't have to be with their mother; just be around," she urged. "Make sure they go to school, make sure they get plenty of sleep, make sure they have plenty in their stomachs nutritionally."

The remarks triggered spasms of guilt. "Maybe I didn't read enough books with her at home," admitted Leon, who was in jail for selling crack. "I shouldn't place all the blame on the teacher." Jackie had given them a handout entitled "Seven Things to Do to Help Your Child Do Homework."

"My wife sends me her report card," said Eddie. "She's on the phone and she can't wait to read me a book. She's only seven, and she writes cursive already. It's amazing for me. She's more advanced than I was!" His voice carried a beautiful lilt of pride.

"They need a safe place at home to practice sounding out the words," Jackie said, "where nobody laughs at them or jumps in with the answer."

Her tidbits of advice provoked a flurry of questions. The men asked Jackie for pointers on giving rewards for good grades (it's OK, but "you need something every week; don't take away a reward"); on encouraging children to write ("Let them spell incorrectly; children get so caught up in that that they forget all their creativity"); and on being the child's advocate ("If parents are involved with school, kids know you care, and teachers know you care"). Michael, convicted of narcotics possession, said of his wife: "Two weeks ago I was trying to stress to her the importance of just listening. If you have a four- or five-year-old that just cries, you say he's trying to manipulate, but there may be some real hurt." He thought that both parents should take a course together.

It was easy enough to be the wise critic from the sheltered perspective of prison. The question was how durable the insights would be in the tough world outside. Within a few months all would be released into the complexities of family, putting their newly acquired parenting skills to the test. Only a couple of the men seemed able to pinpoint how they would behave differently—one pledged to find individual time for each child, another promised to give attention to their schooling. All yearned for deep involvement, if they could find a way back into their children's lives.

"When you're in here, you cherish the times you're missing," said Nick, who was in jail for reckless endangerment and other crimes, "but when you get out you seem to lose focus."

Most of us never get explicit lessons on how to be parents. Whatever we know we learn by osmosis, absorbing unconsciously from our own parents, sometimes repeating their mistakes, sometimes rebelling by turning one error into its opposite—too little discipline into too much, for example. "The way we were raised plays a role in every part of our parenting," Jackie noted, no matter what the socio-economic class. Low-income families have no monopoly on wrongdoing.

Nevertheless, at the bottom of the economy, the task of raising children is vulnerable to the destructive synergy of many hardships. The elements of poverty combine to suck people down, and it takes exceptional parenting to pull a child out of the quagmire. Fragmented programs have appeared across the country to help low-income parents do just that. If they were more extensive, they might have more impact.

Some are based on decades of research demonstrating how crucial the earliest years after birth can be. Watching mothers closely in the late 1960s, for example, the Harvard Pre-School Project found sharp differences in parenting techniques that correlated with the children's later competence in first grade.[4] More recent studies have shown that "sensitive, responsive care in the first few years of life" leads to greater school achievement and less need for special education, fewer behavioral problems, less use of drugs and alcohol during adolescence, and a higher ability to form relationships among peers from preschool on.[5]

Intervention with mothers considered at risk has proved effective. In Milwaukee, training newborn babies of mildly retarded mothers increased the children's IQs from an average of 80 to 100 within three years.[6] In North Carolina, the Abecedarian Project, providing educational day care beginning at ages six to twelve weeks, raised IQs by the time children from impoverished households were four and a half years old. All but one in a group of forty-one scored higher than the median of the general population, and eight to twenty points higher than a control group of forty-five children who were not in the program.[7] A larger contingent of III youngsters, followed for twenty-one years, had a lower dropout and failure rate in school and were less likely to have children out of wedlock. The percentage attending four-year colleges was double that of the control group.[8]

Among the best practices that Lisbeth B. Schorr describes in her 1988 book, *Within Our Reach,* was a center at Yale where "pediatricians, nurses, developmental specialists, early childhood educators, and social workers met with parents and children to provide health care and periodic developmental appraisals for the children and guidance, counseling, and other supports for the parents. Families could also bring their children for day care and toddler school." The staff did home visits as well. Ten years after the program ended, "almost all of the intervention families were off welfare and self-supporting," she reports, "while only half of the control families were." Mothers who had received the services ended up with more years of education, fewer babies, and children who did far better in school.[9]

Today, a privately run program called Parents As Teachers conducts monthly home visits in many parts of the country to instruct parents on playing, talking, and other interactions appropriate to their child's stage of brain development. Children from birth to three who participate show better school readiness in kindergarten, according to studies cited by the project.[10] One difficulty is gaining access to the homes of families that are afraid of being accused of abuse, so the visits may not be reaching the neediest parents.

The coin of good parenting has two sides: first, the specific techniques that can be learned, and second, the personal sense of well-being that enables a mother or father to provide consistent nurturing. To acquire skills and self-confidence, affluent families with child-rearing problems can afford individual counseling or parenting classes, while the poor depend on scattered advice and training funded erratically by government.

The emotional side of the coin is more difficult to address. Many of the poor are single mothers who suffer from untreated depression. Many have nobody to talk to about their problems. Introspection and the capacity to reform are luxuries rarely available to a hard-pressed parent at the edge of poverty. If you have been parented badly yourself, if you have minimal education and a deficient network of family and friends, if you are working long nighttime hours and have no savings, then you have no time or money or emotional wherewithal to recharge your batteries or reassess your parenting. "If you are a middle-class parent, you can get away from your children more easily—buy yourself a baby-sitter, a movie, or a health spa," said Gwen Brown of the University of Delaware. "If you get a break, you can go back fresh." Nor do crises confront you as frequently. "Your car isn't breaking down on your way to taking the children someplace," she noted. "Once every three months there's a crisis in a middle-class family, and once a week in a poor family. Crises affect how much attention you can pay."

The parents Gwen and Jackie saw—prisoners and welfare recipients—had few reserves to draw on, like people with depleted bank accounts. "You don't have much attention to give if you don't get it," Gwen said. "You don't have much love to give if you don't get it. That's what we see with parents hurting their children. It's burnout. They burned out as children because they tried as human beings to reach good relationships and good connections, and they didn't get good nurturing back, and there's a kind of going away inside emotionally. . . . Minds can't think when there's too much stress in there." Furthermore, she observed, in a society where money is power, financial insufficiency may feel like personal inadequacy. So impoverished parents often need assurance that "there's more of a mind in there than you were able to use."

Since Gwen and Jackie both grew up in poverty, they were keenly concerned with the psychological deficits among the parents they instructed, and so their courses were designed to provide a kind of therapy. "When I was a teenager, my mother climbed into bed with me and said, 'I'm so scared,' " Jackie remembered. "My mother had nobody to talk to, so it's so big to me that these people have somebody to talk to." Or, as she preferred to see it, they needed to talk so that they could guide themselves. "All of us as parents need somebody who will listen, just listen to us while we get our turn, because we're taking care of people all the time, and we very rarely get our turn." Parents who were brought together in groups assisted one another just by listening and discovering that they weren't alone.

The classes were designed as safe havens in which parents could uncover their suffering. "People can share at the level they want to share," Gwen explained. "Maybe they want to talk about their deepest, darkest hurts from childhood. Our goal is to help people get to parts where they can release feelings—a lot of crying, a lot of role-playing, yell back at the parent who abused them. . . . This is the place for it, but not taking it out on your children. Just because all the men in your childhood were hateful, negative, hostile doesn't mean that your little boy is going to do something awful."

The approach seemed to help one mother who had been devoting little attention to her eight-year-old son and two-year-old daughter. "I had, like, so much bottled up inside that I didn't never look at spending the time," she said. "Now that a lot of it's out on the table, I'm not as stressed, and I can spend this time. Instead of worrying about what's gonna happen tomorrow, I'm spending it with them. It's like now when I have days off, we go to the park, get ice cream. I didn't do that before. You know, my son would come home from school, he would do his homework and run outside. But now, he's like, 'Momma, we goin' to the park today?' And that was never before. So [I say,] 'Yeah, we can go to the park.' And then he plays baseball, and I've been attending a lot more of his games. When he goes to practice I just don't drop him off. I stay at practice with him."

Therapy doesn't have to mean catharsis, but some form of therapeutic dimension may be necessary for parenting classes to help certain adults. So deep and durable are the ravages of abuse, drugs, mental illness, and other disabilities that "as much as they do love and want to nurture their kids, they can't," said Becky Gentes, a registered nurse who led an intensive program of home visits to help young mothers at risk. The women received parenting instruction and intimate mentoring, and also guidance on how to feed, discipline, play, and even love, but to little effect in cases where the wounds still festered.

With some clients "we feel we're making an impact," she said. "We see families who are dirt poor. They don't have a cent, but by God those kids are cared for. They're sent to school with a piece of fruit, a drink, and a sandwich. There's no fluff, no junk food. They're not gonna have designer jeans, they're not gonna have the latest hairdo, but they're taken care of. You can be poor and still take care of your children.

"Then there's a faction that's really dragging us down—the other extreme. It feels pretty futile." In those most damaged families, she had to measure the program's success by what did not occur. "What we're doing is crisis management," she said, "just trying to keep those kids safe. . . . We haven't had any horrible thing happen, so in some of these cases it's pretty blatant that it is because we were there that it hasn't happened. But if we were to pull out tomorrow, well, there's no long-term change. Most of them would immediately revert right back to the patterns that we started with a year ago." She and her colleagues, who were all middle-aged, middle-class women, spiraled into despair at times. "We are questioning what we are doing," she said one day. "Is this really serving any real purpose? We're working real hard, but where are the outcomes?"

The young clients were first encountered during pregnancy when they visited the prenatal clinic at Valley Regional Hospital in Claremont, New Hampshire, where Becky was director of maternal-child health services. They were then seen frequently at home until their children turned two, and some of them extended their enrollment, in effect, by getting pregnant again before the cutoff date.

"The repeat pregnancies were clearly driven by our attention," Becky insisted, "and that got scary to me. They'd come to the prenatal clinic, and it was the first time in their lives where somebody cared about them. You know, they had a nutritionist, a nurse, a doctor, who are all, 'Hi,' welcoming them in, 'Let's take care of you,' and 'How are you doing?' and we talk and we meet and we have them come back. They thrived on it, and it's sad because for some of them it truly is the only caring person that's ever shown up in their life. So of course it's an incentive to get pregnant again."

The home visitors became surrogate mothers of a kind, available by phone for questions and cries for help. Sarah Goodell once called her mentor, Brenda St. Laurence, and asked: "If he swears can I put pepper on his tongue? Is it all right to hit him?" She seemed desperate for advice and then ignored it. Her household was deemed so dangerous that the visiting program notified the state, which went to court in an unsuccessful bid to have the youngsters removed. Of the forty mothers in the program, four had lost their children under court order, and another two or three should have, Becky said. Most of the others stood in a twilight zone where the parenting was poor but the physical risk was minimal.

In the worst cases, alarm bells went off at the moment the first newborn was brought home from the hospital. Becky and her colleagues looked for that normal, healthy sense of wonder and exhilaration at the sudden responsibility for a tiny human being. "But do you know what? We don't see that with our families," Becky discovered. "That was an eye-opener for us. . . . How they respond is, 'Oh, my God, this means I have to get up at what time? Aw, jeez, my husband's leaving for work and I've got to stay with this baby? I'm not changing the diapers.' There's not this instant bond," no anxiety on behalf of the child's safety or health. "It's almost like a red flag when you see someone who is not asking the questions, who is not wide-eyed on that first mom-baby visit. You're worried."

So, why do they get pregnant and keep the babies? A false sense of independence is induced by the welfare check, some professionals argue, and that dovetails with a yearning for autonomy. "It's a control thing," Becky contended. " 'By God, I have a baby, no one can tell me I can't.' You know, when they've been stripped of control of their life all along. That whole warped feeling of 'somebody in my life who will love me, who needs me.' " And yet many of the young mothers are so needy themselves that their need to be taken care of is more compelling than their need to be caretakers. The child is often resented for stealing the teenage mother's own childhood.

"I'm now in a more difficult phase with my families because they have toddlers," said Brenda. "They can't put them in a little crib and keep them there all day. They just want to walk and get into things. Oh, it's awful some of the things they say to those little toddlers. Like, I have one mom that says her daughter's 'evil.' "

"There was one the other day that wouldn't even call her by name," Becky added, quoting the mother as saying, " 'That one is a troublemaker.' "

The home visitors worried about the effect on children of seeing violence. Advising one mother who often hit her husband, "I try to say, 'Get on the floor, get at their level and make believe you're looking through their eyes,' " Brenda said, " 'and what do they see?' "

What Becky saw was "incredible risk" in some households. In one, where the oldest child was already a mother at age fifteen, "you would see years of substance-abusing people in and out of this home, a mom who is dying [of] terminal liver failure, a stepdad who just died at the age of thirty-six of similar things, foul language, no respect for authority, and a dangerous home in terms of safety. Snakes and dogs and mice [as pets], WIC vouchers may or may not be cashed in, dirty dishes everywhere, law-breaking going on, flare-ups where Mom screams at the kids. The fifteen-year-old would leave the child with whoever happens to be convenient, whether somebody just out of county jail, a neighbor she doesn't know. I've gone into that home where I'm on sensory overload after fifteen minutes. A twelve-year-old comes home from school every day to this. It's not a place I would *leave* my kid, much less *live* there."

Becky, Brenda, and others who do this kind of work get burned out by the scenes of strife. When they contemplate the implications for the next generation, they often feel utterly useless and defeated. And then, sometimes, out of their gloom will come a beam of good news proving that they do make a difference after all, in ways hard to measure.

It happened to Brenda. She had counseled an eighth-grader from a miserably disrupted home, spent hours a day listening to him, and pressed him to finish school. He ignored her, dropped out, and disappeared. Years later, out of the blue, he called from Virginia to tell her that he had "made it." He was nineteen, had gotten his G.E.D., was in the military working happily on helicopters, and was engaged to be married. There is always a spark to be fanned into flame.

So it was with "Melissa," who had been beaten and sexually abused by her father. "She lies all the time," Brenda lamented. "She doesn't trust anybody." At twenty-two, she was living on welfare in a cluttered apartment with her boyfriend and their two-year-old daughter. The boyfriend had been accused of molestation at age sixteen, so he was afraid even to change his daughter's diapers.

"You would cringe if you walked into that place," Brenda said. "It is so dirty. She's been doing good since I've been working with her because she knew what days I was coming, and she'd go down and she'd get her dishes done, she'd clean, she'd be all so proud because someone paid attention that she cleaned. . . . There was rubbish, there was garbage outside. . . . If you saw the mattress you would die. . . . Whenever I walked into that place it was so bad. . . . There was dirty diapers. It was horrible. It was so bad that [the landlord] took pictures and took them to court. It was trashed. A nice apartment, too."

Yet Melissa was devoting extraordinary efforts to being a mother. "She does not let that little girl out of her sight, even with me," said Brenda. As if she were walking along a knife edge of risk, Melissa seemed acutely afraid that what had happened to her might happen to her daughter. At least so far, the anxiety was generating something good for the little girl. "I will say one thing," Brenda conceded. "She reads and reads and reads to her [daughter], and what a difference. That little girl will look like a dirty little Rugrat 90 percent of the time, but she is smart. . . . She loves that little girl and spends a lot of time with her."

Melissa found the time in a way that would not have won any points with welfare reformers: She had quit her $6-an-hour job at a paintbrush factory. "Things are complicated when you don't have any money," she remarked wryly. "I could go out and get a job, but I feel at her age it's more beneficial for me to stay home with her. " And what did she wish for her daughter? "I want her to be whatever she wants to be," Melissa declared bravely. "She's gonna finish high school, because that's the biggest mistake I made. . . . If she wants to be a ballerina, then she'll be a ballerina." Or, a doctor, Melissa added. "Sometimes I'll look at her and say, 'You can be whatever you want to be.' And she will be."

Chapter Seven

KINSHIP

If we have nothing, we have each other.
—Kara King, mother of three

The fragile life of Tom and Kara King fell apart piece by piece until nothing was left but love and loyalty. They lost their jobs, they lost their health, they saw their meager savings melt the way a February thaw eroded the winter's snow, once fresh and deep, into muddy rivulets behind the rundown house they rented. The only asset that remained was affection, which became their sustenance. Its web of support embraced them and their three children, a few of their key friends, and even a stranger who encountered them one evening.

For many weeks, Tom and Kara had collected scraps of cash, enough to treat themselves and the kids to a restaurant meal—not to celebrate, just to soothe their anxieties a little. Kara needed a bone marrow transplant, she had learned, and so the family went to a truck stop in Lebanon, New Hampshire, where the portions were huge. The two boys held a contest over who could eat more. The family laughed a lot. They talked about their hardships, and snatches of their conversation were overheard by a stranger at the bar. He was a truck driver passing through, a man who got little time with his family.

"I asked the lady for the check," Kara recalled, "and she said, 'There's no check.' She said, 'A gentleman at the bar paid your bill.' I was very offended. I tried to explain to this lady that I didn't accept charity." Nothing insulted Kara more than pity. Poverty and sickness infuriated her, and as they drove home to Newport, where they lived beside a junky auto repair shop, she boiled and brooded. She had lost her long chestnut hair from chemotherapy, her teeth from lack of funds for dental care, her stamina, her gaiety. She was not about to lose her dignity as well. So she called the truck stop and demanded the name of the benefactor. He was still there, the waitress said, and she handed him the phone. Kara asked him frostily why he had paid, and he told her. "He had never heard a family discuss problems that openly," she said. "We were so close-knit, and he was a truck driver on the road a lot and just wanted to do something for us. He was touched. This man couldn't believe we could laugh at life like that."

She remembered him telling her: "I counted. Your children said they loved you twenty times."

Her anger suddenly cracked. "I broke down, and I cried."

The family that the driver so admired was unlike anything that Kara had known in childhood. She had been neglected by her mother and molested by her father, also a truck driver. "I can remember eating dog food when I grew up, rabbit pellets," she said, "and I'll be damned if my kids will ever have to go through that—going to school and having my teacher wash me up and bring me clothes. My parents just didn't care. My father was an alcoholic, my mother was an alcoholic." Still, as her father lay dying of cancer, she granted his wish to have his gravestone taken from the top of Cat Hole Mountain, where he could always be found, gun in hand, on the first day of deer season. "So we went and got this humongous piece of marble, white marble," Tom remembered, "and it had one flat face on it, and we got together and we bought this bronze plaque to put on this stone." Kara did not sever family ties easily.

She had repeated her family pattern by marrying two alcoholics in a row. Her first husband, the father of her two sons, Zach and Matt, "used to smack me around and break my teeth," Kara said. Her second, Tom King, plunged into her life after his wife threw him out and he rented a room from Kara and her husband. One day, when Kara's husband "came home all messed up, started to beat on her," Tom recalled, "I said, 'No, I don't think so.' And the next thing I know, we're all out in the street. . . . The last thing I heard him say when we walked out the door was, 'You want that bitch? Take her.'" So the two wandering souls found an apartment and took each other in. "For four and a half, five months, we lived a purely platonic relationship, we split the apartment: She paid her half, I paid mine. And then we just kind of fell in love. Been that way since." They married four years later, after their daughter, Kate, was born.

Tom liked Jack Daniel's, even a shot or two for breakfast with his coffee. Kara worked on him lovingly, steadily, and finally got him into Alcoholics Anonymous. "I never missed a day of work," he insisted, but "in the evening, it was bad, and one night we set down and she said, 'What are you gettin' out of it?' She said, 'If you think about it, you're sick and tired of waking up sick and tired.'"

Tom was forty-six, Kara was thirty-two, and they both looked older still. He smoked Marlboros. Sometimes he wore a black bandanna covered with little skulls and crossbones, or American flags, tightly tied so that his hair, long and stringy, hung back out of the way below his collar. Lean and muscular, his arms were covered with tattoos. One said, "Love." Another read, "Tom -n- Kara." He had a gentle smile and a quiet resilience. When you asked him how things were, he'd always say, "Good," even when they weren't, and then he'd rub his whole face with his hand, as if to wipe away the worry. But he was also willing to admit that he was scared, and even to cry. Together, he and Kara found a mutual blend of vulnerability and strength.

They both worked for U-Haul, she behind the desk for $6 an hour, he as a mechanic for $7. "We were doing fine," she said defiantly, as if to restake her claim to a modest victory that had been stolen from them. "We didn't have credit cards. We didn't owe anybody money." They lived frugally, met their bills, and managed to save a little every month. At work, Kara felt confident enough to cloak herself in a little too much integrity. "I'm a very honest person," she declared. "They said you had to down a truck that came in with bad tires, so I'd do that, and [later] I'd see they'd rented it." When her manager once instructed her to rent out a truck with nonworking headlights "in the daytime," she refused. "They were very unhappy with me," she bragged. She did not get raises. Her applications to become a manager were ignored. Then, after being granted a week off so her son could have surgery on a cleft palate, she returned to find someone else in her job.

Finding other work proved difficult. Because she had epilepsy, Kara was not supposed to drive, although she did anyway at times; otherwise, she would have felt chained down in a rural area without much public transportation. She eventually managed to qualify for a Social Security disability payment of $484 a month, which covered nearly all of the $500 rent on their old house. But the downward spiral continued. Tom wasn't getting along well at U-Haul either. The defective rental trucks were causing him headaches, generating late-night phone calls for emergency repairs. The managers were "kids" in their twenties with no hands-on skills, he complained. After three years without a raise, he got fed up, quit, and went to work driving a truck to and from Massachusetts for a vegetable farmer in Claremont, New Hampshire.

The next blow fell: Kara was diagnosed with an aggressive lymphoma. The prognosis was poor. Without financial means, her best prospect for treatment was to become part of an experiment, "a guinea pig," she said. She began chemotherapy for free in a clinical trial at Dartmouth-Hitchcock Medical Center. If sheer determination could ever defeat a disease, she knew that her iron will would be victorious. "I am gonna get through all this," she declared stubbornly. "It's gonna be a long hard haul. I'm gonna go out and help people. I'm gonna tell these young women with babies that they don't have to get beat up."

Their rental house had a faded joy, its pale blue-green wood and red trim dulled by age and hardship. Anyone walking in through the cluttered back porch met a wall of cloying air thick with the odor from a big round kerosene heater in the middle of the kitchen floor. Kara was at the table. She had wrapped her bald head in a turquoise scarf. Her appearance mortified her sons, who didn't want her to visit their school. She shared their embarrassment, mixed it with a terrible anger, and justified her shame and rage by keeping on display a framed picture of herself with her long, flowing hair. In her eyes, the camera had caught a hint of laughter then. Now, against her gaunt face, they were fiercely bright, pleading, proud.

She had come to feel the mockery of chance, and she couldn't help a wry smile as she told the sour story of her prize at the Cornish fair. New England still loves those quaint country fairs full of wholesome Norman Rockwell faces from communities gathering to see who has baked the best pie, who can eat one fastest with her hands behind her back, who can win a fire department raffle, and who can throw a ball and hit a plunger that will dunk a favorite son into a soaking pool. At the Cornish fair, Kara bought a raffle ticket for a dollar. In the thirty-one years of her life, she had never won a thing. This time, miraculously, her name was drawn for a fat pig named Emma. "I was amazed!" she declared.

But to a star-crossed family, even a delightful trophy can bring misfortune. Tom and Kara housed Emma in a pen at a friend's house. Then the friend's dogs got in, chewed her up, and got Tom thinking that he should build a pen at his place. He called his mother, who had a covered pickup truck, and they got Emma. Tom rode with the pig in the back. A sad comedy followed, one familiar to New Hampshire, where signs warn motorists of the danger. A moose stepped into the road, a car in front of them slammed on the brakes, Tom's mother plowed into the car, and Tom was bounced around inside the back of the truck like a piece of popcorn. The local hospital's emergency room checked him out, sent him home, and made an appointment for him with an orthopedist a week later. The orthopedist discovered that his back had been broken.

Tom King worked with his hands—that's all he knew how to do. He had grown up in the family's cordwood business; his mother had driven a bulldozer in the woods. In tenth grade he'd gone across the Connecticut River to Vermont to live and work with a farmer and continue school, "and then the school system in Vermont found out that I was out of state, so they decided that they was gonna charge me tuition," he recalled, "and I said, 'I think I learn more on the farm than you people can teach me anyway,' so I just quit school and went to work on the farm." He got his G.E.D. later, in the army, which sent him to Vietnam—an experience that he believed led him to alcohol.

He couldn't think of any jobs that his G.E.D. had helped him get. He romanticized his way of learning: from using his hands, he said, not from reading books, which he could not do well in any event. "I can stand there and listen to an engine run and pretty much tell you what's wrong," he said. "A lot of that's from being around the old guys. Back when I got into the field, you didn't have these guys with electronic equipment and that stuff. You had those old boys out there and you'd turn it over; they could tell you why it didn't start or why it didn't run just by listening to what it was doing. I pretty much learned from the ground up."

In other words, Tom was an outdoor man with the wrong skills and the wrong temperament for a desk job. He'd worked in three or four factories, "and after a while they tend to get small," he observed. "You tend to pace." So, he didn't have a lot of job options. In constant pain, he was now confined to the dingy couch in his living room staring at the unrelenting idiocy of daytime television. Like many people with back injuries, he found himself lured by the mirage of SSI, or Supplementary Security Income, the disability payment administered by the Social Security Administration. It helps many and teases many others who hope to qualify. Since his wife was getting it and now he too was disabled, he applied. "I wasn't asking for it to be total," he said. "Partial would be fine with me. I don't want nothing for nothing. I didn't apply for it permanently, just to help me get back on my feet." If he could find a light, sit-down job, he feared, it would undermine his claim that he couldn't work, but as his back slowly healed, he looked a little anyway, in vain. It took Social Security a full year to deny him benefits, on the ground that he could lift ten pounds and stand for more than twenty minutes—not enough to get him work as a mechanic, just enough to disqualify him for assistance.

They had no money. Their savings account, a couple of thousand dollars, had disappeared. Kara owed her lawyer $600 for her divorce. With her former husband in prison, she wanted Tom to adopt Zach and Matt, but she needed $100 to file the papers. Scratching together nickels and dimes, "it took me a year to come up with $100," she said mournfully. "I don't even have $5 today to put gas in my truck to go to the doctor." Most painful was her inability to give to her children. "I have three of the most wonderful children in the world, and as a parent you like to reward them. It kills you when you go into a store and see a little item for $1.99 and you can't get it—a cap gun or something. It kills you. Last year Christmas was the worst Christmas of my life. My kids got three gifts. I didn't even want to wake up that morning. . . . They were OK with it. They were happy." She did not give anything to Tom, and he did not give anything to her. Except the most important thing. "If we have nothing," Kara said, "we have each other."

Kinship can blunt the edge of economic adversity. When a grandmother takes the children after school, when a friend lends a car, when a church provides day care and a sense of community, a parent can work and survive and combat loneliness. One December, Mark Brown, the manager at Claremont's Wal-Mart, mentioned to a meeting of employees that one of them was in need, "without telling them who it was," he said, "just telling them there was somebody here who wasn't gonna have a good Christmas with their kids." They took up a collection. Digging into their pockets, the underpaid workers produced a pile of dollar bills that added up to three or four hundred for the anonymous colleague—and one of those who chipped in a few bucks was the needy one herself.

That was kinship in its broadest meaning, extending further than blood and tribe into a larger affinity and commonality. It is a safety net that improves the material dimension of life; for those who have that network of connectedness and caring within a family and beyond, the brink of poverty is a less dangerous place. In a list of all the factors that make an economic life successful, all the hard skills (such as reading, math, typing, handling tools, reasoning) and the soft skills (such as punctuality, diligence, anger management), kinship stands prominently among them. Its absence facilitates collapse. Its presence can slow the decline, as the Kings discovered.

They could have been called "deserving poor," that condescending label sometimes used to contrast such folks with the mythical "welfare queens" of right-wing fantasy. There was nothing lazy about Tom and Kara, and they weren't looking for handouts. They were hardworking and honest, and they thought the responsibility for their welfare rested not with the welfare system but with themselves. They played by the rules, and what happened to them was not their fault, unless their relative lack of schooling could be considered their own failing. When their reverses piled up one after another, they had no defense.

In desperation, and against their proud principles, they finally applied for welfare and found a few other important strands of the safety net: Medicaid to pay their medical bills, $269 a month in food stamps, and a Section 8 housing subsidy covering their entire rent. They were led through much of the bureaucracy by Nancy Szeto, a case manager who had also grown up poor and proud, and saw much of herself in Kara. Through the private agency where she worked, Partners in Health, Nancy got Kara some free epilepsy medication from pharmaceutical companies that donate drugs—usually when they're nearly outdated. Kara reluctantly accepted vouchers for their daughter from WIC, the federal government's Special Supplemental Nutrition Program for Women, Infants, and Children, which could be turned in at the supermarket for milk, eggs, juice, cereal, and peanut butter.

The Kings also entered the economic realm of barter, a common substitute for money among the poor. Tom took his final pay from the farmer he'd worked for in vegetables instead of cash. "Vegetables do me more good than the money right now," Tom told him, " 'cause I can go home, and I can can, and I can freeze. 'No problem,' he says. 'Tell me what you need, come get it.' "

Barter became a balm of giving and friendship. When a friend with a roadside stand brought them corn and tomatoes, Kara asked how much he wanted, and he said: "Oh, nothing. I know where you are if I need a favor." Without being asked, Kara did him the favor. Fighting the deadening fatigue from the chemotherapy and the advancing cancer, she worked at his stand.

"He'd give us a fifty-pound bag of potatoes, corn for canning," she explained. "We never exchanged money."

Their drafty house was heated mainly by a woodstove in the basement, and as autumn deepened and the nights grew cold, Tom and Kara felt the dread seeping into them, the fear of New Hampshire's winter. There was no money for wood. Their rooms were permeated by the sickly smell of kerosene heaters. And then, a friend of Tom's named Kurt Minich, who owned a small logging company, dumped a truckload of logs in the yard and asked nothing in return. As Tom's back pain eased, he offered Kurt some mechanical work on his trucks, performed as gingerly as he could. Kurt accepted, favor for favor, and the family got through the winter.

As word spread of the Kings' plight, so did the community's generosity. The Women's Auxiliary of Concord raised $450 to get dentures for Kara. The next Christmas, "the visiting nurses, the school, fire department all donated all kinds of stuff to us," said Tom. "People you never thought about having a heart or feelings, you know—and at Christmastime it was like a steady flow of people coming in here. I mean, with boxes and boxes of gifts."

All of the outpouring warmed Kara but also tilted her balance sheet, she felt, putting her in a state of incalculable debt. "I would accept it, but I would feel compelled to do something in return," she declared. "For example, [we] delivered over seventy-five food baskets last Christmas in order to receive one. In order to receive, you have to do. I can't take something. I have to feel good about it. I have to feel I'm worthy of it."

Therefore, noticing on their many visits to Valley Regional Hospital how ill-equipped the waiting room was for children, Tom and Kara had Kate reach into her meager collection of toys to pick some dolls and other playthings to donate. Tom made a wooden toy box for the waiting room. "We wood-burned it and stained it and washed up all the dolls," Kara said. "When my kids go there, they have something to do. So we compensated that way."

Kurt became their centerpiece of friendship, offering everything from work to counseling. "He'd come here in the morning," Tom remembered, "and say, 'What are you doing today?' 'Nothing, really.' 'Well, come on, get in the pickup, let's take a ride.' And we'd go driving around on back roads and look for timber lots. Just to get me out of the house." When Tom's back was well enough to do a little driving, Kurt hired him for a couple of days a week to cruise wood lots and mark boundaries so the loggers could come in and cut. Then he coached Tom through a study guide so he could get a license to drive a logging truck. Then, when the house Tom and Kara rented was being sold and they had to move out, Kurt sold them eleven acres and an old, pale green metal mobile home on easy terms: $30,000 down, paid for out of $36,000 that Tom had just received as an insurance settlement for his injuries, plus $5,000 that Tom paid gradually to Kurt in cash and labor over the next several years. The sense of ownership buoyed Tom's and Kara's spirits, and they went to work putting down roots. They planted a vegetable garden. He put in rosebushes for her to see from her bedroom window. He laid ambitious plans for expanding the trailer. He borrowed a portable sawmill from Kurt, installed it in the back lot, and worked with his sons to cut trees and make boards of various widths, which he hammered together using his crude carpentry skills to add a back porch and other ungainly appendages.

Kara deteriorated. She needed treatment in Boston, but Tom had no reliable way to get her there. The '86 Bronco he'd bought had 230,000 miles and simply wouldn't last the trip, he was certain, so Kurt slapped down his own credit card and rented a truck for him. "Every time Kara goes in the hospital," Tom said, "Kurt calls me, 'You know, if you can't work today, don't worry about it. Take care of what's at home first.' "

The companionship filled the silences. "Kurt's the type of person that if I need somebody to talk to," Tom said, "I can't sleep nights or something, I can always pick up the phone and say, 'Kurt, I need somebody to talk to.' He's the type of person who will sit and listen, maybe for two or three hours and not say a word. Just let me ramble on about my business, my life."

In crisis, Tom and Kara also talked more. Stress and loss bend and break some families, and forge others more strongly. The Kings grew closer, opened to each other, uncovered their fears. "When the kids go to bed, eight-thirty, nine o'clock," Tom said, "we'll set there and talk for hours. . . . Before, I never talked to anybody, you know. I kept everything inside and just let it gnaw at me. And with Kara . . . I'm not afraid to let my emotions show now. It makes no difference if somebody sees me crying, because that's how I feel, you know. This is me. If you can't take me for me, then you better look the other way, because this is the way it is. I got feelings, and I'm gonna show them and make no bones about it. Oh, we got a great relationship now." Tom wiped his whole face with his hand, beginning at his forehead, ending at his chin.

Tom and Kara took in animals: not only her four-hundred-pound pet pig, Emma, but also three ferrets that a relative had kept in squalor, and a couple of dogs and rabbits; Tom later added goats and two steers. He and the boys built pens and a toolshed.

Kara dove into books and pamphlets about cancer, but Tom just felt dumb around doctors, who "use words this long," he griped, holding his hands two feet apart. It is a common complaint that deters many people with little education from seeking timely medical care. "I come home and I say, 'Now, do you understand what he said?' She'll say, 'Well, pretty much of it.' 'Well, I think we probably ought to sit down so you can explain it to me, because I don't understand it.' "

Mostly, his angry sense of inferiority just smoldered, but it flared into the open when Kara needed a donor for a bone marrow transplant. Her case was nearly hopeless, but doctors were working hard at it nonetheless. Tom offered to be a donor, not understanding that only a blood relative's cells stood a chance of being compatible. He was told dismissively that it wouldn't do any good to test him. Why? Tom asked indignantly. Because he'd have only a million-in-one possibility of matching, the doctor replied. "Wait a minute!" Tom remembered himself saying. "We're talking about my wife's life! Even if I don't match with her, somewhere down the line, somebody does match. If I can save somebody else's life, that's fine. . . . If she has to have a donor from the bank, I can give it back." He ordered the doctor to "explain this to me in language that I understand."

"Does this situation make you mad?" the doctor asked.

"No. It pisses me off," Tom retorted.

"I guess I know where you're coming from," the doctor conceded. "Maybe we should test you just for your own mind." They did so, and there was no match. One of Kara's sisters, Kris, made the donation.

"What a great day," Kara wrote in her journal. "I went shopping and had some energy." It was dated February 8, 1998, the first entry in a spiral notebook filled with badly spelled musings written almost entirely in pencil. Many were done as letters to God—in gratitude, in appeal, in desperate pleading for survival. "So, God," she concluded that first evening, "please bless Tom, Zach, Matt, Katie & myself—long life, Love, Happiness, laughter, and to always be close to each other and thank you for Today. Amen. Kara."

Her delights were simple. It was "a wonderful day" when "Tom Bill & virginia went and picked me up a dual range stove, good deal $50.00 bucks—the left front burner don't work but it's better than only two burners and one oven," or when "Tom made Brownies and apple cinnimon muffins for Head Start, & Zach made a date cake—it all sold. I bought Tom a waffle maker for Valentines, he got me a nice slinky nighty. We gave the kids $5.00 a piece."

As the pain of her cancer spread, though, and the money problems worsened, she recorded days of distance from Tom, thinking he'd be better off with her dead. She lost her temper with the children, and she started drinking a lot of Canadian whiskey and ginger ale. On February 19: "Well, I had a most awsome day. I love life, thank you God for all my days. I know all well that I've been indulging in Booze but it does help and that's no excuse but I do feel I need it." That night she was up again and again, and at 4:30 a.m. finally mopped the floor because she couldn't sleep. On February 20: "Well, it's been a day—a good one only because I'm alive. . . . I had to get physical with Zach, push him into the wall and grab him, punish him to his room, for dumb shit, he didn't like the kind of ice cream we had so he got tough with the freezer and Matt, so I got tough with him, and I had to smack Katie on the lips for baby talking." On February 23: "I don't know what my problem with the booze is lately But hey—I can't help it. I need a fix I guess." On February 26 she wrote that Kurt had fallen behind on payments he owed Tom for work. "I'm a booz a-holic—god— Tomorrow I'll regret this. I'll have the shakes. I'll feel guilty—but the shakes is what gets me. But like Tom says—whatever works." By the end of the next day's entry, as she drank and wrote, her handwriting grew indecipherable. On March 5: "Zachary and Matthew got excellent report cards so we are going to give them each $10.00, I've been feeling really depressed lately . . . Tom and I need to talk more—I love the fact that he is in and is my life."

Because she was scheduled for the bone marrow transplant, she feared that she would miss "all the colors of Spring the Brilliant yellow—Sapphire Green—so Green that it takes your breath away." The transplant was delayed, but the spring passed with her journal closed. In late May, after nearly two months without an entry, she scribbled: "Sorry God that I haven't written for a very, very long time." The following day, from the hospital: "I'm in shock and denial, I don't want to die, I have been through to much and gone to far to die now." Two days later, May 30: "The Doctors all have me for dead, But I guess that's okay—no more suffering. . . . My mother showed up today. I asked her to leave." And on June 3: "It is Tom's B-day—he is doing awful—he is having massive panic attacks, I was upset with him last night because he smacked the Ball out of Zach's hand right in the parking lot in front of a lot of people. . . . I have lumps everywhere. I have cancer in my uturus—great huh? . . . I don't want to die, for God sakes—I want to live, please let me live please?"

After Tom took her in the rented truck to Brigham and Women's Hospital in Boston for her transplant, he made the two-hour drive as often as he could, on Kurt's credit card. Helping Tom seemed as natural as breathing. "His heart's absolutely in the right place, but he just got left behind a little bit," Kurt said. "You don't mind bending over backwards to help a guy who's as nice as he is." One day, Kurt's helping hand was gently, seamlessly supported by a salesman at Dartmouth Motors, a dealership at the end of Tom's road.

"I think it was the first Sunday she was down in Boston," Tom remembered. "I had spoke with Kurt, and Kurt had told me, 'Go down to Dartmouth Motors,' he says." Again, Kurt was planning to rent a truck for Tom, but the dealer's last one had already gone out. So the salesman "went and cleaned out his own personal Blazer," Tom said.

"Here, take this," the salesman offered. "Kurt and I already set it up. Bring it back when you get back. It's full of fuel."

"I said, 'Well, when I bring it back it'll be full of fuel,' " Tom reported. "And it was."

On July 3, the day after Kara received the transplant, she wrote; "God please bless Tom, Zach, Matt, Katie, and a special Blessing for me, Kara, and thank you for yesterday. And God, Bless Kris for what she has done for me, Amen. Kara." Three days later, she wrote in a fragile hand: "Well I'm going to Bed soon so god Bless Tom, Zach, Matt, Katie and expecially myself. And god thank you for today. Please god reach out and for me and heal me. Please—so thank you for Today and Amen. Kara." It was her last entry. Five days later, Tom's adoption of Zach and Matt became final.

On the afternoon of July 12, Kara's thirty-third birthday, the doctor called and urged Tom to get to Boston as soon as possible. How about early tomorrow? Tom asked. "OK," the doctor said, "the earlier the better." Tom called Kurt. "He made some phone calls, and then the salesman from Dartmouth Motors says to me, 'When do you need it?' I said, 'I need it before six o'clock tomorrow morning.' 'Come on down,' he said. 'I'll meet you there. I'll meet you there at five-thirty.' He opened the door at five-thirty and handed me a set of keys. I said, 'Where do I sign?' He said, 'You don't. Get out of here. Go.' "

Tom walked into Kara's room by eight o'clock, "and they were in there working on her then. And the doctor come out and he said, 'She wants to see you.' I said, 'OK.' I said, 'How does it look?' He shook his head. So I went into the room, and she reached out to take my hand, and she had her hand like this, so I reached out and took her hand. She had her cross around her neck, her earrings and her rings in her hand, and she dropped them in mine." His voice broke, and a long silence embraced his tears. "And I said, 'Kara, no matter what happens today, I will love you forever.' She nodded her head, she dropped everything in my hand, squeezed my hand, and she was gone."

He drove home in the brand-new borrowed Blazer and told the children face-to-face. He put her wedding ring on a chain around his neck, and continued to wear his own. She never saw the blooming roses he had planted outside her bedroom.

Tom and the boys made a sign, printed in red, and hung it on three poles over the garden:

To My Loving Wife and Mother and our best friend Kara
P.S. We love you

The sign was still there the following summer, but the garden had grown shabby with weeds, the rosebushes needed pruning, and the surrounding grounds had filled up with a junkyard full of rusting machines that embarrassed Zach and Matt when the school bus stopped in front of their place. It was as if everything they had ever owned had been put in their yard. There were four lawn tractors, one of which worked when you held a pair of scissors across the solenoid contacts. The others were useful sources of cannibalized parts. There were two or three rototillers, a couple of lawn mowers, and a weed whacker. A propane tank lay on its side, a picnic table was smothered in junk, and an old wooden wheelbarrow with a spoked wheel was missing one side. A camouflaged metal canoe lay upside down in an aluminum rowboat filled with fishing poles and tackle boxes. An orange traffic cone stood at the edge of the woods behind the trailer, and up among the trees was an assortment of scrap metal pieces, a metal tank, cans, bits of plastic bags, and a pile of old tires. The clothesline sagged under the weight of many pairs of jeans and work pants, and a pile of chicken wire had been cut into sheets for fencing.

Tom and the boys had built a toolshed and a small shed for April and Sylvia, the goats; the rabbits, named Cinnamon, Spice, Licorice, and Minnie; and William, the guinea pig. They had erected the frame of a small barn for the steers, Jesse and Jake. No two boards, cut at their sawmill, seemed the same width, and hardly any were the right length. The fences were random: A single strand of electrified barbed wire kept in Emma the enormous pig, another stretch of fence consisted of incomplete boards that looked like useless crusts of bread. The goats were enclosed in chicken wire, and a gate, made of a leftover door sawed in half, leaned at a rangy angle against a splintered post that wasn't sunk far enough into the ground to keep it upright. Zach and Matt alternated days doing the chores of feeding, which took about half an hour.

Up a dirt road toward the back of their land was a treasure trove of old stuff, most of which had been there when they bought the property: a pile of railroad ties, three snowmobiles, a school bus with half the back missing (Tom planned to put a drying kiln for boards on the back of the bus), five trucks and several old cars, and a big yellow tractor named Frankie with a bulldozer-sized blade against a pile of roots and dirt it had been pushing when "something clogged in the gas tank," Zach said.

It might have looked like a junkyard, but really it was like living in the middle of a grown-up's playground where nothing much worked but you could have a lot of fun fixing things. And that was the way the children were learning—the way Tom had learned, by getting their hands dirty, by making things work, by caring for animals, by taking responsibility. The boys were active in 4-H, where they had won awards, and Zach had cut a sculpture with a chain saw that he'd bought for $5 at a yard sale. He had set a log on end, drawn an outline, and carved a bear with a long snout and two pointy ears. For entertainment, he said, they fished for catfish in Rand's Pond and hunted for rabbits and partridge. A friend who shot deer but didn't eat them supplied them with venison in the fall. What else did he do for fun? "Weed whack!" he exclaimed.

Inside, the trailer had descended into chaos. Zach and two cousins were frenetically working their way through a huge pile of dirty dishes in the sink, probably several days' worth. The bedrooms, strung in a row along a back corridor, were jam-packed with dirty clothes covering beds and floors. But doing laundry was not a priority: Tom and the boys were about to go haying at a farmer's who, in exchange, let them have some of the hay for their animals.

The boys, in seventh and eighth grades, did their homework at the scuffed oval kitchen table, which was littered with stuff and located at the vortex of the household. The bedrooms, small and messy, were sanctuaries for diversions, especially for Matt, the younger, who liked to listen to the radio and fool around. When their phone was cut off after Tom failed to pay the bill, Matt's teacher couldn't call, so she sent a note home; it hung around Matt's room for months, unseen by Tom, who exploded when he saw Matt's miserable report card: E in English, E in Science, D in Math, D in Social Studies. Then, Tom went into school, asking the homeroom teacher, "Why wasn't I told about this before?"

Matt hated school. Zach liked it. He proved to be a good artist, and as he went through high school, he began to think about architecture. At the end of his junior year, I asked Tom if he thought that Zach would go to college. "I think he's already applied," Tom said. "Zach," he called, "what colleges did you apply to?" Zach had not applied, of course, because it was too soon; he had little idea how to go about it, and Tom, for all his love and support, would not be able to give him any knowledgeable help.

The years after Kara's death had plunged Tom into periods of depression, joblessness, and even alcohol. That summer, he couldn't drive logging trucks for Kurt because he didn't have a baby-sitter for Kate. When school started in September, he got a $6-an-hour job with a log yard measuring the board footage of loads delivered by truckers for sale and milling. He discovered one day that the yard was taking his measurements, rounding them off lower, discounting good-quality red oak and ash, then selling the wood at high prices for veneer, and "putting the screws to the loggers," as he described it. "The biggest mistake they made was lettin' me in on it. Three-quarters of the people around here that are loggers are my friends, you know, so me and management didn't see eye to eye." He confronted the foreman.

"That's our business," the man said. "You just do your job. We'll pay you for it."

"No," Tom said, "because at one time, I was on the other end. I know what it feels like." He thought about it overnight, and at noon the next day he quit. "This is what's happenin' and I don't like it, and I'm not working here under false pretenses," he quoted himself as telling his boss. "I try to be a man of my word. I stake my reputation on it, being a man of my word. If you find something wrong with that, time for you and I to part company."

Few Americans have the luxury of acting on such principle, and Tom didn't have it either. He went to work part-time for Kurt fixing equipment, but it barely paid the bills. While the rest of the country was gripped by the impeachment proceeding against President Clinton, Tom let it all pass him by like a great storm beyond the horizon of his concern. "I don't do politics well," he said simply. By February he had full-time work for another logger, making $300 to $350 a week. He loved being in the wintry woods all day. "Right now we're cutting a little bit of hardwood," he said, "mostly rock maple, some cherry, a lot of white birch, and then we're cuttin' pine besides. So we average a couple load of hardwood a week and two, three load of pine. I'm at his house by eight o'clock, clearin' the woods by eight-thirty, and I'm usually home by three-thirty, four. We put in a good day, yet we don't kill ourselves either. Works." He was again on the other end of the log yard business, and he watched the measurements closely. No problems.

"We're doing OK," Tom said. "We're doing OK," and he rubbed his face with his hand. "Yeah, yep. So. Ain't gettin' rich, but. If I can keep a thousand, fifteen hundred in the bank, that way I know if something happens I'm covered for a month, anyway." But then the logger ran out of wood, and Tom was jobless for four months. He started drinking. He let his friendships lapse. He left the TV on all the time, to fill the emptiness.

Into his life walked "Mary," a brassy, plainspoken woman his age, tall and strapping, who fancied herself a rescuer. "The place was a mess," she said. "Books all over, laundry all over. He was a shell of a man. He wasn't working, he'd stopped caring. We both talked and we both cried together." Her yellow hair was in a tangle, her face pleasant, seasoned, almost hard, but she was lovingly firm with the kids, tough and warm, motherly, demanding. She replaced the disconnected phone with another, under her name. When a technician arrived to cut off the electricity because Tom's late payment hadn't shown up in the computer, she insisted that they check, and the power was off for only two and a half hours.

That was long enough, though. "I'm gonna be self-sufficient by next fall," Tom declared solemnly. He and the boys had started work on a dilapidated "barn" for two steers. "I'm gonna raise my own pork, raise my own beef. [Mary] wants to put some chickens in. I'm looking for a diesel generator. There are a couple of emergency generators from Fort Dix, New Jersey. For $1,000. It needs to be rewired." He shrugged as if that were an easy chore. When he laid out his plans, he got a clipped tone of false confidence in his voice, as if he knew that he was saying what he wished, not what would be. Three years later, he was still hooked up to the power grid.

Mary knew about depression; she was on medication. Was he taking anything for his? "Well, Jack Daniel's," she said. "It wasn't prescribed, but that was his own prescription. . . . It was his birthday, and I planned a nice birthday cookout for him, and he decides to start drinking at nine-thirty. So he was drunk by noon." But now it had been four months without a drink. "He's behaving himself," she went on. "The last time he went on a drunk I dumped his bottle down the sink, and he hasn't bought any since. . . . He deals with reality. . . . He's finding his match when it comes to being a jerk. I'm not scared of him."

How about therapy? "The heaviest thing in the world to pick up is that phone," Tom said. Maybe Mary was his best therapy, because she pulled him out of the paralysis that characterizes depression. He looked for work and found a job with Davey Tree company, under contract to trim branches around power lines. "It makes me feel good that I can go out there and swing from a tree for nine hours a day and walk home at night and say, yeah, a day's work. . . . There's things that I can do now that a year ago I wouldn't think of doing because I didn't think I was physically up to it. It don't bother me to strap that saddle on my ass now and head up that tree and spend eight, nine hours up there. Go up the tree, trim it out, go back down." He was teaching Matt, and they were trimming trees on their own land. Somewhere along the way, Mary moved out to her own place, and they continued to see each other, but not at such close quarters.

Tom was laid off the next winter because of too much snow: eight weeks without work. He got a job welding fuel tanks for $10.50 an hour and was then laid off from that, too. In the summer he planted sixty-five acres of sweet corn for a farmer and helped with tomatoes and pumpkins; he was paid $300 a week and all the vegetables he wanted. After the farming season he went back to work for Davey Tree, but they wouldn't let him climb once he turned fifty because insurance wouldn't cover him. So he had no winter work except side jobs cutting and selling firewood. He did some maple sugaring and then got a job maintaining factory machinery at LaCrosse, a boot manufacturer, for $10.50 an hour. It was inside work, and he knew that pretty soon he would start to pace again.

"Eventually," he said with that lilt of false confidence, "I'm gonna put a slider [door] up here on my trailer, and this is gonna be the main entrance. No more parking where they park out front. Slowly but surely, you know. It's been a house long enough. Time to become a home."

A year or so later, though, he replaced the trailer altogether with another used one, bought for $2,500 from a friend who had received it as payment for landscaping work. The job at LaCrosse was too good to quit. His only complaint was that he didn't get to work in the woods. He got full benefits, including medical insurance that cost him just $38.15 weekly, and with a lot of overtime even during the recession of 2001–2003, he made about $550 a week. "It's a pretty decent living, actually," he said.

His boys loved to work. Matt was installing insulation in a neighbor's garage, Zach was doing carpentry for his high school coach, and they were helping their dad with household expenses. Matt was still winning blue ribbons at 4-H, and Zach, with his shy smile, had been elected Homecoming King in the autumn of his senior year. He had scored only 950 total on the math and verbal parts of the SAT and would have no access to the Kaplan or Princeton Review courses that rich kids took to improve their results. His networks of family and community could assist him on their own ground, not on the foreign territory of college. He applied to study architecture at Wentworth Institute of Technology in Boston, but he chose to skip the optional essay, not realizing how attractive his journey along the edge of poverty would be to admissions officers scouting for youths who worked hard to overcome adversity. Wentworth turned him down.

It was a hard winter. The cold was fierce, the snow relentless. Loneliness descended on Tom like an icy silence, and to warm himself he turned again to his old friend, Jack Daniel's. The mechanics of survival in his cluttered trailer began to break down. First, the water suddenly stopped flowing after Christmas. The weight of heavy snow had dislodged a pipe and broken the wires to the pump at the bottom of his well. Then the septic system froze and backed up. Finally, a bearing seized in the heating system's fan, and he came home to find the trailer full of smoke from his overheated furnace. "I lost it," he said. He sent Zach and Kate to stay with Mary, and Matt to his oldest daughter by a previous marriage. Tom took his dog—the only pet he had left—and moved into a friend's camper, heated with propane, on a wooded campsite.

He spent the winter and the spring working and drinking. Every day, he grew more and more eager for the end of his shift, when he and a few other guys at the factory would go to a bar and have some beers. Tom would then buy more beer to take home, and so it went night after night, week after week, as the daylight gradually extended into evening and the snow melted into mud and the brown New Hampshire hills were tinted with the tender green of new growth.

One June night, Tom followed his usual routine. He went to the bar, then bought a twelve-pack of beer. The next thing he remembered was lying in his driveway beside his pickup, whose engine was off but whose radio was on, hearing a female voice announcing the time as 3:30 a.m. There were only three cans left and no empties in his truck. He was jolted into action. He and a buddy from work enrolled in daily sessions at AA, and when I found him one Saturday at his trailer, he had been sober for four days and was digging up his septic system.

Zach's high school graduation would be the following week, and Tom was determined to be in good shape for it. He had a fuzzy recollection of Zach's presenting him with forms for some college in Hartford, Connecticut, something having to do with financial aid. Tom didn't know how to fill them out, though. He thought Zach would be going to college in a few months, but he wasn't sure.

Zach was accepted by the University of Hartford, but he didn't go. The financial forms never got mailed in, and he decided to enlist in the Air Force, which promised to train him in aircraft maintenance. He was buoyant with anticipation, and Tom was proud. By October, the cycle had turned upward: Kate and Matt were back with Tom, who had built an addition to the trailer and was working the night shift, 6 p.m. to 6 a.m., at nearly $13 an hour. He hadn't had a drink since June.

Ann Brash chose poverty. The alternative, she firmly believed, was to sacrifice her bonds with her children by working multiple jobs days and evenings and weekends. That would have yielded only threadbare financial security, she figured, at the expense of their emotional security. "I made a decision to be around them rather than working the fifty, sixty hours a week to let them live a middle-class life," she explained. So she took part-time jobs, accepted help from her church and friends, and managed to stay off welfare. Except for student loans, she steadfastly shunned government assistance: no food stamps, housing subsidies, or Medicaid. After a dozen years "walking along the cliff," as she put it, she saw her son, Sandy, graduate from Dartmouth as a computer specialist and her daughter, Sally, studying voice at the New England Conservatory of Music. Sandy had been granted full financial aid; Sally had been funded by loans, scholarships, and private gifts.

Ann remained poor, however—not according to the statistics (she had found a job that paid $23,600 a year) but as measured by her anxiety over substantial debt, nonexistent savings, and the painful limitations of her life. As it does with many who are nearly impoverished, her tension came less from the present, in which she survived, than from the future, on which she could not depend. Yet her "cultural capital," she said, had defeated the most debilitating characteristic of poverty: its hopelessness. She had strained to enlarge her children's lives beyond the boundaries of their economic circumstances, and she had succeeded. "Both of my children say they've never felt poor," Ann declared with satisfaction. "In some ways, it has made both of them more sure of who they are."

"I know what it's like to be really poor," said Sally when she was sixteen. "I know what it's like to struggle to have money to pay for food for the next week. But I never felt poor." She saw herself as quite unlike other low-income kids in public school. "There was this sort of hopelessness about them, as if they couldn't imagine life any other way." She concluded that poverty was not just a matter of money but also of dispirited loneliness. "If I knew one wonderful person and I was homeless with nothing, and hungry, I still wouldn't be poor," Sally insisted. "As long as I knew just one person that I could love, I wouldn't be poor." Her perpetual smile illuminated her entire face, including her eyes, which gazed merrily at the difficult world.

Sally had been five and her brother seven when they were plunged into hardship by their parents' divorce. She was too young to notice the sudden uncertainties. Her mother's main obsession—not knowing whether they would have a place to live—became normal for Sally, merely "one of the worries," she said, "one of the many worries like getting to school on time in the morning."

For her mother, though, tumbling out of the solid middle-class comfort that she had enjoyed from childhood was disorienting and traumatic. Ann began by sitting down with Sandy and making a list differentiating "wishes" from "needs." She embarked on what she called "a day-by-day take-care-of-what's-in-front-of-me effort." That meant living in the present by figuring out how to pay for the immediacies of rent, heat, and food. "Living in the present means you spend only what you 'need,' and you always distinguish 'want' from 'need,' " she observed.

When she finally gained her footing on that new ground, Ann had trouble recalling the affluent world. "Before the divorce, we would go book shopping as often as we'd go grocery shopping," she mused one day. Now, she added, "I can't remember what it's like to live with dishwashers and somebody that comes in and cleans the house. I can't remember that anymore, but I think it used to free up a lot of time." Confronting poverty kept her busy, but it also adjusted her focus so that she saw not only the basics of food, shelter, and clothing but also less tangible requirements for a healthy life. "We may not be able to even survive without simultaneously addressing our need for things like art, music, our goals, or hope of something beyond our immediate physical environment," she said. "And we can't survive without loving and being loved. So most of us use substitute things, things within our reach—alcohol, TV, drugs, Wal-Mart shopping." She discovered that "when we are/become poor, we need to think more carefully than when wealthy about what contributes to our health as human beings." That means "close healthy relationships, not feeling alone, fresh vegetables, not too much sugar, thirty minutes of daily physical activity. All keep us healthy, or at least surviving when we don't know where we'll live next month or year."

Ann Brash had arrived here partly through aimlessness, which left her with talents but not skills. She would have been financially fine if her marriage had lasted. She loved reading great literature and listening to Bach fugues. She reveled in ideas and spoke with articulate intelligence. Being white, she faced no racial discrimination. But for a woman graduating from high school in 1964, even privileged socio-economic standing did not automatically provide a sense of entitlement or vocational purpose. And that sore failure of American society was not overcome by her parents, who did not instill in her the value of professional self-sufficiency. Her father, a chemical engineering consultant who raised his family in Connecticut and Massachusetts, did not have high aspirations for his daughters.

Ann dropped out of college after a year. "I hated it," she said. She worked briefly as an assistant buyer in a department store. "I didn't like it very much." She then lived in Kyoto for five years, teaching English to Japanese. "I went to the hairdresser and had my nails done a lot." Back in the United States, she worked as a travel consultant to an engineering company in Boston and tried going back to college. "I had no direction," she confessed. She then married a draftsman who started his own business.

After the divorce, she received child support amounting to about $10,000 a year, and she worked part-time—substitute teaching at $50 a day, doing clerical work at a college for twenty hours a week, documenting yachts, copyediting medical texts and other books for a piecework rate per page. The editing "was wonderful," she said, "but last year I think I made $3,000 or $4,000." Throughout, "I also chose to keep long-term goals for the children in focus. That is, I refused to do anything that would mean they hadn't access to me. It made a lot of people mad, or at least they thought me lazy and unrealistic. But I had just enough income from child support to be able to feed the children, and I either found very low rent or shoved myself on my unwilling mother."

Ann and the children lived in her mother's house for nearly four years, until her mother returned from a trip to France, suddenly decided to sell the place, and gave Ann a month to move out. "I was just destroyed," Ann said. "I was clinically depressed. I went to a women's center and got some help." When her mother offered a modest monthly stipend for a year and a half, Ann did some calculations and refused the gift. "I said, 'Please don't do that, because it wouldn't change our long-term financial picture, but it would mean that Sandy wouldn't be able to get his scholarship to go to boarding school that year. So it would end up not really helping us, and it would really hurt Sandy.'" The small amount, she feared, would push her into a borderland where she could neither afford tuition nor fully qualify for assistance.

"Boarding school" sounds like a luxury for the wealthy, as it often is. For Ann, however, it meant an escape from the inferior public schools in the impoverished towns and neighborhoods where she could live. Her own upbringing had granted her an idea of the possible, the attainable, the expected that was far more ambitious than the notions held by generations of impoverished mothers who had inherited only a sense of the impossible, the unattainable, the unexpected. Her children were bright and poor—the perfect combination to draw financial aid—and their education was a central part of Ann's stubborn cause. She tried Sally in a local school, then pulled her out and did home schooling for several years until Sally won a full scholarship to St. Paul's, a boarding school in New Hampshire. Sandy went to private schools as well. This seemed incongruous to Ann's relatives, who judged her irresponsible. "My sister said that Sandy had no right to go to private school and I didn't have the right to make that choice, that we should take what is given to us," Ann recalled. "So that was a very difficult time."

Ann acquired the remaining credits for her own bachelor's degree by passing the College-Level Examination Program exam, but her money shortage didn't ease. Instead, her life was invaded by unending anxiety about where she would find housing. Aside from hollow hunger, there is probably no more frightening void than the looming absence of shelter. A chilling emptiness resides where warm assuredness should be. In Ann's worst moments through the years, when her pleasant features grew pinched with lines of worry and she descended into seizures of despair (always apologetically), she would knot her knuckles together and say, "Things are looking pretty scary," and, "I don't know where we will live," or worse: "I don't really want to live, I'm absolutely without hope, I'm so tired I can't do this."

For a year after eviction from her mother's house, she and the children lived with generous friends, who suffered inconvenience that Ann at last became unwilling to impose. She began to look elsewhere and grew desperate. The rents in New Hampshire, where she had located to find cheaper living, were still beyond her reach. Yet she had the kind of proud, deserving air that made people want to help—financially comfortable people who must have been attracted by her erudition, her introspection, her centered devotion to her children. Her manner and her interests did not betray the socio-economic class into which she had fallen; her children said that they were rarely seen as poor. To the contrary, professionals may have viewed Ann as just like them, someone with whom they could have traded places but for the chance roll of the dice. The results for her were therefore very different from what they were for single black women in urban ghettos. "We're homeless, but we've always been taken care of in some way," Ann noted. At a community college where she was studying, a professor and his wife befriended her, drew first Sally and then Ann into their Russian Orthodox congregation, and finally offered her their unused cabin in the Vermont woods. So Ann found housing and community, shelter for both body and spirit.

The cabin made life hard and pure. It stood a mile from the main road, about two-tenths of a mile up a dirt drive. It had a tiny kitchen and a tiny bathroom that relied on gravity-fed water pumped to a tank on the second floor. It had an outhouse with a spider they named Charlotte, appropriately. The only heat in winter came from a woodstove, the only cooling in summer from an old wooden icebox that had to be kept filled with ice that cost about $12 a week—expensive, by Ann's standards. The only light came from propane lamps and leftover beeswax candles from the church, which made reading hard on Ann's eyes. As soon as the gray, still winter froze the water line, she and Sally had to lug five-gallon buckets up two-tenths of a mile from the well. "Luckily it started snowing," Ann remarked, so Sally, then thirteen, could drag the buckets on a sled.

They got a quick education there. "We didn't have any wood the first winter," Ann said. "We didn't know about it. . . . Sandy came home—he actually wrote his college essay on this. . . . We spent a wonderful Christmas vacation. He came home from the first year of boarding school and we looked and we knew we had about two weeks of wood left. Sandy was going to go back, and Sally and I were going to be there, and I'd never split wood in my life and I wasn't any good at it, so Sandy and Sally decided that they were going to split wood. So down a half a mile from the house, down the hill, was a big pile of some cut-up lengths of wood . . . so Sandy and Sally dug them up out of the snow and Sandy split them and Sally and I hauled them on sleds up the hill, and we got enough to get us through all the way until March." And then someone from church gave them another pile of wood "so we got through the rest of the winter." When food got very short, they were helped by members of the congregation. By the next winter, they were better prepared.

In the cabin, they talked more and read more, "but it's easy to get sick out there, and we did." So after nearly two years they tried to find an apartment with heat and electricity. The rents were too high—$500 to $600 a month. And then, again, the church came to their rescue. In a disused Catholic convent in Claremont, New Hampshire, the Orthodox church had taken a rambling apartment as a place for visitors to stay. Ann was told that she was welcome to live there for the small price of taking care of those who came. It was a sudden joy to have hot running water, warmth, light, and the periodic company. Sally was taking singing lessons, working at a fruit and vegetable store to pay for a piano accompanist. Sandy had also been drawn into the church, befriending Stefan Solzhenitsyn, the son of the Russian author Aleksandr Solzhenitsyn, and was becoming intrigued with computers, though Ann had no money to buy him anything as advanced as his interests.

She pursued her part-time editing and, for a small fee, graded papers for a Dartmouth professor. She carried credit card debt on top of her $18,000 in student loans. And then the church decided to give up the apartment, and she had to leave. As the departure date approached and she could not find housing, she felt herself sliding down into panic. This time, rescue came from one of her church's parishioners, who asked an aunt with a two-family house whether she would rent the upstairs to Ann at a good price. The aunt agreed to $400 a month, and so once again, supported by the kind of church-based, middle-class network inaccessible to most Americans in poverty, Ann found shelter. She disliked the flowery wallpaper in her new place and cared little for her motley collection of furniture, mostly rejects and hand-me-downs. But a few possessions meant something. "There's a little stool with some crewel-stitched material on it that actually is ours," she said. "The silver in the drawers is mine." It was family silver, some connection to roots now withered.

Ann found a full-time job as production editor for the University Press of New England, a small academic publisher that paid her $23,600 a year plus health insurance. She loved the work, but it didn't open a way to financial security. She was strapped by huge debt, and child support for Sandy ended when he turned eighteen. Her new dental coverage, with its ceiling of $1,000 a year, proved inadequate to pay for the extensive repairs she needed to recover from years of deferred maintenance.

Her investment in her children began to pay off, though. Both worked hard, spending one summer together as janitors in a church, demonstrating brilliance along the lines of their respective interests: programming computers and singing opera. Sandy, a lanky, taciturn lad, scored 800 on his math SAT and over 700 on the verbal test. He was accepted with full financial aid everywhere he applied: by Dartmouth, Amherst, Williams, and Carleton. Both kids took their shortage of cash in stride and sacrificed gracefully. Sandy could not afford jazz concerts and movies at Dartmouth, and he tried not to order too much takeout food, although he did run up heavy balances on his credit cards. When Sally, in prep school, went clothes shopping with friends, she didn't buy but just tried things on in the changing room—pretending, acting, playing dress-up. Her small allowance from St. Paul's she spent on pizza for herself and others. Or she walked in the woods and picked bunches of wildflowers to give to her friends. "They give me what I can't afford," she said, "and I give them what they wouldn't give to themselves."

In college, Sandy made good friends, came out of his shell, was plugged into Dartmouth's alumni network of employers, and landed a summer job with one of them at a San Francisco software company for the unbelievable sum of $3,750 a month. He was about to go off to that position one June afternoon when he sat with his mother and sister on the terrace of the Hanover Inn overlooking Dartmouth's green. It might have been a moment of satisfaction for Ann. She was seeing her children heading into the kind of adulthood she had struggled to make possible. But she was not especially proud of herself at the moment, for she had just violated her moral tenets by declaring bankruptcy. That deleted her credit card debt but not her student loans, which could not be legally forgiven. So burdensome had the debt been to Ann that she was frightfully worried about her children ending up with the same from their own student loans. As she carried on in concern and despair, her children looked genuinely pained and worried. "I have no emotion," she said. "I don't care anymore."

"I'll have a job," offered Sandy.

"You took care of us," said Sally, "and now it's about time for us to take care of you—when I'm in the Met!"

There was a burst of laughter, and Ann said, "After you clean up your room!"

Following graduation, Sandy probably could have returned to Silicon Valley at a handsome salary, but his ties to family, friends, and church kept him in New Hampshire, where he lived with his mother and worked as the systems administrator for a company in Norwich, Vermont, that provided computer services to travel agencies. He started at $40,000 a year, more than one and a half times his mother's best earnings, and began to pay off the debt that he had carried out of Dartmouth along with his diploma: $10,000 to $12,000 on high-interest credit cards and $20,000 in low-interest student loans.

When Sally entered the New England Conservatory, she obtained a scholarship and a student loan, but they were not enough. The balance was contributed by a local couple who had been inspired by a newspaper account of Sally's attempt to raise money to study at Tanglewood one summer. They helped send her to Tanglewood and then to the conservatory, and they advanced Ann the funds to pay off her own student debt. Ann and her family were the kind of folks whom people liked to help.

She did not admire the values of her relatives, nor they hers. Money was an obsession to Ann because it was scarce, and to them because it was plentiful. She saw how easily it could sway the moral compass that she struggled to follow. So she watched dismayed in her mother's final years as those responsible for her care moved her to a less expensive, lower-quality nursing home, where attendants called her only "Dear" and "Honey" because they never learned her name. Ann spent hours and days visiting, reconnecting with her mother, feeling grief and bewilderment at the choice to place her there. "I second-guess myself," Ann said. "There must be something wrong with me that I'm not like the others. And I'm not. I don't value what they value. I'm so horrified at what is being done that I can't understand it. It's so simple: It's wrong to trade somebody's welfare, somebody for whom you're responsible, for money."

The self-doubts notwithstanding, Ann remained a true believer in the way that she had chosen. "We've lived for over a decade on no money, and at one point having no house," she said. "And while it sounds awful and sounds like a strange choice to make, I did it. We all did it. And we all did it in a healthy way. We were much better people for the choices we made than if I had ignored the kids, worked seventy hours a week, paid rent, and lived in a poor neighborhood where other kids were left alone. And so I know what it is to be without money and without a lot of things. It's not as bad as having a moderate amount of money but no time for the people in your life."

Chapter Eight

BODY AND MIND

Most of my time I work as a social worker—fight with Social Services, get people housing.

—Dr. Glenn Flores, pediatrician

Food is one of the few flexible parts of a tight budget. Rent is a fixed amount. Car payments are constant. The charges for electricity and basic telephone service cannot be compromised, negotiated, or trimmed. But the amount a family spends on food is elastic; it can be expanded or squeezed to fit whatever cash is left after the unyielding bills are paid. The result is an array of malnourished children in America.

Dr. Deborah Frank sees some of them: the scrawny baby who looks like a wizened old man, the listless toddler who weighs two-thirds of what she should, the bony boy who cannot resist infection. They come to the fifth floor of the Boston Medical Center's ambulatory care center, where the doctor runs the Grow Clinic two days a week.

These are not the skeletal faces of famine, but they are desperate windows into the collection of hardships that consume the American poor. Because food money is not fixed, it succumbs easily to the ruthless costs of

201

other essentials, especially housing, which can soak up 50 to 75 percent of a poor family's earnings. "If there were more subsidized housing there'd be less hunger," Dr. Frank declared. If there were more generous food stamps, if high-nutrition baby formula cost less, if inner-city stores stocked fresh fruits and vegetables, if all day-care centers provided decent meals and snacks, if families could afford varied foods for children with allergies, if new immigrants were not confused by junk-food advertising, if mothers could breast-feed instead of work, if children of working parents were not passed among multiple caregivers, if parents simply knew to sit youngsters down calmly to feed them, if there were less depression among those at the bottom of the economy, there would be less hunger. The clinics that treat malnutrition stand at a devastating collision of problems, most of which cannot be solved by physicians. That is why Dr. Frank and others who address the condition known as "failure to thrive" try to assemble teams of nutritionists, social workers, and psychologists as well as pediatricians. They make a difference, but for only one patient at a time.

The waiting room was crowded with parents and children Wednesday morning when Debbie Frank strode in carrying a red backpack and sporting a colorful smock like a kindergarten teacher. She wore glasses, and her graying hair was cut short. She did not mince or waste words, and she quickly got to work, mobilizing her staff with an intense air of gentle competence. Slightly harried and tightly focused, she directed a blunt friendliness toward patients and an edge of anger at the conditions that brought the children here.

The first on her list, "Juan Morales," made a grim picture of starvation. Emaciated seven months after his birth at five and a half pounds, he now weighed only twelve and was vomiting after eating. His right hand would not open fully, and he needed surgery for a deformed right arm, but no operation could be done while he was weakened with malnutrition. His family was not equipped to help. His father was in prison, slated to be deported. His mother, unable to pay the rent without the father working, had been evicted to a homeless shelter that provided no meals.

"This is one sick little pumpkin," Dr. Frank declared. She ordered a slew of lab tests, and the nutritionist gave his mother a supply of expensive formula, Duocal, which provided twenty-six calories per ounce, compared with the usual twenty. The social worker set out to find government assistance for which Juan, born in the United States, would be eligible as an American citizen. Virtually all aid except emergency medical coverage had been terminated for illegal immigrants. So, against the vast scope of the social, economic, and physical disease that had brought Juan to the Boston Medical Center, the professionals could address only the symptoms.

Then came Jequan Oliver-Bigby, the baby who looked like a little old man. Even his cheeks were hollow, a danger sign that had prompted the family to bring him in. "The facial fat's the last to go," Dr. Frank explained, "which is why people often don't notice that children are malnourished if they're bundled up, because their faces stay round even if their bodies are very skinny. So it was only when this baby's facial fat started to go that people got worried."

Jequan and every other child received an outpatient version of intensive care—first from a nutritionist, then from a pediatrician, then from a social worker. The process began in the hallway, where Jequan was weighed and measured by a caseworker who typed the grim information into a laptop computer. He had lost six ounces, down to nine pounds four ounces, only 63 percent of the normal fourteen pounds ten ounces for a boy his age. He and his parents were then sent to an examining room and seen by a nutritionist, Mary Silva, who had visited them at home two days earlier. She questioned them closely about his feeding, trying to assemble a chronological account of how much high-calorie formula he had taken in. His mother was vague, like many parents who aren't sure about the quantities that their children eat.

"Any vomiting on Tuesday?" Silva inquired.

"A little bit," said his mother, Jaqueta Oliver. Silva asked what time he had been given formula before he went to bed. Oliver fumbled for an answer and settled on one uncertainly. Silva then asked what time before that, and before that, and before that, until Oliver was reduced to guessing. The nutritionist had seen partly consumed bottles standing around the apartment, so she suggested feeding him less each time but more frequently. "It might help him keep it down to get less more often."

Silva then happened upon the key question, one asked routinely in malnutrition cases: "Do you have any allergies?" No, said Oliver. And the subject might have been closed right there had the father not been sitting in the corner of the examining room. He was a smiling man named Jeffrey Bigby, a truck driver earning six-something an hour, not married to Oliver but very attentive to his son. Allergies often run in families, and Bigby offered a clue. He was allergic to bananas, apples, and oranges, he said, as well as pollen, cat hair, and dog hair. "I had bronchial asthma when I was a baby." Silva was taking furious notes—a textbook case of how critical the involvement of both parents can be.

Next came the pediatrician. Gripping the baby's chart, Dr. Frank entered in a state of extreme worry. "His weight is really at a dangerous level," she told the parents. "I think it's really not safe for him not to be in the hospital. You were back and forth to the clinic almost every day. He could get very sick very fast." She checked the boy's reflexes, put him on his stomach to see if he could push himself up; he could, but barely. She stood him up to see if his legs would hold him. "He's not very strong, is he?" she asked. The parents said nothing.

So little Jequan was kept in the hospital, where tests revealed an intolerance for Enfamil, the only formula that the family had been able to get from WIC, the federal government's Special Supplemental Nutrition Program for Women, Infants, and Children. During six days of hospitalization, he gained a whole pound. "The kid probably would not have failed to thrive had he not had the food allergy," the doctor concluded. "On the other hand, if he'd had the allergy in a privileged home he would not have been dependent on the fact that the only formula that WIC supplied was the one that he was intolerant to. Now, with some special letter-writing and stuff we can get WIC to supply some of the other kind," the much more expensive Pregestamil, "which is a very hyper-hydrolyzed formula," she said. "The proteins are chopped up in it so that they're not as allergenic."

As a rule, the Grow Clinic was able to give families a little high-calorie formula and other food for free, plus $10 gift certificates to a supermarket and vouchers for taxis to and from the medical center. Beyond that, the total cost of each examination of Jequan and every other child, including all the time and attention with salaries and equipment, ran to hundreds of dollars per patient. The insurance carried by Jequan's father paid only $40. The hospital donated its facilities. The bulk of the clinic's $600,000 annual budget came from extensive fundraising: donations from individuals and private foundations, and annual grants by the Massachusetts Department of Public Health.

Boston is a city with substantial wealth alongside the poverty, and Massachusetts is a relatively enlightened state. In a less affluent part of the country, a malnourished child lies in deeper trouble, well beyond the coordinated expertise of a practiced team. And even in Boston, if a parent does not or cannot cooperate fully with the Grow Clinic, she might as well be in rural Mississippi.

"Donald," for example, could not be helped fully because his mother wasn't getting the clinic's instructions on the carefully supervised feeding that the boy required. Her unreasonable boss would not let her off work, so she had to send her son with a great-aunt who seemed unreceptive to the staff's advice. Donald was so tiny that he looked only half his age of forty-three months, and he was gaining little weight. The staff gloomily predicted that he would be a "lifer," meaning a kid who never caught up to where he should be. This was a case where a call to the employer from the pediatrician might have helped, but nobody thought to do it.

Few doctors ever do. One exception, Joshua Sharfstein, a young pediatrician who has called about a dozen employers so far in his brief career, saw a baby with a severe rash one day. "When I told her mom she needed follow-up on Monday," he said, "the mom burst out into tears and said that she would lose her job if she took more time off." The next morning, Josh called her boss, who was a physician himself, "and had a long discussion about the girl and the need for follow-up." He didn't have to mention job security. "Once I discussed the medical situation, he said he totally understood how important it was for her to follow up in the hospital," Josh said. "I got the sense he would not punish her, and that turned out to be true. The mom called me back very grateful and said she was not going to lose her job."

Children often fail to thrive because parents fail to comply with instructions. One mother, who had recently arrived from Vietnam, was so misled by advertising that when she ran out of PediaSure, the nutritious formula that had been prescribed, she substituted Coke and Pepsi. "I told her Coca-Cola and Pepsi-Cola is a trick," Dr. Frank said. "We see it on TV, but the bubbles take away their appetite. What would happen if she just didn't buy it? She said she didn't have to. There are no other children in the house. Added a can of PediaSure. That was the Intervention of the Week."

"Intervention" is the operative word. At critical junctures, the professionals can only recommend, urge, intervene to nudge a family's behavior onto a different course. The result can be especially uncertain with newcomers who are plunged into the unfamiliar junk cuisine of America, and whose insufficient English may filter out the good advice. "My classic story is one about an immigrant family where the nutritionist spent, I don't know, a good half hour explaining to them that they shouldn't feed the baby potato chips 'cause he could choke and also it took away his appetite and didn't have good food value," the doctor said. "And they got it, we thought. So they came back for the next visit and proudly held up a bag and said, see, no more potato chips—and held up a bag of Cheese Curls. . . . These are folks who, if they'd been home in wherever they came from, would probably have shopped perfectly competently in their own market for their own traditional ethnic foods. But they're clueless in this country."

So are some Americans, who also make the mistake of filling a kid with soda, chips, and fruit juice, which provide little nutrition and suppress the hunger pangs that make the youngster want to eat good food. Dr. Frank and her team do constant battle among native-born Americans, typically with "the young mom who often lives with her mother and lots of other younger sibs," she said, "and the baby just worships all the big kids, and the big kids are sipping their sodas, and the baby goes up and makes eyes at them and they give the baby the soda and everybody laughs and claps and says, 'See how grown the baby is.'" The syndrome may not be caused directly by insufficient funds, but it flourishes amid the disrupted family life and lack of knowledge that are frequent landmarks of the low-income world.

One young mother, a white American appearing in a Baltimore clinic, didn't know how to scramble eggs; the nutritionist had to teach her. Families in New Hampshire visited regularly by Becky Gentes and Brenda St. Laurence displayed inexperience with basic healthy foods, as a dialogue between the two caregivers illustrated:

Becky: "Some of these kids don't know what fruit is. We ask them."

Brenda: "They get no fruit, no vegetables. None of my kids I work with get any vegetables or fruit."

Becky: "A lot of hot dogs."

Brenda: "Hot dogs, bologna."

Becky: "We're talking about convenience and history of what has been role-modeled to them. They don't know how to peel and cook a carrot."

Brenda: "And they won't."

Becky: "And they won't. It's too much work."

Brenda: "I got a family a fifty-pound bag of potatoes 'cause welfare, they'll give me free potatoes, you sign their name up and stuff. You know, those potatoes rotted. They will not peel a potato. It is not convenient."

It is not a matter of money alone, obviously, since fresh fruits and vegetables are often cheaper than hot dogs and other processed foods. But finances play an insidious role in a parent's incapacity to provide adequate nutrition. Some slumlords won't replace malfunctioning refrigerators, which won't keep milk cold enough. Some families are crammed into shared apartments where the single fridge is rifled by residents who steal others' food. The needy are frequently intimidated by government bureaucracy; those who go off welfare often believe, wrongly, that they are no longer entitled to food stamps, although in some states families remain eligible even as their incomes reach 200 percent of the official poverty line.

Many legal immigrants are reluctant to accept food stamps or Medicaid or the Children's Health Insurance Program, to which they may be entitled, because they are afraid they will be judged "public charges" and therefore denied permanent residence leading to citizenship. Under an executive order issued by President Clinton, only cash payments such as welfare checks and SSI count against the immigrant in this regard. Food stamps and health insurance do not, in a distinction poorly understood by both immigrants and immigration officers.

Welfare reform has also taken a toll on the food budget, especially through its "family cap" provision, which bars welfare payments for any child born while the mother receives welfare, or for a certain period thereafter. About one-third of the malnourished children Dr. Frank sees in the Grow Clinic are family cap babies or their siblings. Furthemore, while doctors think that breast milk is the healthiest, working mothers can't provide that all day without a breast pump, which Medicaid usually won't pay for unless the child is hospitalized.

To be the mother or father of a malnourished child is a most painful price of poverty. Feeding a child is the most intimate responsibility, closest to the heart of a parent's duty. Other essentials feel less controllable. Even the most frugal mother cannot reduce the rent, but when she runs out of money for adequate food, she often blames herself for mismanagement. And so, at the end of a long string of repeated failures—in school, in work, in relationships—her inability to nurture a child seems a final failing at the core.

Embarrassed and humiliated by their children's plight, many parents become delicate clients of the malnutrition clinics, defensive and easily offended. So it was with the mother and father of "Doris," the only white child that day in the Boston clinic. They were very young, both worked part-time at a sandwich shop, and they would not permit home visits or keep records of Doris's food intake. The staff found them resistant to suggestions, and Mary Silva, the nutritionist, thought the only reason the little girl was gaining any weight was the "jet fuel formula" she was getting free from the clinic's pantry.

Doris was six months old and weighed 89 percent of the median for that age, a good recovery from the 73 percent when she was first referred to the clinic. But her developmental test showed serious lags. "She's not moving the way she should," said Silva. "She is not sitting up, not cognitively doing what she should be doing." One remedy would be a variety of good toys, said Wanda Grant, the psychologist who examined her, but she doubted that the parents had the means or the interest to buy such toys. The mother called the developmental test "a load of crap."

Yet the parents cared enough to bring Doris again and again. The mother, wearing her light brown hair pulled back in a plain bun, decorated herself with multiple rings on all but one of her fingers. The father had a button in his left ear and tattoos on both arms: one, a serpent around a knife with the letters "P.O.W." Tattooed on each of four fingers of his left hand was a letter spelling the word "H A T E."

Silva asked for the food records the mother was supposed to be keeping. She didn't have any. Silva asked how many bottles the baby had a day. The mother didn't know. The father guessed eight or nine. Silva suspected an uncoordinated suck, a neurological problem in some babies, so she asked detailed questions about Doris's feeding, spitting up. She got vague answers, as if the parents were reluctant to reveal anything that might suggest failure.

So Silva tried to find ways to praise. "She gained two pounds in a month," the nutritionist said. "Does it make you feel good?"

"Yes," said the mother.

"Does it make you feel that making all those bottles and doing all that work is paying off?"

"Yeah."

"We continue the same formula," Silva said. "We continue her cereal. Two times a day is fine. If she wants it a third time, fine. You feel like giving her a little fruit?"

"Yes."

"Which one would you like? You'll get only one, so pick wisely."

"Applesauce?"

"Sure, that's fine." If Doris had a reaction like a rash, skip a day and try another fruit, Silva advised. Then she asked if the parents had any questions. The sullen mother shook her head. "Are there things you're worried about?" She shook her head again. "Sure?" She nodded.

After Silva left the room, the mother read the psychologist's two-page report on Doris's development lag and slapped the paper angrily at the words "only minimal alcoholic intake" during pregnancy. The information had come from her medical record.

"They made a mistake," she snapped. "I didn't drink at all during pregnancy."

Class, culture, and language place barriers between patients and doctors. Looking up from the lack of wealth and education, many working poor people see an impersonal establishment of white coats and glistening instruments, of incomprehensible vocabulary and condescension. For blacks in particular, anxieties are sharpened by memories of the federal government's Tuskegee experiment, in which treatment was withheld for 399 poor black men with syphilis from 1932 to 1972.

In 2001, the suspicions were reinforced by the delay in providing medical care to 1,700 Washington, D.C., postal employees, most of them black, after two anthrax-laden letters passed through the Brentwood facility where they worked. When the letters arrived on Capitol Hill, public health officials quickly mobilized to evacuate congressional office buildings, test staffers, and administer antibiotics. But the postal facility was not closed immediately, and workers were left untested and untreated until two of them died. One of the dead had been refused antibiotics by his HMO.

From real injustice fantasy may spring, and African-American folklore is replete with tales of doctors experimenting on blacks, kidnapping them for their organs, draining their blood for medicines. Even if such stories are not taken literally, they form a backdrop for mistrust and aversion, used in one case to discipline a child. An African-American boy in the Grow Clinic had no toys to play with. He asked to color, but his mother had brought no crayons. So he started to make toys out of items in the examining room. He climbed up and down on the table and fiddled with the lid of a big trash can. "You want a shot?" his mother threatened. "The doctor come give you a shot? Nasty! Leave it alone!" So the boy went to the curtains at the window, pulled on them, and ducked behind them. "Doctor gonna give you a shot! Want him to give you a shot?"

Even without giving a shot, the doctor can give offense. "For Latinos, there's a big emphasis on *respeto*, which means 'respect,' and *fatalismo*, which is 'fatalism,' " said Dr. Glenn Flores, co-director of the Pediatric Latino Clinic at the Boston Medical Center. This can set up a culture clash between the Latino parent and "the harried, hurried medical care provider in the United States," he noted. "If you feel that you've been slighted, you're not going to follow through with therapy, you're not going to come back for a return visit, and that will affect your health." Fatalism figured in "a classic study showing that Latinos are significantly more likely to believe that a diagnosis of cancer is an act of God and there's not much you can do about it," he said. "They probably won't screen themselves as much, they won't adhere to therapy, and they'll present in the later stages of the disease."

Language also divides, sometimes dangerously. Tape-recording doctor-patient conversations through interpreters, Dr. Flores found that serious errors were made "if you just bring in a sibling to translate, or you grab somebody in the waiting room, or you grab the custodian." When one pediatrician treating a child's ear infection instructed the mother to give liquid antibiotics by mouth, the untrained interpreter told her to put the medicine into the ear. It did no harm there, fortunately, but it did no good either. Trained translators minimize misunderstandings: "It's time for us to start reimbursing interpreter services through Medicaid," Dr. Flores argued. He and other physicians believe that many hospitalizations, especially for asthma, diabetes, and certain kidney infections, could be avoided if language, culture, hunger, and access to care were addressed—if patients could afford medicine, took it according to instructions, and returned for follow-up appointments.

In cases of malnutrition, poverty alone is not always the cause, but it exacerbates the affliction. Nutritionists believe that a toddler should eat six times a day—three meals and three snacks—but no disrupted family can make that happen. Multiple caretakers can't keep track. The household may not have healthy snack food on hand, and the older siblings may hog what there is. A single mother working odd hours, scrounging for cash, confronting the neighborhood dangers of drugs and crime, may not have the patience or energy to create an atmosphere conducive to proper feeding. One skinny Boston child with five siblings suffered because "the other children would just kind of barrel over him," said a nutritionist, Michelle Turcotte. "It's time to eat, they ate, everything was gone. . . . Where the household system can be a little chaotic, sometimes you need to educate that mother that you need to pay attention to the one that's not growing." Mary Silva treated two children whose complaints of hunger simply did not register on their mother, a supermarket employee whose severe depression made her oblivious to their needs.

"There are stressors in any family," said Dr. Frank, "but they wouldn't cause failure to thrive in an economically secure family. And there are also stressors that are so bad, like a psychotically depressed parent, that even in an economically secure family the child may fail to thrive. Or a child can have a medical problem that's so severe that even in an economically secure family they would fail to thrive. But there's this continuum where the problems that would be real but not overwhelming in a framework of economic security become overwhelming and catastrophic" in an impoverished home.

"Nutritionists go in and find no place for the baby to sit and eat," the doctor continued. "The baby is standing on an adult chair leaning against the wall trying to eat off the adult table, or there's not even any table and the baby will be sitting in the middle of the floor on a newspaper. Or maybe the mom is using one spoon for three kids." The Grow Clinic sometimes gives a highchair to a family that can't afford one.

In Baltimore, a desperately poor city, there was no longer enough staff to make home visits from the University of Maryland's Growth and Nutrition Clinic. The $20,000 a year for a half-time social worker disappeared from the budget, so conditions in patients' homes had to be gleaned from careful questioning.

That was the goal of an interrogation by Maureen M. Black, a psychologist who directed the clinic on the ground floor of the University of Maryland's Hospital for Children. She sat in an examining room with a nineteen-year-old who already had three children, one a boy who was three years and four months old but weighed only twenty-two and a half pounds. He had gained merely two ounces in the previous month.

Because of the clinic's budget cuts, the only home visit had been from Child Protective Services, which looked at the basics but not the nuances. The caseworker's report was in the clinic's file: a dirty house but adequate food; nothing about feeding techniques. The children were back from foster care, where they had been placed because their mother had been using drugs. Now she was working at McDonald's at just above the minimum wage, supplemented by $72 a month in food stamps. While she worked, her mother took care of the children, and her boyfriend helped, too. He looked about sixteen, his head bound in a blue bandanna. He wore baggy jeans, a nose stud, and a camouflage jacket. The conversation went like this:

Psychologist: "Where does 'Barry' sit when he eats?"

Mother: "He sits on the floor."

Boyfriend: "And I'll be sitting there with him."

Psychologist: "Does he sit there for a long time?"

Mother: "Sometimes."

Psychologist: "Barry is at an age where he should be feeding himself. Where does your daughter eat?"

Mother: "On the floor."

Psychologist: "Where do you sit when you eat?"

Mother: "On the edge of the bed, watching TV."

Psychologist: "Do you have a table?"

Mother: "Yes."

Psychologist: "What would it take to get you to eat without the TV? Why do you think we don't want the TV on while kids eat?"

Mother: " 'Cause they be watching TV and not eating."

The psychologist was white, the mother was black, and it was hard to tell how the mother was taking this faintly judgmental lesson. The psychologist urged her to make mealtimes more structured and suggested that the clinic might buy a booster seat for her son. She hadn't enough chairs at her round table, however, so she would have to buy more for the family to sit down together.

"If he's focused on the TV he's not focused on eating," Dr. Black explained. "I don't want him sitting there for two hours. How would the rest of your family feel about eating without television?"

The mother laughed, shot a glance at her boyfriend while he played cute hand games with Barry, and said the other kids would probably throw fits.

"Who's bigger in your home?" Dr. Black asked.

"I am," the mother said.

"You can decide," the psychologist coaxed. "Say the TV goes on afterwards. You can absolutely make the rules. You think it's possible to try?"

"I'll try," the mother replied dutifully.

"Tell me what you're gonna try."

So, as if she were doing a recitation in a classroom, the mother gave the required answer: She would go downstairs, eat dinner, then go back up and watch television afterward. Not only was Dr. Black instructing, but she was also trying to empower a young woman who may have felt helpless. "The first time, they'll whine," she told the mother. "What are you gonna do?"

The boyfriend answered: "Let 'em whine."

"Are you gonna yell?" the psychologist asked.

"No," said the boyfriend. "They'll be scared."

"Think you can give it a shot?"

"We'll give it a shot," the mother promised. It would be nice to have the kids "eating at the table, not hollering and yelling," she said. "I'm going to school all over again," she added, a little sadly. Perhaps she meant simply that she had to be taught again, this time how to be a parent. Or perhaps she was reminded of that awful feeling when a teacher disapproved.

Maureen Black's clinic spends considerable effort on parents' interactions with their malnourished children. When youngsters fail to eat sufficiently and parents get anxious, angry, and defensive, mealtime becomes associated in the child's mind with sheer misery. The spiral downward into confrontation can be very steep and fast, as videotapes reveal. On every family's first appointment, a video camera is set up on a tripod in the room, food is brought in, and the family is left alone to feed the child. "You see an amazing array of behavior," said Dr. Black. "You have moms smacking their kids, cussing their kids, ignoring their kids, begging their kids, being very nurturing to their kids." When the tapes are then shown, the staff looks for something to compliment, but many parents are shocked by their own behavior, the psychologist has discovered. "I've had people cry when they've watched themselves."

One session recorded a mother destroying what would have been a reasonably successful meal. While her little daughter, "Cathy," sat at a table that came up to her chin, the mother sat eating pizza and giving commands: "Eat your food. Eat your food." Cathy reached for a piece of pizza, began to eat quite well, then dropped a small piece. "No!" her mother scolded. "Makes a mess! Eat your food!" But Cathy *was* eating, with an empty spoon in her right hand, pizza in the other. She got no praise, only reprimands. When she reached for a carton of chocolate milk meant to be saved until after the food, her mother snapped: "No! Eat! Eat!" So she reached for another piece of pizza, without having finished her first one, and her mother yelled, "No! Eat that! Eat that!"

In fact, Cathy had been eating quietly and happily, but the repeated scolding was finally too much, and now she burst into tears. The mother tried to save the day by handing her daughter two more pieces of pizza, but it was too late. The abrasiveness had rubbed the mealtime raw, and Cathy was in a state. All the mother could say was, "Cathy, hush! Hush! Hush!" Cathy ran off camera, her mother followed, there was the sound of a slap, and then a little girl's scream. The mother yelled: "Cathy! Stop that crying and hush!"

In a later session, the mother took a different tack and withdrew. Cathy spooned macaroni and cheese, blew on it, then ate it mostly with her left hand while holding the spoon in her right. Very little macaroni actually went into her mouth, and the spoon was hard for her to handle. Empty, it became more of a toy than a utensil; she licked it, then bit it. Her mother had nothing to say but, "Eat your food!" Cathy again piled a lot on the spoon, too much for her mouth, so she picked a piece of macaroni off with her left hand, and the rest fell back into the bowl. The struggling little girl could have been helped had her mother noticed what was happening. Instead, the mother sat watching but not seeing, apparently. Finally, when Cathy reached for the carton of chocolate milk, her mother came to her assistance by putting a straw in it.

Another mother on camera, labeled by the clinic as "authoritarian," spoke to her toddler in an ugly voice as she jabbed a spoon at him. "Eat your food! Now eat it! Eat your food, eat it!" She handed the child the spoon; he just played with it. She snatched it away roughly. The boy squirmed off the chair. She seized both his wrists and yanked him, arms above his head, back onto the chair. She smacked his hand, and he cried. Then she tried to force a spoonful of food into his mouth, which sent him into a blood-curdling wail.

"You're gonna eat whether you like it or not!" the mother said harshly. She slapped his cheek and tried again and again to force the spoon into his mouth. Every time, he turned his head away, so she grabbed his head with one hand, twisted it around, and tried to push food in with the other. The boy wriggled out of the chair once more and crawled under the table. His mother jerked him up by his arm, and he wailed. She wiped his face roughly.

The Baltimore clinic saw the boy for years. He was the sixth child of a single mother who had dropped out of school after ninth grade, received welfare, and was obviously overwhelmed. His medical file recorded a loss of weight beginning at six months, and he remained at only the fifth percentile of weight through age eight. Testing showed his cognitive abilities below normal; in second grade, his math and reading were about a year behind.

The damage that malnutrition does to brain development and physical health is stealthy, because it precedes the retarded growth that usually sounds the alarm. "For a child to actually not be growing, you have to have many, many, many episodes of missed meals," said Debbie Frank. "But the health and behavioral effects of hunger, of involuntary lack of access to food, show up, it turns out, before the growth effects." Or even without growth effects. Even with enough protein and calories to maintain body size, a child can suffer from the absence of "micronutrients that are reflected in food quality like iron and zinc, for example, that can affect your immune function, your learning, and all sorts of stuff," she noted.

The hollow sensation of hunger alone interferes with childhood learning. As anyone who has been without adequate food for more than a couple of days can attest, it narrows the focus of attention. Lethargic, light-headed, then intensely obsessive, the hungry person filters out the irrelevant. I experienced this myself when the navy sent me to a survival school run by the marines. After a few days scavenging for food in the woods, I began to slow down and think about little else—not politics, not literature, not even the interesting idiosyncrasies of my survival-class teammates. The only thing about them that mattered was whether they were facilitating or impeding my ability to acquire food. I certainly had no interest in reading a book. Teachers see it in their classrooms, where ill-fed children cannot concentrate. At Dunbar High School in Washington, D.C., an English teacher kept a supply of granola bars so he could toss them to hungry students. "Learning is discretionary," said Dr. Frank, "after you're well-fed, warm, secure."

The syndrome is not easily broken. "Malnutrition impairs certain very important parts of your immune system," the doctor explained. "Besides making your barrier—things like your mucous membranes and your skin—more penetrable, it also interferes with what's called your cell-mediated immunity, which is the immunity that fights viruses . . . and also your secretory . . . immunoglobulin that lines your respiratory tract and your GI tract. . . . And the way the story works is as follows: When any-body's kid in any kind of family gets sick—a little kid—they lose weight. They feel yucky, they throw up, they have diarrhea, they have fever, and fever raises your metabolic rate and you use more calories. And anybody's kid from a perfectly ordinary childhood illness—you know, ear infection, prevailing stomach crud, whatever's going around—can lose a pound or two. But in my house or your house, when the kid gets over the prevailing crud or the ear infection or whatever, they get very hungry and they eat extra. You feed them second and third helpings on everything. Within a few days they're back to baseline, and their immune function's also back to baseline.

"In the families we serve, once the kid gets any kind of a deficit (and it doesn't have to be from a rare illness, just from normal childhood, what-ever's going around) . . . there isn't anything extra." This happens especially toward the end of the month when the food money runs out, or dur-ing vacations when there are no school lunches. "So that the deficit gets established and doesn't get repleted. And then the baby—or the child or anybody—is more susceptible to the next infection, which then drives him still further down. What generally kills malnourished kids in the Third World . . . is infections. Things like measles are absolutely lethal in mal-nourished kids."

The incidence of malnutrition in the United States is difficult to meas-ure. The Census Bureau conducts an annual telephone survey of "food insecurity" for the Department of Agriculture, but it depends on subjective self-reporting and misses families who are too poor to have phones. Dr. Frank thinks it understates the problem. Extrapolating from a sample of 50,000 families, the study found 4.0 percent, or 4.5 million of the country's households, with at least one member who had been hungry at some point during the year 2006. They were part of a larger population of 12.2 million households (10.9 percent of the country's total) who were deemed "food insecure" because they reported themselves as having been uncertain that they could afford enough to eat.[1] Surveying food's insufficient quantity, rather than its quality, may leave uncounted a larger number of families who would not label themselves "food insecure" but have children lacking nutrients vital to healthy brain development. The worsening problem of obesity illustrates the point that a lot of the wrong food is not helpful.

As scientific understanding of the brain has progressed in recent decades, so has the chronicle of damage done by malnutrition. Inadequate iron is a critical example. Sobering studies have found that children who suffer from severe iron deficiency in infancy don't catch up in brain function, even once the iron deficiency is eliminated. In adolescence, they still score lower "in arithmetic achievement and written expression, motor functioning, and some specific cognitive processes such as spatial memory and selective recall"; teachers also see them displaying "more anxiety or depression, social problems, and attention problems," according to a lengthy National Academy of Sciences report, *From Neurons to Neighborhoods,* which compiles research on child development. Iron is necessary in many features of brain development, including growth of the brain in size and the creation of the myelin sheath (the fatty, insulating envelope around nerve fibers), which facilitates the transmission of impulses among neurons, the brain's impulse-conducting cells. The most sensitive periods of brain growth come during the last trimester of pregnancy and the first two years after birth, so the timing of nutritional deficiency can determine what mental capabilities are damaged. Insufficient nutrition even earlier, during the second trimester, can reduce the creation of neurons. Malnutrition in the third trimester retards their maturation and inhibits the production of branched cells called glia.[2]

Premature birth can be a "biological insult" to the brain, with disproportional impact on black and poor mothers and children. Some scientists see a genetic link with prematurity. Others note that racial disparities in maternal health—including inferior medical care, nutritional deficits, and untreated vaginal infections—seem primarily responsible for a higher incidence of prematurity among black than white women, and a consequent rate of infant mortality among blacks that is 2.4 times that of whites.[3] While advances in neonatal intensive care have increased the survival rate of premature underweight infants, other severe results can impose lifetime handicaps, including blindness, deafness, and cognitive impairment. Among the dangers faced by such babies are brain hemorrhages, inadequate glucose in the blood, and the denial of certain intrauterine nutrients and acids crucial for brain growth.[4] "Infants born at very low birth weight appear to account for approximately one-third of children with cerebral palsy and 10 percent of those with mental retardation," write Drs. Barry Zuckerman and Robert Kahn.[5] Even minor brain hemorrhages that do not cause retardation place children "at higher risk of minor handicaps (e.g., behavior problems, attention problems, memory deficits)," *From Neurons to Neighborhoods* reports. "Emerging data strongly suggest that the human brain continues to develop in a unique way in utero until the end of gestation and that early termination of pregnancy disrupts that development with subsequent behavioral consequences." Some researchers have found that toddlers who were premature babies "cannot be assumed to have caught up with their full-term counterparts in all aspects of cognitive development."[6]

My Sunday school teacher, who was also a professor of philosophy, once pointed to a lamp and asked the class what we thought that lamp was least capable of doing. We came up with a few obvious answers: walk, talk, change its own light bulb. But he was looking for something else. There was no way, he told us, that the lamp could ever understand how it worked. He let us ponder that for a moment, and then continued: Nor could we human beings understand how we worked, not entirely. The mind and all its wonders were beyond our thorough comprehension, he said, and would probably be so forever.

That was more than forty years ago, long before the high-tech instruments that now observe the brain with magnetic resonance imaging (MRI) and positron emission tomography (PET). Using those tools and many others, mushrooming neurobiological and behavioral research has made significant discoveries by testing humans and experimenting on the brains of monkeys and mice. My Sunday school teacher would still be mostly right: The human brain remains a vast frontier, largely uncharted. But the newfound knowledge has also created a new discussion, one with solemn implications for the poor. The difficult conditions in which lower-income people live, their vulnerability to disease and stress, are now seen as affecting the brain itself. Many scientists and other researchers from various disciplines no longer recognize rigid boundaries between biology and experience, and between the genetic and the environmental. The dichotomies are mostly gone, replaced by a holistic concept of mental and emotional development guided by the interaction between "nature and nurture," in the words of Jack Shonkoff, a pediatrician and dean of the Heller School for Social Policy and Management at Brandeis. "You've had behavioral scientists talk about what a powerful determinant experience is, environment is, on outcomes," he said. "Now what you have is molecular biologists saying: No gene operates independently of the influence of the environment. . . . that if it's the genes, it's not immutable. It's a predisposition. It has to then interact with the environment."

In this view, the elements of life are tied in an intricate web. No matter how unrelated they seem from one another, none can be dramatically altered without tugging on strands across a distance. Eating and learning, housing and health, a mother's early nurturing and a child's later brain function are connected. Advancing research into the science of children's intellectual and behavioral growth is mapping this web, sometimes with the microscopic detail of laboratory work, sometimes with the bold strokes of systematic observation. Many findings are accompanied by cautionary notes. Because humans cannot ethically be subjected to experimentation involving trauma or deprivation, "a lot of what we say we've learned from brain research comes from nonhuman animal studies—rodents and primates," Dr. Shonkoff noted. "We can infer, but we can't say that's the same thing as studying [human] brain development. Human brains are different from rat brains and even rhesus monkeys."

Nevertheless, the biological development of the human brain is now understood partly as a function of early learning experiences. The number of synapses (junctions across which nerve impulses pass) increases from about 50 trillion at birth to a peak of one quadrillion at age three, then is halved by age fifteen. Such "pruning" is part of a natural process that some scientists call "use it or lose it." Crudely put, it may mean that tasks or functions not performed are deemed unnecessary, and the brain adapts accordingly. In the first couple of years, for example, the brain can recognize any sound in any language; after exposure to a particular language for a few years, the brain loses the ability to perceive sounds that are not heard and used. "Thus, the child's experience, like a sculptor carving a complex statue from a large block of stone, shapes the child's brain," write Drs. Zuckerman and Kahn. "But such 'plasticity' of the neural networks does not last forever."[7] It is not a perfect metaphor because the brain is not carved in stone, of course, and its capacities continue developing well past adolescence. But early interactions can teach lifetime lessons.

Take a two-month-old infant who cries at 3 a.m. Drs. Zuckerman and Kahn offer two scenarios. John's mother picks him up, "cradles him next to her body, then talks to him about being hungry. John nurses for about a half-hour, pausing occasionally to gaze up into the eyes of his mother, who responds by speaking softly to her son . . . puts John in the crib, kisses him, and covers him as he slowly begins to drift off to sleep." The baby "is learning about cause and effect," the doctors note, "that the adults in his life are trustworthy and can be counted on to help him if he is frustrated or in need."

Another two-month-old, Sean, gets different treatment. His mother "has just fallen asleep after a fight with her husband. She has difficulty getting out of bed and shouts, 'Just a minute, just a minute. I'm coming.' . . . She lifts him up abruptly and puts him to her breast. She stares fixedly ahead, going over the recent fight with her husband. . . . Sean responds to his mother's tension by squirming restlessly, stiffening, and finally arching and drawing back from her nipple to cry. The mother responds, 'You don't want to eat, fine, don't eat.' She puts her somewhat hungry baby back into the crib and goes back to bed yelling, 'Shut up, just shut up.' " What Sean is learning, Drs. Zuckerman and Kahn observe, is that "to be handled and held can be uncomfortable and distressing, and that being hungry and crying only leads to a harsh tone, rough handling, and partially met needs. He is learning to be wary and distrustful of others. Even learning about cause and effect is tainted for Sean because of the negative affect. John, by contrast, may develop a love of learning because the brain circuitry connects cause and effect to pleasure."[8]

There is reciprocity here: The mother is also learning that her baby is not cuddly and malleable, and she becomes less warm as a result; child behavior and parenting styles influence each other. Children with a sense of "secure attachment" induce better parenting, according to research summarized by the study *From Neurons to Neighborhoods:* "The children, in effect, are more receptive to the parent's instruction, guidance, and teaching, which then reinforces the parent's sensitive parenting and, in all likelihood, further binds their secure attachment."[9] Maternal depression can be part of the same cycle: The mother doesn't nurture, the child doesn't respond, and that worsens the mother's depression. "Depressed mothers have been shown to display less spontaneity, more unhappy affect, fewer vocalizations, and diminished physical contact with their four-month-olds," write Dr. Steven Parker and colleagues in a 1988 paper. "These infants already manifest fewer vocalizations and happy expressions toward their mothers."[10] Children's cognitive outcomes can also be affected, according to some studies, one of which found reduced reading skills among eight-year-olds who were three when their mothers suffered from depression.[11]

The specific biology of such mechanisms is still poorly understood, but sketches are being drawn, based mostly on animal research into neurochemical changes induced by fear and anxiety. One line of investigation has focused on cortisol, a steroid hormone that is elevated by danger or stress. It is one of multiple "chemical messengers" that affect brain function through receptors in nerve cells and elsewhere. Cortisol "helps to break down protein stores, liberating energy for use by the body," *Neurons* explains, "suppresses the immune system, suppresses physical growth . . . and affects many aspects of brain functioning, including emotions and memory."

There is some evidence that after extreme stress—or its chemical equivalent—cortisol remains high even when stress is removed. Monkeys and rodents that were flooded with prolonged doses of cortisol became more sensitive to stress and showed increased signs of fear and anxiety, which did not fully abate even when the threat was removed. Neglect soon after birth heightened their stress reactions. Nurturing, by contrast, dampened the anxiety and "shaped" their fear-stress system so in adulthood, the anxiety turned off quickly once the threat disappeared.[12]

One of the few studies done on humans found that "in a population of extremely deprived children in a Romanian orphanage, cortisol levels failed to turn off after a mild stress and were highly correlated with the children's poor mental and motor performance and poor physical growth."[13] Other research has shown that human infants in distress do not display greatly elevated stress hormones in the company of warm, responsive caregivers. "In contrast, insecure attachment relationships are associated with higher cortisol levels in potentially threatening situations."[14] This may be a biological component of the behavior seen among parents who suffered trauma, and who cannot modulate their reactions to stress.

Even without the biological mapping, the negative impact of stress on cognitive functioning has long been known. According to a summary of studies in the 1980s, "Children from highly stressed environments are at increased risk for a variety of developmental and behavioral problems, including poorer performance on developmental tests at eight months, lower IQ scores and impaired language development at four years." Class is a factor: At school age, children from highly stressed families of low socio-economic status display "poorer emotional adjustment and increased school problems" than those from upper-income families who are also highly stressed.[15]

Causal connections are hard to trace, and IQ has been seen as more cause than effect by some researchers, most notably Richard J. Herrnstein and Charles Murray, whose 1994 volume, *The Bell Curve: Intelligence and Class Structure in American Life*, argues that intelligence is overwhelmingly inherited. In their view, people with lower IQs naturally do less well in life, gravitate to lower socio-economic levels, and tend to have lower-IQ children who repeat the pattern. Other researchers have found that twins raised apart, in different socio-economic settings, display similar abilities and personalities. But those studies have not been refined enough to document changes in families' circumstances over time, or to pinpoint the family situations during critical periods of early childhood development, when the twins may have shared key experiences—as infants in the same household, for example, to be separated only at a later age.

The contrary view sees synergy between "nature and nurture," the genetic and the environmental. It emphasizes the strong interplay between poverty, with all its disabling factors, and cognitive impairment. Whatever measure of intelligence is inherited—and a great deal is, no doubt—the genetic predispositions are believed to interact with an individual's experience to enhance or diminish not only his biological health but also his intellectual success.

Such a dynamic has been observed in adopted children, many of whose IQs end up closer to those of their adoptive parents than to those of their biological parents. According to a 1999 study, children with low IQs of 60 to 86 before they were adopted at ages four to six increased their IQs dramatically. Most significantly, the increases varied with the socio-economic status (SES) of the adoptive families, as indicated by the father's occupation. By ages eleven to eighteen, the children adopted by the highest-SES parents saw the largest growth in IQ, to a mean just under 100; those adopted by middle-SES parents had the next largest gain, to 93; and those who went into low-SES families had the least increase, to 85.[16]

In this analysis, biological disease becomes a model and a metaphor for intellectual and behavioral difficulty: Just as a complex of vulnerabilities contributes to the contraction of physical illness, so can poverty lead to cognitive and emotional deficits. Just as biological weaknesses inhibit recovery, so can socio-economic handicaps impede childhood development. In the last twenty years or so, the biological and the environmental, once viewed as parts of a dichotomy, have come to be seen as parts of a whole, as a complex array of "risk factors and protective factors" that include not only infections, nutrients, and chromosomes but also love, nurturing, and emotional safety. "Children who live in poverty," Dr. Shonkoff said, "are particularly susceptible to the cumulative burdens of social stress and the greater biologic vulnerability related to a higher prevalence of such risk factors as perinatal complications and nutritional deficiencies."

The risk and protective factors exist in both the child and the environment. "Within a child a risk factor could be some kind of chronic illness, an underlying brain problem, some kind of biological or constitutional difficulty. Or it could be an ornery temperament. An ornery temperament puts you at risk, because unless you've got a really well put-together, adaptive family, that could put you at risk of being abused—or being ignored. Some of it is hard biology, some could be personality style. Another risk factor could be a male child of a single mother who hates that son of a bitch who got her pregnant, and the kid reminds her exactly of that father. That's another risk factor, as opposed to a protective factor, which is anything that increases the likelihood of a positive outcome. And they're usually mirror images of each other. So protective factors in the kid are: good health; a nice, easygoing temperament; good looking; or that kid who reminds you exactly of somebody who's near and dear to you.

"On the environment side," Dr. Shonkoff continued, "risk factors are poverty, economic distress, violence in the environment, lead in the air. So it can be psychological things like family stress. It can be more physical things like environmental toxins. Those are risk factors in the environment. . . . A single, inexperienced kind of a somewhat overwhelmed mother is a pretty potent risk factor. But a nurturing grandmother who lives in the same place can be a very powerful protective factor that buffers the kid against the risk factor of an inexperienced mother. . . . Protective factors in the environment are: an economically secure, stable family; at least one adult who's madly in love with you, who's totally devoted to you; a neighborhood that provides lots of supports for families with young kids."

Dr. Shonkoff has noted that poor children are more susceptible than the affluent to various ailments, among them mild mental retardation. The evidence is indisputable: While severe retardation occurs at similar rates across all economic levels, studies show, mild retardation is increasingly prevalent as household income declines. The reasons are less obvious.

"When it comes to poverty and mental retardation, we don't have all the mechanisms worked out," he explained. "We don't know what gene it's on. We don't know what the environmental triggers are." But there are certainly environmental triggers, he believes. A genetic predisposition to a disease does not always produce the disease; that often requires an external assault. Because the poor have a higher incidence of mild retardation, he reasons, some elements of poverty must play a heavy role.

Among the known factors contributing to mental retardation are malnutrition; chromosomal abnormalities; infections before or after birth; fetal poisoning by lead, alcohol, cocaine, or tobacco; "dysfunctional infant-caregiver interaction"; and "poverty and family disorganization," Dr. Shonkoff said. Sexual abuse may be part of the equation as well. "We have overwhelming evidence from developmental and behavioral research that sexual abuse affects the brain" when the abuse has been chronic and extreme, he observed. "We know that those kids have severe emotional problems. If they have emotional problems, it means something happened to their brains, because that's where all the emotional stuff is going on. It's not your pancreas. Whatever's going on in your behavior, your thinking, your feelings, it's in your brain."

The analysis may apply to Caroline Payne's mildly retarded daughter, Amber, who was sexually abused. The trauma may have deprived the girl of the nurturing sense of safety that specialists see as influential on brain development, but it is not clear how, or whether, that affected her retardation. "Chronic abuse and maltreatment of all kinds, and particularly in a child who may be at risk for other reasons," said Dr. Shonkoff, "are major determinants of the reason for the retardation. We know that the pile-up of all that stuff seriously compromises the development of competence." And because mild retardation is more prevalent among children in poor, stressful environments, "we presume that the stress is an important factor."

The cause of Amber's brain damage was not thoroughly investigated by her doctors, so no firm link with her parents' poverty could be established. Caroline's diet was poor during pregnancy; with her meager wage and her husband out of work, the food budget was squeezed—though even in later years, she was mired in the junk-food-and-coffee habit. Caroline also smoked during pregnancy, and smoking has been linked to brain damage in unborn children. The old housing where she lived had old paint whose chips and dust could have laced the air with lead.

These intricate connections between poverty and health have momentous implications: Physicians cannot successfully treat certain disease without reducing risk factors far beyond medicine's jurisdiction. They cannot always solve a child's malnutrition unless they get the family food stamps and welfare checks. They cannot fully cope with a child's asthma unless they improve the child's housing. That's why Dr. Barry Zuckerman hired attorneys to work on his staff at the Boston Medical Center's pediatrics department. As he saw it, the lawyers "practice preventive medicine."

Dr. Zuckerman is a tired-looking man with an inventive refusal to address only part of a problem. Some years ago, seeing children with poor reading skills crowding his clinic, he and his colleagues stocked the waiting room with used books from their own children's shelves. Soon, however, the books began to disappear as kids stole them and took them home. When a colleague complained angrily that he wouldn't contribute any more to the waiting room's supply, Dr. Zuckerman had a happier reaction to the pilferage. "Well, maybe that's good," he remembered himself saying. "They'll have them at home." Then he made a little joke: "We should just give the books to the kids." The joke became a nationwide program, Reach Out and Read, which has enlisted six hundred clinics across the country to give a book to every child who visits. "Actually," Dr. Zuckerman declared, "we get bigger smiles—I swear to God—for books than for lollipops."

In his own clinic, he confronts the effects of his patients' poverty and Boston's decaying slums. "I became frustrated prescribing antibiotics for kids with ear infections when they were being evicted from their house or the fuel had been shut off in the winter," he said. "My only way of advocacy was to yell at people, and if you didn't have the right telephone number, all you did was feel better yourself for yelling."

You might think that a landlord who gets yelled at by a pediatrician would feel moved to act. Not so, in the clinic's experience. But when the call comes from a lawyer, that's another story. "We had a child here with asthma, was on steroids, could not even go to school," Dr. Zuckerman said. A nurse was dispatched to the apartment. "The mother did what she could in terms of dusting and taking down some curtains, but there was wall-to-wall carpeting, and the house was damp 'cause there was a leak. Our doctor didn't get anywhere, but our lawyer had two conversations with the landlord, and after the second one, the landlord fixed the leak, took up the wall-to-wall carpeting. Four or five weeks later, the child was off steroids, back at school." In other words, "instead of using that money for a doctor, I'm using it for a lawyer," he said, " 'cause I'm real serious about taking care of patients. In this setting, I need a lawyer to take care of them. . . . The sad truth is, it's my fastest-growing division. I started with one, I have three now, and I have a bunch of law students." Needless to say, medical insurance doesn't cover the cost: Most funding comes from foundation grants and other private contributions.

Poor housing is an incubator of physical ailment. Old paint applied before lead was outlawed in 1978 flakes into dust that enters the lungs and poisons the child. Exposed wiring causes injuries. Balky furnaces lead residents to light stove burners or use freestanding kerosene heaters, which cause fires. Overcrowding leads to fights and stress—and "stress is recognized as a trigger" of asthma, said Dr. Megan Sandel, a pediatrics fellow at the Boston University School of Medicine, who has studied the links between housing and health. Poor ventilation and dangerous streets combine to trap children inside apartments with unhealthy air.

Asthma now strikes 9 percent of American children in all socioeconomic groups, 12 to 15 percent of black children in the inner cities,[17] and higher percentages in certain impoverished neighborhoods. For youngsters with a genetic predisposition, "there are lots of allergic triggers in the home," Dr. Sandel said. Exposure to such antigens as mold, dust mites, or the powdery shedding of cockroach skin can activate bodily defenses in the extreme. "You breathe in this antigen, your lungs are irritated, and that irritation causes two things," Dr. Sandel explained. "One, it causes, literally, contraction of the muscles in the lungs themselves. And it causes swelling. Just like if you touched poison ivy, your skin develops some swelling and itching and stuff, you have a similar thing develop in your lungs." This asthmatic condition, which impairs breathing, can usually be controlled by medication administered with an inhaler, but it still results in hospitalizations and numerous days of missed school.

Many parents of asthmatic children are unaware of the triggers because doctors don't bother to tell them. That was the experience of the Baltazars, a struggling family of Mexican farmworkers in Ivanhoe, North Carolina. Although cockroaches infested their small frame house, the specialist who treated the father, Agustin, and two of their children for asthma never asked about housing, never mentioned roaches as a factor. He once called to invite them to a conference on asthma, said Agustin, "and they would give me some kind of machine, an apparatus for my asthma. But I couldn't go. You had to pay $15 to get into it."

Most doctors don't explore problems that they can't address, but that overly narrow focus has been discarded at the Boston Medical Center. There, knowing that lawyers and social workers are available, pediatricians and emergency room staff ask the larger questions. "I've received zillions of referrals of kids who live in poor housing conditions," said Jean Zotter, one of the attorneys in the pediatrics department. "A kid will show up with an asthma attack, and they'll start asking about the housing, and it turns out there's mold growing on the wall. They've refused to let kids go home. They've wanted to keep them there and advocated with the health insurer to keep them there because sending them home would be exposing them to the things that would make them sick again." Insurers won't pay for hospitalization if they know it's because of the housing.

A lawyer's phone call can usually get the Housing Authority to move tenants from moldy apartments into other public housing units, Zotter said, and private landlords often respond to a firm nudge as well. But sometimes it takes more muscle: a demanding letter, a city inspector, a threat of legal action, or even a lawsuit. That's what happened in the case of a nine-month-old boy with pulmonary stenosis, which restricted blood flow to his lungs. He had surgery but then remained dangerously ill in a house whose furnace was blowing toxic fumes and black dust into the air. The landlord, who lived modestly in the same neighborhood, "refused to even look at the furnace," Zotter said.

She used Boston's strong tenant protection laws and called for an inspector, who cited the owner for many violations. A hearing was held, the landlord failed to appear, he was given fourteen days to replace or repair the hot-air furnace, and he did nothing. Zotter then went to court, where the owner claimed that he could fix the furnace himself. Over her objection, the judge gave him two weeks to do so, after which she went back into court, and got a different judge, who ordered the landlord to replace the furnace. He finally complied, "but that whole process took a month and a half," she said, "and in the meantime the nine-month-old baby was in and out of the hospital." Five months later, the boy died from an infection he could probably have fought had his immune system not been so compromised. Although Zotter considered suing the landlord for damages, a clear connection between the furnace and the death would have been hard to prove. The mother, devastated and angry, moved out.

The pathway from poor housing to poor health does not always run in a straight line. One little girl in the intensive care unit, Megan Sandel remembered, had an extreme allergy to cats. The family had a cat. "We said, 'Oh, you really need to get rid of the cat. The child's really allergic to the cat, and we think that's part of the reason why she had this really bad asthma attack,'" Dr. Sandel recalled. "And the parents looked at me dead on and said, 'But the cat kills the mice.' Clearly the house was the problem, and the solution was part of the problem."

When she and Dr. Joshua Sharfstein, also a pediatrician, did a study asking poor parents being offered housing assistance how they thought their previous housing had affected their children's health, the words "emotionally" and "mentally" were spoken again and again. "Emotionally, no space. Too much noise in the house for homework," said the notes from one interview. "Emotionally. Domestic violence, and also the apartment is very cold," said another parent. "Emotionally. We can't be together all the time." "Mentally. Can't go outside to play or do anything [because of street crime]." "Mentally. He needs his own room. He still has to sleep with me." "Mentally. Grandfather is alcoholic and screams. A move is better so the kid won't be scared of grandfather. Sister is mentally sick."

The psychological toll on children was the concern most mentioned by parents, Dr. Sharfstein said. "A lot of families are living with friends or relatives who really don't want them there, and the parents have to share bedrooms with the kids, and the kids have no space, and some of the parents say they can't do their homework because there's no quiet, they're crying all the time, or, 'They hate my aunt.' People fighting in the house. I've heard a couple of horror stories about kids who were abused by people in the house."

And the rats. "The kids are just terrified of rats," he said. "One woke up with rats on him and won't go to sleep, is having trouble in school." The boy is caught in the unbroken cycle: Poverty leads to health and housing problems. Poor health and housing lead to cognitive deficiencies and school problems. Educational failure leads to poverty.

In a tight housing market with high rents, low incomes, and inadequate government assistance, the goal of improving conditions often means getting working poor families the subsidies they have been illegally denied. That occupies the lawyers and social workers in the pediatrics department, which treats many children who should be benefiting from food stamps, welfare payments, and Section 8 housing vouchers. The vouchers, which are federally funded, pay at least part of the rent for privately owned houses and apartments, but there is not enough money or housing in the program, and the waiting lists are long in most areas. With rising wealth driving up housing costs, the working poor have been left practically helpless, unable to get into the market and unserved by underfunded federal and state housing programs.

The system is also plagued by welfare cheats. They are not people who receive welfare illicitly. The more damaging welfare cheats are the case-workers and other officials who contrive to discourage or reject perfectly eligible families. These are the people who ask a working poor mother a few perfunctory questions at the reception desk, then illegally refuse to give her an application form, despite the law's provision that anyone of any means may apply. It is a clever tactic, say the lawyers, because they cannot intervene on behalf of a client who has not applied.

The welfare cheats are the officials who design Kafkaesque labyrinths of paperwork that force a recipient of food stamps or Medicaid or welfare to keep elaborate files of documents and run time-consuming gauntlets of government offices while taking off from work. "I have clients with daily planners that are filled more than mine are," said Ellen Lawton, an attorney at the clinic.

If you want to stay on welfare, you have to provide pieces of paper proving that your children have been immunized and are attending school. If you want food stamps, you have to deliver pay stubs and tax re-turns. If you want a job, you need day care for your children, and if you can't afford it, you have to get a day-care voucher, and if you want a voucher, you have to prove that you're working. Getting a voucher involves multiple visits to multiple offices—during working hours, of course. Caught in this Catch-22, one mother put herself on waiting lists at infant day-care centers all over the city; meanwhile, her caseworker told her that she had to get a job before she could get day care paid for. Lawton quoted the caseworker: "So if you're on a waiting list, you need to find somebody who's gonna watch your kid."

Every demand for a document provides an opportunity for a cutoff, because no matter how meticulous a recipient may be, pieces of paper seem to get lost in the bureaucracy. "I just had a client like this last week," said Lawton. "She had received three different notices informing her in three different ways that she was being cut off. One of the issues was that she hadn't provided a certain piece of paper about her attendance at a [job-training] program. And she said she had provided the paper, but they lost it. Fine, we provided another piece of paper. She receives another notice that she's going to be cut off. Well, it's actually a different computer system that's generating that notice, so she has to take time off from her program to go and get another piece of paper, bring it to the office. . . . Being poor is a full-time job, it really is."

It also promotes absurdity. One mother, desperate to get her asthmatic child out of a harmful apartment, obtained a letter from her pediatrician saying the house was making the child sick, which technically qualified her for emergency assistance, Zotter said. But the welfare department's receptionist turned her away three times, telling her that she already had housing and couldn't even apply for temporary shelter as long as she wasn't homeless. The mother seriously considered moving out and making herself homeless to qualify. As the lawyer was explaining forcefully to a caseworker how the welfare department had broken the law, "she gave up and she moved to Atlanta, because she said she didn't feel like the system was helping her."

Just under half such cases can be solved with an attorney's phone call, Zotter estimated. One involved the mother of another patient who was denied an application for emergency food stamps. "If you're really low income you can get food stamps within twenty-four to forty-eight hours," Zotter said, "and then they do your verification and see if you really qualify. And they wouldn't let her apply for it. I just called them up and said, this is her income, she has no resources, she qualifies for this, you have to give it to her. And they did."

Blessed are the poor who have lawyers on their side.

Chapter Nine

DREAMS

But I, being poor, have only my dreams;
I have spread my dreams under your feet;
Tread softly because you tread on my dreams.
—William Butler Yeats

"When I grow up," said Shamika, age eleven, "I want to be a lawyer so I can help people." What kind of people? I asked her. "The homeless," she replied. "Little kids need help. That's why I want to help the homeless." She made her declaration with the bright certainty of a sixth-grader whose eyes still shone in the conviction that anything was possible.

In her desperate neighborhood of Anacostia, across the polluted river from Washington's marble monuments, that clear gaze of childhood rarely survives into high school. Along the way, somehow, the visions from younger years are dulled—or distorted into fanciful notions of fame and riches on the gridiron and under the hoops.

Virtually all of the youngsters I spoke with in poverty-ridden middle schools wanted to go to college. Some of their parents were unemployed; others moved furniture, sorted library books, and cleaned government buildings. Many worked in supermarkets, factories, nursing homes, garages, hospitals, and hair salons. Only a few had skilled jobs as mechanics, carpenters, electricians, and computer operators. To realize their hopes, most of their children would have to move up substantially through the social hierarchy of education, jobs, and income; they would have to fulfill the American Dream.

Three of the five sixth-graders in Shamika's group imagined themselves as lawyers; one wanted to be an optometrist; and the fifth, Robert, saw himself "working in a office like a [corporate] president or something or a doctor." His goal was to have the power to do good. "Like if my family hurt or something, then I can go over there and I can even help them out," he said. Running a company, "I'd go over and help homeless people out and give them money and help out with charity and stuff."

In a poor neighborhood of Akron named Opportunity Park, a group of sixth-graders wanted to be singers and pediatricians, a police officer and a nurse, a rapper and a mechanic. Their ambitions spilled over the brims of their young lives. Dominique, the daughter of a construction worker and a hair stylist, yearned to be "a archeologist and a pediatrician." At the same time? I asked. "No, a archeologist when I get older and a pediatrician when I'm a little bit younger, like in my twenties and thirties."

Blacks in seventh grade at the Akron school listed the most visible black models: football player, basketball player, and rapper. Whites mentioned artist, veterinarian, and auto mechanic. Don, who was white, explained why he wanted to pave roads for the city: "The pay is good." At schools in two low-income Washington, D.C., neighborhoods, seventh-graders, almost all of them black, mentioned lawyer, photographer, football player, basketball player, FBI agent, policewoman, salesman, doctor, dancer, computer specialist, architect, and artist. Eighth-graders in Akron said: marine biologist, computer engineer, scientist, construction worker, lawyer, and pediatrician. Professions they happened to encounter or read about or see on television entered their hopefulness, sometimes as a passion, more often as a notion carried on a breeze of impulse. Some would realize their aspirations, if overall statistics were applied, but most would not. Many would drop out of high school; few would go to college; most would be trapped in low-wage jobs.

Their ambitions brought a sneer from Mrs. C, a veteran who had taught history for fifteen years at Shamika's school, the Patricia R. Harris Educational Center in Washington. "They come late every day and are out every other day," the teacher scoffed. She was black, and so were nearly all of her students, which freed her to be tough and candid without being accused of racism. "I ask them, 'Where are you going to be ten years from now?' They're gonna be doctors, they're gonna be basketball players. They're gonna be lawyers. They're gonna be football players. I say, 'How many football teams are there, and how many players on each team? What is the chance that you'll be able to do that? And do you realize that if you're gonna be a lawyer, that requires reading skills? If you're gonna be a doctor, that requires math skills, reading skills? You can do it, but you've got to get going.' " She was treading on dreams, and not softly, but she was trying to tell them the truth. "I want them to dream but be realistic in the process."

For Mrs. C and many other teachers, the truth was tainted with exasperation. "They're lazy," she said. "They don't want to read, don't do their homework. Homework is like pulling teeth. A lot of them don't get attention at home, so they want it in school," and they misbehave to get it. Were there rewards and punishments at her disposal? She shook her head. "They're perfectly happy making Fs," she declared. "They don't care. We're the ones who care."

Shamika was already caught in the cycle of mutual resentment. She was cute and talkative. Two charming braids began high on her head and hung down over her ears, testimony to her mother's attentive affection. Her words tumbled out so fluently that her teacher called her parents to complain that she talked too much in class; Shamika insisted that she was being confused with another Shamika. And so her parents did not like her teacher, she reported with relish, and she tried not to care about her teacher's evaluations. "I got a paper back, and she was being smart on the paper," Shamika said acidly. "I had missed this word, and she was being smart, told me, 'You need to study, gril.' and she put it G-R-I-L. And then when my report card came, she gave me a D, and she didn't even know how to spell 'girl'!"

Children can be trapped in corrosive relationships between home and school. Some parents with little education or busy work schedules cannot help with homework, cannot take the time for meetings with teachers, and do not know how to be constructive advocates for their children. Some had such bad experiences as students—sometimes in the very same building— that now, as mothers and fathers, they perceive school as a hostile place to be avoided. When they hear from teachers, the news is rarely good (most teachers call with problems not praise), so the conversation may be humiliating and adversarial.

Across all socio-economic classes, parents adopt various postures in dealing with schools: the confrontational, the conciliatory, the cooperative, the indulgent, the negligent. At the lower end of the spectrum, however, a mother or father confronts particular problems. For many a parent in poverty, love for a child is akin to anxiety. In the context of danger and failure, against a life history of little achievement, raising a son or daughter offers another chance at success. But that goal stands at the end of a long road sown with the land mines of drugs and gangs, of disrupted schools and decaying households. So, for a few parents, the aggressive methods that have worked best for survival in rough families and rough neighborhoods are the favored techniques of interaction. Having defended themselves effectively in their homes and streets, they carry the confrontational manner into their children's schools. It is a crude form of support for their children, and some of their children imitate the style.

"The first day I came in, I was called a white bitch by a kid, like, a second-grader," said Miss V, a brand-new graduate of Columbia who taught second grade at Kenilworth Elementary in Washington. "I was hit on several occasions by the children, like, punched." More frightening, though, was the hostility from parents, many of whom were children themselves when their babies were born. Among the "very young adult mothers and sometimes fathers," she observed, "if you say something like, 'Your child's doing this and this in the classroom,' they're very defensive because they feel that it's a reflection of their parenting. . . . Sometimes they will be like, 'Well, my son or daughter said this about you in the classroom, and what are you doing to him and her, because they've never had problems like this before.' And we also got a lot of, like, 'I'm gonna come and beat the shit out of you white bitches.' "

Normal teaching duties became risky, even such an innocuous gesture as a note home inquiring about a girl's long absence, Miss V said. The child's mother, who had assaulted a teacher two years before, "wrote me a threatening letter in response: 'If I want my daughter to be out of school, she's gonna be out of school.' " Then the classroom next door was invaded by neighborhood toughs brought by another parent to threaten the teacher, who was also a young white woman. "I feared for my life," Miss V said, and both she and her colleague transferred to other schools at the end of the year.

At the opposite extreme, whites are often stereotyped by African-American parents as permissive and unduly lax in disciplining children. It is an image that emerges repeatedly in interviews about attitudes across racial lines. Miss V was seen that way by a few parents who tried to enlist her as an ally by giving her license to hit their kids. " 'Just take 'em in the bathroom,' " she quoted one of them as saying, " 'and I'll give you a letter saying you can do that.'

" 'Well, I can't,' " Miss V replied. "A lot of teachers do a little of that," she admitted, but it was against the law.

Across the gulf of race and class, encounters between parents and teachers can perplex both sides. Miss V was puzzled to find most of her students' parents "very, very concerned with their kids, even the children that were very messed up and whose parents I knew had been through crack." She could not quite sort this out. "They love their kids dearly, and their kids are very precious to them," she said with surprise and admiration.

If the combative parents stand at one end of the spectrum, the absent parents are at the other, and they are much more numerous. Low turnouts at parent-teacher meetings have become a chronic disease of low-income school districts. "They can live one block from the school, they'll never come down and visit," complained Theodore Hinton, principal of Washington's Harris center, which educates children from pre-kindergarten through eighth grade. "Out of my seventy students," said Mr. I, a math teacher at Dunbar High School in Washington, "at my last parent-teacher conferences I saw eight parents." Even where schools have opened their doors to accommodate the odd hours of low-wage workers, or have offered child care during meetings, or have tried to lure parents by requiring them to pick up their children's report cards in person, the successes have not been overwhelming. At Bell Multicultural High School in Washington, parents were supposed to get report cards at the main desk, then walk around to meet teachers. Suzanne Nguyen, who taught math there, usually saw the parents of about ten of her sixty students.

The absence sets a bad tone and is often misread by school personnel. In Akron's Mabel M. Riedinger Middle School, 85 percent of the children were poor enough to qualify for free or reduced-price lunches, and most were black, Latino, or Asian. When I asked several white staff members in the teachers' lunchroom what problems the youngsters had, the answers were brutal. "They don't value education, values that should have been taught at home," complained a librarian. "They don't care if they get suspended." Other teachers at the table endorsed the contemptuous appraisal. It was part of a pattern in which students blame teachers, teachers blame parents, and parents blame schools. The fault always lies elsewhere.

Ted Hinton, principal of the Harris school, set out to break that cycle by seeing through parents' eyes and getting inside their minds to the extent possible. "They don't feel comfortable in the school," he observed. "They feel a sense that the school is somewhat above them, not treating them with respect, or has not shown that love or that we're in this together." The answer? "You communicate with them, be friendly, you talk to them, you welcome them, you put out a welcome policy: Come in, not only when a child does something wrong but a positive thing. You constantly bombard them with information, tell them that your child has done something [good], this child has won a mayor's essay contest. Put everything out. Let them see it's an open atmosphere. . . . Yesterday morning I had a father-son breakfast for the first time, for Black History Month. I guess we had probably thirty, forty-five guardians that came out with their sons. Those are the kind of things. You have to keep on testing all sorts of strategies to get the parents into the school. Parents will come and volunteer in the classroom. Do a side program for parenting training. We're trying anything to get them into the school, no matter whether it's twenty minutes, thirty minutes, or an hour, or a whole day. Take what you can get to get them into your school."

My unscientific sample of teachers turned up no consensus on whether parental attendance at school meetings correlated with their children's performance. Some thought it did, but others could readily think of contrary cases. Mr. N, a black math teacher at Riedinger who described himself as a "product of the inner city," insisted that he could predict which kids' parents would be involved. "The ones who have a row of zeros, their parents won't show up," he said categorically. By contrast, Suzanne Nguyen observed that several of the ten parents who came to her meetings had children who did badly in class. She thought it strange. Miss V, the second-grade teacher who moved from Kenilworth to Webb Elementary in Washington said: "Even some of my most disturbed kids had very involved parents." Mr. I, the math teacher at Dunbar, found that while the turnout was sparse, "I had one of my worst student's parents show up." A team of three teachers at Paul Junior High, who saw about half the parents of their 150 students, told me at first that they saw a high correlation between parental attendance and good schoolwork. Then one exception occurred to them, and another, until one of the teachers concluded: "There are some instances also where parents have been trying really hard and kids aren't performing."

Teachers ought to get to know their students' families, according to Teach for America, a program that accepts eager, bright graduates of good colleges for a summer training session and a two-year teaching assignment in poverty-ridden schools. The fledgling teachers are urged to go to church with families, get invited to birthday parties, and give out their home phone numbers. "I had dinner with probably over one hundred of my students in the two years," said Leigh Anne Fraley, who taught French in the tiny farming town of Lake Arthur, Louisiana. Teachers in urban ghettos find it a much harder task, but many make the effort.

Mr. L, who taught seventh-grade English at Washington's Paul Junior High, put it this way: "I know quite a bit about many of my families. Some families I never see. Some families I have regular communication with. They call up my house once a week, I drive their kid home, I hang out with their kid on the weekends. It just depends on the family. I give them my phone numbers and let them take the initiative." Of his 150 students, 25 or 30 made regular use of his home number.

Having a picture of a student's home life can help teachers interpret a student's shortcomings, make allowances, and give help. "Usually parents don't check to see if they do any homework," said Mrs. M, a middle-aged math teacher in Akron. "Usually parents are in lower-income jobs, they're working the evening shift, the students are home alone, they're usually watching younger brothers and sisters, so the kids are in bed by the time the parents get home, so they're pretty much on their own."

She intervened when she could. "Let's take right here the first child here in my grade book," she said, pointing to a name at the top of a list. "He comes from an extremely poor family, and he's a behavior problem for almost every teacher." She learned of his poverty from his brother, to whom she had given a few cookies and cupcakes after a field trip. The following day, the brother told her gratefully that the meager leftovers would be the family's desserts for a week, which brought home to her the family's deprivation. She saw her student in a new light. "I think he does most of his misbehavior for attention, so I try to give him a little extra attention," she said. "He didn't have the ability to be in algebra, but he wanted to be there. So I said, OK, let him come in. He's in here, and he's getting Cs, but he comes to a tutoring program that we have here, so he's getting extra attention through that, with adult volunteers coming in. And then he comes into my class during a study hall and works on math on the computer. He comes in here at lunchtime every day and gives it up so he can get the tutoring. So I have him three periods a day. He never gives me any discipline problems. Last year he was getting suspended every few weeks. So this year he's hardly ever getting in trouble." Students try to get attention because that is what they need, like food or water or oxygen.

Showing interest and respect is a simple technique that Mrs. M, who once taught in affluent schools, had adopted as a creed. "I try to teach every student as, what if this is the mayor's child?" she said. "Or what if this is the councilman's child? Not that this child maybe doesn't even have a home or a parent. And if you think of them as special and let them think of themselves that way, then they can see that you have respect for them . . . just taking that few extra minutes to listen to them."

That's not always enough, however, and rescue operations by teachers are not always feasible. Some children are hungry. Some suffer from the constant, enervating ache of teeth decayed, abscessed, and untreated.[1] Others need eyeglasses and cannot read what's projected or written in the front of the room. Others, like little Latosha in Washington, just don't make it to school very often. "Her mother works at night," said the girl's third-grade teacher at Harris, and "may be tired in the morning," unable to get her daughter moving on time. This caused the teacher particular pain because she saw brightness in Latosha under the surface of incapability. "She has a lot of weaknesses as far as the mechanics of writing are concerned," the teacher said, "but her thoughts are very good. She's very teachable." She pulled out a page from Latosha's journal, an answer to the question: "If you could give a homeless person a gift, what would it be?"

Latosha had written: "I would give them a per of closs. To were. Becous thay have nouthing. Towere thay hift to were closs, from out the gobitch can."

In Akron, when Mrs. L kicked "Pamela" out of English class and sent her to the office "for mouthing off," the assistant principal at Riedinger couldn't figure out what adult to notify. "Who's got custody of you?" he asked the seventh-grader. She shrugged her shoulders. She honestly didn't know.

"We had a three-week assignment due Monday," said Mrs. L. "She didn't turn it in. She wrote me a long note explaining that . . . she didn't spend the weekend at her house because her mother's boyfriend was hitting her mother around, and they had to leave that house. So she went to somebody else's house, and she said, 'I kept bugging my mother to go back and get my work, but Mom was afraid to go back 'cause she was afraid he would hit her.' " Mrs. L, white and middle-class, felt as helpless as Pamela did. "That's why a lot of these kids are failing," she said. "They don't have the basics, you know. If you don't have a roof over your head, you don't know who you're living with—I wouldn't care about English either."

"About half of my students need a counselor," said Judith Jacob. She taught literacy to immigrant teenagers who brought practically no educational experience from their home countries. One boy of sixteen did not know how to hold a pencil, sit still, or get to classes on time when he arrived at Bell Multicultural High School in Washington, she said. The youngsters were adrift in personal problems. A girl whose father had been murdered in Honduras "was in space, really didn't know how to deal with it." Other students were distracted from learning by drug use, pregnancy, family violence, and the complicated transition into American culture. "They just get really discouraged if they're not doing well in the class," she observed. "Their peers are working and making money and aren't in school. A lot of them told me that, like, 'Miss, I'm not learning. Why am I wasting my time? I'm sixteen, I'm eighteen years old, I need to be working, I have a future.' And they only see tomorrow and they don't see that if they do get an education they'll be better in the long run. They can't see that, and no one in their family is like that. It's all about survival."

The education that they are receiving doesn't open a vista on any expansive universe of possibilities. Unless they happen to find themselves in a classroom with an unusually gifted teacher, or in a home with an exceptionally visionary adult, their schooling limits them, narrows them, closes them down. If it offers a route out of the place they're in, they cannot see it. If it brings deferred reward, they cannot calculate it. So, as the educational machinery processes them year after year, pushing them along on its conveyor belt toward graduation or less, they lose their imaginations about what can be.

When I visited schools and said I was doing a book on the working poor, teachers often had a wry response: "Oh, you can write about me." Because the United States funds its schools largely through local property taxes, disparities between one community and the next are huge, and the poorest districts, which need the greatest services, cannot afford them. Underpaid and low in status, the teaching profession draws an assortment of under-qualified people and mixes them into the ranks of the competent and dedicated.

"It's real easy to work with students who have always gotten As and Bs," said a teacher in Akron. "They have discipline in the home, they have expectations in the home. But I think it takes a master teacher, it takes a teacher who cares, a teacher who's concerned—it takes something special, I think, to work with the students that nobody else wants."

In poor neighborhoods, many dreams are trampled under the weight of struggling instructors faced with large classes, unruly pupils, and insufficient materials. On a Thursday at Dunbar High, Mr. I was trying to prepare his ninth-graders for a math test the next day. He always worked against "a general feeling of dysfunction and chaos," he said. "It's never relaxed. It's never a comfortable place to come in and teach. It's always on edge, worrying about something: conflict between the students and each other, conflict between me and students." That Thursday, his fifth-period students "were bouncing off the walls," and Mr. I couldn't figure out why. He threw some questions at them: " 'How was your day earlier? What did you do?' Finally I narrowed it down. 'What's your fourth-period class, the class before this one?'

"They said, 'We can't tell you.'

" 'Why can't you tell me?'

" 'You'll be mad.'

" 'What'd you do?'

" 'We played Nintendo.' "

It had been a science class, and the teacher had given up and allowed a student who had brought in a Nintendo game to plug it into the television set in the classroom. "If there was like a school-wide, comprehensive structured environment," Mr. I lamented, "things like that wouldn't happen. They'd come into my class ready to work, because in the fourth-period class the teacher would have expected them to work, in second period they'd have been working hard, in first period they'd have been working hard."

The day before, consulting with a boy who had not been doing his homework, Mr. I inquired about assignments in his other courses. The student had no homework from any other classes. "I couldn't believe it," said Mr. I. Teachers also suffer from dying dreams.

It has long been understood that expectations influence achievement. When teachers and parents believe that a child will do well, the child usually does better than when he is thought to be incapable. Teachers' assessments are sometimes based on stereotyping by race or class, as in the longstanding American image of blacks as less intelligent, less competent. That notion, deeply planted, can lead a white Ivy League professor to look straight at the only black student in the room when he warns, "This assignment will be difficult." Many African-American students report such incidents.

But the reduced assumptions are also generated by hard experiences in impoverished schools, where both teachers and children are caught in a whirlpool of low predictions and performance. "My definition of smart has changed," Suzanne Nguyen admitted after a year of teaching at Bell High. "I'll come to a student and say, 'Oh, my God, look at you, you can do this!' when I know if they were my classmates in college I would never think that they were smart for doing the same thing."

Discouraged children and inadequate teachers make a corrosive combination. Even in Washington's Harris school, which was striving hard, some teachers showed signs of fatigue and inability. Harris was a fairly modern building without windows, so bleak that adding a high fence and guard towers would have made it look like a prison. Only one door was kept unlocked, and it opened to a metal detector that was overseen by Board of Education security guards—two young black women in navy blue uniforms. Inside, however, all resemblance to a penal institution vanished. The school had practically no interior walls, because it was built during the open-classroom fad of the seventies. Incomplete partitions now delineated "rooms" and allowed considerable noise to flow among them. Students ambled throughout, and controlling their movements was difficult.

The youngsters, from pre-kindergarten through eighth grade, came from one of Washington's poorest neighborhoods, soaked in drugs and violence. In front of the school on Livingston Road, a bold sign produced by the city's fiction department stated: "Drug Free Zone." Just before school let out one March afternoon, a sporty red car cruised up and parked under the sign. Two people sat in front. As if on cue, a man shuffled down from the apartments across the street, had a word through the driver's window, then loped around the car and got into the back. Five minutes later, he left. A young woman approached the automobile, had a brief conversation, then took a seat in the back for a few minutes. There were no police-men in sight.

The children brought the handicaps from their neighborhood and families into the school, and some of the teachers had deficiencies of their own. "Describe 3 effects of a snowstorm," read a third-grade assignment. A pupil wrote: "Three effects of a snowstorm are that power knockout, people fall, and cars have a hard time getting throw the snow." Under "throw" the teacher wrote a correction in ink: "threw."

A seventh-grade math teacher, Ms. D, was befuddled by her own course in thinking and reasoning skills as she struggled through a problem projected onto a screen: "Slippery Jake bought a pony for $50. After a week, he sold it for $60. Two weeks later, he bought it back for $70. A week later he sold it for $80. How much money did he make or lose?" She set it up correctly as the sum of positive and negative numbers:

$$-50, +60, -70, \text{ and } +80$$

The total came out to +20. To get into this course, students had to have relatively high test scores, but not all the children were following her, not all were paying attention. One who was, a girl in a yellow shirt, raised her hand and went to the projector with a different solution. On the transparency next to the 60 she wrote, "made 10"; next to the 70, "lost 10"; and next to the 80, "made 10." This had enough deceptive logic to stump the class and Ms. D as well. How could you get two different answers? Ms. D couldn't find another way of looking at it: that the first three transactions had cost Slippery Jake a total of $60 before he finally ended up with $80. Nobody could unravel the confusion. More disturbing was how quickly they stopped trying. Neither the students nor the teacher of the class on problem-solving seemed devoted to solving the problem. They dropped it and went on to something else.

The failure was subtler in a sixth-grade grammar lesson at Riedinger in Akron. Miss B, young and agile, watched her twenty-two students like a hawk, never missing a single squirm or wandering eye. Discreetly she glanced at a seating chart to call on students by name (it was the first month of school). She had thorough control of the class's deportment but hardly any command over their intellect. She had taught them about the simple subject of a sentence the previous day, and today it was the complete subject—the noun with all its modifiers. She told them to open their textbooks to page 345. In the sentence "A bright red cardinal sat on the windowsill," she explained, "cardinal" was the simple subject, "a bright red cardinal" the complete subject. Had these youngsters ever seen a cardinal? Why not "a big blue police car" or "a red brick building"? It would not be pandering to limitations if schoolwork were relevant to children's experiences. Decades after progress began toward that end, long after black youngsters in inner cities stopped seeing only blond white suburban kids in their reading books, there is still a distance to travel. In the same school, when a math teacher had given a problem on calculating a 15 percent tip, she was stunned to discover that hardly any of her eighth-graders knew what a tip was. If they had eaten out, it had been at fast-food restaurants only.

"If I said, 'A big red sat on the windowsill,' does that make sense?" Miss B asked facetiously.

"Noooooo!" the class replied. If she felt an impulse then to make the exercise wonderfully funny and entertaining, she suppressed it effectively. Tedium reigned through example after example as many of her students mistook the direct object for the simple subject. "Have you heard the new CD by Gloria Estefan?" She asked for the simple subject.

"CD?" one kid asked.

"No. Who are they talking to?"

"You."

"Right."

What a confusing way to identify a sentence's subject, instead of explaining that it represents what or who is performing the action.

"Those reporters have been interviewing the mayor all day."

"Those reporters."

"Right. Damion, can you tell us what the simple subject is?"

"Mayor."

"No. Stan?"

"Reporters."

"Because reporters is what we're focusing on." With such terrible explanations, it was no wonder that most of the kids didn't get it. But Miss B moved briskly along, leaving a wake of puzzlement.

One measurement of classroom bewilderment is the standardized test, which has become an all-important index of success, justifying career advancement (or derailment) for principals and funding increases (or decreases) for schools. By that yardstick, Harris in Washington was disastrous but improving. The principal, Ted Hinton, had a soft-spoken determination to effect change, and he was making headway. He ran an extensive preschool and after-school program that kept many kids occupied from 7 a.m. until 6:30 p.m. He had obtained plentiful computer equipment, though most teachers didn't know how to make the best use of it. Test scores, still very low, were on the rise: The percentage of students scoring below basic, which meant "little or no mastery of fundamental knowledge and skills," declined from 43.1 to 31.8 percent in math and from 25 to 21.8 percent in reading between 2000 and 2001. The "proficient" rates, which meant "solid academic performance" on grade level, rose from 16.6 to 19.3 percent in math and 19.3 to 24.6 percent in reading. The figures did not include immigrant children with limited English or those in special education for learning disabilities.

How much true learning improvement the numbers represented was a question that divided teachers who were required to devote considerable class time to test-taking preparation. The emphasis permeated the year and rose to a pitch in the weeks before testing every spring. At Bell, for example, it began in the fall with twenty minutes in a fifty-minute period three times a week, then went to thirty minutes every other day starting in January, and finally thirty minutes every single day. Some teachers found the preparation relevant to math and reading skills, but the math teacher Suzanne Nguyen did not. "Not at all," she declared emphatically. "It just makes them more comfortable with the format. I think it's more like a self-esteem builder, nothing else. I don't think it was really helping them learn."

Some teachers found the tests' subject matter biased against low-income children with limited experience. Such expressions as "the center of attention" and "leave up in the air" baffled youngsters who had no way to interpret them except literally. They tried to imagine an idea hovering above the ground. A math problem used "frankfurter" instead of "hot dog," leading to confusion. "Who calls hot dogs 'frankfurters' anymore?" their teacher at Harris asked impatiently.

"My kids are reading this story about camping," said Miss V, the second-grade teacher at Webb Elementary in Washington. "You're supposed to guess what the children in the story are doing, and they come and they get on a bus with their sleeping bags. My children have never been camping before . . . or gone to camps even. They're not going to know that's what's going on." Their attention spans were so short, she added, that they couldn't concentrate as the teacher giving the test dictated math problems to youngsters who couldn't yet read. "They're just gonna zone out," she said.

Furthermore, when a school became obsessed with test results that determined whether money was received or forfeited, the youngsters farthest behind were least likely to get attention, some teachers conceded. "Kids on the borderline get support," said a teacher from Shreveport, Louisiana. "Kids on the bottom, even if they move up a little bit, it's not going to make any difference in the school's test scores."

Drained of spontaneity, the teachers I observed in the months before testing seemed hurried and relentless. They rushed through exercises like speeding trains, scattering the slower children aside like trash blown off the track. It was easy to spot the lost children in classrooms. They were the ones who were talking or dozing or reading something unrelated to the lesson. They were the failing, crushed, insolent kids who stopped understanding the material and stopped trying. As you looked around a room you could pick them out, and they seemed numerous.

A week before the tests at Harris in Washington, most of the twenty children in a fourth-grade class were getting away without putting much effort into the drills, and the teacher was hastily feeding them answers without requiring much thinking. Most didn't know the solution for $1/2 = ?/8$, and most couldn't read a bar graph well enough to figure out which two fruits to combine to get 100 servings in all. The answer was obvious from the graph: 80 servings of apples and 20 servings of grapes. Two girls in back were getting almost everything wrong and weren't working at understanding why. Neither was the teacher. It was not a large class, but she never circulated to find individual students' hang-ups and problems.

Mr. N, the math teacher at Riedinger who could predict which parents would never come to meetings, was doing a spreadsheet instruction one day. His computer projected the grid onto a screen as he led them through a calculation. "Hold on fast and follow my lead," he told his twenty-five sixth-graders, then raced through a lesson that few kids seemed to grasp. The cells of the spreadsheet were set up to compute earnings after entering the time that work started, the time it ended, and the hourly wage. Mr. N was trying to get his class to write the appropriate formulas to stick into the cells, and only one child, Julie, was getting it. She was one of six whites in the class, and one of the few who had a computer at home. Time and again, she put up her hand so high she practically dragged herself out of her seat. The number of hours worked, in cell D2, would be $=(C_2-B_2)$, she said. The total wage at $6 an hour would be $=(D_2*6)$. Mr. N called on other kids to give them a chance, but they never got it. Julie always did, and each time he invited her up to the computer to press the Enter key, she was joyful. Presto! The right answer appeared in the cell—instant gratification, positive reinforcement. She smiled like a pixie.

Most of the other kids were sullen and inattentive. One boy in the back began to hum; others murmured to each other. Mr. N sent the boy to the office and made a girl stand to the side for several minutes. He then walked up and down rows looking at work, saying, "Good job. Good job. You're in the wrong column," giving as much individual attention as possible in a reasonably large class. But his lesson left many youngsters behind.

Sitting there and not understanding must have been miserable. With a whirl of numbers and letters spinning far beyond reach, the mind would surely shut down or wander to more pleasant thoughts, away from the dull throb of incapability. The fun of making a computer display a right answer, the fun of solving a little puzzle, the fun of learning had escaped most of those youngsters that day.

It doesn't look so great from the front of the room, either. "I use the light-switch analogy," said a vocational teacher in Akron. "When the switch is off, there's just no input and there's no output. Certain students have just learned to walk in a classroom, no matter whose it is, no matter who the teacher is, and turn off the switch. . . . And I try to keep the switches on. It's difficult."

In several schools, I asked groups of students what percentage of the time they did not understand what was being taught. Their answers were chilling. Typical were the comments of seventh-graders at Paul Junior High in Washington:

"Half."

"It's not half the time. It's like maybe 25 percent. Some teachers talk too fast."

"Some write sloppy."

"Most of the time I don't understand, but then I just stop listening because they just keep on."

"They don't try to make learning fun."

What do you do when you don't understand?

"You act like you do understand."

"Nod and smile."

" 'Cause if you act like you don't understand, other children will laugh at you."

Do you ever ask the teacher to explain?

"Yeah, sometimes, but then . . . they get mad at you . . . 'Just stop asking. We've got to move on.' "

"Sometimes, teachers, if they see you talking and then you have a question, and you ask them again, they won't answer it. 'Cause it's like your fault 'cause you were talking before."

If you don't understand the homework you're being given, what do you do?

"I don't do it."

"I will call one of my smart friends."

"I still do the homework. I just do it my way. If I got it wrong, it's not my fault because they didn't explain it."

In every school, students could point to at least one or two teachers who stood out because they answered questions and showed the kids respect. More often, though, children felt deterred from asking. "They give you a smart remark or a disrespectful answer," said an eighth-grade boy in Akron. His classmates added that they were made to feel stupid by teachers' tone of voice and body language.

"They give you an answer like you supposed to know it," a girl complained.

"They won't give an answer," said a boy, "so then when you go and ask a friend, they tell you not to talk in class. And all you trying to do is get the answer, but they won't tell you. Either way it goes, you're not going to get the answer."

"It's scary sometimes when you don't understand something," said a seventh-grade boy. "It's scary to ask the teacher."

You don't have to be poor to have this experience, of course. Incompetent, insensitive teachers can be found in wealthy school districts, just as inspired teaching also occurs in classrooms of impoverished children. But youngsters from affluent, highly educated families have a safety net. If they don't understand, they can get help at home. If they have learning disabilities, their parents can hire tutors and consultants and even lawyers to press for services. As trying as it can be for prosperous parents to confront school problems, it is practically impossible for a mother with little education and no time or money or know-how to work the system.

A child with attention deficit disorder, for example, has less chance for a productive outcome in a poor family than in a wealthy one, in the experience of Dr. Robert Needlman, a behavioral pediatrician. As he moved back and forth between relatively well-to-do and low-income patients in a Cleveland hospital and clinic, he saw the vivid contrast. The condition, known as ADD and characterized by inattentiveness and impulsivity, "is not more prevalent among lower-income kids," he said. "What I often see among lower-income kids is that the parent, frequently a single parent, has much less in the way of resources to help them deal with attention deficit disorder. . . . When you're poor you have to prioritize. You can't do everything. You can't pick your kid up from school and go shopping and get the check cashed [and] also go to therapy."

A family of means "can send the kid to day care and to a wonderful school," and the parent gets a break from the strain by leaving the child with a baby-sitter. "Then when I change hats and go down to the clinic, I see children with the same biology, but parents don't have any money. The kids are in crowded classrooms getting yelled at all the time, other kids with similar problems are yelling. If parents take time off they're threatened with the loss of jobs. . . . The resources available realistically to handle solutions are different. The first kid, without too much difficulty, gets sent to a psychologist, and the mom pays every week and brings him. The second, you refer to a psychologist, but the mom can't bring him every week because she's working and can't afford it. The psychologist is a talented intern, but she leaves after a year.

"At the end of the line," Dr. Needlman concluded, "there is a dramatic difference in the two children. One is getting into fights and gets suspended, just a step away from juvenile detention and real-life failure. And the other one is getting Bs and Cs in a fairly well-to-do private school."

In that affluent private or public school, it's a safe bet that that child will have the relevant textbook for the class, access to computers, and a dazzling array of extracurricular activities from orchestra to chess club. That's not necessarily so in a poor part of town. Bell High had no orchestra, just a small jazz band. It had no gymnasium, only a soccer field across the street that had to be shared with a middle school. Some teachers there, including Judith Jacob and Suzanne Nguyen, had no permanent classrooms, so they loaded all their teaching equipment onto rolling carts that made them look like the educational version of the homeless. Ms. Nguyen's students joked with her as she pushed through the hallways behind her two-tier cart stacked with books, files, and a shoebox full of graphing calculators. Her tiny desk stood with two others in a narrow, windowless storeroom among racks of textbooks and paper supplies.

Even paper can be hard to come by. At Harris, a third-grade class got diagrams of a tornado Xeroxed on the back of stationery from the United States Information Agency, complete with the seal of the United States and the legend "Office of the Director." The teacher called it "renegade paper" and paid tribute to the school's principal, Ted Hinton. "Mr. Hinton, he's very resourceful," she said. In an eighth-grade classroom, $300 worth of new maps, replacing outdated versions from the 1980s, stood rolled up along a wall because the school had nobody to hang them; holes for screws had to be drilled into cinder block above the chalkboard. Outdated geography textbooks, on the other hand, had just been replaced with gleaming new volumes at $80 apiece, and there were enough for the students to leave at home while a classroom set was used in school.

That was testimony to the unevenly equipped nature of impoverished public schools—deprived in one corner, suffused in another with sudden surges of supplies. Harris was full of computers—in two computer labs, in the library, in practically every classroom, purchased with a federal grant. Three new turquoise and gray iMacs sat in the back of Mrs. C's seventh-grade math classroom, but the two-day training she received hadn't been enough to teach her how to use them effectively with her students. Besides, the computers didn't have floppy disk drives, the external drives hadn't yet arrived, and she couldn't get them to print, so she summoned a gangly boy from another seventh-grade class to hook them up and get them working. He was part of an after-school computer maintenance group much like the old audiovisual crew of mechanically minded kids who got to roam around schools and run movie projectors.

At Bell High, however, the computers were limited to a lab that was always full, said Ms. Nguyen, who could have used the accounting program Excel in class to run "mindless calculations that current statisticians don't do now," she said. "It would be great to just quickly emphasize a point with that, and to learn the skill." But there were no computers in her classroom.

Dunbar High bought Mr. I a set of sixteen graphing calculators, at $100 apiece. Two students could share one, which would have been a problem if all thirty-six of his enrolled students ever showed up at once. But the usual attendance was about twenty, he said, so the supply was adequate. The usefulness was limited, though. "They spent about $1,600 for this set of calculators," he noted. "What's missing is, there's an extra calculator you can buy that has an overhead projector setup, so you can project the calculator screen on the board. I don't have that, so it's very hard to show them what I'm doing on the calculator because they can't see it. I have this great tool, but then it breaks down because I don't have this extra $300 piece of technology so everybody can see what the teacher's doing."

Mr. I, in his early twenties, was a member in good standing of the technology generation, but he was not enamored of computers as an instructional device. As he watched a colleague entertaining his students with computer games to teach math, he declared: "I like kids writing, thinking, and talking."

So did Kaya Henderson, a supervisor of Teach for America, who had taught Spanish at I.S. 162 in the South Bronx, a school with plenty of computers, internet connections, and pen pals in Japan. "All of that was great and wonderful," she remarked, "except for the fact that I had kids in the sixth, seventh, and eighth grade who couldn't write a friendly letter, let alone communicate with kids in Japan. So the fact that we were getting all these computers meant absolutely nothing when the students hadn't mastered the basic skills. I think that's the hugest issue in urban or in under-resourced education: that people continue to hold these very low standards for students, don't ensure that they master the things that they need to master in order to be successful in this life."

Her own background had shaped her passions. Like most of her students, she was black, although she came from a middle-class family in Mount Vernon, New York, and had graduated from Georgetown University. "You know, somebody can teach you how to use a computer when you get to work," she observed. "You don't necessarily have to grow up using a computer all through school. I didn't. But somebody taught me how to read, so that I could read a computer book and figure it out. Somebody taught me problem-solving skills. Somebody taught me how to multiply.

And my kids were gonna be tip-tapping three words every fifteen minutes to kids in Japan, and they couldn't write a letter across town."

Furthermore, while the school was swimming in computers, Ms. Henderson had only 22 books for her 240 students. "I did everything on a Xerox machine," she said.

"Without enough books, nobody gets books," observed a math teacher at Grape Street Elementary School in the Watts section of Los Angeles. "Teachers put everything on the board or copy stuff." When the Xerox machines aren't broken, some schools control photocopying expenses by denying teachers access or limiting the number of copies. In Ms. Henderson's school, it was fifty a week, ridiculously low. Luckily, she had access to Teach for America's New York office, where she spent hours Xeroxing.

When she became the Teach for America supervisor in Washington, D.C., Ms. Henderson made sure the program's office there served the same purpose. "All 126 of our corps members have a code where they can get into our office twenty-four hours a day, seven days a week to use the copy machine," she said, "and we run hundreds of thousands of copies on our poor little machine every year." An alternative would have been big personal bills at Kinko's; many teachers spent a good deal of their own money. Recognizing the difficulty, the Washington public schools began to give each teacher $250 a year for materials, a sum that provided partial assistance.

"It's amazing, the money I spend," said Judith Jacob. "I copy anything I see." She judged her school library as "horrible, horrible," so she spent time at a Goodwill book sale. "I almost went blind just looking through and finding books my students would enjoy." Elsewhere, too, many school libraries are sparsely stocked and scarcely used. At Harris, the library was an attractive room full of students, most of them on computers, but the book collection was unimpressive. The librarian, Geraldine Hart, had received a stack of boxed new books the previous year and was leaving them unopened behind her office door until the District of Columbia school board introduced a new computerized cataloguing system. She didn't want to put them on the shelves and then have to recatalogue them.

Schools are full of self-fulfilling prophecies. Schools are where dreams and disappointments come together, where children are believed in or defeated, where lights are ignited or extinguished. In Watts, I asked the math teacher at Grape Street Elementary what problems could be solved with more money. "Practically everything except the trauma the kids are exposed to," he said. "And with more money we could provide services to deal with that better."

A grave distinction was embedded in his answer. Poverty or near poverty is not a problem, it is an array of interlocking problems. If schools were staffed and funded as a gateway to an array of services, as is Dr. Barry Zuckerman's pediatrics department with its lawyers and social workers, then some of those far-flung hardships might be addressed, and the schools themselves might function better. To an extent, something of the kind is done when schools provide free or low-priced breakfasts and lunches to improve children's nutrition (and therefore their attentiveness), and when after-school programs serve as day care for working parents.

The broad impact of that larger role was illustrated on the snowy morning of December 5, 2002, when the D.C. superintendent, Paul Vance, tried to keep schools open. Even while the surrounding suburbs were closing in the face of six to eight inches of accumulation, Vance announced that the city schools would operate, and then, just a few minutes before 8 a.m., he had to reverse himself and close down. Politicians and commentators criticized him for indecision and mismanagement, yet his goals were noble. He did not want to complicate the lives of working parents who would have to choose whether to forfeit pay or leave children inadequately supervised at home. And most children in his system were poor enough to qualify for subsidized breakfast and lunch. He knew—as his critics evidently did not—that many children would go hungry that morning if schools were closed. Two months later in the same city, President George W. Bush submitted a budget that would make it harder for children nationwide to qualify for free meals at school.

I have often thought that the best way to learn about a country is to visit its prisons, hospitals, and schools. Inside those institutions, a society's vision and morality are on vivid display against the backdrop of its ideals. In *Savage Inequalities*, Jonathan Kozol quotes bitterly from Lord Acton, writing of the United States in the nineteenth century: "In a country where there is no distinction of class, a child is not born to the station of its parents, but with an indefinite claim to all the prizes that can be won by thought and labor. [Americans] are unwilling that any should be deprived in childhood of the means of competition."

Kozol comments: "It is hard to read these words today without a sense of irony and sadness. Denial of 'the means of competition' is perhaps the single most consistent outcome of the education offered to poor children in the schools of our large cities."[2]

The task seems clear enough: to make it possible for Shamika to be a lawyer, for Latosha to write her good thoughts clearly. However, in the slums and ghettos of misfortune, in the striving migrant camps beside the country's fields, in the dying factory towns of the Midwest and New England, America does not tread softly on her children's dreams.

Chapter Ten

WORK WORKS

There's a lot of talent that's been layered over with
years of maybe drug abuse or alcohol abuse or physical
abuse, no telling what. But the layers have begun to peel
off, and . . . oh, looks like a little diamond under there.
                                        —Leary Brock, a former addict

At first, the job trainer noticed, Peaches could barely maintain eye contact when she spoke. She looked at the floor. Her words were sometimes too quiet to be heard, too halting to be understood. Her face was the kind that attracted photographers and artists who wanted to document suffering, for it bore the ravages of her childhood abuse, her adulthood of homelessness and prostitution. The hard look of hurt had been captured in a portrait drawn by an artist on a visit to a women's shelter where she lived.

Gradually during months of employment training, she raised her gaze and found her voice. A fledgling sense of competence and possibility stirred within. She began a journey of recovery, and once she was well along, she looked again at the portrait and was stunned by the face staring back from across a gulf of healing. "It was amazing to see what was there," she said. "I really looked heavily burdened. There was dark circles under my eyes. You could visually see the weight that was on me, my actual soul."

Peaches was fairly typical of those who enrolled at the Center for Employment Training, off Pennsylvania Avenue about three miles from the White House. Many were so ruined that they had to learn the basics of arriving on time, speaking to people, answering the phone, accomplishing a task, believing in themselves. To make that happen, the trainers had to find the light within each person and turn it on. Then, after four to eight months of instruction, every one had to be matched with a decent job.

Peaches sat at a computer, sliding the mouse, clicking, typing. The instructor, Dewayne Harris, leaned over her shoulder, gently prompting her to create a graphic heading on a document. "Now, click into your text box there," he said. "No, you don't want to do that. Delete your whole box. Now select that text. No, don't paste it. You want to put that cursor inside the box." Softly, kindly, he corrected and taught. Frustrated, she slapped the table lightly, and he finally took the cursor, made the box for her, and then talked her through the rest of the steps. "When did you last save?" he asked.

The trainees, or "team members," were all adults, but they respected an old-fashioned style of hierarchy by calling their instructor "Mr. Harris." He had come to this job after retiring as a sergeant with twenty-one years in the U.S. Marines, where he had learned lessons applicable here. "I had young marines that everybody's given up on," he said. "It was a challenge." It was a challenge he enjoyed. Like all his trainees, he was black, and he had close rapport with them. He was steady, demanding, and warmly supportive, creating in the large classroom the businesslike atmosphere of a real office where you were expected to come to work punctually, dress appropriately, apply yourself diligently, and produce. Random drug testing was done as well: One strike and you were out.

The job-training program had started as a simple soup kitchen. In 1970 the Reverend Horace McKenna, a Catholic priest, began to feed the homeless out of a dining room on North Capitol Street, and the organization So Others Might Eat was conceived. As each layer of problems was uncovered, SOME added a layer of programs. Many of those being fed were drug addicts, so in 1975 a treatment program was added. Even after treatment, many still found it hard to get decent housing and move into a productive life, so in 1988 a halfway house was created where recovering addicts could live for ninety days in a structured setting while they looked for work and garnered support from staff and peers. Housing remained a problem, so the following year a single-room-occupancy building was added for the formerly homeless. Many addicts had trouble kicking the habit in the vicinity of their old temptations, and in 1991, SOME intensified drug treatment by creating a ninety-day program on a forty-five-acre retreat, Exodus House, in West Virginia. Most still lacked the skills to enter the job market, so in 1998 SOME turned an unused Catholic school into the Center for Employment Training, with courses in office skills, building maintenance, and nursing. Trainees were also taught how to write résumés, how to perform in interviews, and how to speak before groups of co-workers.

"Every team member has to experience a success a day," declared the center's deputy director, Scott Faulstick, in recognition of the patterns of failure that had brought the trainees there. "That's part of the motivational technique. Some have never touched a computer. Turning it on and getting into the program is a success. The first thing the building maintenance instructor has them do is build a toolbox. It's fairly simple, but it's a physical sign of their success. Then they get to more difficult things like soldering pipes and hooking up electrical outlets. There's a lot of fear. That's a major barrier. It's like, 'I've never been successful before, why should I be successful now? No one's expected me to be successful. No one's wanted me to be successful. No one cares if I was successful or not.' So there's a lot of fear about trying new things and breaking out of a shell."

One way to crack the shell was a morning routine of brief talks by team members, sometimes on prepared subjects they had to research, sometimes extemporaneously. A great deal of growing took place during the exercise. At first, the experience was excruciating: the awkwardness, the shame, the anxiety, the staring faces of strangers, the expectant silence in the room, the trainee's quiet conviction that nothing she had to say was worth hearing. Gradually, though, as a sense of community emerged within the team, as the problems and burdens of each were revealed as common to all, the eyes came up off the floor, the words came more clearly, the voices grew steady, the confidence built until adults who had failed again and again were beginning to succeed at a crucial element of life on the job: communicating with people.

Peaches remembered little speeches on the topic of self-esteem. "There was not a dry eye in the house, I mean from young to old, man or woman, I mean, somebody was saying . . . 'I know where you're coming from.' Just having a forum where you could let it out, and letting it out in a place where there's no fear. . . . Crying to myself didn't get it out."

One morning Mr. Harris called his trainees to the conference table for impromptu presentations on less personal, office-related topics. "What does 'impromptu' mean?" he asked them.

"Spur of the moment," someone said.

He asked the group for a topic. "Communication between employer and employee," one suggested, and Mr. Harris illustrated with a concise, one-minute discussion of the utility of good communication in avoiding stress, removing barriers. Then he called on Della, a young woman in a purple and cream pants suit, and someone chose "dress code" as the subject.

She jumped in nervously. "The importance of the dress code in the workplace," she began, and then stopped.

"Don't just spit it out," Mr. Harris counseled. "Take a minute."

"Part of the dress code in the workplace is to look presentable," she continued. "Don't just come in looking any kind of way." She fell into a long pause, put her hand to her cheeks, to her chin, searched desperately for more ideas. Mr. Harris did not rescue her. "I think," she said finally, "I look nice, and I just try to." She sat down to scattered applause.

"We're gonna work on that," Mr. Harris said. "It's not that easy."

There was no false praise in this room, but there was more support than Peaches had ever had in her life. She had arrived "dark and dirty and nappy and argumentative," she said, using some of the derogatory words ascribed to her as a child. "I would come here and wouldn't go to lunch because I couldn't afford to have lunch. I sat here hungry. And Shelley [the support adviser] took it upon herself to say, 'Wait, you can't function if you're hungry.' And she just went out, got some peanut butter and jelly and some bread. We made a sandwich. Because you can't function if you're hungry. That's going above and beyond . . . and that Mr. Harris, he walk with you and talk with you. He says, 'You got something on your mind?' . . . When I leave here I can get on the phone and say, 'Shelley, I come up against this,' or, 'Mr. Harris, I come up against this.' 'Mr. Faulstick, dog-gone it, how do I do it? I'm over here and I want to move laterally in this job, and I want to go to school, what do I do? How do I approach this?' I can always ask. It's family here. It's family here. Something that really I have not had. Something that a lot of people here have not had."

So, it was a healing process as well as a training process. "I still have some of those demons," Peaches said, "but I'm feeling much better." She held up SOME's latest newsletter. "I actually produced this," she declared. "This actually went to five hundred people. OK, I can do something. I created this."

The creation came out looking rather grand on her curriculum vitae, thanks to the wordsmithing skills of Kathy Troutman, who ran workshops on the art of résumé writing. She was white and middle class, but if trainees felt a barrier, she quickly lowered it by revealing that she was a single mother and a college dropout. "I don't recommend not going to college," she said, "but you have to survive." Around the table, heads nodded. They were with her.

When they organized their lives, she advised them, they should think about how it would look on their résumés. "It's important," she said, "to do community service and not do dumb things. And not work at McDonald's for four years. What are you going to do with that on a résumé? You learn corporate rules, service, sanitation—OK, do it for one year. Don't do it for four years." Flesh out every bit of education and experience, she urged. "SOME Center for Employment Training. Certificate, name of program," she dictated. "You have to describe the program, number of hours: 960 building maintenance and construction, 810 office skills. Classroom and hands-on training hours." She fed them the lingo, translating the mundane into the special, and suggested that they read the want ads to select the right vocabulary. "The more key words you can use from the industry you're going into, the more you seem to know about it and seem to be part of it," she said. Typing, for instance, became "keyboard skills." Remedial English became "business communication and interpersonal skills."

As Kathy teased out the details of their training and made a list of impressive accomplishments, they all began to sit a little taller. When she learned that the building maintenance class had been renovating the center, she got very excited. "This is a job," she declared. "Major projects. Write them down. 'Building a classroom. Tenant build-out. Tear out the walls, put up new ones. Electrical work to support office technology. Major renovation of an office technology classroom with special electrical and lighting to support computer technology.' You've got to learn to write down what you do." When she heard about the newsletter, she said: " 'Graphics. Publishing.' Let's call it 'desktop publishing.' In parentheses put 'Microsoft Publisher,' because that means you're really going to be a smart office automation person, not just inputting data."

Then, somebody uttered the magic word "team," and Kathy was delighted. "Somewhere we have to get teamwork in there," she declared. "Teamwork is so hot in the real world. So you're completing projects as a member of a team. I like that. I like that. You can talk about that in an interview. They'll fall over."

The interview loomed as a nightmare. As trainees gathered for another workshop, a consultant named Pat asked which of them had ever been through a job interview. Half raised their hands, but half did not. She asked what words they associated with the experience. They said: fear, trickery, worried, confused, intense, inadequate, questions, and overwhelming. One man added: confident. He was targeted with skeptical looks.

"Sit a little taller," she told them. "Sit up straight." They did. Know about the job, she said, arrive at the interview on time. Dress neatly. Ask questions about the company's career possibilities, the job responsibilities. Answer questions by sticking to what's relevant about the job. They worried about gaps in their résumés, owing to stints on welfare, on drugs, or in prison. "Honesty is the code of the road," she advised, and gave them tips: Focus on what they could do right in the job, not what they had done wrong in the past. Then she took them through a drill using the questions they feared.

"Why should I hire you?" a trainee asked.

" 'I get along with people,' " Pat replied. "I am used to being a team player. . . . Don't worry about criminal history. You just focus on your background that applies to your job."

"Do you have any trouble with authority?" another trainee suggested.

" 'No.' That's a confident answer. You're sitting up straight in your seat and you're saying, 'No, I don't.' "

"Tell me about yourself."

"They really don't want your life history. 'Well, I would like you to know that I am a very good worker and I can do this job in a very responsible way.' You don't have to give a sermon for twenty-five minutes."

"Where do you see yourself in two years?"

This time a trainee answered. "I plan on getting myself more prepared to climb the ladder in this field and possibly move up the ladder within this company."

"Oh!" Pat exclaimed. "Music to the employer's ears."

And what if they were asked why they had left their previous employer, or why they had bounced from job to job?

"You have to think of something," she told them. "Let me make a suggestion: 'Yes, in my earlier years I had many terminations, but I am moving forward to turn my life around. I have attended this program, I am basically a responsible person, a hard worker, and'—again, you have to be honest—'I guarantee you will not be sorry you hired me.' But you see what you have to do? You have to have the mental confidence in your head."

All this worked. The Xerox Corporation needed motivated people to staff mail rooms and photocopying centers for lobbyists, law firms, and government agencies; signed up for a welfare-to-work program; got $1 million a year in tax breaks; and hired four from this batch of trainees. Peaches was one of them. So was Wendy Waxler, the single mother whose daughter had cerebral palsy. The company trained them to operate and maintain equipment that could print, sort, and bind full-color reports. Their salaries started at $8 an hour and moved quickly to $10, with health insurance and other benefits. So dramatic was their turnaround that Xerox honored them (and itself) at various ceremonies, including one in Chicago where Wendy spoke with President Clinton in attendance. "He congratulated me on my speech and everything," she said, bubbling, "told me how much he liked it, gave me a hug and had me smile at the camera." She giggled like a schoolgirl. "The picture was all over Xerox, in the Xerox newspaper, in *Jet* magazine." She then accepted an invitation to take her daughter for a visit with Clinton in the Oval Office. Several years later, when her daughter's condition worsened, Wendy had to quit her job to manage medical care for the girl, who at age six weighed just twenty-five pounds. Wendy went back on welfare, but it wouldn't be for long, she was sure, because her training and good performance record propelled her into a school for computer technicians and website designers, paid by welfare. She was confident that she would soon have some real earning power.

Peaches was also pleased with herself, even though she still felt poor. "I'm a working welfare woman," she declared. "Yeah, I'm working, and I'm getting about as much as this woman sitting on her behind doing nothing. I'm a working welfare woman. I don't have enough money to go anywhere, do anything. . . . She's sittin' at home looking at soap operas, getting her hair done and her nails done." Peaches laughed deeply. "And I'm scrambling like I don't know what. I'm a working welfare woman."

The expenses of work, which for women include not only transportation but usually child care and new clothes, make the transition stressful financially. Still, Peaches found ways to dress fairly well in $25 outfits from thrift shops, though they were out of style. She put aside enough money for an apartment. She started a little business on the side, arranging gift baskets of silk flowers. She began to taste the refreshing breeze of freedom, and she let herself dream a little. "I can go to New York and see it if I choose to," she said with a wistful smile. "Let's do lunch, let's do dinner, let's go to—what is the place, oh, my goodness, I can't even think of it—the Kennedy Center. Whatever. I plan on going to the Bahamas. . . . By myself or with somebody, I'm going to the Bahamas, because I want to. New Orleans, because I want to. And not feel bad about it. And do it and be secure in the fact that I can do it . . . so I can enjoy myself and be a real person and have something to talk about besides who screwed who, who shot who, so and so's dead."

Contact with new, more successful people has been a boon of going to work, say many who have moved off welfare and out of stifling circles of indigence. Encounters with achieving colleagues can revive, broaden, and educate. Wanda Roundtree, for example, who made $22,000 as a secretary in a Kansas City office, got unexpected advice on child rearing from her boss. "She says, 'Wanda, try this,' and, 'Wanda, try that. And don't hit 'em. Do this.' And I stopped hitting them and I started doing some of the things that she suggested, and it worked. And I was like, 'Wow! I like this!' She was like, 'Give 'em those.' She told me about the Rugrat books and the magazines and the *Sports Illustrated.*"

Some employers awaken to surprising possibilities as well. Xerox found the ex-addicts and ex–welfare recipients who graduated from SOME's training center more reliable than walk-in applicants, said Beverly Smith, the company's local staffing and development manager, so she decided not to hire anyone who hadn't been through such a program. "They do the work-ready part," she said, "which makes the transition easier . . . to get them motivated and back in the mode of getting up in the morning." In her experience, training courses without the "soft skills" component graduated workers who let child care, transportation, and financial mismanagement defeat them on the job—"getting paid on Friday and by Tuesday not having transportation money," she observed. Hiring welfare recipients through the good training programs "has enabled us to have a larger pool of talent" and "has eased our training efforts."

Here was a key to moving people from welfare to work: Make the process beneficial to business. In many parts of the country, welfare reform stimulated cooperation between private industry and nonprofit organizations. Corporate executives were given a major role in a Kansas City effort that blended government and private funds, and combined business, anti-poverty organizations, and city government to train people for the work-place. In Cleveland, to make sure the instruction focused on jobs that actually existed, the board of the Cleveland Center for Employment Training was dominated by executives from local industries that donated equipment and hired many of the trainees. In other words, the job training was meshed with the demands of the labor market. This may sound like common sense, but it has not characterized every government-funded program.

Success meant a symbiosis between the worlds of profit and nonprofit, a mutual benefit that sometimes looked like a healthy subsidy for private industry. An example could be seen at the edge of a tax-abated industrial park in rural Kentucky, where Jackson County Rehabilitation Industries, a nonprofit job-training enterprise, had contracts to make appliance cables for Mid-South Electrics, a few hundred yards away. Impoverished white women from Appalachia sat at machines that cut brown wires into precise lengths and fastened terminals on the ends. Other women and men, sitting before big tilted boards bearing spools of wire, laced intricate telecommunications cables, tying them together with plastic thread the size of dental floss. A "clean room" encased in hanging clear plastic was being built in the hope of getting contracts from Lucent and Hewlett-Packard. Completed wiring would have been cheaper to make in Mexico but costlier at most other American manufacturers because Rehabilitation Industries had to cover only 70 to 80 percent of its expenses through sales; the rest came from government grants. The trainees, there for ninety days, got minimum wage and lower benefits than at similar jobs at private firms, where most of them would eventually end up working.

Such mini-companies, sometimes called rehabilitation workshops, have no need to pretend that they are a demanding workplace. They are. Since they don't have to make a profit, and they get government funding to put trainees in authentic working situations, they can often underbid profit-oriented competitors who are in the same business of assembling and packaging products for larger concerns. Everybody seems to win—except the small competitors. The large manufacturers save money, and the trainees train realistically enough to become desirable employees elsewhere.

There are downsides. The trainees are non-unionized, and they are sometimes sent with their low wages to do contract labor inside privately owned factories, which don't have to pay for medical insurance, vacation time, or other benefits. This adds to the practice of outsourcing jobs once performed by full-time employees, which undermines benefits and depresses wages. On the other hand, as the corporations get cheap labor, the trainees get valuable work experience. In Chicago about 40 of the 250 workers in a Turtle Wax factory came from Options for People, a job-training program whose executive committee chairman, Denis J. Healy, was also chairman of Turtle Wax. As part of its contract, Options even sent supervisors to the factory to relieve Turtle Wax of the task of overseeing the low-wage workers who stacked boxes and performed other unskilled labor. It was a sweetheart deal for Turtle Wax, but it was also a good entry point for trainees from Options, many of whom became regular employees with opportunities for promotion. Options graduates made up more than half the factory's full-time workforce, and a couple of them moved up to middle management.

On the other hand, such job-training programs rarely train workers in their rights. The entire burden rests on the trainee to be good enough to get a job, not on the employer to be good enough to provide decent pay and working conditions. No true empowerment takes place, and the hiring process itself militates against the worker enjoying even a fleeting sense of leverage. Barbara Ehrenreich observes as much in Wal-Mart's hiring process. "First you are an applicant, then suddenly you are an orientee," she writes. "You're handed the application form and, a few days later, you're being handed the uniform and warned against nose rings and stealing. There's no intermediate point in the process in which you confront the potential employer as a free agent, entitled to cut her own deal."[1]

Hard against the tracks and sidings north of the 59th Street railroad yard, Options for People turned a cavernous warehouse into a bustling factory, and its big-bellied director of training, Richard Blackmon, was busy spreading his zealous work ethic. "This is our contract packaging division," he explained, threading his way among stacks of cartons and barrels. "What this part of our program is designed to do is give people the opportunity to get their time schedules down, get used to working all day, get a baby-sitter in line, figure out transportation routes, to earn some money, 'cause they actually earn money while they're in this division: $5.15. That's our training stipend."

At a workbench, men and women were sticking price labels on cans of air freshener, starch, and oven cleaner for a company called Personal Care, which would distribute the merchandise to dollar stores. "We basically put the stickers on 'cause the manufacturer won't do that," Blackmon explained. "They'll make the cans but they won't put the sticker on. Something that simple." He stopped at another work station. "This is a project that we do for Dominick's [a chain of food stores]. Our chairman of the board is the former president and CEO of Dominick's, so we have a pretty good relationship with them. And they have in-store promotions. When they finish with the in-store promotions . . . they send us all the stuff that's been used for promotions, and we inventory it and repackage it for them and send them back to them so they can sell it. It's been out on display. You can see some of it is still loose, like this bowl and plates and stuff like that.

"This is an inspection job that we just finished for a company called Owens-Brockway. Now, what happened was they had these fancy bottles made up, and the problem with the bottles is that some of the writing and some of the placement of the language is off center, OK? Also, they had another problem. When you handle the bottles, on some of them the ink comes off. So what we did was a tape test on the bottles. We basically put a real sticky kind of a Scotch tape on it and pulled it off a couple of times to see if the ink came off. If the ink came off or it smudged or the bottle got damaged, we got rid of it. Basically took the top off and got rid of it. This is a good one 'cause it still has the top on. So we're gonna ship them back the good ones and ship them back the tops and get rid of the bottles that are bad. . . .

"Back over in this corner is where we handle our paint. We've got a longstanding relationship with Sherwin-Williams paint company where we help them recycle paint. When they have paint that's what they call old age, it's been sitting on the shelf two, three years and the solid part of the paint has separated from the liquid part, well, they ship it to us, we dump it in those fifty-five-gallon drums, and then they rework it. They can reuse it. So all this stuff you see over here is all the paint that we've dumped for Sherwin-Williams. . . .

"This is a project that we're doing for a company called Kendall Packaging. They actually make these legal storage boxes. And what happened was they forgot to put the buttons and the eyelets on the boxes. So what we're doing is we're putting the buttons on. We're putting that in the corner of the boxes and then we're tying the string for closing the boxes. . . . Now, they used to do this in-house, and they decided to job this out to us. We've developed a pretty good relationship with them. . . . We've got 150,000 of these to do."

Blackmon grew up on welfare in Chicago's Cabrini-Green housing project, notorious for its drugs and violence; made his way through law school; worked in corporate law; and was then drawn to a law practice in juvenile court, mostly pro bono, which he gave up to train people at Options. He seemed to keep working his way back through symptoms into causes, trying to find the roots. "You don't walk off welfare," he said from personal experience. "I mean, you kind of have to run, scream, kick, holler, jump off of welfare."

He walked from the cartons and barrels and workbenches into a small classroom, and there he stood, a successful black man from the projects in front of seventeen failed black men and women who wanted to enroll in his ninety-day training program. He made sure they knew where he had come from. He bid them good morning and led them in a churchlike call and response:

"Everybody ready to go to work?" Murmurs of "Yes."

"Everybody repeat after me: I can make change."

The group responded softly, "I can make change."

"Oh, you can do better. Let's say it like you really mean it: I CAN MAKE CHANGES."

"I CAN MAKE CHANGES."

"Or I can make excuses."

"OR I CAN MAKE EXCUSES."

"But I can't make both."

"BUT I CAN'T MAKE BOTH."

Blackmon learned his coaching skills when he played fullback on a football scholarship to Southern Illinois University, and he gave his charges a pep talk as if he truly believed that they could surely win, no matter how far they were trailing at halftime. "What this program is about is helping you help yourself," he said. "We have absolutely nothing to give you. . . . This program is about waking up what's already inside of you, and getting you to see for yourself that there ain't nothin' nobody can do for you that you can't do for yourself." Then he showed them that they had already used what they had inside. "How you gonna tell me you don't have any brains if you've been able to survive in one of the toughest cities in the world? If you are thirty, forty, twenty, fifty years old, and you've been able to survive in Chicago, trust me, you have some brains."

The minimum wage they would be paid was worth more than their contempt, he insisted. "The minimum wage has power. It is a starting point. It's a starting point, $5.15 an hour, forty hours a week, four weeks a month, $824. How many of you get $824 a month in public aid? Nobody's hand is up. OK? So we ain't doin' too bad with the minimum wage, right? If you and your significant other earn the minimum wage, that's $1,648 a month. How many of y'all get $1,648 a month? We understand each other then, right? Don't knock the minimum wage. It's a starting point.

"How many in the room right now got $500 in a savings account? One person, two people got their hands up. How you gonna be grown in Chicago with kids and responsibilities and you can't get your hands on $500? Anything could happen. One of the things that you're gonna learn through this program is the importance of saving money. I'm gonna show you how you can save $10 a week so at the end of the year you have $500. We got to talk about it. You have to save some money. See, the key to saving is not saving a whole lot at one time, just saving a little bit over a long period of time. So we got to talk about that."

He wanted them to rally to their own cause: themselves. "This program is about change. It's about changing your life for the better, and if you don't want that, this is not for you. This is not for you. We can't help you, because we have nothing to give you. Everything you need you already got. We just here to help you recognize that. We just here to help you recognize that."

It took only a few minutes with Ricky Drake to see how smart he was. He flipped through his thick black loose-leaf notebook to explain the math and geometry and engineering diagrams, then took me on a tour across the metal floor of Cleveland's Center for Employment Training, an old factory filled with equipment donated by manufacturers that needed skilled workers. He could run every olive-drab lathe, every drill press and precision grinder. He handled the micrometers and calipers, the tools of his new machinist's trade, with dexterity. He was two-thirds of the way through a six-month course, a bull of a man charged with so much drive and newfound expertise that it was hard to imagine that he had ever done anything except excel.

He had, though. Here was his short version of his life: "I came from a family where my father was very strict, and when he disciplined us he had a wooden slat for the boys, one long, one short. And eventually that affected me, and the [military] service thing affected me. And I had to address those problems. And thinking spiritually and with God, I began to say, 'Well, I can do something better than this and just get ahold of it.' "

As he grew up black and poor, his opportunities did not strike him as dazzling. He was "a little rebellious," so in 1968 he ran away and joined the army. When the army learned that he was only sixteen, they asked and got his father to sign a permission form, and Ricky went off to the Vietnam War—twice. He worked as a cable splicer, field lineman, and radio operator, which brought him an odd sense of freedom and independence. "I should have made a career out of it," he said. He conversed with monks, experimented with Buddhism and yoga, and also with marijuana and cocaine to the point where he had to be put in a military hospital for detoxification. In 1973, when he returned to "the world," as GIs in Vietnam used to call home, he found nothing more than scattered jobs that seemed to evaporate as each one's trial period was about to end. "Just before you hit ninety days, no job," he said, "and you go back to the labor pool. They might not have anything in there, and then you might go be a laborer. You might go work on a truck delivering or something, or the next day come down there they just need somebody to do electrical maintenance. It was over and over, over and over. Then when you go apply for a job, what experience have you had? If I had two months of just menial labor and stuff like that, that's no experience." His affinity for drugs and alcohol overwhelmed him.

Several months after he showed me around the Center for Employment Training, I visited him at home, in a faded Cleveland neighborhood, once middle class. On a corner stood his brick, two-family house, which he and his wife had bought a decade earlier for $40,000. They had nearly lost it because of financial problems. It looked run-down in a comfortable way. When I arrived, Ricky came outside, crossed the street to two young women who were talking, and gave one of them a dime for a cigarette—the sign of a man who was pretending to have quit smoking, I told him. "How did you know?" he asked with a grin.

He had just painted his living room, which was very dark, heavily curtained. He had installed a ceiling fan and was sanding and refinishing the floors. He planned to put a bathroom in the basement. He was getting things together, taking control of himself, but he had worries. He worried about his son, twenty-five, with no job besides belonging to a rap group that had just made a CD but was now disintegrating. He worried about his daughter, eighteen and unmarried, who had a five-month-old; toys and a booster seat were in a corner. He worried about his other daughter, twelve, who had a short attention span and behavioral problems in school. He was determined not to worry about himself.

"I tried the devil," he said. "Drinking, alcohol, drugs, womanizing, you know, it just got so bad, and then I knew the next thing I'd either be dead—someone would kill me or I'd kill somebody, and I didn't want to live that type of life. . . . As you're growing up, you try things for kicks and stuff, but you're supposed to get mature enough to move on and, you know. You try beer, or you try a joint, or you try a cigarette, you know, but as you grow up, those are things you try as you're growing up. These are phases you go through, and you're supposed to become mature enough to move on and learn from mistakes. Some people learn quicker than others. . . . You have choices."

The choice he finally made took him to two sources of salvation, as he saw it: God and work. "Before, I was in different churches: Catholic, Islam, Lutheran. I've studied Masonary," he added, putting his own twist on the word. "I've studied theology, philosophy." For the last couple of years, he had found a place in a Baptist church. But work seemed his most devoted passion. After the job training, he got a starting position for $7 an hour as an apprentice machinist at a plant that made parts for lawn mowers, snow blowers, and the like. "They might make just a piece of it, a catch, a lever, a spring," he said. "They send it back to my department, we might just drill two or three holes where it has to take a specific tolerance, and you may have to de-burr it or you might have to ream it, stuff like that." A year later he was making $8.50 in a steel plant operating a machine that slit metal coil. As a trained machinist, he had a skill to sell, and in the depth of the recession in 2003 he had risen to $9.50 with another steel company that was sending him to school in hydraulics and industrial maintenance. If he stuck with it, he could eventually earn twice as much.

But it wasn't just the potential pay that was making work work for him. It was the process of repair that had begun. He now had focus. He took courses at a community college to upgrade his skills. He got up every morning at 4, caught the 5:40 bus for work, arrived at the plant by 6:30 so he had a little time to read before his shift began at 7, then spent most evenings in classes until 9 or 10.

He did not seem to have time to speak respectfully to his wife, Delores, at least during my brief visit. Even in front of a stranger, his tone was brusque, condescending. When she came home from her job as a food service worker in a hospital, her head was bound in a red bandanna, her frail frame draped in a black leather jacket; she wore white slacks. She sat perched on the edge of an overstuffed couch, and offered her view of Ricky's reform. In the worst time, she said slowly, they had been separated for two years. Then, from the bottom, he came back, and every step of job training was like the rung of a ladder upward. "When a person as he is could support his family," she explained, "then it kind of calms him down and puts him in a better position. That program was the best thing that happened to him." How did she explain his turnaround? "We knew that we had to get back on track with God," she said. "As we came together with God, then God started telling him what he had to do for his family, and then He started telling me what I had to do for my family and my husband." Didn't she give Ricky credit? "We give all the credit to God. We can't even take no credit for the job, for the training, because the way he found the training, it was by God's grace, and the way He bring us together and bless him with the job and then gonna take him another level where he can really make what he really want to make to take care of his family. Yeah." I told her how impressive Ricky had been giving me a tour of the Center for Employment Training.

"Really?" she said, a lilt of surprise in her voice.

Ricky didn't argue. "I take one day at a time, I talk with God, I talk with Him when I go to sleep, I talk with Him when I wake up. I say, 'God, you know the situation I'm in. Help me and keep me straight.' . . . And then He say He help fight off the devil. Now, if you don't put yourself in that situation, you don't have to be fighting too much. If you don't stand around the corner with dope addicts, you won't be tempted. You know what I'm saying? So I know that helps. At first I was hesitant, but as I kept going and going, I relied more and more on Him, and then I was able to put my life in a structure where it was just me and Him, one-on-one. And I didn't have to put my confidence in Joe Blow or nobody."

Leary Brock had been playing hooky, and her mother knew it. On that particular day, however, she left Anacostia High School on time, after the last class, and began to walk home through the struggling black district beyond the southeastern shore of Washington, D.C.'s grimy Anacostia River. It was less than a mile to the small house owned by her parents. A man named Earl was following.

Leary's name was pronounced le-REE, like a small bird singing, and her spoken words sometimes had the rhythm of poetry. She had a fervent gaze, and her light skin, like her mother's, distinguished her from most other African-Americans in her neighborhood. She was restless against the confines of school, family, community. She wanted to defy, seek, and wander, and so she crossed boundaries. "I used to try to interest her in taking law," said her mother laughingly. "The reason I told her she'd be a good lawyer is 'cause she's such a big liar."

Earl, in his late twenties or early thirties, had been hanging around outside the school. He had been watching Leary. On this day, he pulled his car up beside her, jumped out, grabbed her arms, twisted them behind her back, and shoved her inside. He hit her, drove her to Washington's red light district on 14th Street, and forced her into a grubby rooming house. "I remember this big, fat greasy Italian-looking dude signing him in and giving him a key," she said years later. "He tied my hands to a bed top, told me I could scream as loud as I wanted and nobody would help me." She did, and he was right. As he raped her, she heard laughter. If she told anyone, he promised, he would kill her and her parents, and she believed him. "I was pretty damaged goods." Then he actually drove her home.

Leary did not tell, not then. She was afraid both for her parents and of her parents. She was sure that she would be blamed by her mother, Velma, who knew that she was cutting school and suspected that she was doing drugs. A wall had gone up between them, and more than thirty years later its remnants still divided their recollections. "She probably was in drugs to make her act the way she was acting," Velma speculated. "She started going around with a white boy, and sometimes they get in drugs real early, and I think that was happening."

"No," Leary declared.

"She must have not been just coming from school, because she would have told me," Velma insisted. "She knew that I would be upset, because she was where she wasn't supposed to be." No, Leary countered: Although she cut a lot of classes, she hadn't that day. And if she had told her mother about the rape? "Oh, it's hard to say now what my reaction would have been," Velma admitted. "I might have been so mad at her for not being where she was supposed to be—I don't know, really."

"I thought it was my fault, of course, you know the scenario," said Leary. "When I had my miscarriage because of the rape, she wouldn't even come." Her father did, though. He spoiled her, Velma complained with a smile.

Leary then made a choice, and like many choices that teenagers make, this one seemed less momentous than it turned out to be. Instead of finishing school, she moved to New York City. "I had every opportunity to do it another way, and I chose to run," she observed years later. "I was running away from my mother's scorn."

In Manhattan, selling magazines door-to-door, "I ran into some people that invited me to stay with them, because they knew where I was going, what this thing was leading to. . . . That family was what introduced me to a world I did not know before. . . . These people was doing hard stuff, you know. They were sniffing. See, at that age, you take a young girl to an after-hours joint where everybody's sitting around with these black lights—you remember the sixties with these black lights?—and people bringing you the drugs on a $20 bill. Oh, man, you know. I'm like, what is this? And I'm seeing how classy people are dressed and whatnot, not knowing of course, at that age, that that was not class. But that was my beginning. That's when I took my first snort, in that club. I'll never forget it. From snorting, I went to skin popping, from skin popping to mainlining. Heroin. At least two or three years." The drugs helped her "escape the ghosts."

Her parents traveled to New York to try to rescue her, but not until she got pregnant did she want rescuing. She would not do drugs while carrying a baby. "I came off of it cold turkey," she said. "I was twenty by then, and I came home. I tried to clean up my life and did the right thing." She was relieved to hear that Earl could do her no more harm; he had been killed by his wife. "She didn't do no jail time."

Leary's old neighborhood in Washington was a bad place for kicking the habit. "Somehow or other, I started getting back into the same group, because you know once you've been in that lifestyle, that lifestyle is a habit," she said. "Those are the people that you have to eliminate from your life. If you don't want a hot dog, you don't go around a hot dog stand, 'cause the aroma's gonna get you—or you're gonna run into somebody who's gonna buy you one. So that was how it was in my life: on and off, on and off. I would stop for years and then get around people who were in that lifestyle and go right back into it." When she went back into it in Washington, she discovered a new pleasure: crack cocaine.

The introduction came from a co-worker at a school for the mentally and physically handicapped where Leary taught food service skills. It was not a bad job, and she was good with young people, she thought. Her prospects were limited without a high school diploma, and her work record was fragmented by her repeated binges on drugs. But here she was doing well—until her associate, whose husband sold cocaine powder, invited her over one weekend. "We were sitting around having drinks just chit-chatting," Leary recalled. "A thing came over the news about crack cocaine, and I said, 'Why do people do that?' Curiosity killed the cat. She said, 'Yeah, it's really something up there in New York. I've had it once or twice.' And she said, 'You want some?' I said, 'No, I'd be afraid to take it.' She said, 'There ain't nothing to it.' She went back in the back. Before the night was over she had gone through $1,200 of her husband's cocaine powder, trying to make this crack. We wound up having to go out on the street and buy it. That was the beginning. I can pinpoint. That was the beginning. Then it was like every weekend. I had it to the point where I kept the demon at bay for a whole week, but on the weekend I had to be at her house, you know, 'cause I was beginning to get this desire, my brain was wanting it." She was in her thirties, unmarried, with four children by four different men.

"I called it the terminator, that crack cocaine, because it didn't have any physical hold on you. It's a mental hold, a psychological hold, a habitual hold; you don't physically need it. It hits a portion of the brain that has never experienced this sensation before. And when it's awakened, you can't put it to sleep. I'm serious. It's ability that you didn't know you possessed. Now you can become a fast thinker, you're motivated to do this, that, and the other. This is only an allure, because this portion of the brain is not functioning on that level, but it's being stimulated at that level for fifteen or twenty minutes, and then it's really a crash. Oh, no, no, no, no. The brain wants to go back there. All right? It wants to feel that sensation again, and it will make you forget sleep, food, clothes, anything that you normally would do. It just slams that shut. You have to go THERE! It's worse than a physical addiction. . . . It stripped me totally of who I was. It held my spirit in bondage, begging to come out, and it couldn't. It arrested every part of my life and then began to terminate it. *I* no longer existed. *It* did."

She started being late to work, then absent. "They saw a change in my behavior and they figured where there is a problem, 'Let's let her go,' " she said. "I'm glad that they got me out of there before I committed a crime."

She did commit a crime, many times. "I sold it for a little while, me and this Italian guy," she said, "and then we went to Pennsylvania. Believe it or not, I stopped for a whole five years, because the Amish that I lived around, they were able to give me herbs and things that were soothing enough to my lifestyle." She worked two jobs, and felt safely removed from the world of crack. "Little did I know. That stuff is everywhere," she said. "It's everywhere. I'm serious, man, I'm telling you. It may be around the corner—I'm sure it is right around the corner from the Vatican. It raised its ugly head, and with this Italian guy, when we put our two heads together, we were dangerous. We drove to New York, to 143rd and Broadway, bought us a package and started our own business."

Leary bounced relentlessly back and forth between drugs and jobs, often mixing both together. "The weekends started to overlap into Monday, and then Monday into Tuesday," she recalled. "Next thing you know I turned around and it was Thursday and I hadn't been to work. . . . I came on home to my mother's and father's." She used what she had learned about horses from the Amish to get work as a groomer at a Maryland racetrack, where she thought the careful state regulation would keep narcotics out. "Little did I know, the drug is everywhere," she said. "I'm thinking I'm running away from it."

Her methods of financing her drug use became an index of decline. "At first, I had money in the bank," she explained. "I had friends. Oh, I lived the high style. I didn't know nothing about the street life until much later on. I was always catered to and given stuff. I'd be sitting around with bundles of the stuff, you know, traveling up and down from here to Florida. I was gone, I was doing things, I was a mover and a groover, and it was, again, the glamorous life—the life that I had seen when I was younger I was seeing now. That was a trap. The devil is so, so clever, OK? He disguised it with all this glamour and all this other stuff going on. There's so much coming at you, you don't see the snakes slither in. . . . When the money ran out, when the friends ran out, I had to do it on my own. And because I had a networking ability, I was able to get with people who was trying to be incognito about this drug. . . . I was their go-between. That was one way I was able to make my supply. They would give me the money 'cause they could not go out and get it, and I would go get it for them, and

I would get a portion from the drug dealer, a portion from them. I believe because I wasn't larceny-hearted, is why I'm still alive." She once had a near miss when dealers burst into a rival's apartment where she was staying, started shooting, and hit her in the back. Ultimately, she turned to prostitution for her drug money.

Mostly, Velma took care of Leary's children, as so many grandmothers do in such families, and when Velma's grandchildren had children, she took care of those great-grandchildren as well. Velma was bone tired, and sometimes angry about the generations that passed their burdens to her, but she also had an iron spine. She admired obstinacy, drawn from her earliest childhood memories in the hard South. Her grandmother and her grandmother's sister, who were born in slavery, used to reminisce about the steely resistance of their aunt, Leary's great-great-great aunt. "The slaveowner would tell her to do something, and she said she wasn't gonna do it, and he would beat her and beat her, and she said she still wasn't gonna do it, and so he'd put her down in a cistern, a well," Velma recounted. "She never would do it. She was just that stubborn. Just let him beat her."

In its own way, Velma's journey had been as daring as Leary's, propelling her out of the familiar into the adventurous, though with far different consequences. One of eight children on a sharecropper's farm in Alabama, she left in 1940, in her twenties, and made her way alone through Tennessee to Washington, where she found a good husband, a good job in the printing section of the Agriculture Department, and a place in an undergraduate class at Howard University, although she never finished. Her husband, Horace, was an electrician for the Veterans Administration. Leary, even at age fifty, imagined that he had worked in the White House.

Off drugs and on, Leary appeared and disappeared, and each arrival seemed worse than the last. "It got to the point that I wouldn't even allow her in the house," Velma declared, "and she would somehow break in the house. I called the police and explained it to them. . . . She'd come in the house to sleep. So the police told her she had to leave 'cause I didn't want her here. . . . I said, 'No, if you're foolin' with that you can't stay here.' It was hard to do, hard to say it. It hurt me to see the police leadin' her away and all."

Her father never quite gave up on her, Leary remembered. The last time she saw him, she promised that someday he would be proud of her, and he told her that he was proud of her now, "as though he saw in the future," she recalled. "All he wished for me was that I would be happy and safe," Leary said, "and that was a profound statement: happy and safe. If you look at it, if you're not safe, you're unhappy. If you're not happy, you're in unsafe territory."

Then, at a time when she was out on the street doing drugs, her father died. One of her daughters found her and took her the news.

"She got the word that he had passed, and when the funeral was gonna be and everything," Velma recalled, "and she put a note in the door that she would be coming by to go with us. And so you know the funeral cars can't wait for you. So we went on, and to my surprise, people at church told me she was there. . . . She just stayed back in the back and left before we went out."

"That was my spirit," Leary countered. "I couldn't go. . . . Shame. Guilt. He was my best friend. I had to deal with my own grief the way I knew how. That was the beginning of the turning point for me." You have to hit bottom before you come up.

Several months later, in the haze of a high, she spotted an undercover cop in an unmarked car, walked up to the driver's window and said, "Look in your computer for Leary Brock."

"You Leary Brock?" he asked.

"Just look in your computer."

He did and found two outstanding warrants: failure to appear on solicitation charges, and on felony drug possession.

"Are you Leary Brock?"

When she answered yes, he called for a female officer as backup. "I was in jail during Easter," Leary said.

Having stepped into the maw of the judicial system, Leary had placed herself in extreme jeopardy. She could not afford a lawyer. She had no defense, anyway, because the charges were true. She was black, addicted, homeless without the friends or connections or even the know-how to beat the rap or make a savvy plea bargain. When she stepped into the courtroom, she was sure that she was going away to a perverse salvation from the drug-infested streets.

She got salvation of a different kind, perhaps by some random quirk of chance, perhaps because she was finally ready for a different outcome. The District of Columbia had begun an experiment. Instead of jailing firsttime drug offenders (meaning the first time they were caught), those who showed judges a spark of hope were sentenced to treatment programs, monitored closely with unannounced urinalysis, and helped into support groups and job training. Leary's Legal Aid lawyer recommended her, and the judge agreed to send her to a center on Martin Luther King Avenue. She became one of the program's first beneficiaries, so grateful that she would long remember the name of everyone who helped her along the way—the lawyer, the judge, the counselor, each member of the center staff, immortalizing them all in a biographical sketch that she composed. "Drug Court was the turning point in my life," she wrote. "Ms. White was the first counselor to greet us. Her voice and tone was calming and embracing, not what I expected." Leary emerged from "this unreal world I had been living in for so long," as she put it. "During this time my true self emerged with a thirst for life and living that I am still quenching even now."

Once she came to, she saw clearly how bereft she was of the skills she would need to hold a decent job. She took a course to become a certified nursing assistant, worked a little in the medical field, but found herself drawn to the keyboards and screens and gadgetry of the computer world that seemed comfortable to everyone except her.

So it was that Leary Brock walked a couple of blocks from her mother's house and entered Mr. Harris's class at SOME's Center for Employment Training. She put her hands on computers, spoke before the group of strangers, doubted herself and took pride in herself, achieved a small success every day along with many frustrations. Something was happening inside her that had never happened before, some growing sense of competence and drive. "My metamorphosis," she called it.

She had polished her résumé, had gone through the interview training, and had sent her applications. Interview appointments were being arranged, and as she sat by a computer in the classroom, she tried to grab her anxiety, wrestle it to the ground, and make it work for her. "I am afraid, and I'd be a fool not to be," she said. "It's a dog-eat-dog world out there now. I learned that in a seminar. She let us know, they all let us know, your interviewer is not your friend, OK? So don't get friendly with 'em. Don't put your guard down. . . . But you can't let that discourage you. Everybody should have a little bit of fear. That's gonna make you do a better job. That's gonna make you have more determination so that you can face the fear, OK?"

The critical interview came with Xerox, at its offices in Arlington, Virginia. "Beautiful building!" Leary exclaimed. "From the sidewalk going up the steps you're on marble, OK? And when you get in there it's so classy.

Now, look, I've been to some really classy bathrooms, all right? Never with a decanter of mouthwash, never with a hair spray, and a HUGE bottle of Alpha Keri lotion—after you wash your hands, you know, soften them up. The place is very classy, and it shows that they care where their employees work. They look out for your little comforts. Like mouthwash, that was going above and beyond the call of duty there. But people do need it, you know, so they're making sure that they got it! Just go to the bathroom, you know? Freshen yourself up!"

Xerox was hiring to fill its contracts to run mail rooms, do photocopying, and print color reports for firms in Washington, and trainees from SOME's center looked attractive. "The interview was very calming. It was very comfortable," Leary said in surprise. "I talked so strongly about team playing and about being excited with the opportunity that the company could offer, because I'd researched and saw how they were involved in the community and how they had did this and that." The interviewer seemed impressed. "She said the difference between us and the other training programs out here was like night and day because people were coming there from these programs only interested in the hours, 'What is the pay?' You know, I never brought that up. You understand? I never questioned her as to what none of that was at any time. So that let her know that my first interest is becoming a member of Xerox. And whatever Xerox had to offer me I would be gratefully inclined to go with because I knew about the company."

Xerox hired Leary, along with Peaches and Wendy Waxler, and everything about the job seemed to delight her: the classes on the machines, the pension plan and stock options (which she didn't quite understand), the potted plant her co-workers gave her when she arrived. She was first assigned to the copying room of an insurance industry lobbyist. A month later, when she joined her fellow graduates at a SOME reunion, they were all bubbly and excited, like kids who had just come back from a visit to a firehouse. They puffed themselves up into postures of one-upmanship, strutting and bragging about their responsibilities, their access to inside information, and their clients' size and influence. Leary breezed in with a bag full of stationery, binders, and cover pages for reports that she had produced for the lobbyist. "They send stuff to every state!" she crowed. "I work with the DocuTech computer copier, I work with the on-line UPS computer, the Bryce printer, and the Pitney Bowes mailing machine. I also work with a networking machine, where someone somewhere is networking a job to me."

Wendy was at a law firm so vast that "they have an office in Moscow," she boasted. "And they have 250 lawyers here in D.C. I'm a mail messenger. They just made me a supervisor. I've been told I'm one of the best workers that they has."

In another law firm, where Peaches had been assigned, "They have a fax room—eight machines!" she declared. "I'd love to have this in my house—the racks slide all the way around!"

When Leary touted the "high security" in her office, where you need a special key to get onto the tenth floor, Wendy proudly held up the plastic insert key she wore on a chain around her neck.

"I work at Hogan and Hartson downtown," reported Richard Ivory, a big man whose mellifluous voice was rich in pride. "It's one of the biggest law firms in the country—*the* biggest law firm in the country. I work in the mail room. I handle all the mail, UPS overnight deliveries." It was a highly responsible position, he explained to the group, because of the importance of the shipments and the precision with which they must be dispatched. "I have to be very careful about how I send the mail. I've been in my supervisor's office three times for compliments on my work. I'm going to go to the fax room. He sees a lot of potential."

Leary was practically giddy with her newfound worth. She started at $17,000 a year, rose to the low twenties, and stayed there amid financial problems that dogged Xerox in the following years. But the world had opened to her. The previous night, she told the alumni, she had taken her mother and a friend to dinner at John Harvard's Brew House, on Pennsylvania Avenue, and then next door to the Warner Theatre for a gospel musical. Her friend asked, "Who's paying?" Leary said, "I'm paying." When her friend saw the price on the ticket, she said, "What?" and Leary decided to keep the stub as a souvenir of her expanded horizons.

She had gone from victim to victor. She attracted praise from supervisors. One said she had caught on so quickly that she made the job look as easy as eating cereal. Another wrote in praise of her demeanor: "No matter how difficult my day may have been, when I go to Ms. Brock with a job, her attitude and smile remind me that I can take time to breathe and relax. Tasks will get done." Steadily rising, Leary was transferred from the insurance lobbyist to a position overseeing nearly fifty machines at D.C. General Hospital, where she had once flunked out of a detox program, then to the Department of Energy, where she was given the title of Service Coordinator and Technical Service Manager. Along the way, she garnered public recognition. Hers was the story everyone wanted to believe in, the story of redemption. A Washington television station did a feature on her, and she became a celebrated client of Suited for Change, a nonprofit group of well-dressed professional women in Washington who donate clothes and advice to impoverished women who need a decent wardrobe to make their way in the working world. She was chosen one year to say a few words at the organization's fundraiser, a swish affair of which Laura Bush was honorary chair.

In 2000, Leary was invited to speak in the chamber of the United States Supreme Court. The Justice Potter Stewart Award was being presented to the D.C. Superior Court Drug Intervention Program, "in recognition of its success in rehabilitating drug-dependent non-violent criminal defenders." Leary had been selected to represent all who had been given another chance.

She couldn't believe it, and she called me all in a flutter, asking if I would help with her speech. Sure, I said, but she would do beautifully if she just stood up there and told her story in her own words. I sent her transcripts of the interviews I had done with her during the previous two years, and urged her not to write her speech, just talk it. She did, and afterwards, still enchanted by the filet mignon dinner, the august setting, the powerful judges in attendance, she told me that she had looked out at the courtroom full of people wiping their eyes, that Associate Justice Antonin Scalia had walked up to her and said that she had brought him to tears. I did that? she thought to herself.

Another judge, having listened carefully, gave her a more sober reaction: She had to earn her way back into her family. He was right, for that success still eluded her. "My kids have not given me any respect or love because of the way I trashed their lives," she lamented. She was trying now with her grandchildren, bundling them off to the Smithsonian, reading them books, filling the vacuum she had created for her children. This, too, was part of the pattern of failure and redemption—a failed mother whose children also fail as parents, and thereby give her a second chance as a grandmother.

The Brock family tree, which I drew up while sitting one evening with Leary and Velma at their dining room table, looked like the wildest of Alexander Calder's mobiles. It began simply at the top—Velma's parents, married, had eight children, and Velma and Horace, also married, had two. It then descended into a chaotic whirl of offspring from multiple liaisons by Leary and, a generation later, by some of her children. The diagram was so complex that if it had been made into a wind chime, the din would have been unrelenting, and not harmonious.

Leary had been violent with her children, she admitted. In her first year of recovery, when she thought she could suddenly resume a parental role, she got so rough with a daughter that a son had to pull her away. Now, the connections were still frayed sometimes; there was still violence in her tone of voice. In all her elation about her job, she did not seem to have energy left to reconstruct the damaged relationships with her adult children. One afternoon, as she sat watching television in her darkened living room, she saw a daughter come in through the front door carrying a suitcase. Leary's greeting had an edge of accusation: "You movin' back here?"

"No." Then the young woman disappeared into the back rooms. I asked about her.

"I don't know," Leary snapped. "I heard a rumor she's moving to North Carolina. I don't know what's going on with her."

With Leary's recovery, she and her mother had patched together a mutual respect. They lived together in her mother's house, which was still mortgaged but sustained by Velma's pension of $30,000. Most of Leary's children were self-supporting most of the time: one son as a roofer in Pennsylvania, another as a security guard in the Energy Department, one daughter with Xerox, and another cleaning CIA headquarters. Velma's household included a changing cast of Leary's daughters and their children, with Velma the great-grandmother at the hub of the crazily revolving wheel.

"I love babies," said Velma, "but they're a little much. One is enough, into everything." She was eighty-six and frail and critical of her granddaughter (Leary's daughter), who finally put her children with a babysitter during the day. "We had to have a big falling-out for her to do it," Velma said. "She doesn't realize that I'm not as young as I was when I was taking care of her, you know. She thinks I can do the same thing that I did then, but I can't." How did she feel about raising her children, then her grandchildren, and now her great-grandchildren? "Tired," she said with a weak smile. "Don't feel any special way about it. That's just one job accomplished, I think. And always lookin' forward to what is next."

Velma's style with her great-grandchildren, whether from exhaustion or as a practiced method of child rearing, had a harshness to it at times. One evening, at a birthday party for a school principal friend named Sarah, the conversations among adults were sweet and gentle, but they were punctuated by the small-arms fire of scolding words to the children. As if the room were taut with hair-trigger anxiety about the slightest misbehavior, Velma interrupted the pleasantness with staccato bursts like preemptive strikes. Not a kind or loving sentence was uttered to the youngsters. Perhaps these children would have otherwise been hellions, but it was hard to see. Besides twins of three months, there were two girls ages five and seven and a three-year-old boy, Deandre.

When dessert came out, an open gallon of ice cream—half chocolate, half vanilla—was placed right in front of Deandre. What would any three-year-old do? Stick his finger in it, of course. So that's what Deandre did, into the vanilla half, and his great-grandmother, Velma, slapped his hand and threatened to send him to bed. He started to cry, though almost silently, as if he were afraid to cry. "Why are you crying?" Velma asked sharply, and threatened again to send him to bed. "Don't cry!"

Everyone except the two girls gathered to sing "Happy Birthday" to Sarah, followed by "God Bless You" to the same tune. Then Velma scooped out the vanilla with the finger hole in it, gave it to Deandre, and made it sound like punishment: He would have the part he touched, she decreed. He started to cry again.

"Why are you crying?" Leary asked harshly in an echo of her mother. "Don't cry!"

Then, Sarah softly intervened. She told Deandre that she would eat the vanilla that contained his finger hole, and she took over dishing out the ice cream. She asked the boy if he wanted chocolate or vanilla—the first time anybody had inquired about his wishes. Chocolate, it turned out. That's why he was crying. He stopped as soon as Sarah put a dish of chocolate in front of him.

Whatever stresses and strains were being passed down through the generations, though, the family connections were helping to sustain Leary and keep her from falling backward. A year or so later, on Leary's fiftieth birthday, Velma prepared a feast of foods that Leary used to love as a child, and three of her four children came to her party; she was estranged from only one at that time.

"I can't force it," Leary said, giving herself some advice. "Let them come to you. Just let them see that you're a different person."

The dream in America is a demanding standard, the myth is a noble goal. When a man or a woman or a family fills its full measure of possibility, the nation's virtue is affirmed. So the nation should feel very good about the Tran family of Saigon, now of Santa Ana, California, whose accomplishments have demonstrated how powerful the right combination of drive, opportunity, thrift, education, health, connections, and mutual support can be. Within four months of arriving as refugees from Vietnam in 1998, three of the five family members were working at jobs whose low wages, pooled, brought in $42,848 a year. Within five months of arrival, they had saved enough to pay cash for two used cars. Less than a year later, the two oldest children were at a community college.

Their successes demonstrated that work works at the low end of the pay scale only when everything else works: when a cohesive family has multiple wage-earners who believe in their own competence, have the skills, know how to find jobs, manage their money with care, and never retreat in the face of hardship. If this sounds heroic, it is. There is no room for mistake or misfortune—not for drugs, not for alcohol, not for domestic violence, not for poor schooling, not for illness or injury, not for anything less than high diligence. So far, so good for the Tran family.

The model is so rare that it is no model at all, just an exception that highlights the problems for the vast numbers of working poor who can't line up every single factor in their favor. Vietnamese, Chinese, Koreans, and other Asians are often stereotyped as brilliantly hardworking and successful in that perfect American Dream. But millions of Asians also come to the United States and fail, as the Koreans who work in Los Angeles restaurants can testify. Anyone who watches the Trans put the pieces together can see vividly the pieces that are absent for so many others.

Tran Mao, a friendly man in his late forties, wore gold-framed glasses, chinos, and sandals. A few teeth were missing from his smile, and he chopped the air with his hands as he spoke. During the war he was trained in Mississippi as an electronics technician for the South Vietnamese Air Force (hence his good English), and his rank as a noncommissioned officer brought him a year in a "reeducation camp" after the North Vietnamese victory in 1975. A few years later, he and two of his children joined thousands of other Vietnamese in a desperate escape by boat. They made their way to Indonesia and spent seven years in a refugee camp, where he worked for the United Nations High Commissioner for Refugees. Denied refugee status himself, however, he was deported back to Vietnam with his family. He persisted, and two years later he finally gained the refugee designation that brought him, his wife, and their three children visas to the United States.

The Trans began their new life as if they were true Americans: in debt. Their plane tickets had been bought by the International Organization for Migration, which required repayment at $125 a month. They also borrowed $2,000 from friends for a sparse array of furniture. With their three children now twenty, nineteen, and eleven, the two oldest were part of the family's labor force, and they quickly went to work—the son, Tuan, in a bicycle factory at $5.75 an hour, California's minimum wage at the time; the daughter, Phuong, at 10 cents more assembling bicycle lights; the father at minimum wage packing medicine for a drug company. After a month, Mao's fluent English landed him a counselor's position for $9 an hour at a service agency called The Cambodian Family, which helped find jobs for new immigrants, primarily from Cambodia and Vietnam. The debts were soon paid off.

Mao understood clearly that there were two tickets his children would need to excel in the United States: fluent English and higher education. Every day in his agency, he saw how limiting the lack of English could be for the people he tried to help complete applications and prepare for job interviews. Every evening, therefore, he tried to help his children with English, making them read and encouraging them to watch television to improve their comprehension. Since Phuong and Tuan both worked with other Vietnamese, they never had a chance to speak English on the job, so their improvement was negligible, and Mao made no effort to disguise his frustration. "Pronunciation is no good," he said of Phuong, who bowed primly at the waist in respectful greeting. She had learned a precise, heavily accented English in the Indonesian refugee camp. "She should try to practice more and more," her father admonished. He worried especially about her mother and her nineteen-year-old brother, who spoke very little. Soon he had everybody enrolled in English classes, himself included. He was taking a computer course as well, hoping someday to get the college degree that had eluded him because of the war, and then because of the end of the war.

So, five studying people were scheduling the use of their two desks, one in the kitchen, one in the living room. They had pictures of the Virgin

Mary around, and on one desk a Packard Bell computer and printer. Their two-bedroom apartment was crowded, but it cost $675 a month, and they could not afford more. Mao and his wife, Lang Ho, slept in one bedroom, the boys in the other, and Phuong on the living room floor. On the relaxed, pleasant street below, Asians and Latinos casually strolled to and from a run-down little shopping center, where many of the signs were in Spanish. A woman pushed a red shopping cart with a huge plastic bag overflowing with bottles and cans.

By the fall of 1999, both Phuong and Tuan had left their jobs to enroll at Santa Ana College (Phuong in college courses, Tuan to get his G.E.D.), and their mother, Lang Ho, had taken up the slack by getting work assembling pens at a local factory. She was making minimum wage with no medical insurance or other benefits. Mao's pay rate at The Cambodian Family had gone up to $10 an hour. Every weekend the family sat together to plan the week's spending. "We have to write down," Mao said. "We work together. Usually we go shopping for food once a week. . . . We collected coupons from the newspaper. . . . We only buy what we think is most important for our family." There were disagreements.

"Sometimes I want to buy my shoes," said Phuong. "But I think again, I have not money. I don't need shoes right now. I can save money, buy food for my family. . . . My father tell me, 'You can't buy that, you do that or do that.' " Then she added: "But I can decide myself: self-control." They were saving $400 to $500 a month, Mao said, and sending money to relatives in Vietnam.

By spring 2002, the recession had hit some of Mao's clients, who were being laid off by factories and could not get hired by temp agencies because of their limited English. But his family had been spared so far. His hourly wage had risen to $13, and his wife's to $7. Phuong and Tuan, continuing school, were both working part-time and contributing to the family budget. "I have a credit card but seldom use it," said Mao. "I try to manage not to use it. I don't want to be in huge debt."

When she arrived in 1998, Phuong had an ambition. "I want to become a doctor and help poor patients," she declared. Her father laughed, as if embarrassed by his daughter's foolish dream. Four years later, she still had the same goal. He laughed again, as if embarrassed by his hope.

Chapter Eleven

SKILL
AND WILL

Not a place on earth might be so happy as America.
—Thomas Paine, 1776

As the people in these pages show, working poverty is a constellation of difficulties that magnify one another: not just low wages but also low education, not just dead-end jobs but also limited abilities, not just insufficient savings but also unwise spending, not just poor housing but also poor parenting, not just the lack of health insurance but also the lack of healthy households.

The villains are not just exploitative employers but also incapable employees, not just overworked teachers but also defeated and unruly pupils, not just bureaucrats who cheat the poor but also the poor who cheat themselves. The troubles run strongly along both macro and micro levels, as systemic problems in the structure of political and economic power, and as individual problems in personal and family life.

All of the problems have to be attacked at once. Whatever remedy is found for one may help but not cure unless remedies are found for most of the others. Granting a Section 8 housing voucher helps a family move into a better apartment, which may ease a child's asthma and lead to fewer days of missed school. But it won't carry the family far if the child is abused, or if the parent has few skills, works near minimum wage, spends huge amounts on transportation and day care, and can't get affordable credit. As long as society picks and chooses which problem to resolve in crisis—usually the one that has propelled the family to a particular agency for help—another crisis is likely to follow, and another. If we set out to find only the magic solution—a job, for example—we will miss the complexities, and the job will not be enough.

The first question is whether we know exactly what to do. What problems do we have the skills to solve, and where do our skills reach their outer limits? What territory of intractable problems lies unmapped, beyond our abilities?

The second question is whether we have the will to exercise our skill. Would we spend the money, make the sacrifices, restructure the hierarchy of wealth to alleviate the hardships down below?

We lack the skill to solve some problems and the will to solve others, but one piece of knowledge we now possess: We understand that holistic remedies are vital. So, gateways to addressing a family's range of handicaps are needed, and they are best established at intersections through which working poor families are likely to travel. Dr. Barry Zuckerman at the Boston Medical Center has shown how it can be done there, with social workers and lawyers. Principal Theodore Hinton at the Harris Educational Center in Washington has tried to do it there, with scarce resources, by opening his school into the evening, offering parenting classes, and providing information on health insurance. Public housing projects in Los Angeles have referred residents to English classes and job training.

These are embryonic forms of a big idea. If hospitals, schools, housing authorities, police departments, welfare offices, and other critical institutions were bold and well enough financed, they could reach far beyond their mandates, create connections of services, and become portals through which the distressed could pass into a web of assistance. It is a question of skill and will.

Will is a function of power, and the people who work near the edge of poverty don't have very much power. They do have more than they use, however. They have power in their personal lives that many of them leave untapped. They have power in the marketplace that is not organized effectively. They have power in politics that they practically ignore: the power of the ballot.

Whenever liberal Democrats criticize tax cuts for the rich or program cuts for the poor, conservative Republicans raise the fearsome specter of "class warfare" as if they and their supporters in business were not reinforcing class differences by structuring tax breaks and pay scales. In 2003, for example, the Bush White House and Republican congressional leaders excluded millions of low-wage families, with incomes between $10,500 and $26,625, from a $400-per-child payment being made under an increase in the child tax credit, part of a big tax bill that brought immense benefits to the wealthy. But the poor do not fight back. The lower the income, the lower the rate of voter turnout. In the 2000 presidential election, 60 percent of all American citizens over eighteen went to the polls. Three-quarters of those with family incomes over $75,000 voted, 69 percent of those earning $50,000 to $75,000, and so on down to a mere 38 percent of those whose households took in less than $10,000 a year.[1] In addition to those who disenfranchise themselves, about two million citizens over eighteen in prisons, plus ex-convicts, are disqualified in most states from voting. An overwhelming majority of them are from low-income ranks. Twelve percent of all black men between eighteen and thirty-four are in jail.[2]

Therefore, although nobody needs government more than the poor and the nearly poor, they have little influence on its policies. Neither the Democratic Party nor anti-poverty organizations have mobilized sufficiently to encourage low-income Americans to find their voices. In one modest effort, a small sign was placed on the counter of an office in Imperial Courts, a public housing project in the Watts section of Los Angeles:

Mumble
Grumble
Complain
Wallow
Hope
Despair
Worry

Vote

Just a reminder: the one on the bottom changes things a lot faster.
Call 1-800-343-VOTE to register.

The message was clever but probably ineffectual, because Census Bureau surveys show that the lower their income and education, the less inclined Americans are to believe that voting makes a difference. That doubt is a self-fulfilling prophecy. Consumed with the trials of their personal lives and cynical about the power structure, most tell pollsters that they find elections uninteresting and politicians untrustworthy. Without getting candidates' attention at the polls, then, low-income Americans rely on the more affluent to represent their interests. This the affluent do with various degrees of inadequacy, depending on the party in power, the health of the economy, and the current state of the nation's altruism. When it comes to benevolence, we are a moody society.

This need not be. The priorities of the nation and the landscape of politics could change, subject to a few ifs. If people with family incomes under $25,000 had cast ballots at the same rate as those above $75,000, more than 6.8 million additional voters would have gone to the polls in 2000, when Al Gore finished with a slight edge of 543,895 in the popular count over George W. Bush. An upsurge in low-income voters would have overcome even Florida's biased registration and balloting system and (if only a slight majority of them had voted Democratic) would have reversed the results, electing Gore.

Even in landslides, most states' electoral votes are won by margins of 5 percent or less, so the 6.8 million additional low-income voters (6.5 percent of the total electorate) could decide the outcome. In many races for Congress and state legislatures as well, those in or near poverty could hold the balance of power. If large numbers cast ballots according to their own needs, candidates might suddenly find them interesting. If Democrats were able to sharpen their social welfare positions without losing middle-class support . . . If they conducted intensive registration and get-out-the-vote drives among citizens who benefit from anti-poverty programs . . . If a strong low-income contingent in the electorate forced Republicans to adopt more generous platforms . . . If those working at the edge of poverty became visible . . .

In reality, however, most Americans do not vote in line with their class interests, and there is no guarantee that the poor would do so even in a large turnout. Balloting seems driven more by aspiration than complaint. *Time* magazine found in a 2000 survey that 19 percent of Americans thought they were in the top 1 percent of wage-earners, and another 20 percent expected to be in the future. "So right away you have 39 percent of Americans who thought that when Mr. Gore savaged a plan that favored the top 1 percent, he was taking a direct shot at them," wrote David Brooks, a senior editor at *The Weekly Standard*.[3]

When self-delusion distorts behavior at the polls, it has damaging consequences for those of low income. Voting is the basic building block of democratic government, and government is the instrument best positioned to make a difference to the working poor. No key sector of this free-enterprise system, whether business or charity, escapes the pervasive influence wielded by government through tax policy, regulation, wage requirements, subsidies, grants, and the like.

The fact that government is the hub of the wheel puts the country's doubts at the center of the most effective efforts to alleviate poverty. Deep ambivalence about governmental power has shaped the American endeavor since the Colonies wrested themselves from the British monarchy—an aversion defined caustically by Thomas Paine in his 1776 pamphlet *Common Sense:* "Society in every state is a blessing, but Government, even in its best state, is but a necessary evil; in its worst state, an intolerable one."

There is something still to be said for that suspicion. We have owed our freedom to our distrust of government from the beginning, when ingenious checks and balances, the separation of powers, were written into the Constitution. In a time of terrorism, that wariness of the imperious potential of the state has been blunted perilously, but it remains a force in today's political debates over economic and welfare policy. Preaching against big government and applauding private enterprise, conservatives try to prevent state encroachment on the free flow of the market, often to the detriment of the environment, the worker, the consumer. In this view, most zealously expressed by the libertarian wing of the conservative movement, the purpose of government is exceedingly narrow: "The state exists to preserve freedom," declares the Federalist Society, which has successfully promoted right-wingers into the judiciary.

It is a ringing truth, but a stingy statement. The state exists not just to preserve freedom. It exists also to protect the weak. It exists to strengthen the vulnerable, to empower the powerless, to promote justice. It exists to facilitate "the pursuit of happiness." It can behave both as a remote force hostile to the people and as the embodiment of the broad community. It can overregulate and stifle, and it can foster exploration and invention. It should leave individuals alone in their private lives, and it should pool the society's resources for the common good. Government has more than one

personality, and the trick for Americans—one we have been experimenting with since our inception—is how to manage the contradictions.

No system has resolved this quandary. Marxism failed because it mis-
interpreted history: It saw the stages of civilization leading inexorably to
classlessness, a naive assessment of humankind's capabilities. It also failed
because its initial disciple, "the world's first socialist state" as the Soviet
Union called itself, mistook government for the citizenry. The welfare of
the state was elevated above the welfare of the people, producing a bureaucracy of state ownership so vast and smothering that practically nothing
existed outside of it—nothing except the humble kitchen tables around
which the Russian people talked secretly to one another.

Americanism could fail, too. It is devoted to keeping government in its
place, but the question of what place that should be is the centerpiece of
our ongoing discussion. Without our keenest vigilance, government grows
autocratic in a frightening age of terrorism, or loses humaneness in an age
of damaging disparities among our people. We need to restrain and use
government simultaneously.

The entire society needs governmental tools to help those working
at the bottom of the economic hierarchy—both to lend them a hand in
what they cannot do alone and to assist them in developing the capacity to
do what they can ultimately do themselves. No dichotomy exists here
between societal help and self-help. Government can be neither absent nor
all-encompassing. It cannot fail to maintain a safety net, cannot avoid
direct grants to the needy, cannot be blind to its role as the community's
resource. But it also has to blend its power in creative interaction with the
profit and nonprofit worlds, with private industry and private charity.

The most evident point of attack is the wage structure. Business executives
have the skill but certainly not the will to compress salary differentials by
raising the bottom and making sacrifices at the top. Revised tax structures
could induce such policy. Government has the skill to legislate a big boost
in the minimum wage, but it lacks the political will, largely because most
low-income Americans don't vote their interests or don't vote at all, and
can't compete with private industry's sophisticated lobbying and campaign
contributions.

Furthermore, the minimum wage is a blunt instrument, and the skill
to use it is not perfected. Economists disagree over how much it could be

raised without harming entrepreneurial risk-taking, although it is reasonably argued that the federal minimum, which has declined in real dollars against inflation, could probably rise considerably before doing damage. Twenty-five states and the District of Columbia have demonstrated as much by placing their own 2008 minimum wages at $6.62 to $8.08 an hour, above the 2008 federal rate of $6.55.[4]

One idea for making the tool more refined is to set different minimums for different parts of the country based on regional costs of living. Another approach is the "living wage" law. More than 100 counties and cities now require that private companies with government contracts pay $6.75 to $14.75 an hour, levels calculated to support a decent standard of living.[5] Preliminary results show minimal budget increases for localities, reductions in government subsidies to workers' families, and relief among contractors who no longer have to squeeze employees' pay to compete for low bids. Some economists suspect that the living wage doesn't target the right people, however, because those being hired into such jobs are workers of higher caliber, not those at the bottom who need a hand moving up from minimum wage positions.

We have learned other ways to address the discrepancy between what people can earn in the market and what they need for comfortable living. One method, the Earned Income Tax Credit, rewards work. While the payment looks like a subsidy of the employee, it acts as much to subsidize the employer, who can pay low wages without causing the worker quite as much pain. Indeed, the program indirectly benefits many large corporations, from Wal-Mart to McDonald's, and helps make them more profitable. Having cleverly invented this tool, however, we haven't mustered the will to give it sufficient impact; aside from year-to-year growth with the cost of living, the program has seen no increases since 1996. In 2003, President Bush asked Congress for $100 million, not to augment the payments, but to hire 650 new auditors to check for fraudulent claims.[6]

Employers are also heavily subsidized by states, counties, and cities competing to attract new industry, and by the creation of federally funded enterprise zones with tax credits to draw manufacturers into poor areas. As a case in point, Alabama has awarded foreign auto companies hundreds of millions of dollars through property tax abatements, suspensions of income taxes, and payments to boost workers' wages—plus a virtually union-free environment.

In exchange for such handouts, private industry could be asked for a great deal more than its mere presence, but that rarely happens. The creation of jobs is considered sufficient repayment. Here, federalism and local control can interfere with national economic interests, for when localities compete savagely to undercut one another in granting tax relief, they undercut their own tax bases and distort the geographical distribution of work. In Alabama and the rest of the South, which are practically devoid of organized labor, the incentives raise earnings among residents of some of the country's poorest regions, but by diverting jobs, they also undermine unions elsewhere. The proportion of America's workers in labor unions has gradually declined, from 35 to 12.1 percent nationwide between 1950 and 2007; in government, 36 percent are unionized, but in the private sector the figure is only 7.5 percent.[7]

Broader union membership would be beneficial, but even some union jobs yield only low-wage stagnation, as in parking garages and janitorial services. The country's prosperity relies on badly paid workers—that's a fact that is not going to disappear. So the best way to improve a worker's wage is through promotion and upward mobility; new laborers will flow in beneath to take the low-wage positions, and ideally, most of them will eventually climb into decent pay scales.

We know at least two effective methods to help someone starting in the $5- to $8-an-hour range move to $15 or more: One is through sophisticated job training of the kind that rescued Peaches and Leary Brock from the ravages of low skills and disbelief in themselves; the skill is there, now the will has to be mustered to fund such efforts adequately. The second is through a revival of vocational education in high school and a network of apprenticeships for those who don't go to college. There, too, the issue is not one of skill but of will.

Wage differences between high school and college graduates have increased sharply since 1980 as many young people fall through a hole in the economy. Because secondary schools feel growing pressure toward a "college-for-all" curriculum, they send higher percentages to college (nearly 60 percent, up from 30 percent in 1970) but leave many of those who don't attend or don't graduate without the abilities required at well-paid levels of industry. "Doing well in the workplace involves a far more heterogeneous set of skills than doing well in high schools and universities," writes Robert Lerman, an economist at the Urban Institute and American University. Unlike most industrialized countries, he notes, the United States has allowed vocational training to lag, leading to a "weakness in the middle-skill area" that has been cited by foreign manufacturers as reason to avoid investing here. Sweden, Norway, France, England, Japan, Australia, and Germany have spliced technical secondary-school courses into industry-sponsored apprenticeships, producing highly qualified personnel. But when industries come to the United States from abroad, they often invoke dramatic measures to address the American failings; Lerman reports that BMW, the German automaker, has flown American workers to Germany for instruction.

The notion of funneling certain teenagers into vocational school rubs against the American ethic of egalitarianism, which touts the ideal of equal opportunity without actually providing it. Many parents, believing fervently in the dream, oppose vocational tracking for their children, seeing college as the only reliable pathway upward. The trouble is, if you're like Christie the day-care worker in Ohio, your failure to graduate from college may leave you without the technical skills to make you valuable in the hard-nosed labor market. Christie would have done better on a vocational track than by starting college and dropping out.

Here and there, vocational programs operate successfully under the aegis of certain industries, labor unions, and state governments. "In America, there's everything," Lerman says. "Somebody's always doing something well somewhere." State agencies in Wisconsin, for example, have collaborated with private companies to train young people in printing, finance, biotech, and a score of other areas. He believes that Head Start, the federally funded preschool program for poor children, could be a vehicle for creating youth apprenticeships among high school students, which would then provide credentials in the field of child development.[8] But on a nationwide scale, we have not chosen to repair this breach in training our young people for well-paying work.

In broader educational matters, the intersection of skill and will is more complex and controversial. Volumes have been written about improving public schools, but insufficient attention has been given to the unfair way they're financed. The fundamental structure is so flawed that even the efforts of a few generous states to equalize funding between rich and poor communities have made too little difference. Most school districts depend largely on local property taxes, and since most Americans live in areas segregated by class as well as race, the disparities are acute. In New York State's districts, for example, the tax base, the value of all taxable real estate, ranges from $2,395,304 to $184,647 per pupil, producing a per-student annual expenditure whose average ranges from $13,681 in the wealthiest school systems to $7,100 in the poorest—and this in a state that tries to reduce the gap by funneling more aid to poorer districts.[9]

The financing method perpetuates the inequities: The schools that have more money provide a superior education, which helps children improve their earning power so they can live in communities that have more to spend on public education. This, in turn, accentuates the racial divide, for public schools have been resegregated since the late 1980s, thanks in large measure to rulings by conservative judges installed by Republican presidents and Senates. One-sixth of the country's black students now attend virtually all non-white schools, many of which are impoverished, and only one-seventh of the whites attend multiracial schools, defined as those with 10 percent or more minority enrollment.[10]

Breaking the pernicious pattern by funding schools on a statewide or nationwide basis would not end racial segregation, but it would be a step toward redistributing resources. But then, every solution creates at least one new problem. Money comes with strings attached. The ideal of pooling taxpayers' involuntary contributions at higher levels of government to convey it equitably down the line collides with the powerful devotion in this land to local control—and to privilege. Vouchers for private schools undermine the separation of church and state and draw resources away from public schools.

Furthermore, not every ailment can be relieved by money. Even if teachers were paid in accordance with their essential value to society, even if there were enough of them to keep classes small and instruction somewhat individualized, even if they had sufficient books and microscopes and maps, not all the problems that children carry into school would go away. At some place along the continuum of difficulties, our skills weaken. We do not know how to address all those troubles that young people face. However, we do know how to do much more than we choose to do. Our insufficient will has not carried us even close to that twilight region where our competence fades.

The same can be said of every burden that weighs on the working poor. We know how to promote home ownership and make decent apartments affordable, but we don't do enough of it. We know a great deal about how to treat alcoholism and drug addiction, but we don't provide enough facilities to accommodate all who need and crave the help. That is also true of depression and other mental illness.

We know very well that many who work at the edge of poverty fall between the cracks of health insurance plans, earning too much to qualify for Medicaid and too little to buy private coverage. We have made only a partial response. Since 1998 government has filled much of the gap with the State Children's Health Insurance Program (SCHIP), which provides federal matching grants to states that cover children at 100 to 200 percent of the poverty level—or higher, as in New Jersey, which extends coverage up to 350 percent. Few states have chosen to insure parents, however, and reduced tax revenues in a recession make that even less likely to happen. (The program's annual federal budget of $4 billion is roughly the cost of a new aircraft carrier.) Furthermore, nearly a quarter of all uninsured children are ineligible for public coverage, a huge failing that could be changed by federal largess. Then, too, one-quarter of poor children who qualify for Medicaid are not enrolled, either because their parents don't want government help, are deterred by complex application procedures, or simply don't know that the children are entitled to benefits. We have not even had the will to spend extra money for outreach workers to get those kids insured. The same can be said for other support: Only one-third of the households in poverty receive food stamps or subsidized housing.

The larger debate over the country's patchwork health insurance system, which leaves 47 million uncovered, touches on all the big questions about government's role, the private sector's fairness, and the class structure of America. Employer-based policies may be the worst conceivable way to organize coverage. They drive up companies' labor costs, force workers into badly run health maintenance organizations, and create pools of insured so small for some firms that a single employee's cancer diagnosis can send premiums shooting through the roof for everyone. In an age of high mobility, workers bounce from one to another plan as they change jobs, often enduring months without protection. We don't get our auto insurance through our workplaces, and we shouldn't get our medical insurance that way either.

But do we have the skill to solve this? Can we craft a form of universal coverage without stifling efficiency and scientific enterprise? Despite fears about government suffocating the private sector, the opposite has happened in research and development, where soaring federal funding has stimulated a similar growth of private investment. The question is whether the same would happen if a single-payer system of medical insurance were created. The single payer would be the federal government, funding the plan through taxes, as it does now to insure 30 million elderly through Medicare and 45 million poor through Medicaid. That would provide basic care for everyone, regardless of income. You could even call it Basicare.

There are fears that this would lead to rationing of a kind, as in Canada and England. Some Canadians have experienced long waits in getting such treatment as chemotherapy after breast surgery, for example. In spreading finite medical assets more evenly throughout the population, would Basicare also deprive the wealthy of their privileged access to boundless supplies of specialists, high-tech testing, and advanced remedies? Would it constitute "socialized medicine" and sap the profit motive that drives research and draws talent into the profession? Many doctors who resent government regulation of their fees now refuse to see Medicaid and Medicare patients because the payments are so low—or they charge the elderly rich annual subscription fees to compensate for Medicare reimbursements.

The private alternative, however, has brought the nation's medical system to the brink of catastrophe. Insurance companies exact wildly escalating payments from the public, indulge in exorbitant payoffs to their executives, execute dangerous denials of treatment, and reinforce a class-based hierarchy of care that damages the health of Americans with lesser means. Just as government has gradually entered the insurance business through Medicare, Medicaid, and SCHIP, it can't shrink from further involvement without neglecting its duty to the general welfare. Until a single-payer system becomes politically acceptable, some form of federal-private interaction through subsidies and regulation is a must.

Here is where we need the will to develop the skill to have it both ways: to guarantee the benefits without smothering individual choice or medical initiative. That would be quite an achievement for a nation so steeped in aversion to big government yet so idealistic in the pursuit of social justice. Surely this would happen if members of Congress, who enjoy one of the country's best insurance plans, faced the difficulties of Caroline Payne, who had to halt back treatment after being dropped from Medicaid; or Lisa Brooks, whose credit rating was ruined by an HMO that refused to pay for an ambulance; or those malnourished kids at the clinics in Boston and Baltimore.

We know what an unhealthy early childhood does to a growing human being. Neuroscience and other areas of research have taught us about the intricate relationships between the biological and the cognitive, between early nurturing and later functioning. Our understanding of the problems is ahead of the skills we have acquired to solve them, and the skills are ahead of our will to act. Across the country we have developed a multitude of early-intervention programs, many founded on sound concepts. But those that are underfunded and run by undertrained staff set an unhappy pattern: The project receives inadequate resources, which leads to its want of success, which causes it to be abandoned as a failed approach.

Parents' handicaps in raising their children lie along that continuum between the correctable and the unmanageable. At the most accessible end of the spectrum, mothers and fathers may simply lack informed techniques of parenting that can be taught in classes or individual counseling. Plenty of well-to-do parents pay for such training; low-income parents may find sporadic help without charge through social agencies. Parents learn such skills as how to encourage their children rather than focus on their wrong-doing, how to do joint problem-solving and help kids make their own choices, how to manage anger, how to administer discipline sensibly, how to listen and express empathy, and how to achieve mutual respect.

At the distant end of the continuum, though, where serious personality disorders and disrupted families affect parenting, our skills are weaker. Some parents carry such profound disturbance from their own upbringing that lessons and advice don't have much impact. We have not figured out how to curb sexual abuse, for example, other than by removing children to foster families, which are not always model households themselves. These are concerns that cut across class lines.

Given the decisive nature of the earliest years, why doesn't American society muster its most ingenious efforts to guide parents and safeguard children? The successful programs are described with recurring terms: "comprehensive," "intensive," and "highly professional." Another should be "expensive." When you have highly professional specialists in medicine, psychology, and child development focusing on a family the way a trauma team huddles over a patient in surgery, you run up very high bills.

Can the wealthiest country in the world afford to pay? You bet we can, especially if those at the top are willing to sacrifice a little. It might even save us money elsewhere in our social welfare budgets, as suggested by the results of the federal Infant Health and Development Program, a clinical trial aimed at premature babies. From birth through age three, 985 children in eight locations across the country were bombarded with attention from pediatricians, social workers, home visitors, and others who monitored their health, referred families to services, provided educational child care, and the like. At three, the kids had higher IQ scores, larger vocabularies, and fewer behavioral problems than children who had not received the services.[11] In other words, when we do it right, it works. "And everywhere we've tried to do it on the cheap, everywhere we've tried to cut a corner, we end up spending money with no appreciable results," said Representative George Miller of California, who was chairman of the House Select Committee on Children, Youth, and Families.[12] We have known all this for a long time. He made the observation in the 1980s.

Even our extensive efforts don't reach enough children. Head Start, the preschool program for the poor, is funded at an annual amount worth the price of one and a half new aircraft carriers. It enrolls only 60 percent of the youngsters who are eligible, according to the Children's Defense Fund, and its teachers, only half of whom are required to have a college degree, earn an average of just $22,000 a year. The Bush administration has shaken up the program by announcing plans to require it to push reading for preschoolers, a policy disputed as unwise by many educators. Early Head Start, begun in 1995 to tackle the critical years from birth to three, has been deemed effective by preliminary studies, but it touches only 5 percent of the nation's eligible children. Meanwhile, government policies operate at cross-purposes by ratcheting up the work requirement imposed on welfare mothers without raising funds for child care. We don't even do what we know how to do.

To appraise a society, examine its ability to be self-correcting. When grievous wrongs are done or endemic suffering exposed, when injustice is discovered or opportunity denied, watch the institutions of government and business and charity. Their response is an index of a nation's health and of a people's strength.

The United States possesses agile mechanisms for discerning troubling truths and adjusting toward reform. We have done so against racial discrimination, environmental degradation, corporate malfeasance, misguided foreign policy, police brutality, and domestic poverty. The fact that all these ills remain, many of them less virulent than a half century ago, testifies to both the challenge and the accomplishment. If the ideal is high enough, it is never quite attained. If the striving is sufficiently intense, it never runs to completion; at best, it yields success after success indefinitely. That should be our mission against poverty in working America.

If a single cause were identified, a remedy might be readily designed. It would fit neatly into a liberal or a conservative prescription. If either the system's exploitation or the victims' irresponsibility were to blame, one or the other side of the debate would be satisfied. If the reasons were merely corporate greed or government indifference or impoverished schools, then liberal solutions would suffice. If the causes were only the personal failures of parents and children, teachers and workers, then conservative views would hold. But "repression is a seamless garment," as Salman Rushdie wrote. This is repression of a kind, and it lacks the clear boundaries that would define the beginning and the end of accountability. In the fields of North Carolina, the migrants are driven by Mexico's destitution and drawn by America's promise. They are indentured to coyotes and *contratistas*. They are warehoused in squalor and paid a pittance by growers, by wholesalers, by supermarket chains, and by shoppers who enjoy low prices for the cucumbers and tomatoes that the migrants harvest. When accountability is spread so broadly and diffused, it seems to cease to exist. The opposite is true. It may look as if nobody is accountable. In fact, everybody is.

The liberal-conservative divide is not only about how big government should be; it is also about what government should do. Liberalism is the use of the state for some purposes; conservatism is the use of the state for other purposes. Just as liberal Democrats call for increasing grants and programs for the poor, "social conservatives" among Republicans want big government to give or withhold money to promote marriage, dictate local education policies, discourage child-bearing by mothers on welfare, and subsidize religious institutions' moralistic efforts to combat indigence.

The troubles of the working poor will not be relieved by this ideological debate. Political argument is vital for democracy, but solutions must finally transcend the familiar disagreements. The political opponents have to cross into each other's territory to pick up solutions from the opposite side. Just as President Bill Clinton entered conservative ground to impose time limits and work requirements on welfare recipients, so would conservatives do well to step into the liberal arena for the assistance that government needs to provide. Opportunity and poverty in this country cannot be explained by either the American Myth that hard work is a panacea or by the Anti-Myth that the system imprisons the poor. Relief will come, if at all, in an amalgam that recognizes both the society's obligation through government and business, and the individual's obligation through labor and family—and the commitment of both society and individual through education.

Workers at the edge of poverty are essential to America's prosperity, but their well-being is not treated as an integral part of the whole. Instead, the forgotten wage a daily struggle to keep themselves from falling over the cliff. It is time to be ashamed.

Epilogue

Lives continue unresolved. Since the hardcover edition of this book appeared, some of the people in these pages have taken happier directions, others have seen hopeful prospects dissipate, and many remain mired in stagnation. Here is what has happened to a few of them.

Ann Brash (pp. 193–200), still working as a poorly paid book editor, received some financial relief from her son, Sandy, who lived at home and contributed part of his wage as a computer specialist at Dartmouth. But she watched in dismay as her daughter, Sally, dropped out of the New England Conservatory of Music to take a job in a flower shop for $13 an hour. After all, to maximize Sandy's and Sally's opportunities, Ann had chosen poverty as an alternative to working multiple jobs, which would have meant sacrificing the time needed to raise her children well. Nothing scares a dedicated, impoverished parent more than the specter of a child repeating the pattern.

Sally dropped out because she was not succeeding. "I almost failed every single class that I was taking," Sally told me between customers in Brookline, Massachusetts. "I hated being in school; I always hated being in school." Nor could she tolerate the anxiety before she went onstage to sing opera. During two intense summers in Italy and Austria, "I got so nervous that my muscles trembled," she said. "That affected my pitch." When a violinist friend offered her a beta-blocker, usually prescribed for high blood pressure and other cardiac ailments, she tried one "and realized if that's what I have to do, to do what I love, that's just wrong."

So, for the time being, she was applying her creative talents to assembling flowers artistically in vases and baskets, making her choices as she wove gracefully and cheerfully along the aisles, among clusters of riotous colors. Doing arrangements for weddings or theater productions would bring her pleasure, she thought, but she also felt pressure to finish her college degree. The pressure came from her mother, of course, and it came from the New Hampshire couple who had helped pay Sally's tuition. They would continue giving her rent for an apartment, she explained, only on the condition that she continue her studies. She had started one course in Harvard's extension program and dropped it.

"Mom's terrified," Sally said. "She's horrified that I left school and that I'm not immediately going back."

Part of Ann's concern was practical. "I worry about Sally not having health insurance," Ann said, "and worry about her not working toward a degree to enable her to work where she can have health insurance." For herself, Ann had a worry and a wish that could not be resolved: "I would like to be thirty years younger, so I could find a better-paying job with more challenges instead of being stuck in a low-paying, dead-end job."

Leary Brock (pp. 269–81) had a lilt of contentment in her voice when I called to check in. Her career at Xerox continued on a gradual climb. As the technical support coordinator at the Energy Department, where Xerox had a contract, she made $27,000 a year and shouldered increasing responsibility. The company was still investing in her, sending her to a technician's course that would, she hoped, teach her to repair complex machines and, she believed, triple her salary.

Xerox was also paying for on-line business courses from the University of Phoenix, and Leary hoped to get her college degree eventually. She was taking a scriptwriting course at her church, where one of her plays was performed, "and it was well-received," she said proudly. She had benefited from the perfect alignment of her personal strengths and the right assistance at the right moments from society's institutions—the court, the drug rehab program, the job training center, and the private company that recognized her promise. She had come a long way from the addict-infested streets, and she was not going back.

Life at home grew quieter, because children were doing well enough in various jobs that her grandchildren had moved out to live with them. Leary's mother, Velma, turned ninety, enjoyed reasonably good health, and still had a mind as sharp as a tack. A financial uncertainty looms in the future, though, for when Velma dies, the pension and Social Security checks that help pay the mortgage and taxes will end, and the house where they live will become part of Leary's burden. Furthermore, Velma has become an anchor of stability. Her absence will test Leary's ability to maintain the equilibrium she has attained.

Lisa Brooks (pp. 26–7), whose son's ambulance charges propelled her into credit problems, was rescued by marriage and by the skewed values the American economy places on certain jobs. Her meager wage from caring for mentally ill adults in a state home was replaced by her new husband's comfortable income of $500 to $1,000 a week as a polisher for a gun manufacturer. He was paid by the piece, earning enough to permit Lisa to stay home with the six children, ages eight to thirteen, whom they both brought to their new family.

Her husband owned their house and had a sound credit record. He took out a home equity loan to put in a new kitchen and then a mortgage to build a large addition. The house provided a healthier environment for Lisa's son, whose asthma was much improved. The boy was no longer being rushed to the hospital, and so the chain reaction from housing to health to poor credit to higher interest rates was broken.

Medical insurance remained a problem, however. Lisa and the children were insured through the gun company, "but it doesn't cover prescriptions," she said, "so you have to pay yourself. When I need medicine, I buy it, but when we run out, I don't take it."

Lisa wanted to work. She ran a day-care center in her home for a while, cleaned houses, and took a small business management course on-line.

Eventually she hoped to start a private concern to serve people with special needs, like those at the state home where she had been such an effective caretaker. "I absolutely loved it," she said, "and I miss it."

Christie (pp. 39–45), who had earned too little to place her own children in the church-run day-care center where she worked, quit her job and slipped back onto welfare. Her boss had refused to give her time off for the required office visits to renew her food stamps, she said, had denied her the vacation days she was owed, and had refused to pay for a course to get her certified as a child development assistant. The center also assigned too many small children to each caregiver, a ratio of fourteen to one, Christie reported. The tension was raising her blood pressure, and she framed the choice starkly: "Do I want to be dead, working—or alive, not working?"

But she found the life of the welfare mother, sitting at home and drawing a check, utterly boring. By pushing her into a job, welfare reform had given her a taste for the workplace. Furthermore, the time limit under the law was approaching—she had only a year and a half before her welfare payments would stop—so she scrambled to find employment.

From time to time, she earned under the table by caring for children in her apartment in public housing. She applied for a bank teller's position but then learned that the only openings were an hour's commute, a trip she couldn't make with two children of her own at home—kids who were not doing well in school. She applied for a telemarketing job, but smelled a rat when they asked her to spend $120 for "supplies," including the smoke alarms she was to sell.

She seemed to be spinning her wheels, sliding from one idea to the next with no forward motion. She could improve her typing and get an office job, she figured, or work in the insurance industry, perhaps in a billing department. That was especially appealing: She thought it would be nice to send out collection notices instead of receiving them.

Kevin Fields (pp. 41–4, 136), the ex-con who couldn't get a job as a penitentiary-trained butcher, was maligned by Bill O'Reilly, the combative talk-show host of *The O'Reilly Factor*, who carefully selected negative elements of Kevin's story and left out ameliorating details. It was a clear case of not letting facts get in the way of an ideology.

After *The Working Poor* was published, O'Reilly invited me on the show and wanted to find Kevin as well. Kevin had moved, and I hadn't been able to locate him, but O'Reilly insisted that the producers track him down, through prison records if necessary. Without telling me they had done so, a producer called him to update his story. O'Reilly didn't put Kevin on the air with me, probably because he would have contradicted O'Reilly's distortions.

To bolster the familiar conservative position that "some people can't be saved," O'Reilly noted that Kevin had fathered four children by four different women—two more than at the time I had interviewed him for the book. That was true. (A month or so later, another baby was born, bringing the total to five children by four women.)

O'Reilly then proceeded to falsehoods and omissions. "He's been incarcerated time and time again for failing to pay child support," O'Reilly declared. In fact, as I learned after the show, he had been jailed once for one week, and otherwise had made his payments. "Here's a man who's just flat out irresponsible!" O'Reilly huffed. There were people "basically, at their core, unable, unable—all right?—to be responsible. Thus, no one's gonna hire them."

But Kevin had been hired, which O'Reilly failed to mention. As Kevin had told O'Reilly's producer, he had been working steadily for the last three and a half years as a meat wrapper in a Giant supermarket, earning $7.35 an hour.

Kevin is no model citizen; like many in his circumstance, he is a study in contradictions. His responsibility holding down a job stands alongside his irresponsibility in fathering multiple children by multiple women. His record in paying child support is imperfect. But the ambiguities of real life are too complex to fit into O'Reilly's political simplicities. The real Kevin can't quite be squeezed into the right wing's stereotype of the poor as irredeemable ne'er-do-wells whom society can guiltlessly cast aside. Therefore, O'Reilly had to create a caricature of Kevin by deftly concealing from viewers the significant facts that Kevin had a job and that much of his wage went to child support.

Meanwhile, the real Kevin still hoped that he would be promoted by Giant to full-fledged butcher.

Tom King (pp. 174–93), the widower with three kids, lost his job when LaCrosse shut down two of three shifts at its boot factory. "The Chinese are killing us," Tom said, passing on what he had been told. "The same boot, they can make it over there for seventy-eight cents a pair." The sudden vacuum hit his life and his wallet hard. "It was kind of a shock to me to go from twelve hours to nothing," he said. "They let us know a week ahead of time." It was in the depths of January. The water to his trailer froze again, and he had to move in with a friend for a couple of weeks.

Did he vote the next month in the New Hampshire presidential primary? "No, I didn't. I was out lookin' for a job." He might have added, echoing what he had told me in earlier years, that no candidate held the promise of a job or any other improvement in his situation. By the fall, he still wasn't sure whether, or for whom, he would vote. "I don't even bother. I'm on the go most of the time. I don't have time to watch TV."

After the spring thaw, he picked up bits and pieces of construction work and then settled into a routine of collecting scrap iron—rusting trucks and cars and engines and the like—and selling it to a recycling plant in Claremont. "I'm junkin'," he explained. "Everybody gives it to me. The price is right, money's good." And he was also haying on the two-hundred-acre farm where his father worked as caretaker. His daughter, Kate, a sixth-grader, helped out too, stacking bales.

"She's the spitting image of her mother," Tom said. "What's in her head comes out her mouth."

Zach, the oldest who didn't go to college, was training in Nebraska as a mechanic in the Air Force, and he loved it, he told his grandmother. "He said, 'When I get out of the service I can go to any airport and work on the planes,'" she reported. "I said, 'Your mother would be very proud of you.' He broke down. I told Tom later, 'I didn't mean to make him cry.'"

"I'm OK," Tom said bravely on the phone, and I could imagine him rubbing his hand down his face. "I'm up and taking nourishment. Any day above ground's gonna be a good day."

Caroline Payne (pp. 50–76), the mother without teeth, was very busy behind the register at the convenience store when a boy in a long line asked for a pack of cigarettes. "Usually I card everybody," she said, but this time "I was really overwhelmed." The kid turned out to be part of a sting operation by the state, and when he returned with the inspector, both she and the store were given tickets for selling cigarettes to a minor.

"I was crying, and I was scared," Caroline remembered. She would have to go to court, she could be fired, she would have to pay a fine for which she didn't have the cash. She was panicked, and when the store manager backed her up, saying that she was usually very careful in carding buyers, the inspector relented, saying that he'd talk to his boss. A few anxious days later, the inspector called and told Caroline to tear up the ticket, although the store was still fined.

Even with the reprieve, the experience was enough, coming on top of bad hours and bad pay, to push Caroline to quit. "What can we do to make you stay?" her boss asked. "I said I'd like more money and some benefits. They said, 'We can't help you with that.' So I gave two weeks' notice. My last day there, my boss says, 'Can't you work a couple of more days?' because a girl there quit without any notice. I helped them do their inventory, good old kindhearted me."

Eight months later, Caroline was still without work. People who had read about her in an excerpt from this book published in *The New York Times Magazine* had called her to offer help, for which she was grateful. But what she really needed was a decent job, she noted, and that didn't come. "I was hoping maybe Procter & Gamble would call me and offer me a job in a factory." Even after the way the company treated her back in New Hampshire? "They've got factories all over the place," she said.

A jobs program she was counting on to pay for a certified nursing assistant course found her ineligible because she wasn't on welfare and had a college degree. On paper, she looked too good to need help. She was deeply disappointed, because she had hoped to work in a nursing home. "I've got the personality," she said. "It's helping people, and I feel sorry for them."

She was rejected also because it was thought that her back problem might preclude her lifting elderly patients. Indeed, her back worsened. Her chiropractor insisted that she not lift more than ten pounds, walk long distances, bend over, sit or stand more than two or three hours at a time, or raise her arms above her shoulders. So she applied for disability from Social Security, was turned down, appealed, and was turned down again.

Meanwhile, she took clerical classes to improve her typing and learn computer programs. But her teeth remained a defect. She couldn't get used to her new dentures and didn't wear them. "They either need to be adjusted, or I got to quit smoking, or just force myself to keep them in," she declared.

Amber, her mildly retarded daughter, judged the move from New Hampshire to Indiana a good one, given the improvement in schooling. "All they were giving me up there [in New Hampshire] was how to clean, and I was doing it for Mom already," Amber said. In Indiana, she was taking child development, math, government, typing, and other challenging courses. After graduation from high school the next year, she would enroll in a vocational rehabilitation program. She still could not read.

So, the wrenching move from the New Hampshire town of Claremont to the Indiana city of Muncie remained a mixed decision. "Amber has had a good two years," Caroline said, "and has really grown a lot and has matured a lot." Still, selling her house for no profit at $79,000 nagged at her, especially since it was again up for sale, she saw on-line, this time for over $100,000. "It's making me sick," Caroline said, " 'cause I didn't make nothing on it."

"Peaches" (pp. 150–4, 254–7), the homeless woman much abused in childhood, seemed to enjoy a permanent recovery by way of the holistic job-training program run by So Others Might Eat.

She now ran a mail room for one of Xerox's clients, a private firm in Washington, which meant increased responsibility and a salary of $26,000 a year. Her silk flower arrangements began to catch on for baby showers, and she regularly set up a folding table where she sold them in a busy part of northeast Washington, D.C.

She felt good enough about herself to have a homecoming that helped her reconcile with the past. She returned to a church on Maryland's Eastern Shore where she had been raised, spoke to the congregation, and gave gift baskets in appreciation to several elderly parishioners for their support during her painful childhood. "They were stunned," she said. "One lady, I was always welcome in her home. I told her when I was sitting somewhere in a bus stop, hungry and bruised, I was thinking about some biscuits coming out of her oven."

Peaches remembered the church as a true sanctuary, a place of dignity, good order, beautiful clothes. The careful way the women dressed remained a sign, in subsequent years, that life could have beauty and solace. "They were in tears," Peaches said. " 'I didn't know you ever thought of me.'

" 'Yes, sitting there with your hats on, how you held your heads high. It was inspirational, even when I was at my very lowest.' "

To this homecoming on the Eastern Shore came her foster brother, from Philadelphia, for a moving reconnection. His children, embracing her as "auntie," gave her a real family that made her voice bubble as she talked about being part of something larger. "It's just absolutely wonderful to feel like you have someone who really cares about you."

Then, finally, Peaches found a good man, "a nice young gentleman, not hateful at all," she said. He worked for Washington Gas, installing lines and repairing leaks. "I'm hoping to get married," she announced. "We're looking to buy a house."

When I called her to check her address for mailing a copy of the book, I mentioned that she would recognize herself, although I had honored her request to call her "Peaches" instead of using her name. She said in a bright voice, "Oh, you can use my real name now!"

It is Celestine Travers.

Notes

Introduction: At the Edge of Poverty

1. From the poem by Emma Lazarus inscribed on the Statue of Liberty.

2. Richard A. Oppel, Jr., *New York Times,* Dec. 18, 2000, p. A19.

3. "2004 Survey of Consumer Finances," Board of Governors of the Federal Reserve System, Feb. 28, 2006.

4. *World in Figures* (London: The Economist Newspaper, 2003), pp. 76, 79.

5. *Webster's New International Dictionary,* 2nd ed., unabridged (Springfield, Mass.: Merriam, 1956), p. 1935.

6. *American Heritage Dictionary of the English Language,* 3rd ed. (Boston: Houghton Mifflin, 1992), p. 1419.

7. *Webster's Ninth New Collegiate Dictionary* (Springfield, Mass.: Merriam, 1983), p. 922.

8. Michael Harrington, *The Other America* (Baltimore: Penguin, 1963), pp. 173–74.

9. The Census Bureau "counts money income before taxes and does not include capital gains and noncash benefits (such as public housing, Medicaid, and

food stamps)." The poverty threshold is adjusted annually on the basis of the consumer price index. See http://www.census.gov/hhes/poverty/povdef.html.

10. For more on the history of the poverty index, see Gordon M. Fisher, "The Development of the Orshansky Poverty Thresholds and Their Subsequent History as the Official U.S. Poverty Measure," http://www.census.gov/hhes/poverty/povmeas/papers/orshansky.html.

11. Kathleen Short, John Iceland, and Thesia I. Garner, *Experimental Poverty Measures,* 1998 (Washington, D.C.: U.S. Census Bureau), http://www.census.gov/hhes/poverty/povmeas/exppov/exppov.html.

12. "Official and National Academy of Sciences Based Poverty Rates: 1999 to 2006," http://www.census.gov/hhes/www/povmeas/altmeas06/nas_measures_historical.xls.

13. *The NewsHour with Jim Lehrer,* Public Broadcasting System, Mar. 17, 1997.

14. *Weekend Edition,* National Public Radio, Jan. 16, 2000.

Chapter One: Money and Its Opposite

1. Robert Pear, "Aid to Poor Faces Tighter Scrutiny," *New York Times,* February 5, 2003, p. A1.

2. According to Robert Lerman, an economist at the Urban Institute.

3. According to analyses by TRAC at Syracuse University. David Cay Johnston, *New York Times,* Apr. 16, 2000, p. A1, and Feb. 16, 2001, p. A1, http://www.trac.syr.edu/tracirs/findings/national/ratesTab3.html.

4. Rates quoted by H&R Block corporate headquarters were slightly lower in 2001: $29.95 for loans of $200–$500, $39.95 for $501–$1,000, $59.95 for $1,001–$1,500, $69.95 for $1,501–$2,000, and $86.95 for $2,001–$5,000.

5. Details on H&R Block's tax loans and resulting lawsuits are documented by David Cay Johnston, *New York Times,* July 2, 2000, Section 3, p. 1. See also his report of February 28, 2001, p. C1.

6. Christopher Bowe, *Financial Times,* Feb. 23, 2000, p. 11.

7. Peter T. Kilborn, *New York Times,* June 18, 1999, p. A1.

8. Tamar Lewin, *New York Times,* Feb. 13, 2001, p. A14.

9. Richard A. Oppel, Jr., *New York Times,* Mar. 26, 1999, p. C1.

10. *Consumer Reports,* January 2001, pp. 20–24.

11. Geraldine Fabrikant, *New York Times,* Dec. 3, 2000, Section 3, p. 17.

12. Vivienne Hodges and Stuart Margulies, *Stanford 9th Language Arts Coach Grade 4* (New York: Educational Design, 1998).

13. Tom Wolfe, *The Bonfire of the Vanities* (New York: Bantam, 1987), pp. 142–43.

Chapter Two: Work Doesn't Work

1. Alan Weil and Kenneth Finegold, *Welfare Reform: The Next Act* (Washington, D.C.: Urban Institute Press, 2002). Introduction at http://www.urban.org/pubs/welfare_reform/intro.html.

2. Robert Lerman, "Single Parents' Earnings Monitor," Urban Institute, Oct. 26, 2001, and Dec. 26, 2002, available at www.urban.org.

3. Jack P. Shonkoff, Chapter 37.2, "Mental Retardation," in Richard E. Behrman, Robert M. Kliegman, and Ann M. Arvin, eds., *Nelson Textbook of Pediatrics*, 16th ed. (Philadelphia: Saunders, 2000), pp. 126–29.

4. Barbara Ehrenreich, "Two-Tiered Morality," *New York Times*, June 30, 2002, Section 4, p. 15. Also, Ehrenreich, *Nickel and Dimed* (New York: Holt, 2001), p. 146.

5. *Now with Bill Moyers*, PBS, Nov. 8, 2002.

Chapter Three: Importing the Third World

1. Sweatshop Watch's member organizations are the Asian Pacific American Labor Alliance, the Asian Pacific American Legal Center, the Coalition for Humane Immigrant Rights of Los Angeles (CHIRLA), Korean Immigrant Workers Advocate (KIWA), the Thai Community Development Center, the Union of Needletrades, Industrial and Textile Employees, the Asian Law Caucus, Asian Immigrant Women Advocates, and Equal Rights Advocates.

2. Julie A. Su, "El Monte Thai Garment Workers: Slave Sweatshops," http://www.sweatshopwatch.org/swatch/campaigns/elmonte.html.

3. Julie A. Su, "Making the Invisible Visible: The Garment Industry's Dirty Laundry," *The Journal of Gender, Race and Justice*, University of Iowa College of Law, vol. 1, no. 2 (Spring 1998).

4. Nancy Cleeland, "Garment Makers' Compliance with Labor Laws Slips in L.A.," *Los Angeles Times*, Sept. 21, 2000, p. C1. Federal violators in 2000 encompassed 25 percent of clothing firms in San Francisco and 48 percent in New York City. Victoria Colliver, "S.F. Clothing Firms Clean Up Their Act," *Los Angeles Times*, Mar. 29, 2002, p. B1.

Chapter Four: Harvest of Shame

1. "The US-Mexico Border," Migration Policy Institute, June 2007, http://www.migrationinformation.org/Feature/display.cfm?ID=407.

2. "Causes and Trends in Migrant Deaths Along the U.S.-Mexico Border, 1985–1998," University of Houston, http://www.uh.edu/cir/death.htm.

3. Farm Subsidy Database, Environmental Working Group, http://www.ewg.org.

4. Margaret Reeves, Kristin Schafer, Kate Hallward, and Anne Katten, "Fields of Poison: California Farmworkers and Pesticides" (San Francisco: Pesticide Action Network North America, United Farm Workers of America, California Rural Legal Assistance Foundation, 1999). Birth-defect information is from Imperial County, California.

5. Ibid.

6. Anthony DePalma, *New York Times*, Oct. 3, 2000, p. C1.

7. Tim Weiner, *New York Times,* Mar. 3, 2001, p. A1. At the urging of the Mexican government, networks are being established to cut fees through the use of computer transfers, cash cards, and direct salary deposits by U.S. employers into accounts in Mexico.

8. *New York Times,* Jan. 1, 2002, p. C1 and Mar. 27, 2003, p. A12.

9. Maria Panaritis and Thomas Ginsberg, *Philadelphia Inquirer,* Dec. 12, 2002.

Chapter Five: The Daunting Workplace

1. Philip Moss and Chris Tilly, "Soft Skills, Race, and Employment: Evidence from Employers," paper presented at Urban Institute, Washington, D.C., May 6, 1999. Interviews with employers in auto parts manufacturing, insurance, and retail found soft skills mentioned as important qualities in entry-level employees 74 to 100 percent of the time, hard skills 22 to 67 percent.

2. Interview with Parrish Wiggins, job developer at SOME's Center for Employment Training, Washington, D.C., May 20, 2002.

Chapter Six: Sins of the Fathers

1. Judith Lewis Herman, *Trauma and Recovery* (New York: Basic Books, 1992), pp. 96, 111.

2. S. M. Horwitz, L. V. Klerman, H. S. Kuo, and J. F. Jekel, "Intergenerational Transmission of School Age Parenthood," *Family Planning Perspectives* 24 (1991): 168–77.

3. Kevin Fiscella, M.D., M.P.H.; Harriet J. Kitzman, Ph.D.; Robert E. Cole, Ph.D.; Kimberly J. Sidora; and David Olds, Ph.D., "Does Child Abuse Predict Adolescent Pregnancy?" *Pediatrics* 101 (April 1998): 620–24.

4. Maya Pines, "A Child's Mind Is Shaped Before Age 2," *Life,* December 1971.

5. Barry Zuckerman and Robert Kahn, "Pathways to Early Child Health and Development," in Sheldon Danziger and Jane Waldfogel, eds., *Securing the Future: Investing in Children from Birth to College* (New York: Russell Sage Foundation, 2000), pp. 92–93.

6. Pines, "A Child's Mind."

7. "Educational Day Care Can Reduce Risk of Mild Retardation," *Growing Child Research Review* 8, no. 10 (October 1990), from *American Journal of Public Health* 80, no. 7, p. 844.

8. Alexandra Starr, "Does Universal Preschool Pay?" *Business Week,* Apr. 29, 2002, p. 98.

9. Lisbeth B. Schorr, *Within Our Reach* (New York: Anchor/Doubleday, 1988), pp. 163–68.

10. "Parents As Teachers: A Research-Based Program," http://www.patnc.org/researchevaluation.asp

Chapter Eight: Body and Mind

1. Economic Research Service, United States Department of Agriculture, *Food Security in the United States,* 2006, http://www.ers.usda.gov/Briefing/Food Security/.

2. Jack P. Shonkoff and Deborah A. Phillips, eds., *From Neurons to Neighborhoods: The Science of Early Child Development* (Washington, D.C.: National Academy Press, 2000), pp. 204-205.

3. Joycelyn Guyer and Cindy Mann, "Employed but Not Insured: A State-by-State Analysis of the Number of Low-Income Working Parents Who Lack Health Insurance" (Washington, D.C.: Center on Budget and Policy Priorities, 1999). Cited in Barry Zuckerman and Robert Kahn, "Pathways to Early Child Health and Development," in Sheldon Danziger and Jane Waldfogel, eds., *Securing the Future: Investing in Children from Birth to College* (New York: Russell Sage Foundation, 2000), p. 96.

4. Shonkoff and Phillips, *Neurons,* p. 208.

5. Zuckerman and Kahn, "Pathways," p. 96, citing Marie C. McCormick, "The Outcomes of Very-Low-Birthweight Infants: Are We Asking the Right Questions?" *Pediatrics* 99 no. 6: 869–76.

6. Shonkoff and Phillips, *Neurons,* pp. 207-209.

7. Zuckerman and Kahn, "Pathways," p. 90.

8. Ibid., p. 92.

9. Shonkoff and Phillips, *Neurons,* p. 238.

10. Steven Parker, Steven Greer, and Barry Zuckerman, "Double Jeopardy: The Impact of Poverty on Early Child Development," *The Pediatric Clinics of North America,* 35, no. 6 (December 1988): 1234.

11. Niomi Richman, Jim Stevenson, and Phillip J. Graham, *Preschool to School: A Behavioral Study* (New York: Academic Press, 1982), cited in Zuckerman and Kahn, "Pathways," p. 98.

12. Ibid., pp. 213–14.

13. Mary Carlson and Felton Earls, "Psychological and Neuroendocrinological Sequelae of Early Social Deprivation in Institutionalized Children in Romania," *Annals of the New York Academy of Science* 807 (1997): 409–428, cited in Zuckerman and Kahn, "Pathways," p. 91.

14. Shonkoff and Phillips, *Neurons,* p. 237.

15. Parker et al., "Double Jeopardy," p. 1232.

16. M. Duyme, A.-C. Dumaret, and S. Tomkiewicz, "How Can We Boost IQs of 'Dull Children'?: A Late Adoption Study," *Proceedings of the National Academy of Sciences* 96, no. 15: 8790–8794, cited in Shonkoff and Phillips, *Neurons,* pp. 286–87.

17. David Brown, *Washington Post,* Sept. 19, 2002, p. A3. American Lung Association, "Childhood Asthma Overview," Oct. 2007, http://www.lungusa.org/site/pp.asp?c=dvLUK9OoE&b=22782.

Chapter Nine: Dreams

1. Jonathan Kozol, *Savage Inequalities* (New York: HarperCollins, 1992), pp. 20–21.

2. Ibid., p. 83.

Chapter Ten: Work Works

1. Barbara Ehrenreich, *Nickel and Dimed* (New York: Holt, 2001), p. 149.

Chapter Eleven: Skill and Will

1. "Voting and Registration in the Election of November 2000," U.S. Census Bureau, *Current Population Reports,* February 2002, Table B, pp. 6–7.

2. *Los Angeles Times,* Apr. 7, 2003, p. A20 and *New York Times,* Apr. 23, 2008, p. A1. Of the total inmate population, which reached 2.3 million in 2006, nearly 143,000 were non-citizens and over 90,000 were minors.

3. David Brooks, "The Triumph of Hope Over Self-Interest," *New York Times,* Jan. 12, 2003, Section 4, p. 15.

4. Liana Fox, "What a New Federal Minimum Wage Means for the States," Economic Policy Inst., June 1, 2007.

5. The ACORN Living Wage Resource Center, http://www.livingwage campaign.org/shortwins.php.

6. Robert Pear, "Aid to Poor Faces Tighter Scrutiny," *New York Times,* Feb. 5, 2003, p. A1.

7. Bureau of Labor Statistics, Jan. 25, 2008, http://www.bls.gov/news.release/ union2.nr0.htm.

8. The 1994 School-to-Work Opportunities Act, which created vocational and apprenticeship programs, was well funded to the states but was never turned into reality and was not renewed by the Clinton administration. Robert I. Lerman, "Promoting Quality Careers with Intensive School-to-Work Activities," paper for the Association for Public Policy and Management, Dallas, Texas, Nov. 7–9, 2002. Also, interview with the author.

9. For the year 2004–2005. Citizens Budget Commission, "Local Taxes in New York: Easing the Burden," Dec. 6, 2007, http://www.cbcny.org/Bucket% 203%20Powerpoint.pdf.

10. Gary Orfield, Erica Frankenberg, and Chungmei Lee, "A Multiracial Society with Segregated Schools: Are We Losing the Dream?" (Cambridge, Mass.: The Civil Rights Project of Harvard University, Jan. 16, 2003).

11. Jack P. Shonkoff and Deborah A. Phillips, eds., *From Neurons to Neighborhoods: The Science of Early Child Development* (Washington, D.C.: National Academy Press, 2000), p. 211.

12. Lisbeth B. Schorr, *Within Our Reach* (New York: Anchor/Doubleday, 1988), p. 293.

Index

Deandre (three-year-old boy), 281
Delgado, Hector, 17–8, 106–7
Delgado, Maribel, 17–8, 106, 107
Democratic Party, 287, 288, 299
dental care, 37, 52–3, 198
depression, x
    maternal, 168, 211, 220
    self-neglect as symptom of, 53
    treatment of, 190, 195, 294
    work performance affected by, 63
Dickerson, Frank, 8
diet, *see* malnutrition
dissociative reactions, 144, 161
divorce, 95, 118
Docusort, 127, 140
domestic abuse, 35, 149–50, 171
Dominick's, 264
Dominique (sixth-grader), 232
Don (seventh-grader), 232
Donald (malnourished child), 205
Doris (malnutrition patient), 207–9
Drake, Delores, 268–9
Drake, Ricky, 266–9
drinking, 43–4, 119
    see also alcoholism
driver's licenses, 116–18
drug addiction, 119
    crack cocaine, 156–8, 271–6
    employees with history of, 137–8
    treatment for, 158, 255–6, 275–6
drug trade, 8, 241–2
Dunbar High School, 215, 235, 236, 240, 250
Duocal, 202

Earned Income Tax Credit (EIC), 13–5, 16,
    38, 291
earning gap, 89–90
Eby, Sharon, 128, 136, 138, 139
economic recessions, 53–4, 72
Eddie (jailed father), 165
education, 231–53
    for associate's degrees, 60
    career aspirations vs., 231–3
    computer use in, 245, 249–50, 251
    curriculum relevance in, 243, 244–6
    extracurricular programs and, 248–9
    family values in, 235–6

home-life deprivations and, 237–9
homework assignments in, 240, 247
of immigrant children, 239, 283
learning disabilities and, 59–60, 73–4,
    247–8
loans for, 60, 73, 199, 200
local funding of, 59–60, 239–40, 293–4
malnutrition and, 215
of migrant workers' children, 113
parental involvement in, 233–7
in poor neighborhoods, 239–42
as predictor of further education, 140
of preschool children, 167, 298
private vs. public, 195–6, 294
production quality vs. availability of, 134
racial stereotypes in, 235, 241
school-supply levels in, 248–51
standardized testing used in, 243–5
teaching deficiencies in, 233, 240, 242–3,
    245–7
vocational training, 266, 268, 292–3, 306n
see also employment-training programs
egalitarianism, 293
Ehrenreich, Barbara, 67, 263
EIC (Earned Income Tax Credit), 13–5, 16,
    38, 291
elections of 2000, 69–70, 287, 288–9
El Monte, Calif., Thai garment workers
    exploited in, 80–2
employers, deference to, 71
employment
    application process of, 122, 135–6, 140–1,
        258–60, 276–7
    criminal records and, 42, 122, 124–5, 136–8
    educational requirements of, 135
    in factory jobs, 47–9, 50, 62, 68, 70–1, 72,
        78–84, 262–6, 302n
    fears about, 121–2, 123–6
    of former welfare recipients, 127–8, 129,
        134–5, 159, 160–1, 261
    health insurance tied to, 295
    from homeless shelters, 128
    levels of, 134, 135
    production quality vs. availability of, 134
    racial stereotypes in, 128, 135–6, 282
    role models in, 124, 129
    soft skills in, 7, 126, 127, 139, 261, 304n
    turnover rates in, 126, 133, 135

Los Angeles, Calif.
  cost of living in, 93
  garment industry in, 77–82
  Korean section of, 93
lotteries, 21
Lynn (librarian), 31–2

Mabel M. Riedinger Middle School, 235–6,
    238, 242, 245
machinists, 266, 268
McKenna, Horace, 255
Macy's, 123, 124–5
maintenance jobs, 20, 137, 292
malnutrition, 201–17, 224–5
  brain development damaged by, 215,
    216–17
  feeding behavior and, 210–15
  food allergies and, 203–4
  immune function impaired by, 215–16
  infant formula and, 202, 204, 205
  and junk food, 205–6
  parental embarrassment about, 207–8
  U.S. incidence of, 216
Maria Bianca Nero, 85–8
Marine Corps, U.S., 255
marriages
  emotional support of, 183, 185
  of Korean immigrants, 95
  of migrant farm workers, 118–19
Marxism, 290
Mary (Tom King's friend), 189–90, 191, 192
Maryland, University of, health services of,
    211–13
maternal depression, 168, 211, 220
math skills, 74, 139, 242
mechanical skills, 131
Medicaid, 180
  breast-feeding and, 207
  dental coverage of, 52, 75
  eligibility for, 64, 295
  for immigrants' U.S.-born children, 107
  interpreter services and, 210
  numbers of recipients of, 296
Medicare, 296
Melissa (young mother), 172–3
mental health problems, 34
  see also depression

mental retardation, 58, 59–60, 74, 167, 217,
    223–4
mentoring programs
  for children at risk, 142
  for parents, 163–73, 297
Mexico
  factory wages in, 79, 102
  illegal border crossings from, 99–100, 107
  migrant farm workers from, *see* migrant
    farm workers
  money sent to, 114, 115, 304*n*
  number of undocumented immigrants
    from, 114
Michael (jailed father), 166
micronutrients, 215
Mid-South Electrics, 262
migrant farm workers, 96–120
  border-crossing journeys of, 99–100, 107
  as Catholics, 118–19
  children of, 106, 107, 112, 113
  contractors of, 98, 100, 101, 108–10
  environmental health risks of, 112–13
  hours worked by, 102, 106, 115
  housing loans for, 105–6
  illegal status of, 114; *see also* immigrants,
    undocumented
  job mobility of, 107–9, 116
  limited visa program for, 114
  living conditions of, 96–9, 101, 102, 103,
    105–6, 108, 109–10, 113–14, 115, 299
  money sent home by, 106, 109, 114–16, 304*n*
  payroll deductions of, 102
  personal problems faced by, 119–20
  recent security crackdown on, 116–17
  seasonal travels of, 97
  shift to settled residence made by, 105–6,
    120
  union activism of, 110–12, 113
  wages of, 100, 102, 104, 106, 115, 299
  work availability for, 101, 102, 105, 106
Miller, George, 298
Minich, Kurt, 181, 182, 184, 185, 186, 188, 189
minimum wage, 290–1
  in California, 78
  federal vs. state, 19, 291
  other wages affected by, 105
  piecework wages vs., 78–9
  price rises vs., 90

Tambrands factories, 62, 68, 71, 72
taxes
    audit policies and, 15–6, 20
    corporate breaks on, 291–2
    cuts in, 287
    earned income credit in, 13–5, 16, 38,
        291
    payroll withholding and, 102
    professional preparers of, 13, 15, 16–8,
        302n
    undocumented workers' involvement
        with, 14, 102
Taylor, Glenda, 123–5
teachers
    confrontational responses to, 234
    inadequacies of, 233, 240, 242–3, 245–7
    low socioeconomic status of, 240, 298
    racial stereotypes and, 235
    school materials purchased by, 251
    see also education
Teach for America, 237, 250, 251
television, 7, 27, 28, 29, 42–3
temp workers, 72
terrorist attacks
    employee background checks and, 137
    government power and, 289, 290
    immigration laws emphasized after,
        116–17
    survivor compensation for, 90
textile industry, 85
Thai immigrants, garment industry
    exploitation of, 80–2
Third World
    child deaths in, 216
    U.S. wages vs., 79
throwaway society, 131
Tillmon, Carla, 134
Tran Mao, 282–4
Tran Phuong, 283, 284
Tran Tuan, 283, 284
Travers, Celestine, 309
    see also Peaches
Troutman, Kathy, 258–9
Truong Cam, 126
Turcotte, Michelle, 211
Turtle Wax, 263
Tuskegee experiment, 209
Tyson's Foods, 116

U-Haul, 176–7
unemployment rates, 134, 135
Union of Soviet Socialist Republics, failure
    of, 290
unions
    of bakery workers, 48
    decline of membership in, 292
    of farm workers, 110–12, 113
United Farm Workers of America, 113

Valley Regional Hospital, 170, 181–2
Vance, Paul, 252
Victorian Paper, 129, 136–7
Vietnamese immigrants, 282–4
Vietnam War, 103, 178, 267, 282
violence, 35, 135–6, 171, 280
vocational training, 266, 268, 292–3, 306n
voter participation, 287–9, 290

wages
    bonuses vs., 88
    differentiation in, 89–90
    in garment industry, 78, 79, 80, 82–3, 84,
        85, 88
    of high-school graduates vs. college
        graduates, 292
    of migrant farm workers, 100, 102, 104,
        106, 115, 299
    minimum standards of, 19, 78–9, 90, 105,
        265–6, 290–1
    of Third-World workers vs. U.S.
        immigrants, 79
Wal-Mart Stores
    co-worker collection for employee of,
        179–80
    employee turnover rate of, 66
    hiring process at, 263
    net annual income of, 65
    overtime pay avoided by, 67
    price structure of, 65
    promotion policies at, 51–3
    suburban locations of, 11
    wages paid by, 64–5
Ward, Terrence R., 134–5
War on Poverty, 5, 6
Waxler, Kiara, 148–9, 150

Waxler, Wendy, 21, 146–50, 158, 260, 277, 278
Wayne (job seeker), 122
Webb Correctional Facility, 163
Webb Elementary School, 236, 244
welfare recipients
    bureaucratic demands on, 41, 60–1, 229–30
    childhood sexual abuse of, 146
    new children born to, 207
    parenting instruction received by, 164
    spending restrictions on, 28–9
    successive generations of, 160
    undeclared jobs of, 46–7
welfare recipients, former
    employment of, 127–8, 129, 134–5, 159, 160–1, 261
    psychological barriers of, 135
    stereotypes of, 128
welfare reform
    family cap provision of, 207
    immigrants and, 107
    job-training programs and, 47, 134
    low-wage employment spurred by, 40, 46–7
    time limits set by, 4, 13
    work mandates of, 4, 47, 159
W-5, 15
WIC (Special Supplemental Nutrition Program for Women, Infants, and Children), 37–8, 180, 204
William Mead Houses, 126
Winterowd, K. B., 128
Within Our Reach (Schorr), 167
Wojciechowski, Maria, 85–8, 89
Wolfe, Tom, 32–3
women
    childhood sexual abuse of, 144; *see also* sexual abuse
    family concerns vs. work commitments of, 128
    as majority of working poor, xi
Woodruff, Camellia, 123, 124, 125
Woodruff, Judy, 6
worker's compensation, 94

work ethic, 126, 138, 263
working poor
    criticism of spending habits of, 23, 27–30, 196
    economic recessions and, 53–4, 72
    financial exploitation of, 16–27
    former welfare recipients in, 40–50
    invisibility of, 3, 12
    personal support system of, 174–200
    spending habits of, 27–38, 54
    women as majority of, xi
    see also poverty
workplace
    accountability developed in, 130, 131
    collegial relations in, 126, 131–2, 134, 135
    cultural differences in, 132
    dependability in, 126, 127, 129–30, 131, 138
    family problems vs., 128, 131, 140, 205
    as foreign culture, 122, 125–6
    initiative in, 126
    invisibility in, 129–30, 133–4
    personal grooming and, 126, 127, 128, 257
    repeated failures in, 122
    supervisory support in, 133–4, 135, 138
    therapeutic benefits of, 122–3
    transportation to, 138
    violence in, 135–6
    see also employment
World Trade Center, survivor compensation after attack on, 90
World Trade Organization, 79–80
worthlessness, sense of, 126, 129–30, 133, 151

Xerox Corporation, 260, 261, 276–7, 302, 308

Yeats, William Butler, 231

Zabounian, Joe, 82–4
Zotter, Jean, 227, 230
Zuckerman, Barry, 217, 219–20, 225–6, 252, 286

ALSO BY DAVID K. SHIPLER

A COUNTRY OF STRANGERS
Blacks and Whites in America

A Country of Strangers is a magnificent exploration of the psychological landscape where blacks and whites meet. Pulitzer Prize–winning journalist David K. Shipler bypasses both extremists and celebrities and takes us among ordinary Americans to show how blacks and whites see each other, how they interpret each other's behavior, and how certain damaging images and assumptions seep into the actions of even the most unbiased. Shipler penetrates into dimensions of stereotyping and discrimination that are usually invisible and discovers the unseen prejudices and privileges of white Americans, and what black Americans make of them. Black-white stereotypes are dissected: the physical bodies that we see, the mental qualities we imagine, the moral character we attribute to others and to ourselves, the violence we fear, and the power we seek or are loath to relinquish.

Shipler's book is unstinting in its criticism of society's failure to come to grips with bigotry, but it is also, happily, crowded with black people and white people who struggle in their daily lives to do just that. He makes clear that we have the ability to shape our racial landscape and to reconstruct, even if imperfectly, the texture of our relationships.

Current Affairs/0-679-73454-6

VINTAGE BOOKS